Dr Prem's Guide

Medical Tourism

http://DrPrem.com/Medical-Tourism

Contents

Chapter 7
What could go wrong during Medical Travel?   62

Chapter 8
Why I should or shouldn't opt for Medical tourism   67

Chapter 9
Understanding your Medical Tourism Needs   72

Chapter 10
Pre-Operative Preparations   76

DESTINATION GUIDE   179

Introduction

Medical Tourism is a growing phenomenon where people opt to travel to other countries for quality health care services. Several factors contribute to medical tourism – these include high cost of treatment, lack of availability, high waiting time, or poor quality of care at the home country. Medical tourism portrays a highly promising scenario to achieve quick healthcare services with personalized care. Lots of planning and research goes into it to make it a successful venture. Poor planning and improper execution can be disastrous for the health care seeker, upsetting the objective.

This comprehensive guide offers a sincere and honest attempt of bringing the concept of medical tourism to light – its evolution and the benefits it offers to the tourist. The book efficiently guides you towards proper step-wise planning, creating due awareness about possible lapses and flaws.

Each chapter is a meticulous exercise and not merely a bland compilation of facts and data. The finely woven text drives home the need for medical tourism in the context of an era where achieving a disease-free body is the prime need. The language is lucid and understandable that touches the basics of medical tourism with its rising demand and the enormous benefits waiting at the end of your journey.

The opening chapter is expressive of the fact that the existing medical facilities that a country might offer may not adequately address the problems suffered by a patient. The human body is vulnerable to a host of diseases that can leave one frail and distressed, irrespective of the medical capabilities of a patient's home country. This certainly gives rise to the necessity to travel and explore the avenues available in other countries, which may not be available back home due to some limitations.

The patient need not necessarily choose cross-border travel, but can avail medical support in a different region of the same country. However, the cost of the treatment in one's own country might be prohibitive compared to that in a foreign land, even if we include accommodation and travelling costs. Legal implications and social customs of a particular country may prevent one from availing upgraded medical support for a particular health issue. There is always a chance that the treatment may be accessible in other countries.

A fine distinction has also been made between medical tourism and health tourism. While health tourism aims at achieving complete wellbeing of the body and mind, medical tourism deals with the diagnosis and treatment of specific diseases. Both could lead to travelling if local doctors fail to offer a solution.

The author has emphasized on exploring the potential of the developing world in terms of quality health care facilities available. The term 'third world' is often misguiding. It portrays a less developed and economically backward nation with crude scientific developments where travelling for medical support may put your life at risk.

On the contrary, many of these countries have made stunning progress in certain domains of medical science. They are equipped with world-class medical infrastructure and qualified, experienced professionals with wide international exposure. Many of these professionals are internationally qualified from prestigious institutions in nations like USA and UK.

Affordability is a vital factor driving the growth of medical tourism. A surgery with equivalent quality of treatment and care in India, Thailand, Malaysia, Jordan or Mexico can cost remarkably lower in comparison to a developed western country. Moreover, a new destination and environment help in quick healing. The book explains this aspect, very logically presenting authentic illustrations.

Chapter 1 also deals with dental tourism, an important offshoot of medical tourism where patients from developed nations like the USA and high-profile Euro nations seek dental treatments at a much lower price in developing nations like India, Turkey and Poland. Expenses related to dental treatments, including the cost of dentures are astronomically high in affluent nations. This encourages people to look for economic options in developing countries.

Chapter 2 portrays interesting facts on medical tourism drawing anecdotes from historical records. The author has done extensive research to establish the fact that medical tourism was very much in vogue through much of recorded history. It is amazing to learn that during the pre-Christ era, people migrated from one corner of the world to the other in search of solutions to their ailments.

In old texts, we often come across tales of people suffering from incurable diseases moving to different lands in search of a miraculous cure. Hot spring baths that were rich in minerals were recognized for their therapeutic value and attracted visitors. The custom of drinking from bronze cups was believed to be therapeutic too, and was a treatment often prescribed.

The book goes into the depths of time to inform us of interesting facts like the ancient Greeks laying the foundation stone of the temple of Asclepiad, the god of medicines. It was considered a potent healing center for medical tourists from around the globe. The Greeks took pains to set up travel networks so that people from near and far confronted no difficulty seeking answers to their health issues.

It would be interesting to note that the post-Christ era saw a rise in the trend of medical tourism as Egypt started establishing advanced hospitals open to patients irrespective of their nationality. We find that Japan, which was a remote island in the Pacific utilized its wealth of hot healing springs for amazing healing benefits.

Medical centers in medieval Europe and South American ethnic settlements offered gratifying treatment to the sick and diseased. The book is a fascinating compilation of such authentic information from different periods. The history of medical tourism and its need-based growing popularity over the years is very categorically illustrated in this book.

The book's narration of immense benefits of medical tourism is based on sound analysis and reasoning, rousing the interest of the reader. The book clearly explains that commercial benefit is not the lone factor that drives a person to choose medical tourism.

Who would not like to have a pleasant vacation amid pristine landscapes and breath-taking sea beaches as a break after an appointment with the doctor? People today are bent more on overall mental and physical well-being that can be achieved through a medical tourism venture.

Some countries have come up with groundbreaking treatment facilities of disorders related to vital human organs, thus attracting the global crowd. The upgraded infrastructure of such countries has made them hotspots of medical tourism. In some cases, one may risk social embarrassment in the treatment of certain diseases locally. Many people choose medical tourism for privacy and for the sake of preventing such unwanted attention.

Medical tourism is highly cost saving, especially if you successfully locate proper treatment centers in developing countries. The book explores the financial angle of medical tourism as well and is informative about details like insurance coverage. This is a clear financial benefit to the tourist seeking treatment abroad. A hair-split analysis is done in successive pages as to why medical treatment abroad is often cheaper, logically dealing with the factors like quality of treatment and the associated cost, accessibility to treatment, and a desire for personalized care.

The book handles travel and tourism aspect of medical treatment very well, providing an expert's viewpoint. The scratch to end guidance provided in well-framed chapters helps in the effective planning of medical tourism. It covers issues relating to organizing the trip, booking the flight and other modes of travel, getting through with passport and visa formalities, and selection of a decent accommodation.

Issues that are generally sidelined or ignored are given due importance in this book. Travel medicine, for example, is an important area in medical tourism and the book emphasizes this factor. How many of us have a good knowledge of this? Taking vaccination, preparation of a comprehensive list of medicines and arranging the medical kit are all covered methodically.

The striking feature of this book is that it doesn't overlook ground realities. Everything related to medical treatment and wellness has its pros and cons. The subsequent chapters handle the subject of medical tourism from the realistic perspective revealing the possible obstacles in pursuing healthcare services abroad.

Language and cultural hindrances might become a serious issue, as would an incorrect estimation of travelling and accommodation costs The book guides you on accessing authentic information about the medical treatment center abroad, while highlighting the checkpoints.

Pre and post-operational care could be a serious issue if not anticipated. These issues are dealt elaborately, with solutions and tips for prevention.

Somebody should accompany the person going for medical tourism. The importance of taking the right companion with you abroad for medical treatment cannot be emphasized enough. The companion selected should be level-headed and capable of taking decisions under crises. He/she should be aware of the patient's condition, and resourceful enough to share workload under stress.

The book states that while being optimistic in selecting the best possible treatment center to the right kind of accommodation, you should prepare yourself for the worst and work out contingency plans.

Organizing medical and legal documents properly has been duly stressed in the book so that you can pull the required piece when required, instead of wasting time on desperate searching that often gives rise to a panicky situation. This may seem to be a trivial issue but comes handy.

The importance of medical facilitators is also stressed expressively. The narrative has rightly explored this factor, giving due weightage of positive and negative factors.

Collecting authentic information from reliable websites, understanding the ethical, cultural, legal issues and assessing the quality, safety and the track record of the facilitator are very important, as emphasized in the book.

The world is not a small place and picking the right destination for medical tourism is not simple. Medical Destination section provides basic information with statistical data of 68 global medical tourism destinations. Available healthcare facilities as well as the tourism activities are highlighted for the convenience of the reader. This is perhaps the most interesting part of this book, where you discover various destinations that offer quality medical support.

Medical jargon is tough to understand, but the glossary provided at the end of the book makes the terms and words understandable. You can flip through the pages and learn the meaning of these terms arranged alphabetically.

No human being is spared from the onslaught of diseases and ailments, and medical tourism is a very effective approach to achieve a cure, enhancing your well being, and a well-framed guidebook like this is worth reading not once but several times.

Understanding Medical Tourism

CHAPTER 1

Understanding the concept of medical tourism

Medical Tourism is quite a self-defining term. To explain it broadly before we go into specifics, medical tourism means traveling to some other location or place to avail medical facilities and services. Several causes fuel medical tourism in our modern world.

Medical Value Travel takes a lion's share in Medical Tourism numbers and revenue. This particular term defines the phenomenon of patients traveling from a developed nation to other parts of the world for medical care. The motivating factor behind such movement is usually a desire to get treatment at a lower and more favorable cost.

There is also a reverse flow as people from underdeveloped countries, or from countries that lack in sufficient healthcare, travel to other parts of the world for medical support.

In some cases, people travel to other countries to get medical procedures that are unwelcome or denied in their home countries.

To be clear, Medical Tourism does not essentially imply cross-border travel or globetrotting. It could as simply mean traveling to a different region or state in your home country, owing to a number of factors both personal, and medical. One could decide to go to a different region looking for better facilities, the fame of a particular institution and surgeon, or for a personal reason like being together with friends and family.

While many believe medical tourism to be a new and modern concept, it is in fact a tradition that is as ancient as tourism itself. Before traveling to another country to get a surgery for economic reasons became fashionable, physicians asked people suffering with various ailments to travel to towns and hamlets like the Belgian town of Spa or even Bath in England where natural hot or cold water springs sprouted.

Traveling to remote monasteries where monks used rare herbs to cure specific ailments, and pilgrimage spots like Lourdes in France (renowned as places of healing) were the most common established practices.

With the progress in modern medicine, healing and recovering from ailments of the body isn't so much a matter of faith as it is of having access to the finest yet the most affordable medical facilities. The big buzzword one needs to consider in terms of healthcare these days is "affordability."

In some countries, even the basic surgeries could mean huge bills to a patient. While in second or third world countries, the same surgery costs much less despite any major difference in the quality of care provided by hospitals in the two respective nations. That is what, in a nutshell, provides the required impetus to the medical tourism industry.

Quite simply put, medical tourism – both domestic and international – is all about traveling to another destination that offers medical care, surgeries and therapies at a considerably reduced cost when compared to a local facility, which would charge you more for the same treatment.

It is vital to understand that traveling to another place to receive better treatment is nothing unusual or new. Medical tourism is vastly different from medical travel of yore since it promotes cost saving.

In essence, the concept of medical tourism is exactly what it sounds like – it is essentially tourism with medical treatments at discount prices. So when you travel to a South East Asian country to get a knee replacement, the overall cost of the trip will include you expenses on travel, surgery, postoperative care, necessary physical therapies, sightseeing and souvenir shopping. Even so, it is likely to cost an average American patient less than the same surgery and post-surgical care would cost in a local facility.

WHY DOES IT MATTER?

For many of us, the very notion of traveling to a third world country for medical treatment might sound riskier than traveling there to explore the local haute cuisine. While the risks associated with traveling to another country and placing your health in the hands of a total stranger are real, patients with limited means should not ignore them altogether.

In fact, a large chunk of medical tourists includes retirees and pensioners. This part of the population essentially lives on their life's savings, pensions and whatever investments they have made. Government sponsored healthcare for this section of the society often doesn't cover expensive surgeries and experimental therapies. For example, a heart valve replacement in the US costs $160,000 while the same surgery at a super specialty hospital in Thailand costs roughly $10,000. For a pensioner, this means a huge saving.

Another section that finds medical tourism rather attractive includes patients traveling out of the country for nonessential or cosmetic procedures. In the US, a simple breast augmentation procedure could cost around $10,000 plus the cost of postoperative care. Getting the same surgery in India would cost around $2450 and the postoperative care would cost lesser given the exchange rate. If you choose not to go sightseeing or shopping, your entire trip would cost you roughly half of what you would pay for the procedure alone in the US.

Another key reason that drives the multi-billion dollar global medical tourism industry is the fact that the drug and medical care-regulating agency of a country may not approve some new procedure or therapy. The FDA in the US, for example, was quite reluctant to approve hip resurfacing surgery until some years ago. Hence, anyone who wanted to enjoy the benefits of this surgical process needed to travel out of the country.

Hospitals and medical facilities in many popular medical tourism destinations now flaunt top-notch standards when it comes to offering the highest level of care, treatment and surgeries to patients.

HEALTH TOURISM

Health tourism is yet another segment that has boomed along with medical tourism. Some may consider both terms interchangeable and synonymous with each other; nevertheless, the fact remains that there are stark differences between the two. Health tourism looks at one's wellbeing in a more holistic way than medical tourism which is inherently an industry driven by curing the ailments of the body by using modern medicine and allopathic or contemporary surgical methods only.

Medical tourists with non-life threatening ailments often visit international centers, which are quite famous for providing therapies derived from the principles of ancient medicinal techniques. Generically speaking, a good example of health tourism would be a visit to one of the renowned Ayurveda centers in Kerala in southern India, to an acupuncturist in Seoul or even to a Reiki expert in Hong Kong. These centers follow ancient medical traditions and systems while following a multi-pronged approach to cure a physical, mental or spiritual ailment.

Health tourism, thus, represents the concept of medical tourism itself. When you visit a renowned holistic health center attached to a five-star resort, you get the benefit of a top class trip along with a rejuvenating therapy. However, one cannot expect a higher end establishment to offer premium services on similar or more discounts.

On the other end, the super cheap, local health centers are family run establishments whose services are not often five-star rated, but locals and travelers recommend them for some obvious reasons. Since you can visit these centers during your stay at a cheap hotel, the overall cost of your entire health tourism trip will be less than otherwise. Nonetheless, health tourism does not guarantee results in the true sense of the word. You cannot sue the establishments even if their therapies failed to deliver the expected results.

DENTAL TOURISM

Also known as dental vacation, dental tourism is a quickly growing subset of the larger medical tourism sector. Patients embarking on dental tourism are usually ones who seek dental care abroad and outside of the local dental care and health systems.

The general flow in this sector sees patients from developed countries like the UK, Australia, and the US seeking dental procedures and dental care in developing countries like

Ukraine, India, Turkey, Poland, Hungary, Northern Ireland, Peru, Slovenia, Slovakia etc. This flow of patients from high-income economies to developing countries represents huge savings for patients in terms of overall costs of treatments and savings made through currency exchange rates.

For host nations, dental tourism provides the boost to their own tourism industry as patients wish to "make the trip count".

One of the key concerns that patients in high-income countries have about dental tourism is quality. For example, in Mexico, a general practitioner can obtain a certificate in dental implants and begin practicing without any prior experience in the field of dentistry. Similarly, in many other developing nations, certification standards for dentists vary which heightens the risk factor for dental tourists. It is very important for you to ensure that the person is well qualified and experienced in the field. On the other hand, the lower cost of education and access to low cost materials and tools allow reputed dentists in such countries to offer services at par with international standards at a considerably lower cost.

A simple comparative study of popular procedures is enough to make the differences in dentistry costs more obvious. The cost of dental implants costs an average of $1800-$3000 in the US. The same procedure costs $650-$900 in Costa Rica. Root canals that cost $650-$900 in the US cost just $75-$80 in Turkey. Even when we add travel expenses, the overall cost of getting the same procedure at a dental tourism hotspot abroad means significant savings for American patients. The low cost of materials required for dental procedures like porcelain veneers also becomes yet another important factor.

WELLNESS TOURISM*

As fitness does not merely mean your ability to run a marathon with ease, wellness tends to go beyond perfect health. In fact, wellness focuses more on prolonging life, improving the quality of life and preventing diseases than curing ailments.

When compared to traditional medicine and even alternative medical practices, wellness seeks to make changes to a patient's lifestyle and equip them with tools that would help them stay immune to lifestyle diseases in the future. Accordingly, individuals opting for wellness treatments stay at a treatment facility for durations between weeks to multiple months.

Wellness tourism, of course, has been a part of human society since the dawn of history. In olden times, people traveled to monasteries and places of worship seeking enlightenment or divine knowledge that might improve their quality of life. Before the advent of medical tourism, general practitioners advised patients with ailments to visit a famous tourist spot.

In modern times, the concept of wellness tourism has become a lot more multidimensional, individualistic and holistic through destinations and centers offering wellness tourism packages. Such packages focus on restoring inner peace in an individual through guided meditation, spiritual counseling, slow-paced physical therapies, and controlled breathing.

---

*We recommend you to read Dr Prem's Guide - Wellness Tourism for more details.

For average patients, a wellness tourism trip is a matter of personal beliefs and preferences. Someone who innately does not believe that yogic breathing can restore inner peace will not benefit too much from a wellness regime that includes it. Other factors influencing wellness tourism include preference or leaning toward a certain ancient culture or its philosophies.

Of course, wellness tourism is not limited to these activities alone. Depending on the destination and the package a patient has opted for, a wellness regimen may include physical, mental and spiritual exercise, aside from socializing and nutrition.

Unlike medical tourism, costs incurred during a wellness trip can range from dirt cheap to exorbitant depending on your personal lifestyle preferences. For example, a trip to a wellness center run by expat Tibetans in northern India may cost you nothing at all; however, a stay at a premium wellness resort in Tijuana may cost you hundreds of dollars per night.

SPA TOURISM

The spa tourism industry is akin to wellness tourism and health tourism subsets of the larger medical tourism industry. Visits to spa centers for spa treatments have profound psychological benefits on patients as a massage, facial or a similar cosmetic treatment helps restore their self-confidence.

One of the key factors that drive spa tourism is its projection of spa therapies as services that come included with the package when one books a stay at a spa resort. Since a trip to a spa for treatments alone has a slightly negative connotation, bundling a bunch of spa treatments into your vacation becomes psychologically acceptable. Men who would otherwise consider getting an exotic fish pedicure or a mud body wrap demeaning or a feminine pursuit can benefit from these therapies without delving into their gender-specific connotations.

One of the key advantages of spa tourism is the fact that it blends seamlessly with mainstream tourism, such as medical tourism, health tourism and even wellness tourism. Therefore, you find the most high-end spa resorts and spa therapy centers within close proximity to major global tourist resorts.

Hence, when a couple or a single male executive from a developed nation stays at a high-end spa resort, his package would include local sightseeing and a number of therapies provided at the in-house spa.

Apart from the de-stigmatization of essential cosmetic therapies, spa tourism caters to an aspect of human wellness that mainstream medical, health and wellness tourism segments often neglect completely: the need to look good.

Beauty is a prized characteristic for any member of any species on the planet. Similarly, humans look for outer beauty in other members of our species. Hence, what skeptics would consider a vanity becomes the heart and soul of an essential medical service through spa tourism.

If we keep cost factor in mind, spa tourism caters to a whole range of budgets. Higher end travelers can stay at posh spa resorts and avail exclusive in-house therapies. The budget travelers can stay at cheaper hotels or hostels and visit local spas to get popular therapies, such as Thai massage, Dead Sea mud wrap, etc.

ALTERNATIVE WELLNESS TOURISM

In the mainstream medical industry, alternative medicine has garnered a lot of attention, respect and credibility and hence, many specialists prescribe alternative wellness treatments to patients receiving mainstream treatment.

In certain cases, wellness physicians recommend cancer patients to consider therapies from Unani and Ayurvedic alternative wellness systems to cope with the side effects of chemotherapy etc. Some alternative wellness specialists, on the other hand, ask their patients to consult an allopathic specialist to overcome an ailment when alternative medicines are not sufficiently effective on their own.

Even though most alternative wellness treatments do not guarantee 100 percent results for every patient every time, they are excellent supplements to a conventional course of treatment, especially for an aggressive one with known side effects.

Interestingly enough, what we now acknowledge as alternative wellness treatments were once the conventional courses of medicine and treatments. Some alternative wellness treatments come from very ancient medical systems, which involved highly evolved and complex use of herbs and holistic methods of treating the body, mind and spirit.

Also referred to as holistic medicine, alternative wellness treatments include herbal medicine, homeopathy, Ayurveda, chiropractic, osteopathy, acupuncture, acupressure, reflexology, yogic breathing, Reiki, and even cyma therapy (sound healing).

It is vital to note that some of these treatments like acupressure, acupuncture and Ayurveda have their roots in ancient medical practices, while others, such as cyma therapy, reflexology, chiropractic and homeopathy are recent inventions. While mainstream medical science does accept that alternative wellness therapies do work, it also concedes that scientific research does not completely support most modern AW systems.

For a patient planning alternative medical trip, it is vital to remember that any good institute or facility offering these treatments would have some form of recognition, certification and license from an authority regulating these practices in that country or region. Just as you would not walk into a Bikram Yoga class run by an unlicensed practitioner, you should also remember to check the credentials of the facility offering alternative wellness before investing in a package.

COMPLEMENTARY MEDICAL TOURISM

Complementary medical tourism is a relatively new subset of the mainstream medical tourism industry. Unlike alternative medical tourism and wellness tourism, complementary medical tourism helps one receive a specific kind of treatment from an alternative/

wellness medical practice to tackle problems caused due to a mainstream or conventional course of treatment.

The biggest difference between complementary medical tourism and other forms of medical tourism is that the former aims to relieve the stress or side effects caused by a mainstream course of treatment. Hence, a doctor or specialist consulting or treating a patient would usually recommend a complementary medical treatment that conventional medical methods cannot alleviate.

Some of the best-recommended complementary medical treatments include Tai Chi, which is a system of postures and rhythmic movements developed from martial art postures used in the 12th century in China. Tai Chi bases itself on the Yin and Yang principle or the principles of the two opposing life forces as theorized by Confucian and Buddhist philosophies. The purpose of Tai Chi is to restore emotional and physical balance by restoration of Yang and Yang energies.

Japanese stress relieving therapy Reiki is also popular with patients seeking complementary medical treatments. It helps promote physical relaxation, reverence for life and spiritual awareness. For someone stricken with a life-threatening ailment, Reiki can provide physical relief from the rigors of conventional treatment and mental relaxation from the stress as well.

As an alternative medical system, Ayurveda is perhaps the best known but one needs to understand that it is a full medical system in its own right. However, since Ayurvedic treatments rely entirely on the use of herbs, organic materials and massages, they do not interfere with a conventional course of treatment and can even boost the effectiveness of allopathic treatments.

INTEGRATIVE MEDICAL TOURISM

Before one can understand what integrative medicine and integrative medical tourism is, it is essential to know the basic differences between this subset of medicine and medical tourism and all the others that have become popular recently.

We have many kinds of alternative and wellness medical streams. Each of these disciplines claims either to stem from an ancient system of medicine or to be a recent invention based on ancient medical philosophies.

For therapies like cyma therapy, aromatherapy, magnetic therapies, hot stone therapies etc., a proper scientific basis is not always present. Not all ancient and alternative medical and wellness therapies are bogus.

Integrative medicine, basically, seeks to examine and find the best of ancient therapies and modern treatments and combine various methods of both worlds to treat the patients with the least invasive, least toxic and least costly treatments. Briefly, the unification of nature and technology emphasizes healing with the best of both worlds.

CRUISE SHIP MEDICAL TOURISM

Even if one has never personally been on a cruise, the industry is famous for providing all material comforts known to man on land aboard a floating vessel. The cruise ship industry experienced considerable growth in the 1970s when the economic boom in the western world filled both young and mature travelers with optimism.

Unfortunately, cruise ships lost some of their charm when the airline industry began attracting middle and low-income tourists. These tourists are the ones who were short on both money and time, and needed a budget and time friendly vacation.

In the second decade of 21st century, cruise ship tourism is making a grand comeback while bracing itself with medical, health and wellness treatments. Traditionally, spa treatments and health & wellness treatments had been a part of a regular cruise package. Activities including sporting lessons, nutrition and cuisine lessons, arts and crafts, dancing and dance lessons, massages, nail treatments, hair and skin treatments were available on cruise lines – both on and off board.

However, it was not until the mid-2000s that cruise lines realized the potential for medical tourism within their existing infrastructure. Since most cruise lines are required by law to have a nursing and hospital staff on board, it didn't take too long before cruise ships began employing cosmetic surgeons who could offer procedures like Botox, breast augmentation, various other cosmetic procedures and even minor non-life threatening medical treatments.

With the growth of medical tourism in its own right, it only makes sense for the cruise ship industry to offer an increasing range of medical treatments both on board as well as at key stops and destinations. The industry is in its infancy, but it still offers the potential for exponential growth in the cruise ship tourism as well as the medical tourism industry.

Imagine a top cruise liner roping in the services of the best-known dentist, cosmetic surgeon or even heart specialist for the duration of a cruise. Patients on board can consult the specialist, get treatments done, have follow up checkups and recover post-procedure right on the ship that also provides them with a number of other luxuries and activities. It would be like staying at an excellent hospital where you feel at ease to entertain yourself during recovery.

CHAPTER 2

History of Medical Tourism

IN THIS CHAPTER

- Medical tourism through history
- A look at how medical tourism developed over time
- Medical tourism in the 21st century
- The future of medical tourism

"Healing is a matter of time, but it is sometimes also a matter of opportunity."

–Hippocrates

The history of medical travel is not different from that of medicine itself. Humans have voyaged to the end of the world to find remedies for their ailments and the best possible cure, sometimes at the cost of all their possessions, severing ties with their homeland and even life. Had our ancestors not explored the realms of earth to find cures, today we would not be where we are in terms of curative knowhow.

We will acquaint you with a brief history of medical tourism divided into three major parts: period before Christ, period after Christ and the developments in the 21st Century.

PERIOD BEFORE CHRIST

Thermal springs

As early as 4200BC, health recuperations included baths in thermal springs or fountains housed in lofty, grandiose temples. The Sumerians were the first to host these temples of yore and provide people from all over the world with a cure that was missing in their respective countries.

Bronze cups

As civilization advanced and entered the metal age around 2000 BC, people started to use bronze utensils to drink from the mineral-rich thermal springs.

Asclepiad temples

During 1500 BC, the Greeks laid the foundation stone of Asclepiad temples in honor of their God of medicine. These temples were the Mecca of convalescent centers. They opened up a vast network for travelers seeking recovery from their illnesses.

Epidauria

In the year 300 BC, the Greek civilization showed promising growth in the budding infirmary field. A small province in the Saronic Gulf – Epidaurus housed centers providing abundant services like temples, gymnasiums, steam baths, curative farms, baths, etc. Some examples of such establishments were the Olympian Sanctuary of Zeus and the Delphian temples.

Thermae

Around the same time, the Romans popularized Thermae or ancient public steam baths, which, aside from offering treatment, helped commoners develop a sense of social life as well.

Yoga and Ayurveda

India made great contributions in bringing the ancient healing measures to the present stage. Yogic healing and Ayurvedic medications attracted several civilizations to the Indian civilization, seeking cures for their physical and spiritual woes.

PERIOD AFTER CHRIST

Onsens

During the 12th-13th centuries, another Asian nation, Japan, emerged as a major remedial contributor. Hot mineral springs, widely known as Onsen, captured the attention of warriors for their miraculous curative properties.

Egyptian hospitals

Cairo was yet another ancient medical tourism hub where an advanced infirmary, Mansuri, flourished sometime during 1250 AD.

Salude per aqua

The term salude per aqua or 'spa' was coined for iron-rich hot springs located in the town of Waters (Ville d'Eaux) in erstwhile Europe. In the subsequent years (14th and 15th centuries), people toured European destinations like Bath, St. Mortiz, Ville d'Eaux, Baden Bade and Aachen not just for treatment but also for tourism.

New World therapies

A growing trend of residing near medicinal springs until the complete recovery gripped the Europeans towards the 17th century. However, newer therapies emerged after the discovery of the New World, wherein natives provided herbal remedies for serious ailments. Comparable to Far Eastern or African cultures, the natives of America were accomplished in ancient healing techniques and thus boosted the influx of health travelers to their nation.

Sanatoriums

The earliest form of hospitals, called sanatoriums, surfaced during the 18th and 19th century. Serious diseases like liver disorders, tuberculosis, gout and bronchitis were surfacing rapidly and sufferers frantically searched for places to cure and isolate these highly infectious syndromes. In such an era, sanatoriums provided welcome relief and patients did not mind traveling to distant countries to avail themselves of such therapeutic opportunities. The kind of resources, physicians or services offered by the sanatorium depended on the national origin and opulence.

THE INDUSTRIAL REVOLUTION

Few things have had as massive an impact on our world as the Industrial Revolution. As the steam engine first chugged and new transport methods became available, medical tourism got a huge shot in the arm. People could now travel to different locations much faster, at lower costs, and in greater volumes. Traveling distances for medical needs actually became practical. Doctors increasingly started suggesting treatments like "a change in scenery," made possible and affordable on the large scale by the facilities brought forth by the Industrial Revolution.

Specializations:

The late 20th century saw the several developing countries offer specialization surgeries as part of medical tourism initiatives. The specialized surgeries were available in advanced nations, but executed at a dear price. Developing countries took advantage of the gulf in pries to promote medical tourism facilities of their own. For example, Cuba started propagating its capabilities worldwide and gained eminence in cardiac, cosmetic and even optical surgeries. While countries in Central America became quite famous for dental procedures, Thailand started gaining prominence for plastic surgery and even customary medical procedures during the late 90s.

Emergence of Medical Tourism in 21st Century

The rich history of medical tourism and its continuous growth over the years is enough to give anyone an idea about emerging trends in 21st century and events that contributed to it. This is the only reason why millions of people are now considering taking a trip to other countries to obtain surgical, dental, or even regular medical care.

The medical tour offers cost saving, better accessibility to treatment, and having fun at a tourist destination that would not be otherwise possible in your home country. However, these are not the only reasons that made medical travel a success.

Though medical tourism's current massive scale is a comparatively new development, the niche industry already has impressive statistics related to its operations. The annual cost of medical travel is around $40 billion all over the world, whereas the average expense of a medical tourist is approximately $3,000 to $5,000 for each visit.

As medical costs skyrocket in developed countries like United States, Australia, United Kingdom, Canada, etc., there is a continuous increase in patients' tendency to travel to developing countries to seek healthcare. The countries that are becoming hot destinations for the patients from the developed countries include Thailand, India, Singapore, Malaysia, Mexico, Korea, and a few other nations in the Middle East.

The primary reason behind this rising trend of medical tourism is excellent healthcare at a fraction of the cost in developed countries, which is attributable to:

- Significantly lower labor cost
- Much less expenditure associated with the litigation for unprofessional conduct

- Flexible laws and regulations
- Restricted engagement of third-party clients

Some other factors that contribute to the growth of the medical tourism industry include:

- Huge uninsured population and insured people bearing the costs of elective surgeries and 'pre-existing' medical conditions
- Aging population, considered a 'burden' for the healthcare industry
- No accessibility to alternative therapies like Ayurvedic treatments, Homeopathy, naturopathy, and others
- Long waiting period for several surgical procedures

However, the competition in the industry is also escalating with its rapid growth. Owing to this increasing competition, countries have started offering excellent services at competitive prices, which certainly works very well for the medical tourist. Certain other commercial considerations like benefits of insurance, tourism, and trading, have played a part in boosting medical tourism and have successfully turned it into a global industry. All these facilities help various medical destinations attract more medical travelers and strengthen their global presence at the same time.

RISE OF DEVELOPING COUNTRIES

When it comes to medical tourism, developing countries always remain ahead of developed ones. Be it cutting-edge technology or healthcare costs, western countries lag behind the less-developed nations in terms of several aspects of medical travel. The majority of developing nations coming up as great medical destinations are accredited by the Joint Commission International (JCI) and offer world-class, specialized, customized, and cost-effective healthcare along with insurance benefits.

Thailand, the beautiful country located in Southeast Asia, is one of the most preferable medical destinations. Patients from developed countries can get a highly positive medical experience in Thailand at a very affordable cost. From staying at a lush hotel to undergoing a last-minute medical procedure, the Thai Government has made each and everything possible for medical tourists without burning holes in their pockets. The country provides advanced treatments like stem cell therapy along with traditional healthcare services. As there is no threat of strict regulations or mismanagement grievances in Thailand, the industry runs quite smoothly.

The 'incredible' country India also has an international reputation for its growing business of medical tourism. Accessibility to state of the art healthcare infrastructure at low to moderate costs is the specialty of Indian medical tourism. Thousands of medical practitioners in the country have obtained their degrees from the world's top medical universities. Nurses and technicians working in India have also earned fame for their excellent care, cooperation and skills. Indian hospitals and medical facilities have access to advanced medical equipment, which turn the dental, surgical and medical procedures into faster and smoother ones. Alternative medicine or treatment is another major attraction of the medical tourism in India. The country has also made the concept of surrogacy tourism popular throughout the world.

Mexico is another prominent addition to the list of developing countries having the best medical tourism destinations. The country draws around 1 million foreign patients each year. Healthcare at an economical rate is one of the major attractions of Mexican medical tourism. The services offered by the hospitals and other medical facilities in the country are so reasonably priced that one can visit a doctor at $25 and stay hospitalized for a whole night at $35 only. Medical tourists mainly go to Mexico for dental treatments as well as weight loss surgeries.

Many other developing nations like Singapore, Malaysia, Costa Rica, Indonesia, Turkey, Taiwan, and some from the Middle East have already earned fame and admiration from medical tourists.

ENVISIONING THE FUTURE OF HEALTHCARE

With advantages like cheaper costs, world-class services, alternative therapies, well-qualified doctors, medical tourism is the future of global healthcare. An increasing number of people from developed countries are visiting developing countries for obtaining surgical, medical, dental, and cosmetic treatments. As the multiplicity and intricacy of various diseases are increasing, the trend of visiting foreign countries to undertake treatments is also going up.

Non-emergency surgery is the most popular choice of medical tourists. They choose this exclusive form of healthcare mainly for undergoing elective surgeries or non-emergency surgeries including joint replacement surgeries (hip replacement, knee replacement, etc.), laser eye surgeries, and so on.

Plastic surgeries or cosmetic surgeries are also highly in demand, which further include facelift, liposuction, rhinoplasty, breast augmentation, etc. People are also opting for dentistry works like veneers and dental restoration (crowns).

A recent report shows that the number of medical tourists surpassed 10 million all over the world last year. Among them, 1.6 million were Americans and constituted a major chunk of medical tourists. China and Japan are in second and third positions respectively. Almost 29% of worldwide medical tourists are Chinese and 18% are Japanese. Certain Asian countries like Thailand, India, and Malaysia are drawing a huge chunk of American medical tourists each year.

Quality is one of the biggest aspects of medical tourism, and medical travelers do gain the maximum value for their investment. Medicine has always been a great career option and with the inception of medical tourism, the trend has gone even bigger. Many staff doctors working in the health care facilities in developing nations have obtained their training and education from the UK or USA. The majority of hospitals in these countries have accreditation from the Joint Commission (US).

Besides, the invention of new drugs, launch of new pharmaceutical patents, introduction of cutting-edge surgical technologies, use of advanced machineries, thriving national infrastructure, affordable traveling, and fast and easy loan procedures contribute to the global healthcare sector.

CHAPTER 3

Benefits of Medical Tourism

IN THIS CHAPTER

- The various benefits medical tourism offers
- How medical tourism can offer you cost savings
- How medical tourism can provide better quality care

Affordability is the biggest advantage of medical tourism. As patients from highly developed nations are traveling to less-developed countries, they are obtaining treatments and care at reasonable prices. From simple medical procedures to complex surgeries, everything has become cost-efficient through medical tourism. The services offered by major medical tourism destinations are generally low-cost, but that surely does not mean that the facilities compromise with the quality of the care. International patients can get almost similar medical facilities without spending an arm and a leg for the same.

Easy accessibility of hospitals, doctors, nurses and other staff is another reason for which patients become eager to step out of their geographical regions. It ensures immediate treatment without prolonging the waiting time, which further makes the entire procedure faster.

For those seeking secret treatment, medical tourism is a perfect option. A variety of insurance coverage offered by various medical tourism destinations is also a great attraction for medical tourists. As a final point, the perception of recovering from an illness and exploring the scenic beauty of an amazing place is quite exhilarating too.

AFFORDABILITY (COST SAVING)

The major reason lying behind the extensive popularity of medical tourism is its affordability. Investing in traveling, lodging and treatment in another country is much cheaper than being treated in your home country. Due to the low labor cost, lesser involvement of middle parties, inexpensive misconduct litigation procedures and lenient rules and regulations, the healthcare services offered by medical tours remain a lot easier on the wallets of people. Therefore, opting for medical tourism can eventually result in huge cost savings.

Cost-effective medical travel is not only for insured patients, it has multiple benefits for uninsured people as well. It is an outstanding solution for those who have insurance policies but need to undergo certain surgeries or medical procedures that do not come under the coverage.

Many factors regulate the healthcare costs in foreign countries. Traveling costs, accommodation expenses, costs of food, costs of medical services etc. are some of them. The location also plays an important role in deciding the estimated cost of the entire affair. People can save anywhere between 25 to 80 percent during a single medical vacation.

EASY ACCESSIBILITY, IMMEDIATE TREATMENT

Promptness or easy accessibility to the medical services is another amazing benefit of this exclusive form of healthcare that foreign patients can really enjoy. The number of medical tourists flocking to developing nations like Thailand, Malaysia, India, Singapore, Costa Rica, and Taiwan is escalating at a rapid pace as the healthcare services that these countries offer are much faster than the services that developed countries offer to their citizens. It is truly helpful for people who are in need of emergency cures.

Countries like Canada and UK run a public healthcare system, which faces extreme challenges to serve several patients simultaneously. As a result, everybody – from regular patients to critically ill ones – needs to wait to get the necessary treatment. It is very problematic for those who are suffering from chronic diseases or are in urgent need of medications. Medical tourism has turned into the best alternative to healthcare services for these people as it offers easy accessibility to medical facilities as well as fast treatments.

Several developing countries do not have public healthcare systems and hence, they do not have waiting lists either. Every patient is considered as the 'priority' in these places, which makes the entire system amazingly fast. All leading hospitals and nursing homes in these nations are equipped with highly qualified and experienced doctors, nurses and other staff. They make use of the most advanced medical equipment as well as sophisticated technologies. The infrastructure of these medical facilities is also top-notch. Above all, patients can receive excellent care and access all these facilities any time they need them. As the waiting time is shorter, patients do not have to suffer much. They are diagnosed, treated, and sometimes even recover just within a few weeks.

More and more global patients, who prefer traveling overseas for the sake of their health and skip the queue, are opting for medical tours. It is a quick and convenient way for them to get rid of pain. In addition, it ensures satisfaction as well as peace of mind for patients, which can be a major factor in accelerating the time of recovery.

ACCEPTABILITY OF SERVICES AT OTHER DESTINATIONS

While a few governments in western developed nations do not accept certain medicinal therapies or complicated surgeries, some developing countries offering medical tourism consider the requirements of patients as their first preference and allow them to receive those treatments with utmost care.

Availing the medical services at the foreign destinations that are not otherwise legally accepted in their home countries wasn't possible for patients before the concept of medical tourism came into being. Many countries have put regulations on certain non-emergency procedures as well as complex surgeries. Some of them have even banned those treatments due to several reasons. However, when it comes to other destinations like developing nations, people can take advantage of the lenient laws and regulations and get services that they wish. Besides, they do have a selection of countries to choose from, so even if the preferred treatment is not available in some countries, it may be available in another country.

FACTS AND INSIGHTS RELATED TO MEDICAL TOURISM

Mexico, one of the most popular medical tourism destinations in the world, has gained much popularity for its stem-cell therapy. The U.S. Government does not accept the unique intervention strategy that is useful in treating a range of injuries and diseases. Therefore, an almost wheelchair-bound U.S. patient of Parkinson's disease (PD) had to fly to Mexico a few months ago in order to undergo the therapy and got some relief from the problem.

Similarly, the U.S. Food and Drug Administration (FDA) kept Hip Resurfacing, which is a surgical substitute of Total Hip Replacement or THR, under regulation for a long time. The procedure is recognized as one of the most helpful solutions for patients suffering from non-inflammatory degenerative joint diseases.

Furthermore, it has an excellent success rate at more than a few well-known medical tourism destinations. None of these was enough to receive approval for the surgery from the American Government. However, the issue has been resolved now and the U.S. Government finally allowed the surgery in the year 2006.

The situation is quite clear from these two facts. You can say that if a person wants to undergo any of those elective surgeries that are either not legal or available at his or her home country, going across the border can be a better option. In short, medical tourism works as the great savior for such patients.

AVAILABILITY AND BETTER QUALITY OF HEALTHCARE SERVICES

There is a myth that patients need to compromise with the quality to get affordable treatments and care during medical vacations. Countries offering medical tourism always focus on the superiority of their services and try to maintain excellence in order to ensure the highest quality of care to lure a greater number of international patients.

The majority of hospitals, nursing homes and other medical facilities present in developing countries have accreditation from Joint Commission International (JCI) and International Organization for Standardization (ISO). Both of these global accrediting bodies have strict prerequisites that every healthcare organization needs to fulfill prior to getting the accreditation. Some of them also get affiliation from various well-known American establishments like the Johns Hopkins University School of Medicine, the Harvard Medical School, etc. and work in collaboration with those. The objective of such associations is to provide the best possible healthcare services to foreign patients.

Quite a few other factors also contribute to the amazing quality of services offered by medical tourism. Governments of various developing nations are investing lots of money in the healthcare sector for improving their infrastructure as well as giving a significant boost to the entire medical tourism industry. As a result, well-equipped medical facilities are coming up with each passing day, which are ultimately enhancing the quality of services and making healthcare accessible for all.

Developing countries now boast of having numerous qualified and talented doctors as well as medical consultants. They are skilled, efficient and have many years of working experience in reputed healthcare organizations in the USA or UK. The nurses and other hospital staff are also quite proficient and helpful. Therefore, global patients can always get a more customized as well as personalized service for themselves during medical vacations.

The application of a range of cutting-edge medical tools and equipment has also turned these medical facilities into the best ones in the entire world in terms of the standard and quality of services.

PRIVACY

Patients often look for privacy in the medical facilities available in their home countries but usually fail to find it. Though the need for secrecy or confidentiality can vary from person to person, it plays an important role in the case of certain surgeries or medical procedures. Many people want to keep their healing procedures as furtive as possible, especially when it comes to various cosmetic surgeries. They do not even mind flying across the border in order to maintain their confidentiality. Medical tourism is bliss for these people as it provides a perfect environment to keep them away from prying eyes.

Cosmetic surgeries or procedures are medical specialties that many people opt for these days. These are non-emergency or elective surgeries, which patients intend to enhance their appearance or eliminate the appearance of aging from their face or body. People who undergo these beauty treatments often try to stay away from their surroundings during their treatments in order to avoid inquisitive eyes and uncomfortable questions.

There is a great variety of cosmetic surgeries, such as rhinoplasty, liposuction, breast augmentation, facelift, etc. offered by various medical tourism destinations. Those who want to undergo any of these can opt for a medical tour and obtain the best possible treatments at a reasonable price, without people knowing about their decisions.

Medical professionals working in the healthcare organizations of different medical tourism destinations ensure the utmost privacy of their clients by making use of all those standards of confidentiality that are maintained in American hospitals. They never disclose personal as well as treatment related information of their patients to guarantee the excellent services.

CUSTOMIZED AND PERSONALIZED SERVICES ABOARD

Sometimes, saving money or getting better quality healthcare is not enough for patients. They look for something more that can give them a sense of satisfaction and help them recover fast. Customized medical services and personalized care can work best in such situations, which usually the public healthcare systems of most of the developed countries do not offer. However, medical tourism can come up as one of the excellent solutions for this issue.

Leading medical tourism destinations like India, Thailand, Costa Rica, Mexico, Malaysia and others have the necessary setup that can keep the entire process easy, smooth and streamlined. The idea is to ease the process for foreign patients who know nothing about the destination country. The doctor-patient ratio in such nations is also very impressive. As there is no long waiting list, medical professionals can spend enough time with each of their clients, know their problems in detail, identify with their requirements and finally come up with personalized healthcare services for them.

Like the doctor-patient ratio, the staff to patient ratio maintained by the hospitals and other healthcare organizations in these countries is also quite low. Nurses working in these medical facilities are very friendly and efficient. They receive proper training to manage their tasks successfully. They can easily provide professional attention and care to foreign patients, even after their treatment.

Technology also plays a key role in providing personalized care to overseas patients. Most of the hospitals and clinics present in various medical tourism destinations are equipped with highly sophisticated equipment and use the latest technologies. It helps medical practitioners offer the right treatment to the patients as per their requirements.

COMPETITION

As said in previous sections, the most important benefit of medical tourism is its affordability. While the medical expenses incurred by the public healthcare systems around the world are out of people's reach, several countries offering medical tourism are coming up with a number of cost-effective solutions. Moreover, with the ever-increasing competition in the thriving industry, most of the medical service providers are trying to keep the costs at the lowest point and the quality at the higher end, which adds to the advantage of the patients.

Medical tourism has opened up a completely new industry. As the healthcare costs in developed nations are rising dramatically, more and more people around the world are opting for medical tourism. Though it was limited to a few countries like India, Thailand, Malaysia, etc. at first, the scenario has changed a lot. In order to compete in the global marketplace and gain huge profit from the boom, several other nations like Mexico, Costa Rica, Taiwan, and Singapore have joined the industry and the number is still growing. As a result, it has become very important for every medical tourism destination to offer quality services at unbelievably low prices in order to fetch the maximum number of foreign patients.

While the countries are trying hard to sustain the highly competitive market, patients are enjoying amazing low-cost high-quality services. This setup contributes to the advancement of the entire medical tourism industry significantly and hence, the business is growing at a 30% annual rate around the world.

Here is how the foreign competition is driving the costs of healthcare down for patients:

- A Cardiac Bypass surgery that costs $144,000 in the U.S. can be availed at $25,000 in Costa Rica, $24,000 in Thailand, $24,000 in Korea, $20,000 in Mexico, $13,500 in Singapore, and only $8,500 in India
- U.S. patients need to spend around $50,000 for a Hip Resurfacing surgery. But it costs $20,900 in Korea, $16,000 in Thailand, $12,800 in Mexico, $12,100 in Singapore, $12,000 in Costa Rica, and as little as $8,000 in India
- The average cost of Rhinoplasty is $8,000 in the U.S, while it costs approximately $5,500 in Costa Rica, $4,165 in Mexico, $3,500 in India, $3,400 in Thailand, and only $2,700 in Singapore

INSURANCE COVERAGE

Insurance benefits of medical travel are also very important from the customer's point of view. The number of insurance agencies offering policies for medical tourists is progressively increasing.

It can help the foreign patients in two ways. Developed countries still have a large number of people who cannot afford health insurance. Special insurance coverage intended for medical tourists can assist them in undergoing expensive as well as complicated surgeries without burning holes in their pocket. On the other hand, patients who already have health insurance policies but need to undertake certain medical procedures that their health insurance does not cover can reap the benefits of the affordable healthcare services offered at leading medical tourism destinations.

There are a number of surgical approaches, such as orthopedic surgeries (hip replacement, hip resurfacing, knee replacement, etc.), cosmetic surgeries (breast augmentation, facelift, rhinoplasty, etc.), eye surgeries (cataract, LASIK, etc.), which do not come under regular health insurance coverage. However, at the same time, the demand for these elective surgeries is escalating at a rapid pace. Hence, an increased number of developing countries have started offering these services to their international patients at remarkably low prices along with optimal care.

Offering insurance coverage to medical tourists is also a great deal for the insurance agencies as it can save costs to a great extent. That is why the majority of companies focuses on the requirements of their clients and come up with tailored policies for them and their companions as well. From comprehensive travel insurance to coverage for medical procedure complications – there is a wide range of choices for patients. Certain features of these policies include:

- Coverage for the cancellation, interruption or disruption of medical trip
- Benefits for the delay of trip
- Coverage for baggage as well as personal effects
- Coverage for emergency medical conditions
- Benefits for regular medical procedures
- Accidental coverage for medical travel
- Coverage for complicated surgeries
- Coverage for the companion of the patient

Typically, the insurance coverage intended for medical tourists covers all sorts of conventional healthcare including surgical care, medical care and dental care. Furthermore, there is no co-pay or deductible associated with the policies. Patients can take advantage of 60-day travel insurance that is effected from the date of leaving the home country and get around 40% off all their prescriptions. On top, there are some exclusive facilities offered by such insurance coverage, which are not even available in the U.S.

MEDICAL TOURISM BENEFITS

Apart from getting all those materialistic benefits, medical tourists can enjoy a wonderful vacation too. Patients from developed countries often travel to other parts of the world, especially less-developed ones, for obtaining high-quality healthcare services at reasonable prices. It means that while going out of the country for medical purposes, people can expect to get the best possible medical care as well as a fast recovery in a beautiful surrounding or for that matter, in the lap of nature.

The concept of adding some fun, enjoyment and adventure to the medical needs of a patient is certainly a positive move. Though critics often say that the amalgamation of tourism with healthcare is a wrong approach, the medical tourism industry has already proved its success. It gives those ill people a comforting break from those day-to-day stresses so that they can stay relaxed and get well quickly. Even if the patient is unavailable for conventional tourism, friends or family members accompanying the patient can enjoy a small vacation.

Medical tourism attracts a huge number of foreign patients each year by its usefulness, low-cost high-quality healthcare services as well as the pleasure of a peaceful vacation. They can also enjoy exploring the food, culture, major attractions, fun activities, etc. at those places.

Generally, medical tourism destinations offer lucrative package deals for their potential patients. They consider each and everything that a medical tourist might need, expect, and want. From the medical expenses to the costs of traveling, everything is included in these packages. Foreign patients can get some of the most intricate surgeries done while staying in boutique hotels or luxury resorts with first-rate services. Even the private rooms available in the hospitals or medical facilities for the patients and their companions are decorated so well that patients would always feel like spending time in one of the best accommodations in the world.

Medical tourism can often also prove to be lifesaving. Several countries do not allow patients to undergo procedures like organ transplants. However, the same surgery might be available in some other country and could be availed with medical tourism.

Medical tourism also gives a wonderful opportunity to patients to take pleasure in the scenic beauty and awesome environment of their destinations. Depending on the location, they can enjoy the sunset across a white sand beach or get a full-body massage at one of the best spas in the world. It could help them recuperate more effectively and at much cheaper prices than their home countries.

Since patients and their attendants travel to a foreign land, it can be difficult for them to find the appropriate hospitals, doctors, or even arranging for a stay in their intended destination country. These problems are generally taken care of with the presence of Medical Tourism Facilitators. These professionals manage the entirety of a patient's medical tourism trip. The facilities offered range from being an interface of the patient with the medical facility and arranging documentation for travel and treatment, to arranging conventional tourism visits for the patient and/or their accompanying friends and family members. Having professional support in a foreign land can prove to be advantageous and help remove issues one might face in these countries.

CHAPTER 4

Challenges and Issues of Medical Tourism

IN THIS CHAPTER

- Different challenges involved in medical tourism
- Unexpected events that could arise from medical tourism

Nothing in this world comes with the benefits alone. The various benefits that medical tourists can reap have been elaborated at length, it is now time to introduce the other side as well. This section will focus on the challenges and issues that a potential medical tourist could face on foreign soil, or even during planning a medical tourism foray.

As things are wont to be when concerning medical conditions, and complex trips, you obviously cannot rule out the chances of things going haywire in several stages – during your stay, when the treatment is in progress, and/or during post-operative care. The possibility of anything going wrong in a foreign land makes it prudent to be prepared for eventualities. The challenges are worth considering for anyone and everyone planning to undertake medical treatment overseas. A potential medical tourist should know about these to make the best out of his journey abroad.

It is important to note that countries may have varying authorization codes and quality measures across the globe, that one might not entirely feel comfortable with. Therefore, in the lack of effective regulations and standards for medical tourist destinations across the globe is likely to present a problem. Proper medical tourism, however, does not fall into an entirely unorganized sector. As mentioned in a previous chapter, several hospitals are accredited by associations like JCI, ISO, or have affiliations with other major institutes. It is in the best interest of patients to look for, and consider only such accredited institutions that follow international standards for patient safety.

These problems and challenges not only include certain risks but one could face language and cultural barriers and problem with pre and post-operative care if things have not been planned meticulously. You might surely not know exactly as to what type of services a particular facility on a foreign land provides and of course, not the quality of the services either.

Also, you might be landing in a different environment altogether and you do not know whether your body will act in the new environment. You never know how active your immune system will be against the infections and other diseases prevalent in the destination country. You do not know their law, nor have time to know the same either.

ACCESS TO CORRECT INFORMATION

Internet is a boon and a bane too. Everyone who is active on the World Wide Web knows this. Another thing that we all know is that the internet is a vast source of information. As the number of websites increases with each day, distinguishing between authentic sources and those that are less reliable is becoming increasingly difficult, even for the net savvy.

In such a situation, accessing the right information is not an easy task and patients face major problems accessing the right information while they search various websites for the availability of different treatments on many foreign medical tourism destinations.

The lack of information regulation and the freedom to post anything on internet ends up in cluttered information that has the power to baffle a medical tourist. Therefore, accessing correct information is a challenge. The potential medical tourists should ensure that they access information from the right sources and never forget to crosscheck and confirm before they finally travel overseas to seek healthcare.

PROBLEMS WITH PRE AND POST-OPERATIVE CARE

Another challenge that a medical tourist faces while seeking healthcare abroad is availing good and timely pre and post-operative care. This becomes even more difficult if the patient has traveled long distance to avail treatment. For patients seeking healthcare abroad, proper pre and post-operative diagnoses are not just necessary but can also save them from unnecessary expenses.

For example, if a patient is travelling overseas for surgery and his/her blood sugar level is high; a doctor might ask the patient to wait and/or can refuse to perform surgery until the sugar level drops. Therefore, timely pre and post-operative care is necessary and the medical tourists can avoid any discrepancies in the same by developing a good communication strategy.

Returning to the case of post-operative care, it forms one of the greatest concerns for the medical tourist. Availing the right and timely post-operative care on a medical tourist destination for an extended period might be too expensive at times. Even if you avail it for some time abroad, you cannot rule out the possibilities of post-operative complications arising when you are back at your home.

One can have complications like blood clots or pulmonary embolism to name a few, during a long journey back to the homeland. It should also be noted that unnecessary alarm is unwarranted. Hospitals generally will allow the patient to travel only after sufficient post-operative care is provided, and the patient is seen fit to travel. However, such possibilities should not be entirely dismissed. It is likely that some post-operative care might also be needed once the patient returns home. In such a situation, finding the post-operative care on time is challenging. However, one can deal with this problem to some extent by keeping in mind the following:

- Check in advance whether the post-operative care for the treatment or surgery you seek abroad is available in your country or not and how much it will actually cost. If not, do not consider the option of medical tourism.
- In another case, a patient is at a potential risk of health problems like swelling and/or infections by exposing his/her fragile body to exertion too early. Planning everything in consultation with your physician is the key to successful treatment abroad.

LANGUAGE AND CULTURAL BARRIERS

Language issues and cultural barriers are formidable challenges in the medical tourism sector. If the people of the destination country do not speak or understand the language of the medical tourist, obtaining the accurate information can be fairly difficult. It also lands you in a situation where you find yourself unable to ask relevant questions and the healthcare service provider fails to provide you with the right information.

The chance of a medical tourist facing cross culture misunderstanding is also as high as it gets. To avoid these, a medical tourist should avoid traveling to medical tourist destinations that do not speak and understand his/her language in the first place.

On the other hand, if you wish, you could hire a translator, but hiring one will mean you spend more. Apart from this, the medical tourism destinations and facilities catering these services should make conscious efforts to include resources required for the purpose and even offer a translator to ensure that the patients get accurate information. It will help patients make an informed decision regarding an issue as sensitive and important as their health.

The healthcare service providers should also be well aware of the cultural competency and include these to their treatment policies to avoid any hassles arising due to this factor. Patients should also know the basics and try understanding the culture of the destination country to make their experiences as medical tourists as pleasing as possible.

In several instances, important documents, healthcare reports, patient history, and other documents of the tourist might be in the native language of their country. This can pose a problem in case the native country and destination country do not follow the same language. A (relatively) small expense on medical transcription would be very useful in dealing with such a problem.

MAINTAINING QUALITY OF HEALTHCARE

Every medical tourist does a qualitative analysis before opting for medical travel, and rightly so. The primary concern is to know if the medical tourism facilities are well up to international standards. Usually, the healthcare facilities under medical tourism industry try attracting medical tourists with the promise of highest level of quality care as demonstrated by international standards. However, there sometimes remain discrepancies if we compare facilities offered in developed countries to what the developing countries offer.

One can see the efforts of developing countries to provide high-class facilities and healthcare. Even then, what makes medical tourists from the developed countries skeptical is the implementation of high quality standards when the basic medical infrastructure is perceived missing in general.

Another cause of concern for medical tourists is to know if the affiliate centers to the accredited medical facility operate at the same level of quality as is set by the accrediting authorities. Checking it on internet and believing it is difficult, and to ensure the same by personally visiting the facilities is not practical.

COPING WITH INFECTIONS IN FOREIGN COUNTRIES

Another big challenge that medical tourists face at a foreign location is the fact that they are usually exposed to various infections and diseases prevalent in the destination country. The native people usually have natural inborn immunity to these diseases. They are not at high risk of these diseases; however, these diseases might gravely affect new visitors. Knowing and keeping themselves safe from these infections and allergies is a big challenge before and particularly after the treatment or surgery. This is because of the reason that the immune system of a patient after a procedure may not be as sound to protect the body from an infection.

LEGAL ISSUES

Legal issues are of greatest concern to patients while they seek healthcare at a medical tourist destination in a foreign country. In case anything goes wrong during a surgery, or for that matter, during a treatment, it puts the patients in a difficult situation.

The intra country laws and legal procedures pose a big challenge too and hinder medical tourists from getting meaningful legal support. Most of the time, lack of recourse makes medical tourists apprehensive about seeking healthcare abroad.

Further, medical tourists from developed countries find considerable differences when it comes to legal rights in the destination country and what they are accustomed to in their home country. Coping with such a situation can be difficult, particularly when they have valid reasons to sue a doctor or medical facility but they cannot.

If there are some technical problems, some medical facilities are unavailable for a particular time, doctors are unavailable and many other reasons might cost heavily to medical tourists. They have to wait and that will increase their stay in a foreign land and thereby their expenses. If the medical facility does not compensate for the same and doctor(s) refuse to correct any surgical errors initially or delays correcting them intentionally, getting legal aid in a foreign country, and getting any error corrected on time becomes difficult for the patients.

The situation becomes even more gruesome for a patient who has undergone some major surgery. In such a situation, seeking legal aid is really challenging. The course of retribution is of prime concern.

INCORRECT ESTIMATION OF COSTS

Patients often end up facing trouble due to incorrect estimation of cost involved in medical tourism. Potential medical tourists should get the right information about the total cost involved before seeking healthcare abroad. Before entering into an agreement, potential medical tourists should understand that the overall cost would include the expenses for treatment, travel, accommodation and other hidden hospital treatment expenses.

Getting the right estimation will help them avoid any unlikely situation arising due to lack of funds on a foreign land.

AUTHENTICATING QUALIFICATIONS OF DOCTOR/SURGEON

A medical tourist might feel the need to verify the qualifications of the physicians and surgeons when considering a medical facility abroad. Having a suitable doctor is important for better results of any treatment.

Knowing everything about the doctors and their qualifications is also important due to other reasons. For example, the chances of one doctor being struck out of the medical register in one country but continuing practice in another country cannot be ruled out.

Most accredited institutions deal with this problem by sending doctor/surgeon profiles to the prospective medical tourist, along with details of their sojourn, and the price quotation. Respectable institutions will often also make it possible for the medical tourist to confirm and crosscheck doctor profile documents, should they wish for it.

INSURANCE COVERAGE

Insurance coverage is a wise move. Not barely in terms of expense, but also as a protection in the event of anything going wrong. Insurance is just like a protective cover that will reduce your financial and mental burden. The need of insurance is even higher during treatments, particularly when one seeks treatment in a medical facility abroad.

An increasing number of insurance companies are now offering their services to medical tourists. It is important for the tourist to understand the requirements of their insurance cover, and find an institution acceptable to their insurance provider. Most of the time, the latter is taken care of by the company itself, by providing their customers guidance towards the selection of a medical facility. Advantage of such an arrangement to the visitor is that quality of care is generally ensured in the recommended institutes. The coverage however, remains limited.

On the downside, many capable hospitals in developing countries offering healthcare to medical tourists are not a part of the network of payers of the developed markets. This results in lack of opportunity for many medical tourism facilities to work directly with the insurance companies and other healthcare funding providers in the market.

ETHICAL ISSUES

The concept of medical tourism also revolves around many controversial ethical and moral issues. Seeking legal protection in such a situation is difficult, time consuming and expensive in a foreign country. It becomes practically impossible for a medical tourist to come out of this difficult situation.

Further, there might be issues like some medical tourist seeking an organ transplant at a foreign location for reasons like the facility is not available in his/her home country or there are long waiting times that might affect his health adversely. In such a case, the patient is left with no other option but to choose a medical tourist destination for organ transplant.

This also has the power of making things appear suspicious, and could be tempted to the folly of illegal organ trade. As with other scenarios, government organizations take such procedures very seriously, and put minute scrutiny on such operations. It would be extremely unlikely for a patient to be caught up in something as heinous as illegal organ trade.

DOCUMENTATION AND VISA

To be certain, it is mere formalities like documentation and visa that trouble medical tourists the most. These processes often move slowly, and to someone keen on getting treatment as soon as possible, the insipid process might as well seem like a lifetime. Some countries might also insist on interviews before providing a visa, which might seem like a nuisance to the prospective tourists. These processes do often require mounds of documentation that will further discourage the medical tourist.

Fortunately, most of the preferred medical tourism destinations are well aware of this problem and are working to cut through the bureaucratic red tape. Many countries now offer "Medical Visa," a visa especially designed for medical tourists. The idea is to make the process more bearable and less taxing to the medical tourist. While progress has been slow, things certainly are taking a turn for the better.

CHAPTER 5

Why healthcare costs are cheaper abroad?

IN THIS CHAPTER

- Examples of why the cost of healthcare in developing countries is cheaper
- How lower real-estate costs and cheaper medications bring about a less expensive hospital bill
- Reasons why lower cost healthcare does not compromise on quality

Low manufacturing cost of medical equipment and low labor costs in developing countries like India, Thailand, and Malaysia play a vital part in making these nations the preferred medical tourist destinations that they are today.

There are many other reasons that not only enable developing countries to offer economical healthcare services, but also world class healthcare that may not be available in developed countries like US, UK, Australia, and France.

LOWER COST OF LABOR (HUMAN RESOURCES)

Lower cost of labor is one of the principal reasons for any commodity being priced cheaply in any sector, and medical tourism is no exception.

The high cost of labor accounts for more than half of any hospital's operating cost on average, which is, of course, high in the developed countries. However, the lower cost of labor enables medical tourist destinations across most of the developing countries to offer healthcare at a considerably lower price.

LOWER REAL ESTATE VALUES AND CHEAPER CONSTRUCTION COST

Lower construction cost and lower real estate values also contribute to lower cost of healthcare in developing countries. Real estate forms one of the major investments for the healthcare sector and real estate values are considerably lower in developing countries, as compared to their developed counterparts.

Hospitals and health centers require large areas for installation of various machines, infrastructure and diagnostic facilities. With the increased cost of real estate, healthcare costs will undoubtedly go higher and this happens everywhere – be it the developed countries or the developing ones. On the other hand, lower cost of real estate contributes immensely in keeping investment low, which then reflects in a lower price for services.

Further, medical facilities require big buildings and constructing these will not be cheap in developed countries. Here too, the high labor cost adds more to the overall cost of constructing buildings and infrastructure.

LOWER GOVERNMENT TAXES

Any product manufacturer or service provider has to pay tax to the government in order to sell the products and services. Therefore, the cost of a commodity that you buy for regular use more often or any service that you avail occasionally is subject to government taxes. Several governments in developing countries provide tax benefits to healthcare institutions, sometimes with an eye towards the medical tourism market, thereby allowing a lower cost of services.

CHEAPER MEDICAL SUPPLIES/EQUIPMENT/MEDICATION

Keeping in mind medical tourism industry in particular, supply, equipment and services offered form a significant portion of the overall cost. Like many other things, these are also cheap in the developing countries. The cost effective manufacturing of medical equipment and medicines and easy availability of medical supplies at lower cost help reduce the overall treatment cost. This is particularly important in the case of long-term illnesses.

In addition to medical supplies, equipment and medication, the prescription drugs are also usually cheaper at medical tourism destinations in developing parts of the world. Prescription drugs form an integral part of the total cost of the treatment. Governments in various medical tourism destination countries subsidize several drugs, which simply means that these destinations are able to offer medicines and treatment at a lower cost for the benefit of medical tourists.

India, for example, was in news recently for a government mandated reduction in costs of several important medicines, including lifesaving drugs. Additionaly, the country has a well regulated and fledgling pharmaceutical industry, which is one of the largest and amongst the most competitive industries in the world. With an increased focus on medical tourism and resulting encouragement to the pharmaceutical industry, India can offer very well priced drugs to medical tourists.

The high cost of medication in developed countries will inevitably raise the cost not only in the case of hospitalization but also in the case of ordinary treatments and medical consultations as well.

PRICE DISCRIMINATION

International medical suppliers tend to, and usually do, quote increased prices for countries with higher income as compared to the countries with lower income. Consequently, the same generic product is sold at a lower rate in developing countries, as compared to Western countries. It is possible that the same products are priced differently depending on where you seek the treatment.

LOWER ADMINISTRATIVE & DOCUMENTATION EXPENSES

Easy availability of resources at an economical rate in the developing parts of the world further helps reduce the administrative costs significantly, which are usually too high for the healthcare providers in the developed world. The administrative costs include government requirements, documentations, affiliation costs, licensing fees as well as administrative fees and these are far cheaper in developing countries.

LOWER COST OF LEGAL PROCEEDINGS

The legal systems of many developed countries like the USA, come down very hard on health related cases and it is litigious many times. There are special laws to deal with crucial issues and rightly so because in the healthcare industry, the life of an individual is at stake. The cost of seeking legal help if anything goes wrong during a treatment or surgery is high and cumbersome in healthcare sector. This is mostly dealt with by relying on malpractice insurance, which inevitably raises the cost of operation, and consequently, the cost of services offered.

Reports have it that as much as one third of hospital costs go toward fighting legal battles and settling various issues associated with malpractices and treatment errors. The overall expenses also include court costs and insurance. However, legal proceedings and settling health related cases are relatively less expensive in developing countries.

CHAPTER 6

Deciding for Medical Tourism

IN THIS CHAPTER

- Why opt for medical tourism
- General reasons for people traveling abroad for healthcare
- Patient experiences from across the world

The ever-increasing numbers and statistics demonstrate the immense popularity of medical tourism. People from all over the world are traveling to other countries for healthcare. By doing so, they are not only enjoying the benefits of travel packages but also saving time and money.

Before you make your mind to embark on a journey for medical purposes, it is important that you make a right decision about the destination and kind of care you are looking for. Every individual has different needs and tolerances, particularly if we talk about health issues. One should choose the right destination where the care isn't just world-class but economical too.

Medical tourism offers huge benefits, suited for the needs of the medical traveler. The monetary benefits come with a simple logic that the cost of living or say living healthy is higher in developed countries compared to the developing or underdeveloped ones. Hence, there is every reason for people to seek healthcare abroad than in their home country. The travel for healthcare abroad becomes even more logical when there are little or no differences in terms of care that developed countries offer.

On the contrary, while people from developed nations travel to save on money, people from underdeveloped nations often take trips to developing or developed nations to access medical care that would otherwise be unavailable to them.

THOSE WHO WANT TO SAVE MONEY

The cost of living in the developed countries is comparatively higher. People need to buy new technology, spend on insurance, make car payments, mortgage, regular expenses, and the list goes on. In such a situation, incurring heavy medical expenses could be a jolt strong enough to destroy anyone's savings and budgeting plans.

As per the WHO, this isn't a trouble for the individual alone but for governments of the developed and developing countries across the globe. A WHO report also indicates that this unlikely situation has made hundreds of millions of people poorer than ever before. Hence, the need for alternative and medical tourism comes out to be a viable solution. By doing so, you may combine treatments with vacation plans to make the best out of this otherwise unfavorable condition.

When patients decides to travel abroad to seek healthcare, they pay for travel, lodging, and medical services. The whole thing, taken as a package or booked individually, costs far less (one tenth at times) than what patients have to pay for medical services alone in a developed country. As a result, those who have less means, and/or who want to save big on their medical treatment while enjoying a visit to a different country, become medical travelers and potential medical tourists.

Medical tourism becomes even more logical when we know that we need some medical treatment every now and then and we plan vacations at least once a year. Combining both to save time and money won't be a bad idea either.

Patient experience# 1:

Susie Philips residing in Cleveland, Ohio, in the United States was living the American dream. She had a great husband, two wonderful children and an excellent job where she could see her 401K in the distance. She had dreams of retiring with her husband once her kids would be in college and begin their own life. However, similar to many others, Susie got hit by the recession and ultimately, she and her husband lost their jobs. She had had a bad knee for a while, but she always knew that her insurance would help her bear the expenses with ease. However, with the loss of the job, she lost her insurance coverage.

They were thousands of dollars in debt, and on top of that, her knee was hurting more than ever. Susie was researching on the internet for alternatives and came across a wonderful facility in New Delhi, India. She saw how cheaper the treatment costs as opposed to getting it done in the US (especially now without insurance). After thorough research on the facility's quality standards and her doctor, she booked a medical tourism package through a facilitator.

Susie describes her medical experience as "life altering." The doctors were able to provide her with personalized service, and she was able to see a country she had always dreamt of. Susie used this medical treatment as her last resort as there was no way she could afford the cost of care in her own country. She recommends medical tourists to undertake comprehensive research before engaging in any medical related travel and have all the facts available.

THOSE WHO ARE NOT ABLE TO WAIT FOR TREATMENT

Only financial concerns don't force patients from the developed counties to travel to developing countries for healthcare. Many developed countries like France and UK have very effective nationalized healthcare system that offers excellent services to their patients through their flawless procedures. These healthcare systems are good if we talk about catering to the basic health services.

A coin always has another side too and these healthcare systems are no exceptions. Those who admire these healthcare systems should not forget that patients have to wait, sometimes for a long time, for some specialized and complicated treatments as well as procedures that may further deteriorate their health or at least leave them in discomfort during the conditional wait for care.

On the other hand, medical tourism offers you an opportunity to travel to a different part of the world to seek the best and economical healthcare. Equally important is the fact that waiting time for a procedure or medical treatment is comparatively less if medical vacations are planned on time. Popular medical destinations do their level best to reduce wait time, offer options and provide best possible care with word-class facilities and highly qualified doctors.

Medical tourism might see a rise due to two other factors as well. One, there are approximately 47 million people uninsured in US alone even when Obamacare came to the fore.

Many of these uninsured people seek healthcare abroad and many more will continue doing it in future since affordable healthcare for all is still a distant dream.

Secondly, aside from patients opting for medical tourism, health insurance companies have also started sending insured patients overseas for various treatments. The aim is to keep the medical costs down for treatments and procedures that are too costly to afford in the native land. It's a win-win situation for both – companies save money and patients don't see waiting lists.

THOSE WHO SEEK QUALITY TREATMENT

Many countries across the world lack proper healthcare infrastructure. This is true even about the developed ones that have well-established and quality healthcare systems – but for primary services only. However, there might be little or no options for high quality and complex procedures. In such a case, people who can afford quality services but don't find any in their own homeland will, of course, decide on traveling overseas for the same. Medical tourism offers such patients an opportunity to travel to other country where the treatment isn't just easily available but is world-class and cost effective too.

Popular medical tourist destinations across the world have implemented strict regulations set by Joint Commission International (JCI). The organization sets stringent standards for healthcare services providers. These healthcare facilities provide treatments, various highly sensitive surgeries and procedures as well as high-class postoperative care to their patients.

Seeking quality care isn't just about people from the developed countries traveling to the developing countries. Any affluent person from the third world countries or a developing country can seek healthcare in other developing or developed countries that offer the best care at the lowest price. In this case, the first and the foremost aim of such tourism is to seek quality care.

Patient example: 2

Steve Leeds, a wealthy Canadian residing in Toronto was thoroughly satisfied with his country's healthcare system. He mainly saw his physician whenever he had an infection or flu and was happy with services. Steve was also a keen motorbike enthusiast and frequently rode his motorbike around the Canadian countryside for a ride away from the city.

Unfortunately, Steve had a terrible accident while he was on one of his motorbike excursions. This caused serious injuries to his spine and his skin. He needed several surgeries, and some cosmetic work to graft some of the skin he lost during the accident. In addition to this, he required several MRI and CT scans to determine the complete extent of damage that his body may have suffered.

Steve quickly realized that it would be impossible to schedule all the cosmetic surgeries and tests with any healthcare facility in Canada as there were likely to be long waiting times, and his medical bills were piling up very fast. He got on the internet to search for alternative medical options in close proximity to his home country. He found an excellent hospital in Costa Rica that performed the required surgery at a very cost-effective price.

The doctor who treated Steve spent a lot of time with him and gave him thorough information about the process of the surgery and how he should proceed post-surgery. Steve is now recovering following his treatment and is extremely pleased with his decision to avoid the inevitable waiting lists in his home country. He received high quality care at a very affordable price and now, he recommends this option to anyone needing emergency services if his or her region or country can't provide it.

PEOPLE WITH LIMITED OR NO ACCESS TO CERTAIN TREATMENTS

Then there are people from the developed and developing countries with no access to certain treatments in their home country. In such a case, those who are in dire need of a treatment and cannot afford to wait have to travel abroad to seek care well on time. Here, medical tourism comes to the rescue as it offers the patient with the best available healthcare at the minimum possible price.

Lack of infrastructure is a huge motivator for people to travel abroad for medical treatments. There are even legal bondages and some regulations in many countries, which lead people to travel abroad for various treatments. These regulations allow treatments to some patients and forbid others. There are countries where there are strict laws, and strong legal and ethical guidelines that categorize treatments and procedures. While this setup is desirable, some procedures may take a very long time to get approval from the regulatory authority. However, there are also countries with loose structure that offer relaxed regulatory laws and allow patients to choose the treatments in certain cases.

Talking about USA, FDA regulates some stem cell therapies. Coming to the Middle East, most of the countries here prohibit any form of abortion and discourage patients from receiving organs from donors that they are not directly related to. In India, fetal sex determination is illegal and is subject to severe imprisonment, whereas certain countries permit it legally. In some countries, even seeking private infertility treatments is prohibited.

Many countries across the world have varying levels of research and technology within their medical competence. It happens at times that a particular country has recently discovered some lifesaving treatment that is not available anywhere else in the world. This makes certain facilities within a country or a country itself the only place where you can avail specific medical care. If you are in dire need of the treatment, you have to travel to these countries

Patient experience: 3

Cathy Price, residing in Denver, Colorado in the United States, is a mother of a beautiful 7 month-old daughter named Eva. Eva unfortunately suffers from blindness as she was born with optic nerve hypoplasia (where the optic nerve fails to develop properly in the womb). The doctors told Cathy that this condition has no current cure or treatment which could successfully restore her daughter's vision.

Cathy searched for alternatives for her young daughter and found one unbelievable facility. However, it was located in China, a country she would have never even have dreamt of going to. The facility offered a breakthrough treatment pioneered by a biotechnology company and she immediately sought the advice of her family doctor. The physician advised her against it, but Cathy's determination and love for her daughter soon found her on a flight to China.

Eva is currently undergoing stem-cell therapy in China and Cathy is spending less in comparison to the cost of common treatments in the US. The procedure is based on the infusion of stem cells harvested from umbilical cords (less controversial than the embryonic stem cells, which are frowned upon in several parts of the world). The US utilizes these umbilical stem cells more commonly for blood diseases, but not for conditions similar to Eva's.

THOSE WHO WANT TO KEEP THEIR TREATMENT PRIVATE

Medical tourism serves well to those who do not want others to know about any treatments they are getting or for that matter, surgeries that they undergo. In most cases, this is applicable to the stars, celebrities as well as VIPs who do not want their treatments and procedures made public.

The treatments that they prefer hiding from others include some cosmetic surgeries, infertility, or any condition they wouldn't want to be public knowledge. In these cases, medical tourism offers such people a chance to leave their country and seek their desired healthcare overseas.

THOSE WHO WANT BETTER, PERSONALIZED CARE

With increasing population in the cities, there are a few efficient doctors and too many patients to take care of. The number of doctor/s serving people, if we talk in terms of doctor(s) available/per thousand patients, is quite less. It is, therefore, quite natural that these few doctors cannot pay attention to every patient and his/her needs.

An efficient practitioner charges more for personalized care. In some cases, people are ready to pay extra for personalized care, which, in turn, results in increased number of patients. Now, in a bid to earn more, medical practitioner ends up rendering second-class services to patients.

Unavailability of eligible physicians or medical professionals leave patients with no other choice but to look for alternatives, wherein medical tourism comes out to be the best one. Medical tourism caters well to those who want better care or personalized care at a fraction of the cost that the patient might need to pay in his home country.

Patient experience: 4

Alan Cole was traveling from Germany to Thailand for a routine business trip. He picked up an infection when he decided to experiment with an exotic culinary dish at a restaurant, ending up with disastrous consequences. He was hospitalized in a foreign land with no one to care for him. The bacterial infection in his digestive tract threatened to compromise the rest of his system.

Fortunately, this gastronomic disaster led him to experience the wonderful Thai hospitality and medical care. He could have never imagined the same in his own city, Frankfurt. Sick and bedridden following his unfortunate gastronomic disaster, he was in no condition to drive to the nearest clinic. Hence, he contacted a local doctor who made a house call at the nominal charge of USD30.

Alan was also able to access medication at a fraction of the cost he might normally have incurred in his home country. He also arranged to have a nurse attend to him for a week until he had completely recovered. The special care included change of sheets, making tea or hot soup when he needed, a light massage and a face wash. He was very happy with the quality of medical care he received. Because of his emergency, he was able to appreciate the affordable, high quality personalized healthcare available in the Asian destination.

THOSE WHO WANT TO RELAX, ENGAGE IN TOURIST ACTIVITIES AFTER TREATMENT

When you receive quality healthcare treatment in a foreign land, you also get enough time to rest and recover and that is included in your package. This gives people another good reason to opt for medical treatment – meaning recuperating while having fun. Medical tourism also offers potential patients a chance to recover in a relaxing atmosphere.

After a treatment, medical procedure or a surgery, the patients need to relax and take enough time to rest to not only recover fast but also have long positive health effects of treatment. This makes them opt for medical tourism than seeking healthcare at home.

A recent study affirms that a patient in an atmosphere away from home – preferably at a tourist destination or a new place – recovers quicker and better. The reason being, a patient gets some good moments on a tourist destination abroad and gets more time to focus on his health. This makes the healing process quicker for a patient on a foreign land than in his native country. Anyone and everyone will love it.

Patient experience: 5

71-year-old Jimmy McPherson was worried about his deteriorating knee. His local physician was unable to treat his case any further without surgical intervention. Unfortunately, by that point, Jimmy's savings had dipped and he was unable to afford the surgery required to correct the problem, as it would cost him USD 45,000-50,000.

Following a documentary on medical tourism, his son urged him to travel to India for affordable and high quality healthcare. In comparison to the cost of care in the US, the entire trip to India including all related expenses would only cost him a third of the amount. What's more, he would also have funds left over to travel and discover an exotic new land.

Jimmy contacted a medical service provider and did not regret it one bit. He was given a choice of three surgeons. In addition, he also received assistance with his passport and visa requirements as well as travel arrangements to nearby destinations. For him, it was a dream come true, as he was able to avail excellent treatment and engage fully in fascinating tourism activities. He visited some ancient attractions, shopped for his grandchildren and participated in the vivacious local culture.

THE EXPATS WHO SEEK HEALTHCARE IN THEIR HOME COUNTRY

Then there are people who love to travel back to their home country for a treatment. There is no specific reason/logic for such people opting for medical tourism back at home but only the fact that they feel at ease in their homeland and a visit will give them an opportunity to meet their relatives and family members.

However, people residing in foreign countries opt for medical tourism, in most of the cases, in emergencies. They choose traveling to their home country only in conditions wherein they are familiar with healthcare system available in their country. Most of the patients plan to travel their home country during their annual leave and spend less money on treatments that otherwise would have cost them more.

For example, Indians – non-residing or citizens – living in US would prefer traveling to India for a heart surgery or for heart valve transplant than spending 10 times or even more to what they would pay in India.

Another benefit may fall their way if they already know the doctor/s back at home. In such a case, they would get personalized care. In doing so, they would also get care from their friends, relatives and family members. They can arrange things required for a procedure and surgery far more conveniently in their native country. Another potential reason why expats love traveling back to their homeland for various treatments is the fact that they don't face any language and cultural barriers.

Patient experience: 6

58 years old Atul Chauhan worked for years in the Gulf region to support his family back home in India. While visiting India for holidays, he decided to take advantage of the cost-effective healthcare and so, he undertook a complete general check-up and full health screening. He was diagnosed with a heart blockage; hence, he immediately decided to have the angioplasty procedure in Mumbai.

Instead of doing the surgery in Doha, Qatar, he thought it more beneficial (not to mention cheaper) to avail the service in his hometown of Mumbai. He decided to seek treatment at the esteemed Asian Heart Institute in Mumbai and took 10 days off work to that effect. By the time he returned to work in Qatar, he was hearty and healthy. The close proximity between Qatar and India made additional follow-ups relatively easier too.

INSURANCE COMPANIES, EMPLOYERS ENCOURAGE PATIENT TO TRAVEL ABROAD FOR HEALTHCARE

Insurance companies and employers are responsible to pay their employees for any health needs. As a result, the number of insurance companies and employers who encourage insured people and employees to travel abroad for healthcare is increasing with each passing day. The insurance companies have taken measures like including medical tourism in their policies to obtain the maximum monetary benefits and urging more and more patients to travel abroad for treatments. People who have high deductible plan should opt for services overseas, which are more economical as well as more beneficial for insurance company and employer.

Patient experience: 8

Ellen Jaye, residing in San Diego, US, always had a good working rapport with her boss. The transparent management style of her office meant office communication was always encouraged. Even though the office had an established culture of interaction, they were going through serious financial troubles. Her boss, Jerry, could just no longer afford to pay for his staff's medical care. Even though Ellen was one of his favorite employees, her medical history of diabetes (acquired at an early age) meant that she required medical attention more often.

While Jerry did not want to lose Ellen merely because of his inability to shoulder her medical expenses, it was getting unaffordable, and his situation desperate. He then came up with the idea of sending her across the border to Mexico to avail treatment for her eye, which had worsened due to the enhanced diabetes condition. Ellen went to Mexico and much to her surprise, received world-class treatment; her medical condition was dealt with in the most efficient and professional manner.

Ellen was back at work within the next two weeks and was much healthier. She didn't lose her job, and Jerry was able to save on the necessary medical expenditures – funds which he could use to reinvest in the company and in Ellen's potential.

THOSE WHO WANT TO COMBINE MEDICAL CARE WITH CAM

There aren't too many people who opt for medical travel for the sole purpose of combining medical care with Complementary Alternative Medicines (CAM). Still, we cannot and should not drop these medical tourists from the list of reasons why people are opting for the medical tourism.

Some of the chronic diseases and some diseases that are simply incurable after their primary stages come very hard on people; for example, cancer which requires powerful treatments like chemotherapy and radiations to eradicate it fully during the primary stages or even at a later stage. In such cases, complementary alternative medicines come to the rescue and help mitigate the sufferings of patients. CAM helps alleviate suffering and take away the pain to make patients feel better and relaxed.

Complementary alternative medicines are nothing but ancient techniques that have resurfaced to provide relief to a number of ailing patients. As a result, people have now started combining medical care with alternative practices or more aptly known as Complementary and Alternative Medicine.

If you want alternative treatments, you have to travel abroad in case you don't have access to CAM in your home country. To benefit from CAM therapies, traveling to regions like India and China makes more sense since alternative practices are a specialty in these countries.

Patient experience: 8

Loren Watts, a South African national, was devastated when her doctor informed her that her skin biopsy indicated she had cancer. However, after the intense support of her family and friends, she decided to fight the disease.

She researched hundreds of different treatments and procedures that could help her with her condition. Being the hippy she was, she preferred any treatment that didn't require intense chemotherapy prescribed to her. She searched for a natural cure. To her delight, she was able to find a hospital in China that offered something called complementary and alternative medicine which combined allopathic treatments (such as radiation and chemo) with natural Chinese herbs.

She is in her third month of treatment at the Modern Hospital in China, and truly feels the herbs have helped decrease the side effects such as nausea and vomiting, which are synonymous with cancer treatments. She often travels to China and is extremely happy with her physician who explains the medical and herbal aspects of her treatment clearly.

CHAPTER 7

What could go wrong during Medical Travel?

IN THIS CHAPTER

- What could go wrong on Medical travel
- Problems that patients could face

After knowing the benefits and reasons why many people from the developed countries are opting for medical travel, it is fair for potential medical tourists to know about the possibility of complications that one could face at a medical tourist destination.

If you seek any medical treatment in your home country or abroad, the possibility of problems and risks remains. Therefore, possibility of risk isn't new or surprising to someone looking for treatment. However, the dangers and possibility of any complications increase to a greater level, particularly when one seeks medical treatment in foreign country. The patient even considers these things at times especially when it comes with a logic as strong as that you are in a land that you know nothing about

MORE POST-OPERATIVE CARE THAN ANTICIPATED

It is understood that every surgery has a certain amount of risk – be it in your home country or in a medical tourism destination. Sometimes, the best doctors make mistakes or things go wrong even when the medical tourism destination provides utmost care and takes best precautions to treat the patient. Irrespective of your reason for medical travel, there always remains a firm need for more postoperative care at medical tourism destinations.

The incidents of patients not reacting well to the anesthetics dose, or something unexpected happening during a surgery are some of the risks that one might experience. However, this is something that could happen anywhere. The only thing is that it adds more to the woes if it happens in a country that is very new to the medical tourists.

DOCTOR/S REFUSING TO CORRECT SURGICAL ERRORS

Patients might have to face troubles and/or end up paying more, if doctors at any foreign destination refuse to correct any error in treatment or in a surgery for different reasons. The doctors might refuse to correct any surgical error for the simple reason that it asks them to put in more effort and devote extra time that they otherwise could utilize to earn more.

As a result, the prime concern for every patient who intends to seek healthcare abroad is 'what if something goes wrong' and rightly so. There are many cases of cosmetic surgeries going wrong and patients traveling back to their home country without any fixes for the medical errors. As a result, many patients decide against traveling abroad.

Correcting any error in treatment or in surgery is the moral responsibility of doctors and the medical facility that entertains medical tourists. In any such case, getting surgical or other treatment errors fixed with no extra cost involved should be the (legal and moral) right of the patients. To encourage more people to opt for the medical tourism, all the destinations and countries involved should answer this prime concern to satisfy every potential medical tourist and thereby, encouraging them to travel overseas to seek healthcare.

CORRECTIVE SURGERY AND POSTOPERATIVE CARE IS MOSTLY UNAVAILABLE OR MORE EXPENSIVE IN HOME COUNTRY

Once you complete the medical procedure overseas and return home after the postoperative period is over, finding adequate and right care in home country would not be easy or economical. It is possible that the home country of the patient isn't suitable owing to lack of infrastructure or high costs involved to handle any post treatment complications. This situation will leave the medical tourist with no other option than to travel again to the same country where the treatment was done earlier. Moreover, the idea of patients traveling back to medical tourist destinations to remediate postoperative complications does not make any sense either.

LACK OF RECOURSE FOR PATIENTS

Legal framework of a country differs (sometimes considerably) from another and so does the process of addressing the grievances of patients, if any. It might happen that a patient finds the legal system of a country inept or inapt to serve his/her interests. For example, in US, there are strict rules, regulations and guidelines to hospitals about protecting the rights of patients. While several medical tourism destinations have laws to protect the interests of patients in general and medical tourists in particular, getting legal recourse can be a difficult and time consuming effort.

Seeking legal remedies against any medical mishap happening in a foreign country might not be just expensive but cumbersome too. It will come out to be an additional burden on the patient. In such a situation, the country seems a no man's land for the patient where finding the right legal protection against any medical error is not only difficult but also expensive and time consuming.

Things come out to be even more difficult for a patient when he/she has to return home without any legal justice. In some cases, the legal system of the patient's home country has no legal provision for providing justice against the negligence of the medical team of the treating facility on a foreign land.

CULTURAL AND LINGUISTIC BARRIERS

Usually, a medical tourist hails from a different cultural background to that of the destination country. This thing is more prevalent for medical tourists traveling from Middle East countries to the USA or Asian countries that are coming up as cheap medical tourist destinations. The language and cultural barriers prove to be quite a daunting barrier for the patients.

Medical tourism destinations are trying their best to relieve this trauma. As many medical tourism experts opine, understanding culture is not a one-way process. The need to understand the culture of the patients and their beliefs and behavior is important for the medical tourism destinations. This doesn't mean that a patient has no need to understand the culture and behavior of the destination.

In order to mitigate the borders in Medical Tourism, it is the responsibility of the provider to make cultural documents related to their destination available to the patients. The reasons why patients and the healthcare provider need cultural understanding is to mini-mize gaps for better outcome, avoid miscommunication arising from cultural differences, build awareness, and increase positive results for the higher satisfaction rate.

CONTACTING TROPICAL DISEASES OR POST-OPERATIVE INFECTIONS WHEN ABROAD

We have seen that prime medical tourist destinations (or countries) are located on some exotic locations all over the world for the simple reason to combine travel with healthcare in a better way. However, there is also another side to this thing as well. The prime med-ical tourist destinations on exotic locations can have tropical or foreign diseases running rampant within that specific area, region or the entire country.

The local populace within that particular region might have natural inborn immunity to such diseases. However, this could make things worse for a foreign tourist and therefore, they become more prone to contacting such infections.

Once the surgery or a treatment is over, the immune system of the patient goes weak during the recovery period. Consequently, the immune system would not be able to with-stand infections. As a result, a medical tourist needs to be extra careful against contracting any infection. Though medical tourism facilities take extra care of hygiene, you should know and take precautions well in advance to mitigate the risk of contracting hospital-ac-quired infections.

POSSIBILITIES OF NATURAL AND MANMADE CALAMITIES

No one, on the other hand, can rule out the possibilities of natural disasters or manmade calamities hitting the destination country during travel. Unforeseen events like natural disasters, can put uncertainties about patients reaching their destination facilities.

Aside from natural disasters, manmade calamities like terrorist attacks, political unrest and other upheavals might leave you stranded in the host country, leaving you with no other choice but to wait and watch until the dust settles. To know about the natural disas-ters in advance is difficult, but one can avoid traveling to a country for medical purposes where there are signs of some political unrest.

UNDESIRABLE RESULTS

Undesirable results aren't all that unexpected for anyone who seeks medical care at home or in a foreign country. The chances of things going haywire are as high at a medical tourist destination as in the home country. The medical tourist should be aware of this problem and be mentally prepared to face such a situation. Medical tourists need to take certain precautions in advance to face such a situation overseas.

You should be especially on the guard against exaggerated promises and miracle treat-ments that physicians or a hospital might promise. They might come up with patients' miracle postoperative pictures. If you have a family doctor or you know one related to the field, you should confirm whether the claims are real or simply overstated.

MEDICAL MALPRACTICES/WRONGDOINGS

Medical malpractices can be of varied forms – ranging from mistakes committed by surgeons to the very serious and heinous crime of organ trafficking, or using fake credentials and failing to do what the surgeon initially promised. In addition to this, things might go even worse if the treating physician has no related education or experience. Faking medical credentials to earn more money is another problem to keep in mind. This can often lead to a catastrophic situation for the patients. There are many examples of medical malpractices and wrongdoings in the medical field.

It is best to stick to well reputed and accredited institutions, where such problems are unlikely to arise. The cautious traveler might also consider malpractice insurance to be confident that they would, at the very least, not suffer a monetary loss should an issue of malpractice arise. These steps also make the hospitals more careful in their approach, as they would not want the unwelcome attention or ire of insurance or government agencies.

DOCUMENTATION AND VISA

Medical travel comes with its own set of comprehensive documents, and formalities. If the medical stay of a patient increases beyond the intended duration, there is a risk of the visa being expired, and it might be difficult to get a renewal if the patient is in the hospital or otherwise engaged. While most countries have made an effort to make the medical visa more streamlined, there is always a chance of trouble, and no one really wants to be caught in paperwork.

Some medical tourist destinations also include formalities and regulations. For example, many companies employ a Foreign Regional Registration Office (FRRO) in India, where travelers are meant to register on arrival. If the tourist failed or forgot to complete the registration, they might see trouble at departure and could be stuck for an uncomfortably long time.

CHAPTER 8

Why I should or shouldn't opt for Medical tourism

IN THIS CHAPTER

- Things you should consider before opting for medical tourism
- What you should know before seeking healthcare abroad
- What to ensure before traveling for medical procedure

The first section, 'Reasons people travel for medical care', highlights the main motives that lead potential patients to seek healthcare abroad and provides personal testimonials so that patients can relate to their experiences.

The 'Reasons people travel for medical care' provide you with significant guidelines. However, it is important to note that these experiences do not apply to everyone. As an individual, you should consider personal factors before making your mind up to seek medical services overseas.

The next section, 'Reasons people are opting for medical tourism' aims at acquainting potential medical tourists with all possible reasons as to why anyone should seek healthcare abroad. The section, 'Things that could go wrong during medical tourism' discusses the possibility of natural calamities, post-operative complications that lack any legal recourse for the patient or potential lingual/cultural barriers as well as all the worst-case scenarios possible during medical travel.

The last section of this chapter will assume that the potential medical traveler reading this book understands why people generally access medical services abroad, and all the possible problems that could occur. This last section i.e. 'why I should or shouldn't opt for medial tourism' is crucial in shaping your thought process leading up to the major decision of whether or not to travel abroad to seek healthcare. The advantages and disadvantages are clearly stated and further highlighted with examples.

This section will provide some crucial questions that you as a patient should consider and ask yourself before you actually take the medical tourism related decision. Based on the information in the previous two sections, here are the individualized questions and factors any potential medical tourist should read and consider before deciding on medical tourism.

HOW DO YOU FEEL ABOUT TRAVELING ABROAD?

If you are not an avid traveler, have not boarded a plane so far either, and have an innate fear of flying, traveling overseas for a medical procedure or a surgery may not be a good decision for you. It will only add more stress to your already beleaguered health condition to complicate things further and that too, on a foreign land that you know nothing about or had never visited in the past.

Try to get and exploit the best deal available within your home country to avoid traveling overseas. However, if you find nothing affordable and good enough to suit your medical requirements, try finding the closest destination to your home country that fits your parameters of affordability and accessibility.

A potential medical tourist should know how to swiftly travel abroad and manage different things at various airports on his way to a medical tourism destination. You might have to change your flights if you are traveling for example from USA to India. In another case, if you do not have to change any flight, you should not worry about spending (sometimes even more than 3-4 hours) time on different airports as your flight might remain there for hours to refuel.

If you are going for long distance air travel for the first time, you should know about Jetlag. When you travel over multiple time zones, the contradictory time zones might leave you feeling fatigued. You should not only know about this, but should also be able to handle it. It can sometimes take around 3-4 days at times to thoroughly recover from the jet lag. Feeling good about traveling through plane is an essential trait that a potential medical tourist should possess.

DO YOU ENJOY INTERACTING WITH DIFFERENT LANGUAGE AND CULTURE GROUPS?

In order to be a potential medical tourist, you should not necessarily be a jovial person or the one who loves interacting with people and traveling different countries. However, you should be at ease to interact with people. During your medical trip, you are supposed to interact with people from different cultural, religious and racial backgrounds.

Even when you travel to a country where people speak your language, you should do your utmost to understand their cultural, racial or religious background. For example, if you are traveling from US to Australia, UK, etc., the language might be the same but the culture can differ considerably.

This skill is extremely important when it comes to communicate with the healthcare professionals at a facility who do not understand and communicate in your native language. English is widely spoken throughout the world, but even so, there is a possibility that the people you interact with are not fluent in the language. If there is a possibility of a language barrier, and the very thought of using a translator to discuss your medical history or things related to your treatment makes you nervous, you should reconsider your decision.

Many people love traveling. Such people enjoy the idea of traveling abroad to interact with people they never met before, know more about a new land and prevalent cultures. For such people, medical tourism combines tourism with healthcare to provide the added bonus of exciting new experiences, besides the affordability and accessibility factors that encouraged them to travel abroad for medical care. Hence, it is critical to evaluate your likings, dislikes and your nature to maximize the benefits of medical tourism and obtain optimal care at a foreign location.

CAN YOU TRUST A FOREIGN FACILITY OR PROVIDER?

If you are fundamentally uncomfortable with the idea of medical treatment in a facility abroad, you should reconsider you decision to use the medical tourism option.

If you are at ease with the type of facilities you enjoy back at home, decide against traveling abroad for healthcare, because this decision will put you out of your comfort zone. You should also consider the socio-political scenario of the destination country. Take into account the political stability, unrest, any foretelling of natural disaster like heavy rain and storm that could occur anytime, or crime rate to ensure your safety.

You need to check for credibility and accreditation of the medical service provider in a country overseas in detail. Confirm from those who have already been to the facility and read customer reviews on various online portals to know the kind of care that particular facility provides.

Many facilities participating in medical tourism have affiliation from renowned medical institutes. You might find hospitals at medical tourist destinations having collaboration with reputed institutions like Harvard Medical School or Johns Hopkins to attract US citizens, as they are familiar with these affiliations. JCI accreditations also ensure quality of care and availability of facilities.

Know and confirm everything in advance and use various online and offline sources. If you are able to trust any facility, only then decide on visiting that facility for medical care. Check if the hospital has affiliation from a renowned medical institute.

DO YOU HAVE ALL THE MEANS READY FOR THE MEDICAL TRAVEL?

Confirm if your passport is still valid. Know the time duration that you are going to stay in a foreign country. How long does it take to obtain a visa to the said country? Also, check if you have all the documents ready to apply for a visa to the destination medical tourism country.

Do not forget about one of the most important travel requirements, i.e. funds. You need to have enough funds to cover your health services abroad. The budget includes the expenses for treatment, postoperative care and travel fare to and from the destination medical facility. Though medical tourism is all about saving big on medical treatments abroad, it is wise to have enough budget for other aspects including postoperative tourism activities to recuperate, and boarding and lodging expenses, to name a few.

HAVE YOU TAKEN A SECOND OPINION?

The importance of second opinion in medical tourism is as important as it is in any other case. You cannot and should not forget to consult your family doctor or a local physician regarding your decision of traveling abroad for treatment.

Before embarking on medical travel, you should consult your doctor who knows all about your health condition and is familiar with your relevant medical history. Consulting your doctor about your health and discussing everything will help you make an informed decision.

DO YOU HAVE TIME AND RESOURCES TO PLAN MEDICAL TOUR METICU-LOUSLY?

Planning a medical tour is a big challenge for anyone. The act of medical tourism will increase the chances of errors and discrepancies if you did not plan everything meticulously and well in advance. When you decide to travel abroad for healthcare, you need plenty of time to plan your tour, arrange things with the treating facility, and talk to physicians abroad. Other than this, booking flights to and from the medical tourism facility, getting over the visa hurdle and arranging ample funds for the purpose requires your valuable time and finances.

If you cannot manage everything on your own, that does not mean medical tourism is not an option for you. Instead, check if you have an option of using a facilitator, who can handle most of the formalities and requirements for your journey and medical stay. If that option is not on the table, take help from friends and family to organize your trip.

The availability of time and resources – monetary or otherwise – remains crucial in deciding for medical travel. These factors play a role in properly organizing the medical tour and deciding whether it is an option for you or not.

DOES YOUR HOME COUNTRY OFFER THE POST-OPERATIVE CARE YOU MIGHT REQUIRE?

Yet another factor that you need to consider and confirm for sure is whether the postoperative care of a medical treatment you plan to seek overseas is available in your country. Ignoring this factor could cost you all the benefits guaranteed by medical tourism. Most procedures will require regular consultations with a doctor, even after the procedure is complete. While your medical tourism destination might offer sessions with the doctor through teleconferencing, it is desirable to have the possibility of consulting a doctor in person.

Even before you embark on a medical tour, you should know that medical tourism is not a foolproof plan to seek healthcare at an affordable price and with ease at a foreign land, it is also about imperfect results at times.

Millions of individuals will tell you about their success stories as medical tourists and show their commitment to travel abroad to seek every treatment in future. Still, you cannot rule out the chances of you being one in million who is not satisfied with the healthcare services you received abroad.

Additionally, you also need to think as to how you will handle any specialized treatment like stem-cell treatment or proton therapy and the follow-up care. Traveling abroad for follow-up care is not just costly, but cumbersome and time-consuming too. However, if the patient is in a region that does not offer treatment for a health issue, or the treatment is unavailable, by all means, choose medical tourism.

Most medical tourism destinations do make acceptable arrangements for post-operative care, and minimize the risk of complications by ensuring that the patients are in good health before returning to their home country. This would be especially useful for patients traveling from underdeveloped countries like Tanzania, Uganda, and Ghana, where multi-specialty and super specialty healthcare is unavailable.

CHAPTER 9

Understanding your Medical Tourism Needs

IN THIS CHAPTER

- Familiarizing yourself with your healthcare condition
- Importance of researching and educating yourself on your condition
- Importance of communicating with your foreign healthcare provider and physician

FAMILIARIZE YOURSELF WITH YOUR CONDITION

Before you start the quest to search for facilities in different parts of the world where you can get the required treatment, it is essential for you as a patient to understand your medical condition completely. You should gain in-depth knowledge of your diagnosis before you start diagnostic procedures such as screenings and check-ups. Self-assessment of your medical condition is critical, as this will help you in understanding what you have to do and what treatment options are available.

Moreover, if a physician has already diagnosed you in your country, you should be familiar with all that the diagnostic reports say, and the recommended treatment procedures that will benefit you. If you find it necessary, you can even consult a different physician to get more information and recommendations. In addition, consider using the internet to get valuable advice and precautions that you should take while dealing with your healthcare condition. You should also try to speak to patients who have been dealing with a medical condition similar to yours, and get valuable advice that will help you determine the best treatment options available.

Once a physician diagnoses a medical condition for you, the best course of action is usually to gain complete knowledge about the condition. Knowing answers to key questions such as, what effects it can have on you, what kind of precautions you have to take, how long can you delay the treatment, and above all, where in the world can you get the best treatment, can make a lot of difference. With these answers, you will be in a better position to take good care of yourself, while understanding the different treatment options available. Also, familiarize yourself with the complications that can arise during treatment and how you can deal with any unforeseen problems.

Once you have gained enough information and have familiarized yourself with your condition, share all the information with your physician and your family members too. It will help you verify the knowledge that you have gained, and sharing it with your family members will ensure that they do everything they can to take good care of you and make you feel better.

RESEARCH AND EDUCATION

After a physician diagnoses a disease, it is often difficult for the patient to accept, or get accustomed to the diagnosis. The initial time is a lot more cumbersome for a patient as they do not exactly know what is wrong with them and how much worse the condition can become. The best way forward is to relax and start researching everything you can about the diagnosis.

The more equipped you are in terms of knowledge; the better your position will be to find treatment options. One of the common mistakes that patients make is that they do not educate themselves about their condition, but start looking for immediate solutions. However, the fact is that with the right information and knowledge, you will be in a better position to understand and find the right treatment options available for you.

The better you equip yourself with the power of knowledge, the more you will know about your disease, and the less will be chances of any unpredictable conditions cropping up.

Although there are hundreds of ways to get knowledge about a medical condition, the best and the easiest way is to use the internet. The internet is full of sources where authentic and verified information is available at just a click. You can easily visit reputed and credible website like webMD.com, NHSdirect.nhs.uk, nlm.nih.gov, etc, which offer free knowledge to patients seeking detailed information about specific types of diseases. With the right information, it is easier to understand the current condition and symptoms.

Additionally, by doing ample research, you will be in a better position to read and understand different treatment options available in different parts of the world, and what these procedures involve. Patients without the right information and complete knowledge about their condition tend to take decisions in haste and end up facing problems. Before you start making any medical tourism arrangements, knowing your disease and illness in detail will help you make the right decisions.

You should keep an eye on the treatment options available in different parts of the world, and take recommendations from your physician. Once you have settled on a treatment, read about it in detail to gain valuable insight into the treatment process.

COMMUNICATION IS KEY

Once you have familiarized yourself with the disease or illness and have done ample research on the same, the next thing you should do is to start looking for treating facilities in different parts of the world. Learn more about the healthcare structure of your destination country and the kind of facilities that they have. Carefully analyze patient testimonials of the facility and learn about the education of the physicians.

After you have chosen a destination and a hospital/clinic within the region, you should immediately start communication. Usually, every reputed healthcare facility that caters to medical tourists has an international patient department to facilitate communication. Find the contact details of the department and immediately get in touch with them. Approach this department, and ask for details. As the communication progresses, you might have to send them your diagnostic reports, and receive brochures, details, and documents from them.

Different countries have different laws pertaining to medical tourists and it becomes essential for you to have complete knowledge about these laws. Carefully read the consent form, which is a legal document that provides vital information about the hospital and the procedure. Further, ask the department about the physician who will perform the procedure. Get to know as much about the physician as possible and reassure yourself that the physician is duly licensed to perform the procedure.

If possible, speak with the physician and understand the possible complications associated with the procedure, and how well the facility is prepared for an unexpected hospital stay. While many facilities offer onsite hospitality and would not refer you to another facility for an extended stay, it is best to know the answers beforehand. If you are currently on medication, be sure to share these details with the treating physician, you might also want to ensure the availability of such medicines in the destination country. If not, get the names of the medication they will provide you, and verify these with the physician in your local country.

Have a list of all the medications that you will have to take prior to and after the treatment. Make sure that they are safe and are of the same, if not better, standard as the medications available in your country. Also, make it a point to get in touch with your healthcare insurance provider to ensure that they will cover and reimburse the healthcare expenses that you will have to bear in the destination country.

TAKE ADVANTAGE OF TELEMEDICINE

We will discuss the importance of telemedicine in greater detail in a later chapter, but a mention of telemedicine is relevant for the current objective as well. Formally defined, telemedicine is the exchange of medical information from one place to other using electronic communication techniques. This helps remove the distance barriers between the patient and the physician while improving access to medical services.

Since you would only be reaching your destination country after you have the date when your treatment will begin, it is important to remain in touch with the physician in your choice of medical tourism destination. With telemedicine, the physician will be in a better position to prepare you for the treatment.

Telemedicine is not a technology or a process in itself, but it encompasses all methods that bridge the geographical limitations and allows physicians to provide healthcare services from a distance.

Telemedicine is especially beneficial for potential medical tourists as it allows them to start receiving care instructions and directions from the physician who will eventually treat them. This helps in reducing any additional expenditure that would otherwise have been borne by the patient. Communicating with the physician helps reduce stress in patients, who would otherwise travel to another country much before their treatment began.

The initial use of telemedicine was to provide healthcare services to patients living in remote regions of the world where healthcare facilities were negligible. It has found itself to be of utmost use to medical tourists, as they no longer have to wait for their arrival in the destination country for their treatment to begin. With telemedicine, potential medical tourists can get in touch with the physician in a distant country and start the pre-treatment procedures right at their home.

With tele health and telemedicine, excellent healthcare services are just a click away for potential medical tourists. Telemedicine can make advice and information from the physician easily available. It has the advantage of providing valuable information about the disease and the treatment procedure, much before the patient actually visits the country to start the medical procedure.

CHAPTER 10

Pre-Operative Preparations

IN THIS CHAPTER

- Pre-operative check-ups prior to travel
- Gathering your medical documents necessary for your medical trip
- Importance of asking as many questions as possible to your local and treating doctor

PLANNING PRIOR TO TRAVEL

Traveling abroad for medical treatment is a global phenomenon. With the rising costs of healthcare in many countries, an ever increasing number of people are traveling overseas to get high quality and affordable healthcare. Once you have educated yourself on the basic concept of medical tourism and have made the initial communication with your physician, you have to start with pre-operative preparations for traveling overseas for medical procedures. When traveling overseas for medical or wellness treatments, you should pay proper attention to all the pre-operative check-ups prior to travel.

It is very important to plan and prepare a timetable of all your travel proceedings. You should mark all the important dates of consultation with the physician, or surgeon in advance, and keep all your appointments. Since you are moving abroad for medical care and want a speedy recovery, you must make the necessary preparations to avoid any stress during the journey.

Another important thing to consider prior to traveling abroad for low-cost, quality medical care is your medical history and pre-operative medical check-up. You will have to go through a number of physical assessments and diagnostic tests abroad, but there is a possibility of completing some tests in your home country. Before embarking on a medical journey, it is crucial for patients to make proper arrangements in order to stay safe and avoid any problems. The purpose of traveling abroad for medical care is health recovery, so you cannot afford to make any mistakes where the relevant procedures and information are concerned.

Before you start your medical trip, communicate with the healthcare facility and the concerned physicians or doctors regarding your medical condition and other important things related to your treatment. This will help you plan and prepare the necessary medical documents needed for your treatment abroad.

SENDING MEDICAL REPORTS

If you want to save some money on your medical trip abroad, you must get accurate quotes from the doctors or the treating facility. It will help you make an informed and cost-effective decision when considering medical treatment abroad. In order to receive accurate quotes, you might have to gather and send your detailed medical reports to the treating facility, which will then provide you with an accurate quote for the cost of treatment. Communication with your treating facility and physician abroad is extremely important in order to ensure a smooth and successful treatment. Since the concerned physician or surgeon is located in a different country, your communication will be done over telephone and email.

Many patients also contact the medical tourism providers or facilitators to avail medical services abroad. In such cases, the medical tourism provider asks the patients to furnish their medical reports. As per the instructions of the treating facility and the doctors overseas, your medical report could include the nature of the ailment, opinion of the local medical professional, your medical history, diagnosis reports and other information related to your medical condition. The cost of medical treatment abroad depends a lot on the international healthcare facility and the country to which you are traveling to avail healthcare services.

Sending medical reports helps the physicians or consultants located abroad study your medical history in detail and come up with the best treatment options for your ailment. By sending your detailed medical reports to the concerned healthcare provider, you will get the best online consultation and an accurate price quotation for the medical treatment.

This book will cover the process of digitizing medical documents, such as MRIs, CT scans and X-Rays and telemedicine further in later chapters.

ENQUIRE AS MUCH AS YOU CAN

You should get in touch with the hospital where your pre-op consultations will be located and ask about different things, such as the treatment location, treatment procedure and the availability of transfer facility after you go through the surgery. It is important for you to ask your treating facility about the transfer services post-surgery, as you might have to make the transportation arrangements yourself if they are not providing the transfer facility.

Before you embark on a medical journey to a foreign country, you should completely understand your healthcare condition and the recommended treatment. Once you have chosen the hospital or the clinic abroad, you should initiate communication immediately in order to make your medical vacation as smooth and safe as possible. Most of the certified healthcare facilities abroad have the international patient department to ease the process of communication. You can contact them via telephone or email and ask them about various things related to the healthcare facility or the doctor who will treat you. You can also take advantage of telemedicine to receive information from your potential provider.

It is important to enquire about the treating facility's standards and its history of serving overseas patients. Moreover, you should also enquire and ensure that the chosen hospital has international accreditation. The most important person you should be communicating with is your doctor. You should consult in detail about your medical condition and the treatment options. It is important to know that you are receiving surgical treatment or any other medical treatment from certified and experienced medical professionals. You can also use the internet to know more about your treating facility and the services they provide to the patients.

FAMILY HISTORY

In order to receive accurate online consultation and ensure a successful treatment overseas, it is important for a medical tourist to collect and create a detailed family and medical history. The detailed reports will help the physician or surgeon abroad to review the nature of your ailment in a better way. You should document and store all the relevant family medical conditions, current and previous medications, and other key information, as it could help your treating doctor to decide the best course of action for your case.

Your treating physician or surgeon can go through your complete family and medical history to know more about your health condition. Before you get in touch with the healthcare provider in a foreign country, you should have all the documents of your medical history at hand. It will ease and speed up the entire process of your medical treatment.

GETTING PRE-OPERATIVE MEDICAL CHECK-UP DONE

If you are traveling as a patient to another country for low-cost, high quality medical treatment, you can expect to undergo a number of medical screenings and tests. This is a mandatory requirement for all new patients, as the treating facility overseas does not have any prior records of your health condition. Therefore, the medical tourists should perform all the necessary medical tests in their home country, which will save you both time and money during your trip overseas. You can collect the test reports from your local physician and bring the copies of these documents along on your medical journey.

Pre-operative medical check-up is also important to ensure if you can travel safely in an airplane for long hours without developing health troubles. Medical screening may include the examinations of important body systems to assess the state of your health. A potential medical tourist should always consider speaking with the local physician and taking a second opinion.

Medical tourism providers and healthcare facilities abroad usually urge all the medical tourists to do as many tests as possible in their home country related to their condition. If you are traveling abroad for affordable and quality healthcare services, you should get the pre-operative medical check-up done in time.

CHAPTER 11

Selecting a Healthcare Destination

IN THIS CHAPTER

- Criteria for selecting a good healthcare destination
- Generalized factors that all medical tourists should seek
- Personalized factors based on your specific care and medical condition

WHAT ARE THE CRITERIA FOR SELECTING A GOOD HEALTHCARE DESTINATION?

The internet dominates the information landscape of the modern world. Information, which was earlier accessible to just a selected few, is now publically available with just a click. This sharing of information across borders is enabling individuals to take control and get essential knowledge. Similarly, rising consciousness and access to information about matters that affect people's lives have enabled individuals to opt for healthcare services in parts of the world that are more suitable to their requirements.

Improved communication, access to information and the development of the global healthcare industry has provided individuals with the convenience to choose a healthcare destination that suits them on all fronts. The internet and other means of electronic communication have transformed the world into a global village.

At least 35 countries have already been selected as established medical tourism destinations, and more are about to join the list. With those many destinations and hundreds of good healthcare institutions in each country, several sources provide a potential medical tourist with information that leads to confusion. At present, it has become hard for you, as a potential medical tourist, to decide the destination that most suits you. Even if you have decided on the country, it could be hard to finalize the healthcare facility where you can get yourself treated.

The decision of choosing a medical tourism destination depends on different factors for different individuals. While some might consider the presence of relatives in a foreign land as a deciding factor, others believe that they should be visiting a country they have always wanted to see. While there is nothing wrong with such decision-making, you should definitely consider your own health as the top priority while making a choice.

Listed here are some of the most essential factors that you should look for while selecting a healthcare destination. It is suggested that these factors be used only as a guide to help you understand the important aspects involved in selecting a medical tourism destination. These are just general factors, and things might differ according to the medical condition that your physician has diagnosed.

GENERAL FACTORS

Quality of healthcare

If you are a potential medical tourist and looking to choose a suitable medical tourism destination, the first thing that you should consider while making a sound decision is to acquaint yourself with the quality of healthcare in your chosen destination. Make sure that the quality of healthcare in your chosen destination is up to international standards and these internationally renowned agencies are monitoring these standards.

The destination you choose must fit your needs and preferences, and be ideal for treatment. As a rule of the thumb, a good healthcare institution will be ready to serve you without any unnecessary delays. In addition, they will make sure that they have all the medical tests and the equipment necessary for treatment.

Quality of healthcare at a medical destination will make you feel safe and secure in a foreign environment. A good healthcare destination will be ready to provide the best in healthcare services to you, irrespective of your gender, language, age, income or race.

The second thing that you have to consider while rating a healthcare facility on the quality scale, is the country's level of advancement in health and healthcare technology. Since technology does not advance at the same speed in different countries, some countries have developed a better position over the others about their medical capabilities. These advancements not only mean that a facility is better equipped and trained to carry out the required procedures, but also ensures that the patients recover early.

Additionally, consider going through the websites of all the healthcare facilities that you have shortlisted, and go through the profile of their physicians. This will help you determine the level of education that they have gained, their specialty and their experience. Moreover, in some cases, reputed healthcare facilities display patient testimonials on their websites, which help you gain valuable insight.

Popularity and recognition of the medical tourism destination

No matter what a medical tourism destination claims for itself, if it is not popular in the world, the chances are that the healthcare services provided will not be of high quality. In addition to great healthcare services, a popular medical tourism destination will also have abundant facilities and offer a wide variety of treatments, common procedures and medical specializations. The destination should also give the assurance of providing high quality healthcare at affordable prices.

As a potential medical tourist, you should look for the presence of a comprehensive system of healthcare or an extremely strong private sector, which is able to cater to the demands and requirements of foreign patients without sacrificing and compromising on the care facilities for its own local citizens. You will be able to identify, or speak to several medical tourists who have availed of services in a popular medical tourism destination. This can help you gain valuable information about the process, procedure, and quality of the intended destination.

While rating a healthcare facility on a popularity scale is essential, you have to make sure that the destination is also gaining international recognition in the field of medical tourism. Many renowned medical tourism destinations have established differentiation in the medical tourism industry. For instance, Cuba is recognized for eye-related medical tourism destinations, China is known from its unique combination of modern and traditional medicine, Dubai is quickly becoming a hub for cosmetic surgery, and Thailand is renowned for being a versatile and a highly affordable medical tourism destination. Look for a medical tourism destination that is recognized in a specialist field related to the type of healthcare services and treatment you require.

In addition to gaining comprehensive knowledge about the medical services that a potential medical tourism destination can provide, many medical tourists look for tourist attractions within the country. Apart from just the obvious tourism attractions, a country with a strong tourism sector will be able to provide medical tourists with all the amenities, tourism attractions, comfort, safety and international connections that they are looking for. With a strong tourism sector, a destination will also gain popularity as a good tourism and medical tourism destination, hailing more potential medical tourists from around the world.

Accessibility of the destination

A crucial factors that you should keep in mind while choosing a medical tourism destination is easy accessibility to the region. Since most potential medical tourists reach a destination when it is time for their treatment to begin, they cannot risk being delayed during their travel. The destination should be accessible from all corners of the world through basic transport systems, such as air, road, and rail.

The region where your healthcare facility is located should have an established international airport or a domestic airport. For most medical tourists, time is the biggest deciding factor, the less you lose in travel, the better it is.

In addition, you should have basic information and important facts about the destination available to you through different channels of communication. Look for the information provided on the internet by various government agencies of the country or other web-based services. Understand the rules that you might have to follow in that country as a medical tourist. Gain as much information about the standard and the reputation of the hospital in its country. Read patient testimonials of the hospital to ascertain that the facility provides the same level of services as they claim.

Government support system and other tourism indicators

Another critical factor that a potential medical tourist should evaluate while looking for a suitable medical tourism destination is the type of government support for foreign tourists, both travelers and medical tourists. Other tourism indicators that guarantee a safe tour should also be considered. Governments in all reputed medical tourism destinations have set up various policies that govern medical tourism traffic and assist in the orderly integration of tourism and healthcare services. These policies also ensure that medical tourists get the best healthcare services.

In addition, a potential medical tourist should seek a destination which has a known history of catering to foreign healthcare seekers, and ensure that the conditions in the country are safe. Go through recent news archives and look for information that could be troubling for foreign tourists. Make sure that the country is politically stable and has friendly relations with your country. If the country has high crime rates and conditions are not favorable to even the local residents, it would be nearly impossible for medical tourism to flourish.

Judging a potential medical tourism destination by crime rates not only helps you choose a destination that is safe for you and your family during your visit, but can be a good indicator of the quality of healthcare institutions in the region. Before you finally choose a medical tourism destination, it is always best to discuss the claims with your physicians so that they can be crosschecked.

Another good way to check the tourism structure in a country and its openness is to do some research about the number of tourists who visit the country and what they say about their visit. Go through the political and law enforcement structure of the country, and look for the presence of departments that facilitate and help foreign tourists in the region.

Presently, only a few countries have established themselves as reputed medical tourism destinations. Others are joining the list too, and hence it becomes important for all potential medical tourists to ascertain the credibility of a medical tourism destination before they start planning their travel. A section of this book lists indicators for the 70 countries that are either established as medical tourism destinations, or quickly making it to that list.

PERSONALIZED FACTORS

While the above-mentioned factors include general considerations that you should take into account to find a suitable medical tourism destination, the choice also depends on several personalized factors. Needs and expectations are different for different people, personal requirements and personal factors influence the decision too. These factors might range from budget constraints to the understanding of language and culture of the country you are traveling to. Below are some of the personal factors that will largely influence your decision about choosing a suitable medical tourism destination.

Affordability

One of the biggest factors that influence the choice of a suitable medical tourism destination is the tourist's budget. While there are patients who opt for medical tourism to get access to high quality healthcare services, others just want to save money. Since treatment costs and quality differs in different parts of the world, most people living in the developed regions visit developing countries as medical tourists for saving money, while getting access to the same quality of healthcare services.

This inflated cost of healthcare facilities in the developed and industrialized nations has caused a surge in the number of medical tourists, who head over to the currently developing nations, such as India, where cost of healthcare services is drastically less.

Countries such as India and Thailand have made a name for themselves in the medical tourism world by providing key treatments at a small percentage of what is usually charged in countries such as the United States of America or the United Kingdom. With air travel becoming feasible to the general population, it has become possible for middle-class families to travel to these countries in search of better and affordable healthcare services.

As healthcare costs skyrocket in the western world, the benefits for potential medical tourists are clear. They can end up getting the same level and quality of treatment as is available in the home country, while paying up to 90 percent less. Reputed medical tourism destinations have set up dedicated departments that ensure fast and high quality treatment to foreign patients.

Expats travelling back home

One of the biggest factors that expats take into consideration while choosing a medical tourism destination is the quality of healthcare in their home country. It is usually noticed that non-resident Indians prefer to avail healthcare services in India, as the quality of healthcare in India is on a par with that of the western world, and comes at a fraction of the cost. Chinese and Thai citizens living abroad also follow the same ideology. Similarly, if you are an expatriate and want to avail yourself of healthcare services, you might consider the possibility of traveling back to your home country.

However, before you make up your mind to travel back to your home country for healthcare services, do make sure that the services provided in your home country are of high quality and meet your criteria. The quality and standards of healthcare might be entirely different to the country in which you are presently living.

One of the biggest reasons for expats moving back home for healthcare is that it gives them the opportunity to reconnect with their relatives and friends, while enjoying the attractions of a famous destinations either after or before the treatment by using the money they've saved on their treatment.

Language and cultural understanding

Language and culture play an important role in the decision making process of selecting a potential medical tourism destination. Not many medical tourists want to visit a country in which they will not be able to communicate with people. It is important to note any language and cultural differences at your potential medical tourism destination. Even if the country's residents do not speak your mother tongue, you must make sure that people in the country know and can communicate in English, which is widely spoken throughout the world.

Also consider the culture of the country that you intend to visit as a medical tourist. Many communities in the world can be very sensitive about their culture and religious values. If you are a strong believer of your culture and don't want any possible breach of your cultural and religious values, they you might want to consider traveling to a country for medical tourism to maintain the integrity of your cultural and religious values.

PRIVACY

Laws pertaining to personal privacy of any individual are different around the world. While in some countries a person's privacy gets the highest priority, you will find no or insufficient laws to govern the media in others. If you want your treatment with complete privacy, you should choose a destination where various government bodies are set up to regulate the flow of private information. While the privacy factor will not hold much relevance for some, for others, especially celebrities, the privacy aspect of a potential medical tourism destination is something that they cannot ignore.

Media privacy is the reason why many celebrities travel to Dubai for cosmetic surgery procedures. Laws in Dubai ensure that the government has complete control over the media, and hence it becomes impossible for reporters to broadcast or reveal personal information about anybody without the person's consent.

WEATHER AND CLIMATE

Ideally, you should rate a potential medical tourism destination according to its climate and how comfortable you are with it. While in some popular medical tourism countries, such as Thailand, the summer temperatures can be oppressing for many tourists, the conditions can just be the opposite in other parts of the world. Do your research and ascertain that the weather during your time of visit would be pleasant and the healthcare facility that you have chosen for treatment has ample equipment to monitor and regulate temperature.

If you have planned your medical tourism visit to coincide with a holiday season, make sure that you are visiting the place when the climate is at its best so that you can completely enjoy your visit while availing the best of medical and wellness procedures. In addition to weather, make sure that you are fully aware of the atmospheric conditions of the country.

Some countries, such as China, are well known for high levels of atmospheric pollution, which is simply intolerable for medical tourists. Make sure to select a clean medical tourism destination where the pollution levels will not put you at risk. There have been incidents in the past when medical tourists have been diagnosed with additional diseases once they have returned from their medical tourism visit. Keeping yourself abreast of the living conditions in a potential medical tourism destination will help you keep at bay from such incidents.

Make your choice of a potential medical tourism destination after carefully evaluating both the general factors and the personal factors.

MEDICAL VISA

While the quality and availability of care are the major concerns of the medical tourist, the documentation and government controls required for the visit should not be forgotten. In essence, try to choose a destination where traveling to and from will not be a problem. This requires being aware of the Visa laws and requirements of the selected country. As a rule of thumb, if it is difficult to obtain the visa of that country, or the visa's given are of insufficient duration, it is better to skip traveling to that destination.

Most popular medical tourism destinations do make allowances for medical tourists. Dubai and India, for example, offer Medical Visa to people looking for treatment. Generally speaking, this makes it easier for the tourist to travel to such a destination. Some procedures might require several visits to the medical tourism destination. Easy and affordable visa laws, which also allow the patient to be accompanied by family and friends are he factors that should figure prominently in your decision.

CHAPTER 12

Finding and selecting the right healthcare facility

IN THIS CHAPTER

- Seeking out accredited hospitals
- How to evaluate the quality of a non-accredited facility
- Understanding the importance of outcomes and success rates of the facility
- Importance of communication between patient and the treatment facility

SELECTING THE BEST HEALTHCARE FACILITY

When preparing for traveling overseas for medical treatment, one of the most important things to consider is the selection of the right hospital or clinic. After you have chosen the perfect medical tourism destination for availing healthcare services at an affordable cost, you need to choose the best healthcare facility. Choosing the right hospital is an important step that could largely shape your medical journey.

It is important that you engage in meticulous planning and research when selecting a hospital abroad for your medical treatment. While the cost of treatment is quite reasonable in many medical tourism destinations, one should not compromise with the quality of healthcare. Most patients are clueless about the factors they need to consider when selecting the ideal treatment facility. Many medical tourists face serious problems in gaining access to accurate information regarding the various treatment options. With so much information available online, choosing the right clinic or hospital can be an overwhelming experience for patients going overseas for medical or wellness treatments.

In your home country, you are usually accustomed to accessing medical care through your local physician. Even in emergency cases, you know the right contacts and the best medical facilities in your hometown. However, when you opt for medical travel, you are likely to find yourself outside of your depth. You may face many problems in the foreign land if you are not aware of the best and accredited healthcare facilities that offer the desired treatment. Since there is an overabundance of information and resources online, you should try to be an informed consumer and familiarize yourself with what to look for in a reputed and accredited treatment facility overseas.

It is important for a medical tourist to know about the specializations and accreditation of the treatment facility. Moreover, you should also check for certifications of the physician or the surgeon handling your case. Most of the medical tourism providers have contacts with renowned medical institutions in different medical tourism countries, you can always seek their help. This section will help the medical tourists understand everything they need to know, from accreditations to international affiliations. I hope that it will guide your thinking process on the important factors to consider prior to selecting the right healthcare facility for your medical treatment.

CHECK FOR HOSPITAL ACCREDITATION

All medical institutions have a system of quality measures that they implement within their facilities. In each country, the government sets the regulations. The healthcare providers follow these regulations stringently or loosely in different countries. In some countries or segmented sectors, governments or health authorities launch mandatory accreditations for the healthcare facilities. For instance, Dubai Healthcare City has its own regulation body, which ensures that all providers operating within Dubai Healthcare City follow standard practices set by DHCC, which are based on international standards and as part of ISQUA. Hospital accreditation is one of the most crucial factors that medical tourists should consider to ensure safe and successful treatment abroad. The body that 'accredits the accreditors' is known as ISQUA, which ensures that the accrediting organizations are also following strict guidelines and international codes.

Internationally accredited medical institutions provide quality healthcare to their patients. Proper accreditation also provides a hospital or clinic competitive advantage in the health care industry. Accreditation is a crucial factor that could help a patient to determine the quality of care, treatment and services. You can always expect to get better services from a hospital that is internationally accredited by a prominent organization like JCI (Joint Commission International), Australian Council on Healthcare Standards International (ACHSI) and Quality Healthcare Advice (QHA) Trent. With medical tourism on the rise, international accreditations are gaining more importance with each passing day.

A foreign facility can demonstrate the fact that they take the issue of quality healthcare seriously by ensuring their accreditation by one of the esteemed accrediting international bodies. Organizations like Joint Commission International (JCI) have stringent requirements that a hospital needs to follow in order to get a JCI accreditation stamp. Other influential and well-known accrediting bodies are QHA Trent Accreditation based in the UK, International Organization for Standardization (ISO) and Accreditation Canada.

During the process of accrediting a hospital, JCI and other such organizations perform a series of inspections and examine the important components within a hospital, from the ventilation systems to the quality of food served to the patients. If the hospital or treatment facility selected by you has the accreditation from an international organization, you can breathe a sigh of relief, as this demonstrates the treatment facility's excellent healthcare quality standards.

By choosing an accredited hospital or clinic, you can enjoy the cost benefits of getting quality medical treatments out of the country. When people travel overseas for cost-effective medical treatment, they also wish to seek the best in medical care and treatment.

The best way to identify and evaluate the quality of the healthcare providers is by their accreditation. A medical tourist should always select a healthcare facility that operates on an international code of quality practice. Patients coming in from the UK or the USA for medical treatment are accustomed to a certain level of treatment quality and always seek the same level of quality medical treatment in the medical tourism destination they visit. This is ensured, in large measure, by accreditation organizations.

IMPORTANT NOTE

While the international accreditation is the best way to determine the healthcare standards of a particular hospital or clinic, you cannot overlook the fact that many non-accredited medical facilities might provide healthcare services to the patients at the same or higher level. There is no denying the fact that there might be many facilities in different medical tourism destinations that have not yet applied for an international accreditation, or are following through the long path of receiving accreditation.

Usually, such facilities have accreditation from local accreditation body, which in most cases is the particular country's local health authority. It guarantees that the facility offers high quality services to the patients.

EVALUATING QUALITY FOR ACCREDITED OR NON-ACCREDITED HEALTHCARE FACILITIES

Affiliations with international organizations

We have already discussed about the significance of choosing an internationally accredited treatment facility for the patients who travel overseas for medical care and treatment. As a medical tourist, you should also know about the hospital's affiliations with international organizations. Other than the stamp of international accreditation, most medical facilities that provide healthcare services to foreign patients tend to have affiliations and associations with the leading medical organizations from across the globe. The medical institutions with genuine international affiliations truly demonstrate their ability to associate with world class institutions.

Some examples of renowned institutions that have paired up with medical tourism facilities are Harvard Medical International, Johns Hopkins Hospital, Cleveland Clinic and Mayo Clinic. These hospitals have a proven track record of serving patients traveling overseas for specific medical needs. A number of hospitals in different countries around the world have exclusive agreements with these renowned institutions. These international organizations ensure that the treating hospital takes the issue of patient satisfaction and quality care very seriously, as their reputation is also at stake. They will visit the treatment facility and conduct training sessions to bring the quality up to an international level.

If a hospital affiliates with an American or European hospital, patients coming in from the countries in those regions will be quite familiar with the name, brand and reputation of the organization. It ensures that the treatment facility you have chosen overseas will be operating at a similar or higher level than the institution in their affiliation list. These institutions review the quality of the care and medical treatment to maintain the standards. The affiliations with leading organizations help in making the healthcare global in the true sense.

OUTCOMES AND SUCCESS RATES

If you are considering medical treatment overseas, it is important for you to investigate the quality of the treating doctors and the services you can expect from the treatment facility. As a medical tourist, you should always take your time in choosing the right hospital or clinic that maintains high standards of patient care and safety. International accreditation is one of the key factors that can influence a patient's decision-making process. The leading international accreditation institutions help promote the much-needed transparency between patients, healthcare providers, and insurance companies.

When choosing a healthcare facility overseas, you must consider the potential outcomes and the success rates, so that you can make an intelligent decision of choosing the right hospital for your treatment. If you are using a medical tourism facilitator, you should always ask him or her to show you the outcomes and success rates of the recommended hospitals in your medical tourism destination.

In order to maintain high standards of global healthcare, all the established hospitals in the different parts of the world should have detailed and transparent data on the outcomes of medical treatments offered within the facility. Along with these outcomes, the treating facilities should also have the detailed information about the success rates of different procedures carried out in the facility.

The success rates are simple to understand. The success rate of a hospital refers to the ratio of the successful and smooth procedures in comparison to the total number of procedures carried out within the facility. It is the responsibility of the hospital's management wing to collect this type of data within the hospital and crosscheck the same for accuracy and authenticity. All the healthcare facilities have to provide this data about the success rates of the procedures to the patients and other important members of the healthcare industry.

While medical tourism industry is booming, there are many concerns with the entire concept. One of the biggest issues is the transparency within the healthcare industry. In the ideal scenario, any healthcare facility that does not have transparent practices in place should not function as a medical tourism destination. In simple terms, transparency is simply the practice of making all data available to the public, herein the patients, while at the same time ensuring that the available information is anonymous and cannot be traced back to individual patients without their explicit consent. Within the realm of transparency, it is important to make certain that an average consumer can understand the data easily and make a knowledgeable decision. If you are using a medical tourism facilitator for your medical trip overseas, you can ask him or her to provide you with the success rate and outcomes of the medical facility where you wish to seek treatment.

Any potential medical tourist should never choose a hospital that has a success rate lower than 98% for routine procedures. The 2% discrepancy could account for human errors, unforeseeable errors and the best success rate set by international accreditations. However, there are established standardized protocols for most medical procedures. These protocols define the ways of performing a procedure the right way. If you are unable to find the relevant data on the hospital's website, you should personally enquire with the international patient department and it is their responsibility to provide genuine answers for all your queries.

CONSIDER THE LOCATION OF THE TREATMENT FACILITY

When choosing a hospital overseas for your medical treatment, you should ask yourself some basic questions that will help you make a smart decision. If you do not choose the right location of the treatment facility overseas, you might have to face unexpected events when you reach there. You should do thorough research online about the location of the treatment facility where you wish to seek medical treatment. Some of the important things you need to consider are:

- Is the facility at a favorable location in the city?
- Will you require a great deal of transportation to access the treatment facility?
- Is the treatment facility located in a safe area?
- Is there a high crime rate in the area surrounding the treatment facility?
- What are the accommodation options in the area?

In order to choose the right facility, you must know the answers to these common questions. Many tourism destinations have a poor transportation infrastructure and medical tourists should avoid going to such places or ensure proper arrangements with the help of a certified medical tourism facilitator. You should determine that the location of the facility is within close proximity to the area you will be staying in, so that you do not have to waste time stuck in traffic, or being otherwise delayed.

It would not be a wise decision to choose your treatment facility in a location where the crime rate is high. Since your focus will be successful treatment overseas, you would never want to face any legal or other complications overseas. You should always consider using a map service, such as Google Earth or Maps.com, to help you find the exact location of your treatment facility with utmost ease. Using these services will help in getting to and from the facility overseas and save you a lot of time.

It is important for the medical tourists to familiarize themselves with the exact location of the healthcare facility, so that they do not have to run around in a place new to them. One of the important aspects of medical tourism is the vacation. Therefore, you should also check for the tourist attractions located close to the treatment location.

LEVEL OF FOLLOW-UP CARE

A good follow-up care can greatly speed up the recovery process after the treatment. Usually, your treating physician or surgeon will list screenings and other medical tests as an integral part of your follow-up care plan. The follow-up care is of utmost importance, especially for the medical tourists, as it could have a great effect on their health and lives if they do not take proper care after the treatment. Poor follow-up care can further lead to health related complications, for which you might have to take more treatment.

Prior to arranging any deals with a particular hospital, internationally traveling patients need to ensure that their treatment facility takes the issue of following up with the patients very seriously. If the treatment facility overseas does not pay proper attention to the follow-up care, you should never choose that facility for your treatment, as you will require regular checkups and care when you get back to your home country.

You need to ask yourself a number of questions before you choose a medical facility in a foreign country. Some of them are as follows:

- Will the treatment facility assist me in case any medical complications arise after treatment?
- Will the treatment package include any post-operative care or will I have to pay for it separately?
- Will the same doctor look after my follow-up care or will the hospital refer me to another provider for the treatment?

You need definite and clear answers to these serious questions before you finalize any healthcare facility for your medical treatment. If you do not find the answers to these questions satisfactory, you must talk to your facilitator regarding the same and should start looking for some other treatment facility that guarantees a high level of follow up care to their patients. With the right follow-up care, you can monitor your health and share your concerns with the healthcare team anytime. It is important to consider that while a healthcare facility might provide a high level of follow-up care within the facility, they might not attend you properly once you are back home.

Considering these factors, it is important for medical tourists to select a hospital or overseas clinic which has a good record of providing long-term follow-up care for the patients. You can always ask the hospital for referrals of internationally traveling patient who have received treatment within their facility. You can get in touch with the individuals and ask about their experiences with the level of follow-up the hospital provides to the medical tourists.

PROVIDING ARRANGEMENTS FOR THE PATIENTS

While the major responsibility of a medical facility should be to provide excellent health-care services to the patients, many hospitals also provide extra arrangements in order to attract more patients. Other than the basic health-related advice that a hospital normally provides, there is a lot more information the hospital will provide you if you agree to avail treatment at that particular facility. This additional information can greatly help make your medical journey more comfortable.

It might also eliminate or minimize the need for the medical tourists to make some particular travel arrangements regarding their medical trip overseas. While some treating facilities will provide the patients with the transportation service to and from the hospital, the others might have affiliations with some hotels within close proximity to the hospital. Since you will receive treatment at their facility, you might get accommodation for a very reasonable price. It is advisable to ask your treatment facility if they provide other arrangements for the international traveling patients.

All medical tourists should enquire about these arrangements prior to traveling, as it could ease out your preparations checklists and make your medical trip as smooth and comfortable as possible. The complementary transportation for the duration of your medical needs can make your stay more comfortable, and save you a good deal of money. Since more and more hospitals in different countries have started to accept the potential of medical tourism industry, they are willing to throw in more benefits to please foreign tourists.

COMMUNICATION IS IMPORTANT

If you want your medical journey to be as smooth and successful as possible, you need to understand the importance of proper communication with your treatment facility abroad and the medical tourism provider. It is obvious that as a medical tourist, you will have plenty of questions and concerns about your medical journey.

There is no better organization than the treatment facility in your home country to provide you with information and advice. Since you will be receiving treatment at their facility, they would be in the best position to provide answers to all your queries. They will have all the information and resources you would require to make an appropriate decision when choosing the right treatment facility out of your country. In order to make sure that the hospital or clinic is worth your time and investment, you should pay proper attention to the way the treatment facility communicates with you.

If they do not emphasize on interaction with their patients, it would be wise to move on with your search for a better treatment facility. Most hospitals in medical tourism destinations have an international patient department, which you can contact for all your concerns and queries and they will be more than willing to comply. An international patient department creates a proper channel of communication with the patients traveling overseas for medical treatment. They should be able to respond to all of your queries and provide first-class customer service, before and after your treatment.

For any medical tourist, it would be better to initiate the communication with one key person at the treatment facility and build a healthy bond. This person should be available to answer your questions and concerns. Apart from the availability factor, the treatment facility should be able to communicate in a clear language that you can understand easily. If there is any communication barrier during the process, it could affect your entire course of treatment. Since you are going to a foreign destination, chances are that you may not find someone who can speak your mother tongue. If that is the case, you should ensure that the hospital has a translation service on board that can translate the conversation between you and the treating doctor in order to ensure a healthy communication.

As a medical tourist, you should ask the concerned department or the people about any documents you might need during the entire process of your treatment, such as informed consents and medical itineraries. Since you are going to receive treatment from a facility in a foreign country and would not want to face any potential problems or complications, you should ask for guidance regarding anything you do not know.

SELECT A FULLY INTEGRATED HEALTHCARE FACILITY

When choosing the right hospital, give preference to a healthcare facility that has a wide range of features and offers multi-specialty treatment. Selecting a fully integrated hospital will save you a lot of time, effort and money during your medical trip. This is because you will need to make yourself familiar with only one location and you will not need to waste any time running between facilities in a place unknown to you. A fully integrated medical facility will always strive towards improving patient care.

In most cases, a clinic or smaller medical facility will have limited selection of available services. They also might not have all necessary medical equipment to perform the medical procedures efficiently. While a small treatment facility may have a room where they can provide consultation to the patients, it might not have the necessary resources or facilities to carry out many diagnostic, laboratory or other medical tests. A small clinic might not have an operating room to handle the procedure. Therefore, you should always opt for a hospital that offers a full suite of healthcare services and specialization in treatment for which you are traveling overseas. When you select an internationally accredited hospital with the best facilities and expertise, you can always expect the best treatment. A good healthcare facility must have qualified and experienced doctors, high-end medical equipment, state-of-the-art research facilities, emergency care units, an international patient department, and the latest in technology.

As a medical tourist, you have to make sure that you receive the best possible medical care and treatment abroad. A hospital that is fully integrated will be efficiently able to cater to patients that are coming in for common, routine procedures as well as more specialized, complex treatments. A fully integrated medical facility will always have separate areas for consultations, an area to conduct all the relevant medical tests, a pathology and laboratory division to analyze the tests, and pharmacies that can dispense medication. These integrated healthcare facilities have several benefits. Owing to this, the patients can simply put all their focus on preparing for the treatment and the healing process after the treatment. In addition, such integrated facilities are more efficient in handling the emergencies, as they also have ER facilities.

REPUTATION OF HOSPITALS (IN INDUSTRY AND AMONG LOCALS)

When choosing the right treatment facility for your treatment, you should always consider the reputation of the hospital, in the healthcare industry and among the local residents of the area. There are certain hospitals and clinics, such as Johns Hopkins and Mayo Clinic, which have a good reputation within the healthcare industry and among patients as well. They operate at a high level of quality and never fail when it comes to patient and customer satisfaction. They are the leaders in the field, in terms of the medical staff they hire and the treatments they provide. With Mayo or Cleveland clinic, you can always expect to have a pleasant experience, as they will thoroughly take care of your needs. While the selection of a hospital will largely depend on the type of treatment and the physician or surgeon who will treat you, you cannot overlook the hospital's previous record of serving its patients. Clinical results, waiting times, emergency care and the parking facilities are some of the key factors that can influence your decision of choosing a hospital overseas.

The examples above are those facilities that have a strong global presence. However, patients should find out through word-of-mouth or do online research if the facility where they wish to seek treatment has a decent reputation within the country of their practice or at an international level. If patients and the industry leaders speak highly of the institution, you can always make an informed decision. There is a stiff competition in the healthcare industry these days, many hospitals around the world are working hard to attract internationally traveling patients, experienced doctors and collaborating organizations.

You can always ask your insurance provider about their knowledge of a facility, as the insurance companies usually keep quality pointer records for hospitals and clinics in a particular area. Another option is to contact the health and government organizations that rate the quality and reputation of the hospitals. In a nutshell, you should always research the reputation of your treatment facility overseas long before you travel to that location.

PATIENT EXPERIENCE (TESTIMONIALS)

When choosing the treatment facility abroad, you should always check for the patient testimonials and reviews in order to get a broad idea of the hospital's reputation and services. You can browse the online forums and patient websites to find the patient testimonials about a particular treatment facility. Many hospitals provide patient testimonials themselves and you can find them on the hospital's website or ask the international patient department to provide you with the same. Internationally traveling patients thinking of selecting a hospital to seek a certain treatment should search about the patients' experience with the quality of medical care they received at that facility. Here are some of the key questions you should always take into consideration:

- Do patients speak highly about the services provided by the hospital?
- Are they willing to come back to same hospital for treatments, if any, in the future?
- Are there some patients who have had a horrible experience, and why?

You can have answers to such questions by doing your own personal research and by communicating with the patient departments at the hospital. You can also ask them to provide you with the names and contacts of the patients who have undergone treatment at their facility lately, so that you could speak to them on your own. It is recommended that you ask the treatment facility to provide you with patient satisfaction findings. You may find patients in similar conditions or situations like yours who have taken treatment at the particular facility. By asking them all the aforementioned questions, you can get to know the quality standards of the treatment facility in detail and their commitment towards providing quality medical care to the patients.

Following is a condensed version of the questions medical tourists should ask from their chosen destination facility, and perhaps, to themselves.

GENERAL CONCERNS REGARDING THE TREATING FACILITY

- As a medical tourist, will I have the right to use all exclusive and modern amenities at the hospital?
- Is the treatment facility air-conditioned, as I am accustomed to the air-conditioned facilities in my home country?
- Does the hospital have cable, television, internet access, and other means of entertainment?
- Does the hospital provide newspapers, magazines, and other reading material for leisure time?
- On request, would it be possible to contact and talk to other medical tourism patients who have received treatment at the particular facility?
- What privacy policy does the hospital follow and is there anything in particular I need to know?
- Should I travel alone or should somebody from my family accompany me?
- Do I need a translator? If yes, will the hospital provide one or will I need to arrange one on my own?

OTHER QUERIES REGARDING THE HOSPITAL

- Are the facilities in the hospital up-to-date? Does the facility have all the modern medical equipment for the complex treatments?

- Are the doctors and surgeons well qualified as per international standards? Can I check the certificates that could guarantee this?
- Is the hospital easily accessible? How can I reach the hospital? Does the hospital provide transfer facility to and from the hospital for internationally traveling patients?
- What are the different services billed in my medical estimate?
- What are the acceptable modes of payment? Do they accept cash, credit cards or any other means of money transfer?

REGARDING TREATMENT

- Will I have to sign a consent form before any invasive procedure? If yes, can I review it in advance and make changes, if required? What would happen in case any complications arise during the treatment?
- In the event that the hospital is unable to provide the treatment when I arrive, will I get my money back? If yes, what would the process be for this?
- Do you provide nursing service round-the-clock during recovery?
- I follow strict dietary restrictions. Will the hospital provide the necessary support or will I have to arrange for this on my own?
- When do I leave from my country for the treatment?
- When can I go back to my country after the treatment?

REGARDING FOLLOW-UP CARE

- Will I be able to take the medications back home with me? If not, how will you provide the necessary follow-up care in my home country and what alternative medications can I take in my country?
- Are there any medicines which I may not carry when traveling? In such a case, how do I continue my treatment when I get back to my home country?
- Will you give some prescription that can be filled in my country? If not, how will you handle the follow-up care?
- How will you provide the follow-up care? Who will look after this – the treating doctor or the hospital's patient department?
- Suppose I return back home and develop some minor or serious complications; how will you communicate with me and arrange for the required treatment? Whom should I contact in such a case, as I will need guidance at the earliest opportunity?
- Will my primary care physician administer follow-up care or will you refer to any other healthcare provider for the follow-up care?

REGARDING SAFETY OF DATA

- What precautions will you take for ensuring the safety of all the medical records? What if my medical records are compromised or fall into the wrong hands?
- How will you transfer the medical reports, such as the X-ray, MRI, CT and PET scans, if my primary care physician needs to consult them?

LEGAL CONCERNS

- I have a medical insurance policy issued in my country. Will it cover the procedure performed in a foreign country? Does it also cover any complications that may arise out of the treatment?
- Does the medical expense paid as part of medical tourism affect the tax payment?
- As a medical tourist, whom should I approach in case of malpractice or negligence of care?
- What are my rights to seek legal recourse in your country in case any medical complications arise during the course of treatment?
- Are there any established laws related to medical practices in the country I am visiting to seek medical treatment?

CHAPTER 13

The right physician for your treatment

IN THIS CHAPTER

- Understanding the credentials of a doctor
- Decoding a physician's abbreviations
- The importance of a licensed and certified physician
- The necessity of constant communication with your treating doctor
- Insisting on personalized care

SELECTING THE RIGHT PHYSICIAN OR SURGEON FOR YOUR TREATMENT/PROCEDURE

By now, you have already done everything you could to find an appropriate medical tourism destination and have also selected the best healthcare facility within the region where your treatment will be carried out. The next thing you have to consider is to find the best physician for your condition. While it sounds relatively easy, the fact is that finding a good doctor or a surgeon in your own country takes a lot of time and research. Since as a potential medical tourist, you have to find a good doctor or surgeon in a destination foreign to you, the process can be a lot more daunting and tedious.

After you have arrived at your selected medical tourism destination and have reached the facility, all you can do now is to trust the doctor and his skills. Selecting the one, who is credible, experienced, has complete knowledge of your condition and the various treatment options available can be a little tricky. The first thing you have to ensure is that the doctor or the surgeon has a great educational background, precise experience, expertise and appropriate credentials. Understanding these credentials is important to ensure that the doctor can accurately perform any tests, diagnose and ascertain the seriousness of your condition, and ultimately treat it in the best possible way.

It is always a good option to research the healthcare facility that you have selected for the list of doctors that work there, and then shortlist the ones who have specialized in treating medical conditions similar to yours. Before you select any physician, speak with the healthcare facility's foreign patient department and get the contact details of all the doctors available there. Make a telephonic appointment with the doctors and speak with them regarding your medical condition and your travel plans. Make sure that they will be available during your time of visit and will be in a position to serve you.

Additionally, make sure that the physician will offer post-operative and post-treatment services. Finding a good doctor overseas is a difficult job and apart from doing thorough research, you should get in touch with your local doctor or your medical insurance provider for some recommendations. This chapter aims to help you in your research of finding the best possible doctor in an overseas location.

EXPERIENCE, KNOWLEDGE AND CREDENTIALS OF THE DOCTOR

The list of doctors available at any healthcare facility in a potential medical tourism destination will be long and you will have to meticulously screen the list to shortlist the doctors who you think are perfect for treating you. One of the first things that you have to do is to rate the doctors according to their experience. Just like in any other profession, experience only betters a doctor's skills, and an experienced doctor will not just be able to treat you quickly, but will also be ready to take up unexpected challenges that can come up during treatment.

Start by scrutinizing the past and the current endeavors of the doctor you are planning to seek care from. Find out more about their educational background and ensure that they are affiliated with a facility catering especially to medical tourism. Since the diagnosis and medical reporting in your home country can be entirely different from the standard of reporting and diagnosis in a medical tourism destination, affiliation to a medical tourism facility ensures that the doctor can understand and seek important information from different report and diagnosis documents. Once you are satisfied with the credentials of the doctor, ask them for their complete Curriculum Vitae, which will contain all other relevant information.

Try to contact the physician personally and ask him/her if he/she has ever treated a medical tourist with a medical condition similar to yours. If yes, ask about the outcome and how long did the patient actually had to stay at the healthcare facility and what kind of post-treatment services did they require. If possible, try to get in touch with the patient by seeking contact information from the physician. This would help you get valuable information about the physician, his skills and how he was able to prepare the patient for treatment and what kind of post-treatment services he offered.

In addition, by getting in touch with a past patient, you will get to know more about the treatment that was offered to him/her and how effective the treatment really was. Once you have crosschecked the claims of the doctor with the actual patient testimonials, you will be in a better position to make an informed decision.

UNDERSTANDING A PHYSICIAN'S CV

There is no better way to know more about a doctor than by carefully going through his/her curriculum vitae. The curriculum vitae, or simply CV, carries all relevant educational and professional information about a physician. Utilize this CV to understand the various aspects pertaining to the doctor's medical background. The first thing you should look for in the doctor's CV is his educational background. Go through the country's medical education infrastructure and then check the information with the doctor's CV. For instance, some universities in the United Kingdom only require a few years of tertiary education for a student to be labeled as a doctor, while in the United States, it is essential for students to attend four years in a pre-medical school and then four years in a medical school to be labeled as a doctor.

The next thing you should do is to check the name of the college or medical school from where the doctor has completed his medical education. Do internet research to ascertain that the medical school or college is reputed and accredited by government authorities of the region. Once you have completely established the doctor's educational background, it is time for you to start looking at his/her record of accomplishment following his/her medical graduation. Gain enough knowledge about the doctor's past work experiences to find out the total years that the doctor has spent in the profession.

In addition to the doctor's medical background, you as a patient should also gather information regarding the doctor's involvement in medical research or affiliation with various medical organizations. Since medical science is an ever-evolving field of study, a doctor's involvement in medical research will ascertain that he/she is fully abreast of the latest in medical science, diseases, and treatment options. As a member of reputed medical organizations, the doctor will be able to continuously try and improve his/her medical practice and will also remain in touch with qualified peers, which is essential for his medical profession. Ideally, you should choose a physician who is deeply involved with medical research and is associated with globally renowned medical organizations.

There are regional and international associations for almost every specialty in medical science, each with like-minded doctors and peers. Therefore, you initially have to understand which groups your potential physician is a member of, to judge his/her knowledge about the specialty, his experience and the desire to grow within the field and specialty.

DECODING THE ABBREVIATIONS

Unlike in the curriculum vitae of any other professional, doctors usually list their qualification and education in abbreviations, which might be thoroughly confusing to a layman. The list of abbreviations which you might find in a doctor's curriculum vitae is seemingly endless, as the abbreviations differ in different parts of the world. Moreover, several doctors also list the associations of which they are a member, in abbreviated form too, making it nearly impossible for you to find out what they mean. Since you want to know everything about a doctor before you visit him in a foreign country, decoding these abbreviations is your responsibility.

Abbreviations differ in different parts of the world. For instance, MD stands for Medical Doctor in the United States of America, and this is equivalent to M.B.B.S (Bachelor of Medicine and Bachelor of Surgery) in India. Some other abbreviations that are commonly used by doctors are MS, which translates to Masters in a specific field, DMD that translates to Doctor of Medical Dentistry, and DDS translating to Doctor of Dental Surgery.

In addition to abbreviations denoting the educational background of a doctor, several physicians also list abbreviations of the associations that they are a part of in their curriculum vitae. For instance, ASPS is a prestigious association entitled 'American Society of Plastic Surgery' and if you read this abbreviation in a doctor's curriculum vitae, it means that the doctor is renowned and has established himself as one of the premier plastic surgeons in the world.

Other commonly used abbreviations are PHP, which stands for Primary Health Physician and GP, which stands for General Physician. Doctors having these abbreviations in their CV can make general diagnoses for common treatments but they are not specialized within a specific field of medicine. Although these doctors are fully qualified to prescribe patients with medication for commonly occurring diseases, they will not be the best for a specialized treatment. However, these doctors can definitely refer patients to a specialist.

Unlike a normal GP or a PHP, a specialist has spent additional years in obtaining advanced training and education to treat a patient with special needs. Specialists focus on a particular area of the human body; for example, a cardiologist is a heart specialist, allergist is a doctor specializing in treating allergies and surgeons are doctors that have the skills to operate on specific organs.

AVOID QUICK-FIX DOCTORS THAT CHARGE LESS AND PROMISE MORE

The growth in medical tourism has not only brought quality healthcare services to millions, but has also given professionals a way to promote their services. While most experienced healthcare professionals promote quality services, a few incompetent medical practitioners promote quick-fix treatments to gain attention. Hence, it becomes essential for potential medical tourists to verify these claims with a registered medical practitioner in their own country, long before they plan their travel. In most cases, these quick-fix treatments are not effective, and the worst case scenario is that they are relatively expensive and can prove to be harmful for patients.

As an example, many people simply neglect their oral hygiene for years, and only when their teeth start deteriorating and the pain becomes unbearable, they frantically look around to find the best and the nearest dentist. Dentists who advertise easy solutions, quick relief and package deals should be approached with caution. The best you can do is to stay away from enticing commercials such as "Walk home pain-free in just 30 minutes", as these fixes could potentially be dangerous.

A good dentist who follows standardized procedures will not have the time, or the need, to advertise his/her services. A good dentist relies on his patients to promote his/her services. If you, as a patient, got good dental care services from a dentist, you will definitely share his name with your friends and coworkers.

It is nearly impossible for any dentist to claim results without actually diagnosing the problem in your teeth. A qualified dental surgeon will be willing to conduct an initial consultation to determine the cause of your discomfort, before putting you in the dental chair. Only after some X-rays and tests, he/she will be able to give you an estimate about the time it could take for your problem to be corrected.

It is extremely important for patients, including medical tourists, to judge the credentials of a reputed dentist or any healthcare professional by looking at his/her past patients, and verify enticing healthcare claims before opting for any one of them. In some countries, healthcare professionals are banned from making claims which cannot be verified. However, in some countries, such laws do not exist and healthcare professionals do everything they can, such as making false claims and offering inexpensive services to entice patients and potential medical tourists looking for a magical cure.

ONLY LOOK FOR LICENSED, BOARD-CERTIFIED DOCTORS

Unlike the common misconception that any doctor can treat a foreign medical tourist, the fact is that not every medical professional is fully equipped and trained to handle foreign patients. This is because the needs and requirements of patients in different parts of the world are different, and so is the type of treatment that they are looking forward for. In countries which have established themselves as reputed medical tourism destinations, the medical council provides practicing license to trained and equipped medical professionals.

As a potential medical tourist, it becomes essential for you to look for this important certificate. With a simple research, you should be able to generate enough results to provide you with information about a physician's credentials. In addition to the license, many doctors also furnish a board certificate. Doctors who are board-certified are specialists in a specific treatment.

The medical field has widened its scope with continuous research and discoveries. Each specific field has a medical board, which allows practitioners to continue practicing under their support. Being a part of such a reputed board keeps practitioners abreast of the latest developments in their field of practice.

Many doctors fail to upgrade their board certificates and hence are not fully capable of understanding the new developments in their specific field. This could also mean that the doctor is lagging behind on his/her knowledge about new pharmaceutical drugs, treatment options, patents and laws of expertise. It is extremely important for you to look for a medical practitioner who has an updated board certificate and the license to treat foreign patients.

Doctors who have updated board certificates are members of esteemed and affiliated associations, which encourage doctors to progress with tireless education. Since these doctors always remain in touch with the current technology and treatment options, they are always in a position to share their acquired knowledge base with others through workshops. Such doctors always make sure that their patients achieve optimum health and treatment, which in fact, is the motto of every good doctor.

Make sure you crosscheck the doctor's medical certification with the board that he/she claims to be a member of. The first thing you should check is whether the board is certified and is a recognized medical specialty board. The second thing is to verify the doctor's association with the board. You can simply browse the board's website to ascertain if the doctor's name is listed on the board's members list.

CONSTANT COMMUNICATION WITH THE PHYSICIAN

Communication between a medical practitioner and a potential medical tourist is desirable, and in fact, necessary. You should ascertain that you can communicate with your doctor via a common language, failing which your treatment can be affected. While you should ideally choose a doctor who can easily communicate with you, in the worst-case scenario, you should consider taking the services of a translator.

You cannot undermine the importance of proper communication with the doctor. While most of us feel relatively comfortable while communicating with members of the hotel staff before we check it, we usually get more submissive in matters relating to medical treatment. It is essential for you to understand that if you are willing to pay a good amount of money for top-notch healthcare, you also have the right to ask as many questions as you want. The physician also has the responsibility to clearly explain the need for various treatments and services that will be introduced during your visit.

Always keep a check on the responses given by the physician to your queries and look for signs if the physician is unable to explain something. In addition, ask questions pertaining to the routine of the doctor. Ask how many patients the doctor sees each day; if the number of patients is too large, the doctor might not be in a position to give you personalized service and care, which could affect your treatment. Also, check if the doctor has successfully treated other patients with the same ailment. If he/she has, then ask about the outcomes and the side effects.

INSIST ON PERSONALIZED SERVICES

If you have chosen a doctor who is already attending several patients each day, he/she might not be able to give you personalized care and service. Such doctors accept new patients and after doing the initial diagnosis, they often refer patients to their interns for follow-up treatment and appointment. As a prudent medical tourist, it becomes your responsibility to discuss these things with the doctor in advance. Demand that the entire fees of the treatment should be directly paid to the physician so that you don't end up getting treated by an intern.

However, do keep in mind that it is a common practice for healthcare professions to coordinate with other healthcare professionals of the same expertise and experience if it becomes necessary. You might also require a team effort of reputed healthcare professionals during the treatment.

Along with personalized care and services, a good doctor should also make their patients feel at ease. If you have chosen a good doctor, he/she will reply to all your enquiries even after your treatment is over. If you call your doctor, he/she will not refuse to respond to any follow-up enquiry. If you are a woman and have chosen a male doctor, he will do everything he can to make you feel comfortable in his presence.

Also, keep in mind that not all doctors have clinical labs and tools at their disposal within their facility. In such a case, you should ask the doctor to tell you about the facility where all the necessary tests will be conducted. Research about the testing facility and verify its credentials and credibility. In addition, make sure that the doctor is capable of answering all your insurance related questions. Do check if the doctor's services and your treatment comes under your medical insurance bracket, you should need to be informed about whether the doctor will release bills from his/her office or will they be issued by another facility.

The last thing to keep in mind is that you should not undergo any examination on the very first visit to the practitioner. On the other hand, prepare a list of questions to ask so that your time is not wasted.

Most facilities and doctors will provide a teleconferencing option before you leave your home country. This will facilitate your communication with your physician, and allow him to explain your course of treatment, and clear any doubts you might have, and answer your questions.

CHAPTER 14

The Medical Tourism Facilitator

IN THIS CHAPTER

- How a facilitator can help a patient
- What a patient can expect from a facilitator's services
- Advantages and disadvantages of hiring a facilitator
- Tips on how to select a good facilitator

IMPORTANCE OF MEDICAL TOURISM FACILITATOR

There has been a significant increase in the number of medical travel companies over the last few years, which aim to make the complex process of global healthcare easy for the patients. A medical tourism facilitator, often referred to as a medical tourism provider, sets up a comprehensive support system that goes far beyond the obvious arrangements. A facilitator is usually an organization that offers travel, accommodation, medical services, pre- and post-operative care, and tourism activities. Medical tourism facilitators have an important role to play in the medical tourism industry. The facilitator is of great help to patients who are busy with their work schedules and are not comfortable with the complexities of international travel.

A majority of people who seek affordable healthcare overseas are not aware of the entire process and have a lot of questions and concerns. A patient thinking of traveling abroad for treatment will have tons of questions, and very little experience about dealing with medical facilities in other countries. This is where a medical tourism facilitator can be of great help. The responsibility of a medical tourism provider is to educate the potential medical tourist on all things regarding their medical journey.

Facilitators provide a combination of various services, which often require meticulous planning from patients. However, the selection of an incompetent medical facilitator could lead to dissatisfaction. In a recent survey conducted by the author, the respondents deemed the role of the facilitator within the medical tourism industry quite significant. Sixty-one per cent (61%) said that facilitators were 'Very important', 27% said that they were 'Important', 10% regarded them as 'Optional' and 2% said that they were 'Not important'. Integrated knowledge of medical services, tourism and travel facilitation and concierge services, which form a three-dimensional support to the traveler are central to the business and a medical tourism facilitator should be completely familiar with these concepts. This chapter provides essential information about the role and responsibility of a medical tourism facilitator in the medical tourism industry and most importantly, this chapter discusses how patients can identify a good medical tourism facilitator.

WHY USE A MEDICAL TOURISM FACILITATOR?

A medical tourism facilitator plays an important role in directing patients towards quality healthcare providers in different medical tourism destinations. A facilitator helps medical tourists get access to detailed information about destinations, treatment facilities and wide-ranging health services. Let us take an example of how a facilitator can assist a medical tourist. Let us suppose that a family based in California is looking for the best options to get a heart bypass surgery done for their ailing grandfather. While all the facilities were available in the neighborhood, including a great team of experienced doctors and superbly appointed facilities, they had some minor problems with the health insurance. Therefore, they started searching online for better value but equally good quality options. After a thorough online research, the family was able to find a good medical provider in a foreign country and started making the necessary travel arrangements. While they were planning the whole thing, they also thought of combining some fun with the entire journey by considering some sightseeing options in the chosen destination.

As it appears, the process was not easy, considering the various legalities, visas, pickups and drop offs, accommodation and the inner-city travel arrangements in the medical tourism destination. With the help of a fully functional team of hands-on professionals, the family was effortlessly able to make all the travel arrangements, along with a confirmed appointment with the most capable yet cost-effective service provider.

This example shows how professional help made things easier for this family. Experienced medical tourism facilitators have the right contacts in place, which can help make your medical journey as smooth as possible. Once you have decided your medical tourism destination and the treating hospital overseas, the facilitator takes care of all your travel arrangements, which include flights, lodging, and transportation services during your stay abroad.

For any potential traveler, the process of opting for medical tourism and taking care of all the travel-related things is undoubtedly challenging. If you decide to avail yourself of medical treatment abroad, you will need to find reliable healthcare providers and make trouble-free travel arrangements. Moreover, you will also need to make sure that you are familiar with the pre-operative and post-operative necessities in order to avoid any complications. Because of the complexity of this decision-making process, some medical tourists seek help from travel agents, the international patient departments of hospitals, or concierge service providers.

While all these agencies can help patients a great deal by acting as intermediaries, none can offer comprehensive medical tourism support services like a medical tourism facilitator. The medical tourism facilitator understands a patient's particular needs and manages all aspects of the entire medical journey in the best possible way. From flights to accommodation to medical assistance, a medical tourism facilitator takes care of everything important in the medical tourism process.

Starting from the point of contact, a facilitator takes care of all the things important to a medical tourist, such as flight reservations, patient's medical history, appointments with the treating doctor, transport facilities in the area, and hotel bookings. Since facilitators have good relationships with international healthcare providers, they can assist you with the selection of an accredited treating facility in a safe medical tourism destination. Mostly, the medical tourism facilitators have traveled to different locations around the world. Therefore, they are more knowledgeable about the exact conditions of different destinations and the healthcare standards of the treating facilities overseas. They also help in transferring your vital medical information across the borders with utmost ease.

Professional facilitators can be of great help in making an informed decision regarding the selection of a medical tourism destination. When it comes to medical tourism, the language and culture barriers could be a major concern, as you will have to contact the treating hospitals overseas. A medical tourism facilitator also makes sure that the language barriers and the cultural differences do not get in the way of the communication process between patients and the medical facility in a foreign country.

WHAT CAN A FACILITATOR DO FOR A PATIENT?

A medical travel facilitator company, which many people refer to as a medical tourism agency, can make things considerably easy for the medical tourists. Since you, as a medical tourist, are moving out of your comfort zone, you cannot afford to make any mistakes that would create problems during your medical journey.

A facilitator acts as a one-stop solution and provides you with all the necessary information regarding medical services, tourism and travel facilitation, and concierge services, which will help ease the medical tourism process for the potential tourists. From flights and lodging to consultations with the treating doctors, a medical tourism facilitator takes care of all the important things. Since facilitators are familiar with the legal and ethical issues associated with the medical tourism, they can guide you properly.

The medical tourism facilitators play a key role in blurring the geographical borders and connecting the medical tourists with quality healthcare providers from different parts of the world. Let us discuss the key things a facilitator can do for the potential medical tourists.

One stop solution: Since facilitators have a clear understanding of all the important things associated with the medical tourism sector, they can offer all-inclusive support services, which could include pre-travel arrangements, medical arrangements, concierge services and healthy communication between the medical tourist and the treating facility.

Relationship management: A good facilitator with industry experience can provide comprehensive relationship management in case the patient needs to communicate with insurance companies, governments or their employer bodies that sponsor medical tourism activities. The basic idea is to build a comprehensive support system for the potential medical tourists.

Know how: The medical tourism facilitators are expert in their field and are familiar with all the ways of handling different situations that may arise during medical travel. Except the medical service itself, they are efficient in providing all necessary help to the internationally traveling patients. A facilitator can provide the patients with information on the healthcare providers, treating physician or surgeon, local attractions, and the infrastructure.

Negotiation skills: Negotiations can play a major role in bringing down the costs of your medical journey. An expert facilitator will negotiate better on your behalf, and therefore might be able to reduce the costs where possible. Since a patient might not be able to understand additional expenses charged by a treating facility abroad, it is always better to seek the services of an experienced medical tourism facilitator who will guide you along the complex medical tourism process.

Travel and logistics partner: Making travel arrangements can be challenging task for a first-time medical tourist. A good medical travel facilitator can take care of all your travel and logistics requirements. A facilitator understands the exact needs of the patients and can make arrangements accordingly.

Representative: The medical tourism facilitator could also function as a formal representative on your behalf to communicate with your family and friends in your home country about your medical condition and other important things your family members or friends should know.

Continuity of care: Post-operative care is extremely important for a speedy recovery. A medical tourism facilitator ensures that your medical provider has prepared sufficient arrangements for your post-operative care. The continuity of care is of utmost importance for the patients.

WHAT SHOULD ONE EXPECT FROM A FACILITATOR?

It is very important that all the medical travel facilitators should have a clear understanding of medical procedures. Before they suggest any destination or treating facilities to the potential medical tourists, they ought to research different treatment options and success ratio of the medical facilities in that particular destination.

This diligence is bound to benefit the medical tourists, as they can compare different options of treating doctors, healthcare providers and the medical tourism destinations. As a medical tourist seeking the best healthcare services, you must ask the facilitator on what criteria they have chosen the hospitals, clinics and spa facilities in a foreign country. If your facilitator can explain the reasons, you can be sure that you have made the right decision.

However, seeking opinions is not the same as receiving advice on various treatment options. Before you receive any advice, you must ensure that the physician in question is a doctor or a specialist in the particular field in which you are seeking treatment. Since you will receive your treatment in a foreign country, it is better to ensure that your life is in safe hands. After all, you are putting in so much effort to have a successful treatment overseas.

A facilitator should have well-established connections with the hospitals in different countries. A facilitator should be aware of general medical terminology related to treatments, so that they can understand your needs and concerns in a better way. This also helps a facilitator to explain things in detail and in a proper way to the potential customers.

Before you enter into an agreement with a medical tourism facilitator, you should ask a number of questions to clear all your doubts regarding your travel and medical arrangements. One of the most important questions to ask the facilitators is whether they are associated with some overseas hospitals in particular, function as a tourism agency, or simply work as an intermediary. One of the major concerns for any patient while opting for medical treatment overseas will be the transfer of medical information. It is important to ask facilitators how they will handle and transfer your medical information and other important confidential files, such as X-Rays, MRIs and CT Scans, across the border.

A good facilitator will not just sell you a foreign trip, but will also explain the terms and conditions with all the associated advantages and disadvantages by offering you an honest advice. These terms could include legal jargon and any other contracts you sign with the healthcare providers in a foreign nation. The facilitators should not only educate the potential medical tourists about the entire process of medical tourism, but should also understand their liability towards the patient in case anything goes wrong during the trip. A facilitator should also educate patients about the various legal issues they could face overseas.

WHY SHOULD YOU BE VERY CAREFUL IN SELECTING A FACILITATOR?

In order to avoid any complications during your medical journey, you should be careful in selecting the right facilitator and the healthcare facility. To understand it better, let us discuss various concerns covering the medical tourism industry. Since there are no specific government instated legal rules and regulations, the medical tourism sector has become an easy "quick start." Owing to this, many people have chosen the profession of medical tourism facilitation and if you search the internet, you will find so many facilitators and facilitator companies, which might make it difficult for you to make the right decision. All these new facilitators are raising major concerns for the growth of the medical tourism industry.

When it comes to health care services and especially medical tourism, more and more people are using internet to access the information. Therefore, it is important to select a medical tourism facilitator who can properly educate you about the concept of medical tourism, and can guide you through the overwhelming process of all the arrangements required to undergo medical treatment in a foreign country. Since facilitators know the medical tourism industry inside out, they can offer expert advice. There are associations and organizations that certify medical tourism facilitators, such as the Medical Tourism Association. Certified facilitators are in general very useful, as this chapter illustrates.

The entire process of selecting a medical tourism destination, making all the travel arrangements and receiving treatment overseas can be very confusing, especially if you are a first time global healthcare patient. Hiring a facilitator makes good sense, but you must make sure that you choose an experienced and certified facilitator in order to enjoy the best medical retreat experience overseas.

WHAT ARE THE MAJOR DISADVANTAGES OF USING A MEDICAL TOURISM FACILITATOR?

If the facilitator you choose does not know the medical tourism industry inside and out, there might be more cons than pros to choosing a facilitator. Hiring a facilitator ends up as a bad decision in cases where there is lack of transparency. If the medical tourism industry has to flourish, it is important for the medical tourism intermediaries to maintain transparency. A facilitator should educate the potential medical tourists about every single fact and information that could affect their medical journey overseas. Let us discuss the different disadvantages of using a medical tourism facilitator.

Limited choices: Chances are less that a facilitator has visited every medical tourism destination, which he or she recommends to the customers. Most of the time, facilitators will only suggest certain healthcare providers and hospitals where they have the contacts. They can simply recommend those hospitals from where they receive a handsome commission. As a result, the medical tourists are left with limited choices, and they might not be able to make an informed decision best suited to their interests. Therefore, if you are planning to get medical treatment overseas, you should ask the facilitator for wide range of options, so that you can make a smart decision.

Price: There are so many medical tourism facilitators and related companies on the internet, and choosing the best one can be an overwhelming task. Since most of the potential medical tourists are unfamiliar with the entire concept of moving overseas for medical treatment, the facilitators might charge steep fees. In many cases, these patients end up paying a lot of money to the facilitators.

Ideally, a patient should not mind paying a small percentage of his or her total medical tourism expenses to a facilitator company, for the services offered. However, if there is no transparency in the price structure they put forth, a medical tourist could get into troubles later. Paying a high price can upset you even more if they do not offer you the services they promised earlier during the initial meetings.

Communication: There is no denying the fact that a medical tourism facilitator functions as a bridge between the patients and treating facility overseas by minimizing the cultural and language barriers, if any. Miscommunication by the facilitator could possibly lead to big problems. In order to address the issue of miscommunication, it is better that the patient is directly involved in any communication pertaining to the actual treatment. While you can let your facilitator to communicate with third parties regarding travel arrangements, you should consider communicating with the treating facility directly.

Arrangements: There is a possibility that facilitators will be biased towards certain hospitals or medical providers, as they might be receiving good commissions from them or might have entered into an agreement. This could lead to biased decisions and arrangements. While it can be a tough task, the medical tourists should take extra precautions and try to find out if the facilitator is conducting any biased practices. You could ask the different medical tourism facilitators for referrals. Get in touch with people who have previously received their services and ask about their experiences. Doing this will help you make a better choice when it comes to using a facilitator.

Using a medical tourism facilitator for your medical trip has both advantages and disadvantages. Therefore, you should do the proper research and should never rush in choosing a medical tourism facilitator.

SELECTING A COMPETENT MEDICAL TOURISM FACILITATOR

Selecting the right medical tourism facilitator is of utmost importance. In the best scenario, the medical tourism facilitators function as a one-stop solution for patients traveling to foreign countries. They should operate upon four essential and some optional functions in order to make the medical journey as smooth and comfortable as possible for the potential medical tourists. You will find many medical tourism facilitators in the market who claim to offer the best services to the patients traveling abroad for treatment. However, a medical tourist should do proper research and assess whether or not a medical tourism facilitator stands true on the four essential components, which are listed next.

UNDERSTANDING OF MEDICAL SERVICES

It will make no sense in choosing a facilitator who does not understand the concept of medical tourism in detail. Whether it is the traveling checklist for medical tourist, the standards of the healthcare facility or the ethical and legal issues associated with medical tourism, a facilitator should have a clear understanding of everything that could be of importance to a potential medical tourist. Like any other industry, consumer is the king in the medical tourism business, and it is of utmost importance that the facilitator understands the exact needs of the medical tourists. It is essential for a facilitator to initiate and develop a healthy communication between patients and medical care providers.

Since one cannot rely entirely only on the information available on the internet, which often tends to be misleading, it is the responsibility of facilitators to act as reliable and sensitive consultants, and assist patients in the best possible way.

UNDERSTANDING OF ETHICAL AND LEGAL REQUIREMENTS

Many patients seek treatment options that are not available, or are illegal in their home countries. Some of the examples of such options are the reproductive technologies, abortion, and stem cell treatment. There are many issues associated with receiving treatment overseas, which includes the quality of medical care, right documentation, and the relationship between patients and the doctors. Some of the key factors that play an important role in the medical tourism are the awareness of ethical medical procedures, medico-legal laws and accreditation systems of the healthcare providers. In addition, the pre- and post-operative arrangements are of utmost importance.

Before entering into a contract, it is crucial that you go through all the terms and conditions in order to establish a healthy legal relationship with the service providers. The contract should protect the interests of the medical tourists in a foreign country. It is important for every medical tourist to check the accuracy of all the documents or contracts you sign with the healthcare providers or the medical tourism facilitators.

Considering all these things, it is important that the medical tourism facilitators should have a clear understanding of the medical subject and the concept of medical tourism, so that they can assertively explain all the services with all the technical details to the customers, thereby guaranteeing a better healthcare experience to the medical tourists.

A medical tourist should always choose a facilitator who has a clear understanding of the ethical and legal requirements of the medical tourism industry. A facilitator with in-depth knowledge of the ins and outs of the medical tourism industry can efficiently manage the entire trip for a patient traveling abroad for affordable medical care.

SUPPORT SERVICES

Medical tourism facilitators work to facilitate a smooth medical tourism process for both patients and healthcare providers. Whether it is the transfer of medical records, arranging travel logistics or follow-up care, a medical tourism facilitator takes care of all arrangements in order to make things easy for the medical tourists. Therefore, a facilitator's understanding of the medical tourism industry should not only be limited to apparent activities, such as travel booking, accommodation arrangements and tourism exposure guidance, but should also include an understanding of environmental, cultural, political, security and community factors that could influence your stay in a foreign country.

All medical tourism facilitators need to be efficient in handling certain important things, such as the development of customized benefits with special needs arrangements, interpreter provision, and preparation for unexpected services in case of an unsuccessful medical treatment. A facilitator should properly take care of the travel logistic services, which includes passports, flights, and accommodation and transportation in the foreign land. These facilitators should have a comprehensive list of hospitals, clinics, surgeons and physicians in different medical tourism destinations. Moreover, a facilitator should be knowledgeable enough to educate patients about all the minute details that could affect their stay overseas. When choosing a facilitator, you must make sure that you ask about the support services these professionals provide to their customers.

CONCIERGE SERVICES

Traveling out of your home country for medical treatment can be a challenging task for any medical tourist. One of the key components of a wholesome experience for medical travelers deals with destination management by third party providers. The concierge and destination management offer a range of services, which usually include the contact details of medical service providers, scheduling appointments with treating doctors, planning a medical trip, lodging arrangement, transfer facilities, and rehabilitation services.

Usually, the medical tourism facilitator companies get in touch with local travel firms to provide the required services for the medical tourists. These professional firms help organize all the necessary details of your medical trip. Moreover, such professionals also offer special services for patients with disabilities. These specialized professionals take care of a medical tourist's entire trip, right from their airport pickup to booking hotel accommodation, from a hospital consultation visit and surgery to assistance in the post-op check up, and finally delivering the patient back to the airport.

A medical tourism facilitator should always be available for assistance in case some unexpected incident occurs during the patient's medical journey to a foreign country. A facilitator must have a proper understanding of the concierge services in order to provide the much coveted "doorstep" service experience to the medical tourists. This is extremely important, so that the patients do not have to face any trouble either in finding accommodation or the hospital or in getting back safely to their home country post treatment. The ever-growing need to lift up the quality of medical care has led to the escalating availability of the concierge services in most of the medical tourism destinations.

OPTIONAL COMPONENTS:

Insurance coverage

The concept of patients traveling from their native countries to overseas destinations for medical treatment has totally transformed the global health care industry in the recent years. If a medical tourist is traveling with an international insurance policy or through an employer, he or she may not be aware of the mandatory formalities required by healthcare providers and insurance companies. Being unfamiliar with medical insurance solutions can lead to trouble in getting medical treatment at the right time. In such cases, a medical tourism facilitator should prearrange all the necessary documentation to avoid any unnecessary delay in the treatment.

You must understand that the standard travel insurance would not be enough when you are seeking receive medical treatment abroad. An insurance policy that covers urgent complications or readmission post treatment is beneficial. While you may find a variety of insurance products in the market for your travel needs, it is important to find one that offers wide insurance coverage in a foreign country. It is important for all medical tourists to check if their medical insurance covers the entire cost for medical treatment overseas. You should know the medical issues your insurance policy covers and the clauses that could reduce the chances of receiving compensation. If you are thinking of obtaining quality health care in a foreign country, you must make sure that you have proper insurance coverage to protect you. It is up to the facilitator to be aware of, and inform the medical tourist of any conditions or complications that might show up in their insurance coverage.

Expecting the unexpected

Complications can arise anytime with the medical services. Even after you do complete preparation regarding your medical journey, things could go wrong. In such cases, a facilitator should make allowances for unexpected events, which may include long stay for treatment, additional expenses, complications that arise from treatment, and death related arrangements, among others.

There is a wide range of insurance options to protect internationally traveling patients from various complications that may arise during the medical trip overseas. Obtaining medical or wellness treatment overseas can be an overwhelming experience, especially for the first-time medical tourists if they do not hire the right person to facilitate their travel and medical arrangements. A medical tourism insurance policy could highly benefit a medical traveler by minimizing the chances of any nerve-racking events during the medical journey.

International certification

For any potential medical tourist, it is always important to find a certified medical tourism facilitator. The presence of International certification for medical tourism facilitators helps them to be prepared in the best possible way in the field of healthcare protocols. These healthcare protocols include patient protocols, pre-operative and post-operative protocols, communication protocols and legal liabilities that help protect organizations. This is in addition to receiving continuous education on latest trends in quality management practices in the field of medical tourism.

Accreditation not only helps in improving the quality of healthcare services, but also instills confidence, trust and creates credibility for a facilitator in the eyes of patients. Placing the right processes and procedures in position can reduce the likelihood of errors.

Choosing an internationally accredited facilitator can certainly increase the chances of getting positive results. Considering the fact that facilitator companies are popping all over the planet, every internationally accredited facilitator is a value addition to the booming medical tourism industry. When choosing a facilitator for your medical journey, you should always choose one who has received international accreditation.

Knowledge management is important

There are many ethical, cultural and legal issues associated with medical tourism. The facilitators should be familiar of all such issues, so that they can deliver the best services to the patients. The Knowledge Management Consultancy services provided by renowned, recognized and reputed consultants can help understand these different aspects in the best way. One of the major ethical issues with medical tourism is that a medical procedure ethical at one destination can possibly be considered unethical at another. Medical tourism is on the rise and many patients are seeking options that are illegal in their home country. This adds to the already existing inequalities in the global healthcare system. A medical tourism facilitator should be familiar with all the legal and ethical issues of medical tourism, and should make potential tourists familiar with the same.

Cultural differences in global healthcare

A facilitator should clearly understand the cultural differences between different medical tourism destinations in order to prevent any misinterpretations and provide services as expected by the medical tourists in their home countries. Usually, the differences in topography, ethnicity, nationality, religion or language lead to the cultural differences.

Before embarking on your medical journey to a foreign country, you should do proper research and understand the cultural values of the host country. Bilateral cultural understanding is of utmost importance in the medical tourism industry. In this way, a facilitator promotes a healthy flow of information and organization of services between patients and medical providers.

SPECIAL PRECAUTIONS FOR PATIENTS

Finding a good facilitator/agency

As mentioned above, finding a good medical tourism facilitator is one of the important tasks you need to perform when you consider medical treatment overseas. A facilitator with vast experience can organize your trip much better than you could have imagined. In short, a medical tour facilitator makes the touring experience much more pleasant and stress free, leaving you free to look after other issues during your medical tour.

You should never make a hasty decision when it comes to choosing a medical tourism facilitator. You need to communicate freely with the potential candidates and choose the one who completely understand your concerns, the medical issues and the medical tourism industry as a whole. It is also important that the patients choose a facilitator or a company that has certification from leading organizations like the Medical Tourism Association.

Avoiding the online trap

Patients from all across the globe primarily adopt the Internet and web-based tools to gather information. Since there are so many facilitators in the market these days, you should carefully select one with utmost care and attention without falling victim to the online frauds. It is important to avoid the online traps and only choose a reliable, trusted and recommended medical tourism facilitator.

A competent and knowledgeable facilitator would always be available at your service to listen to all your concerns and provide you all the necessary assistance. While you can always use email or telephone service to get in touch with the facilitator, it would be wise to arrange a face-to-face meeting. On the other hand, if your facilitator does not communicate with you in a proper way or is unable to understand your requirements, you should better start looking for another facilitator.

You should always make sure that the facilitator you choose maintains transparency. When you first contact a facilitator or a facilitator company, always ask questions regarding their previous work. It makes sense to ask for referrals in order to check for the quality of their services. In addition, you must confirm if whether they are an independent agency or are associated with any particular organizations or healthcare facilities.

Developing one-on-one communication programs

Communication is the key to a successful medical journey overseas. From the very moment you choose your treating facility abroad, it is important to initiate the communication process. However, since you will be going to another country for your medical treatment, chances are there that you might face the language barriers, which might create a problem in communicating effectively with your treating doctor or the healthcare facility.

If you cannot understand the language, the treating facility would not be able to tell you about the treatment process effectively and you may not able to be clear your concerns. This is where a medical tourism facilitator plays a major role. Since most of the facilitators have already established connections with the different hospitals in different medical tourism destinations, they will be able to work as intermediaries and remove communication barriers.

An experienced medical facilitator will be able to provide you with expert advice on the proceedings of your medical journey. Facilitators function as a bridge between the patients and the medical providers, thereby encouraging a healthy communication. It is important to ensure that the facilitator you use takes the process of follow-ups and feedback seriously and is in touch with you over the telephone instead of email services. A face to face conversation is more desirable than other means of communication. As a medical tourist, you should be very comfortable with your facilitator, so that you can discuss your concerns, if any, without hesitation.

Things you should not discuss with the facilitator

While a facilitator is the person who guides you through the entire medical journey, there are certain things you should not discuss with a facilitator. Although, you should have a detailed discussion with your facilitator, so they can understand your needs completely and recommend you packages and services accordingly. However, it would be better to discuss the complex medical matters with the treating physician or surgeon instead of a facilitator. It makes some good sense, as the treating doctors are best placed to give accurate advice.

Why should you pay a facilitator?

This is as simple as it could be. We usually pay in return for the services we receive, and same is the case here. While many people avoid availing the services of a facilitator in order to save some money on their medical journey overseas, using a facilitator can benefit you in a number of ways. The task of booking flights, hotels and paying for your treatment abroad might seem easy enough for you, but you should not forget that a medical tour entails a whole lot more than that. Many other things you need to know when planning an international medical trip include the selection of right destination and treating facility, and a clear understanding of legal and ethical issues associated with medical tourism.

A competent facilitator will be able to help you manage your budget efficiently. Therefore, if you have managed to find a good facilitator who can manage every aspect of your medical retreat experience and promise you a pleasant experience, you should not mind paying them for what you will get in return.

Again, it bodes well to remember that a medical tourism facilitator is not usually a single person, but an organization. As such, there will be several people working in tandem to ensure quality of service, or simply to make arrangements. A destination program manager, for example, will be responsible for setting up the necessary arrangements like lodging and traveling at your destination country. Similarly, a medical officer will offer expertise in selecting the best medical facility and location for the patient. A travel coordinator will take care of the travel and tourism needs of the patient and accompanying people. More or fewer people may be involved in such an exercise, depending on the size of the medical facilitation company, and the requirements of the medical traveler.

CHAPTER 15

Budgeting for Medical Tourism

IN THIS CHAPTER

- Understand various costs associated with medical tourism
- Different costs you are likely to find on a hospital bill
- Differentiate between medical and non-medical costs
- Different ways of paying for medical tourism

Medical Tourism is widely considered a cost saving exercise, yet it can very well get harsh on your wallet and bank accounts. Remember, it is cheap, not free. Prior to making a decision, it becomes essential for potential medical tourists to make an appropriate budget for the entire trip. Careful planning can help alleviate the stress from your medical tourism journey. Many medical tourists do not do enough budgeting and are unaware of the different expenses they might incur during their visit.

While some tourists simply consider the cost of the physician, others just prepare a budget for their airline tickets. While preparing a budget for your medical tourism journey, you have to take into account several non-medical costs, which in particular account for a large part of the entire cost.

Since the amount and the type of payments you will have to make during your overseas medical tourism trip are different from what you will pay in your home country, it is important for you to be aware of the related costs in order to prepare a budget for your trip. It is essential for you to understand the type of costs that you will incur during your trip. You should be able to estimate the expense of traveling abroad, while including the cost of medical treatment, traveling, and other expenditure. While initially you might consider the cost of the treatment as the most significant payment, the other costs are not negligible.

This section of the book aims to help you understand the intricacies that a medical trip requires. This section provides a breakdown of the most common expenses you will incur during a medical tourism visit. This section also highlights several non-medical costs including travel, tourism, and accommodation. After you have understood the different costs associated with medical tourism, you can go through the section where we discuss the various ways you can make payments.

UNDERSTANDING THE COST OF TREATMENT AND SURGERY

Although planning your budget for a medical tourism journey seems difficult to most patients, the fact is that your overall expenditure can be divided into two main categories – medical expenses and non-medical expenses. In the following pages, we will discuss the costs that a medical tourist has to bear without taking help from insurance agencies. Those who have comprehensive health insurance need to get in touch with the insurance provider to check what is included and what is not covered in your policy so that you can appropriately plan your budget.

While there are many costs that you should be prepared for while opting for medical tourism, healthcare facilities in some of the most reputed medical tourism countries offer package prices for commonly sourced healthcare treatments, which includes all the different types of expenditure that you will have to bear. Choosing this option means medical tourists will not have to make separate payments, going for a complete healthcare treatment package eases the journey for medical tourists. However, if the healthcare facility that you have chosen doesn't offer you a package for your specific requirements, you should be aware of the various types of payments, as they will show up on your bill.

We have done our best in listing down all the possible types of payments, which you will have to make while overseas for medical tourism. However, we urge all potential medical tourists to keep in mind that the type of payments they will have to make depends a lot on the type of medical condition for which they are seeking remedy. Different people have different requirements, the cost and the type of payments they will have to make varies.

MEDICAL TREATMENT COSTS

Since you are traveling in pursuit of good healthcare services, the majority of the expenditure will include the cost of medical treatment. Medical treatment costs include the amount you will have to pay to the medical practitioner as his/her consultation fees, cost for diagnostic tests and additional expenditure for subsequent visits to the healthcare facility or to the practitioner, before the treatment is finalized. All these costs contribute directly to the total costs of the visit. These costs could be broken down into some major sections that are listed here.

Physician fees

The most significant cost on any medical journey is the amount one has to pay the physician. The cost of the physician usually makes up a major percentage of the total medical bill that you have to pay and hence it requires careful planning. Usually, medical practitioners with more experience and better skills charge more. It includes their pre- and post-consultation charges, treatment charges, and charges for all procedures that are required during the treatment phase. These charges contribute significantly to the overall invoice that is shown to you after the successful completion of the treatment.

However, if the patient does develop any complications during or after the treatment, additional charges might also be included. This usually happens if you are going for a medical treatment that requires surgery. All reputed doctors will warn you about any possible complication that might come up during your treatment when you first approach the physician for consultation. As an example, a patient with diabetes will need special care and services that will stabilize his blood sugar before a cataract operation can be performed. Here the doctor will have no other choice but to monitor all vital parameters to ensure that the operation can be performed in a safe way.

Patients with other complications, complex history, or other diseases and illnesses require extra time and effort from the physician for which the patient has to pay. This results in the addition of extra charges to compensate the additional effort of the medical practitioner. In situations like this, where the treatment depends on previous medical history of a patient, it becomes difficult to stick to the original budget. It is advisable to share your medical history with the physician beforehand so that you can prepare your budget accordingly.

Anesthesiology fees

Anesthesia, as you might already know, is an essential medical requirement for all procedures that require surgery. At times, especially if you have chosen a package price for your medical treatment, the fees for the anesthesia are charged separately and are likely to be higher if a complex surgery is required during your treatment. In most cases, healthcare facilities make you pay additional fees to the anesthetist, which is independent of how much you are paying to your treating doctor. It is thus important for patients to find out these charges prepare an accurate estimate of the budget. Healthcare facilities usually recommend an anesthesiologist who is attached to the facility and hence they know the amount you will have to pay them.

The fee for anesthesiology generally includes the fees of the anesthetic and the administration of the drug. It can also include the cost for the special care that is required during the procedure and for post-operative care. Since anesthesia is critical during surgeries, you should select a hospital that has competent anesthetic facilities, qualified and reputed staff, and includes modern anesthesia equipment.

Surgical implants

Medical tourists who require surgical implants will see them in the bill. Some surgeries require surgeons to install artificial devices, such as artificial pacemakers, which are quite expensive. Moreover, surgical implants are also required in certain cosmetic surgeries such as breast augmentation, where silicone inserts have to be surgically implanted. A medical tourist who is availing himself of such a procedure should inquire about the cost of these implants prior to the commencement of the procedure in order to prepare an accurate budget. It is very much possible that the implants cover the better portion of the bill.

Consumables

The word consumable in medical terms refers to items that are non-reusable, and are used during the procedure. Examples of this include cotton, IV lines, gauze, sutures, gloves, etc. The cost of these consumables varies from facility to facility and on the type of procedure. If you are interested in preparing an accurate budget that includes the cost of consumables, you should inquire about the cost of consumables from the international patient department of the healthcare facility you are planning to visit.

Post treatment prescription drugs

Some treatments are finalized at the healthcare facility and you don't require taking any prescription drugs after returning home. Most treatments however, will require that the patient take regular doses of medicines and prescription drugs after the completion of the medical treatment. Medical tourists should be aware of the fact that after all discharge procedures are completed, the hospital and the doctor would not be responsible for providing the prescribed drugs. In most procedures, the use of the drugs ceases after the patient has completely recovered, some patients may need to take regular medication for extended durations. Since patients have to bear these additional expenses, it is important that they understand the regular cost of drugs that they will have to pay after their treatment is complete.

Lab and imaging fees

The lab and imaging fees varies according to the medical conditions for which you are seeking treatment. It includes the cost associated with the number of lab tests that are required before and after the treatment. The treating doctor usually prescribes these tests and the hospital will charge additional fees for the various tests that are conducted during the course of your treatment. However, if the healthcare facility is not fully equipped to carry out all tests, they may recommend facilities where you have to get some tests done. You might have to pay these facilities separately. Tests such as X-rays, MRIs, CT scans and blood tests are the most common tests, which have to be conducted during the pre- and post-operative treatments.

Blood transfusion fees (if required)

During surgery or other unavoidable situations, when a patient loses a lot of blood, a doctor might advise a blood transfusion. This is usually done if the patient loses an un-controllable amount of blood, which could potentially be fatal.

The blood transfusion procedure is usually a lifesaver in such circumstances. The patient has to pay for the blood bags and the special care that was needed during the treatment. This cost is separate from the otherwise agreed-upon medical expenses, since the need for it arises only during an emergency, which are near impossible to predict.

Operation theatre charges

For procedures that have to be carried on within the safe and equipped confines of an operation theater, additional expenses are charged as operation theater charges. Due to the various resources that are utilized within an operation theater, which include the monitoring tools, surgical equipment, additional surgeons and nurses, the cost may figure prominently in the bill.

Intensive Care Unit charges (if required)

After a procedure has been carried out, the physician might recommend shifting the patient to an ICU or Intensive Care Unit, where the patient will be kept in special care. An ICU environment allows doctors and nurses to give critical care and closely monitor the condition of the patient until the patient stabilizes. In an ICU, multiple nurses and healthcare professionals tend to the patient so that he/she can be quickly restored back to health.

The need for an ICU can rarely be predicted in advance, as it mostly arises due to complications which cannot be predicted either. Hence, these charges cannot be budgeted in advance. However, if you require medical services for a complicated medical condition, it is a good idea to ask about the price of the ICU services that are charged, just to gauge the possible addition to your medical bill.

Treatments

Different patients have different medical conditions when they enter the hospital premises. While some of them might be in a good condition, others are serious and require immediate attention. Treatment needs vary according to the condition of a patient when he/she reaches the healthcare facility and hence, the cost of treatment differs too. In some cases, a combination of treatments would be recommended, which will involve multiple skilled medical personnel and a large number of auxiliary services, such as nurses and lab attendants. If the patient's condition is critical, doctors might advise hiring a full time nurse, which costs more.

Recovery

After the successful completion of the treatment or procedure, patients are not normally allowed to go back home immediately. Rather, patients are kept under surveillance during the recovery period. A proper recovery pattern ensures that the doctors can keep an eye on the patient, so that they can keep tabs on the patient's recovery. A well managed recovery phase is essential for the patient to return to a normal healthy life at the earliest possible point. This is the reason why doctors recommend proper medical assistance during the first few days after the surgery or treatment has been completed. This too incurs some costs depending on the recovery period and the facilities that are used during the phase.

Hospital stay charges

The hospital stay charges come into effect once you enter the hospital premises and are calculated to the date you are discharged. Patients need to pay for all the services and facilities they use during their stay. It includes the cost of the hospital rooms and the bed they occupy during the course of the treatment. Hospitals usually have several types of rooms, such as, single room, isolated wings, double bed rooms, dormitories, etc. The choice of room depends on your budget. Single rooms are usually the most expensive rooms, where, apart from good healthcare services, you will have access to several amenities such as a television, entertainment options, and en-suite bathrooms. On the other hand, dormitories are the least expensive, and here you will have to share the hall with several other patients.

Use of nursing services

In addition to healthcare professionals such as doctors, a patient definitely needs several auxiliary services, such as the ones provided by the nursing staff. Nurses come in very handy during the treatment phase as they provide full time care to the patient when the physician is not around. Apart from tending to a patient's daily needs, nurses constantly keep in touch with the doctors and monitor the patient's health regularly. Thus, patients have to pay for their services additionally.

REHABILITATION OR PHYSICAL THERAPY CHARGES (IF REQUIRED)

Certain surgical procedures such as hip-replacement surgery or knee surgery require that the patient spend some time in rehabilitation after the surgery is complete. A physical therapist is employed to check the patient's mobility while in rehabilitation. The physical therapist will dedicate his time to bringing back normal mobility after the surgery, by using special exercising techniques and equipment. The fees payable to the physical therapist will not necessarily be added in your hospital stay charges. It you are planning to undergo a surgery that requires you to spend additional time with the physical therapist, it would be great if you can calculate their charges and prepare your budget accordingly.

Hospital meals

The hospital room charges do not include the meals that are served to patients during their stay, and are often billed separately. Medical procedures require patients to adhere to a strict diet plan prepared by dieticians and nutritionists. Apart from the fee that has to be paid to the dieticians, the hospital staff will also add the cost of the meals to the total bill that has to be paid by you.

Follow-up care in home country

There is no denying the fact that follow-up care after a surgical treatment is just as vital as the treatment. It is wise to have a clear picture of the entire treatment to find out the type of follow-up care that you will require. Many surgical procedures require expensive follow-up treatment and hence, it is vital for you to know the type of expenses you will have to bear. Get in touch with the physician to understand the procedures that you will have to undergo in your medical tourism destination and the ones that you will have to go through after you return to your home country.

Non-medical costs

For most patients, opting for medical tourism is a way to save money. Even though you can definitely reduce your treatment costs by opting for medical tourism, the act of leaving your home country to get medical treatment abroad requires you to bear considerable expenses. In addition to the medical treatment costs, patients have to prepare a budget for non-medical costs too. You have to think about lodging expenses, travel expenses and visa/passport expenses. Since you will be traveling to a foreign country, which you might not have visited previously, you should also plan your expenses for any possible sightseeing and shopping activities. These non-medical costs also constitute a significant portion of the total expenses of medical travel. Here are a few non-medical costs that you should consider while preparing an accurate budget.

Traveling expenses

Travel costs are the most significant cost that all medical tourists have to bear. Preparing a travel budget in advance is extremely important. If you are making your travel expenses without taking any help from a facilitator, you will have to take the services of a travel agent, or book your flight using the internet.

It is also crucial to note that it is not just another trip where you can sit in the economy section for an extended period. Traveling as a patient requires you to consider spending a little extra for added comfort. Consider buying a flexible ticket, even if it does cost a little more. Also, consider buying a business class ticket, especially if you are traveling for surgeries, such as hip-replacement surgery or knee surgery, so you can have some comfort during the flight.

Accommodation

After you have carefully planned for your travel, the next thing you should consider is the accommodation. Comfortable accommodation forms a very important part of your entire medical treatment journey. You must act in advance and arrange suitable accommodation for the pre- and post-treatment phase of your trip.

You should attempt to find a suitable accommodation, which is near to the healthcare facility and is cost-effective too.

Visa and other documents

In addition to booking airline tickets, you also have to keep in mind that you will require a valid passport and visa for visiting a foreign land. Traveling to and from certain parts of the world also requires a valid visa. Your budget should have space for Visa and document fees.

Vacation expenses

There is no denying the fact that for most patients, tourism is one of the driving forces behind the medical tourism plan. It is an integral part of medical tourism, which acts as a treat for patients, but also increases your travel bills. Many medical tourists want to explore the beautiful places situated close to their treatment location.

Food and related expenses

For survival in a foreign land, you need accommodation, food, water and other daily products, which are based on your lifestyle and habits. Nonetheless, all these contribute to the total expenses. Keep in mind that the food you eat should adhere to the diet plan recommended by your physician or dietician.

Shopping and souvenirs

For many patients and travelers, traveling to a new country is synonymous with shopping. Shopping adds a good amount of charm to the journey. Shopping and souvenirs do come with expenses of their own, and obviously are a part of your budget.

Budget for unexpected expenses

The element of surprise resulting in unexpected expenditure is inherent to any vacation. However, when you consider that medical treatment is the essence of your tourism, budgeting for unexpected expenses becomes even more important. Medical tourists should keep "emergency funds" at their disposal for unforeseen circumstances.

Cost of travel insurance and air ambulance insurance

Travel insurance is extremely important for any traveler, and its need only increases if you are a medical tourist. Just like travel insurance, air-ambulance insurance is also vitally important, especially for patients who could need emergency services. This insurance will protect you in the case of an emergency that might necessitate air-ambulance services.

Expenses for companion

So far, the focus has been solely on the budget of the medical tourist. It is very likely that friends or family accompany the medical traveler. Thus, it is important to consider the expenses of the companion, which will include all non-medical expenses listed here. Sometimes, the companion decides to undergo some checkups or basic treatment, this cost also has an effect on the budget.

HOW TO PAY FOR A MEDICAL TOURISM TRIP

After you have planned your budget, and are mentally prepared to travel overseas for treatment, the next thing you should consider is your mode of payment. There is no dearth of payment methods, such as the use of personal savings, taking help from insurance providers, utilizing your company medical claim policy, taking help from relatives, using credit cards or even, if you are just as lucky as some Arab patients, you can even ask the government to pay your medical bills. While the payment amount could be large, several hospitals and clinics in reputed medical tourism destinations offer flexible payment options allowing you to pay the entire medical bill in easy installments.

Each patient has a unique, preferred way to pay his medical journey bills based on his or her financial condition.

Asking insurance to pay for medical travel

There is a dedicated section in this book, which deals with insurance companies' take on medical tourism and why people with a health insurance policy should consider medical tourism. Since medical tourism is often cheaper than similar healthcare services in your home country, insurance providers have started including provisions for the same too. It is in the interest of medical tourists to check with their insurance provider on cover related to medical tourism.

Asking employer to pay for medical travel

Several employers offer medical aid to employees. Since you are planning to seek medical treatment in an overseas location, you might have to present your case effectively. Try to tell the employers the various monetary benefits of medical tourism. Since medical tourism can cut down on medical bills, the employer is likely to have a positive response. Prepare a list of the potential benefits of medical tourism, including cost saving, better healthcare and speedy recovery, and share it with your employers.

Asking the government to pay for medical travel

Governments of most countries do not usually pay the medical expenses of their citizens, but some do offer the privilege. In several Gulf countries, GCC governments sponsor medical tourists if that specific treatment is not available in their home country. These governments spend billions of dollars annually to sponsor their nationals. In order to apply for government sponsorship, the patient has to prepare a case study with evidence that proves that the services required are not available in the home country and necessitates medical travel.

A certificate from a local government facility affirming the need for medical tourism needs to be furnished. The application is reviewed, and if approved, receives sponsorship from the government.

OTHER WAYS TO PAY FOR MEDICAL TRAVEL

Savings

Saving money is a fundamental need of every member of the family. People usually save their money in bank saving accounts or in the form of a fixed deposit. Assessing your financial condition is extremely important as some medical treatments can cost a fortune and you want to ensure that you have enough funds, not just for your treatment, but after that as well.

Asking relatives for help

It might not be possible to depend on your relatives to sponsor your entire medical tourism expenses, but you can take some help from them. No matter how awkward it might sound, most patients will be surprised at the support they can get from their family and friends in case of an emergency. Always remember that when you are sourcing funds from your family and friends, every cent counts and you can use this extra money to get back to normal health.

Taking a loan

Many financial aid companies provide loans for medical treatment also provide financial help to medical tourists. As with any other loan, a loan for medical treatment also attracts interest on payment. Search for financing institutions, such as banks, which charge a lower interest rate. An institution affiliated with some organization can help you in case a dispute arises.

Several financing organizations have included medical travel as a valid reason to apply for loans. If you have a good credit score, banks will be more than happy to lend you money for your treatment.

Paying through credit cards

You can pay your pending dues with your credit card and later pay the credit card bill along with the international transaction fees. Keep in mind that credit cards have limits and may not be able to foot your entire bill.

Healthcare tourism intermediaries

Special agencies and medical service providers have made it possible for individuals to seek financial help from them. One of the biggest advantages to seek financial help from these institutions is the fact that they help you identify good and highly affordable healthcare facilities. These institutions will provide you funds after considering the severity of your medical condition and the recommended treatment. Instead of giving cash directly to the patient, these institutions work directly with the healthcare facility. Such schemes are ideal for patients who do not have a health insurance policy, and cannot get sponsorship from their employers or the government. These institutions also provide financial help in certain cosmetic treatments as well, such as facelifts and liposuction, which health insurance companies do not usually cover in their policies.

Charity and support

Patients traveling from underdeveloped countries or those in a financial crunch can approach certain organizations to help with their medical expenses. Several NGOs (Non-Government Organizations) provide relief and assistance to medical travelers. The hospitals might also consider a discount to support patients through their MSW (Medical Social Work) department or similar programs.

CHAPTER 16

Travel and Tourism

IN THIS CHAPTER

- What to consider before you book your flight
- Information regarding your passport and visa
- Learning about a new culture
- Importance of safety and security while abroad

MAKING TRAVEL ARRANGEMENTS

When traveling overseas for quality affordable medical care, you should give attention to travel arrangements in order to avoid any hassles during your medical journey. Once you have decided on the medical tourism destination and the hospital where you will receive medical treatment, it is time to focus on how you are going to get there. Most often, reaching a medical tourism destination will require air travel. Usually, if you are traveling from a major city, you are likely to find direct flights to your destination. Otherwise, stop-overs will be included in the itinerary.

The travel arrangements also depend on the country you are visiting for medical treat-ment, as many countries have their own rules and regulations with respect to international travel. If you are traveling internationally, you must purchase travel insurance in order to protect yourself from unpleasant situations, such as flight cancellation and travel delays due to different reasons. Moreover, you should also check if your medical insurance covers you for overseas travel. Let us talk about a few important things you should keep in mind when making travel arrangements.

BOOKING THE FLIGHT

You can book the flight through a facilitator that offers an entire medical tourism pack-age, or by whatever means you have employed in the past to make travel arrangements (either online or through a trusted travel agent). Considering the fact that the long flights can be very uncomfortable, you should pay attention to certain factors when booking a flight. Always remember that you are traveling as a patient and you need to consider the factors that could have an impact on your health. For example, if you are traveling for a knee-replacement surgery, you might want to consider upgrading your ticket to business class, so you will have the comfort of more legroom and will be able to sleep in a fully reclined position. Price and comfort are the key factors you need to consider when booking the flight. Consider the fact that some airlines charge you with extra costs during the booking process. Therefore, make sure you get to know the exact amount you will have to pay. When booking the flight, you should always check for the fees and the cancellation policy.

When comparing different airlines, do not forget to check the cost of check-in luggage, as it could vary between different airlines. You should always select flights with more than enough time during layovers. Book international flight as soon as possible, as making your travel booking the flight at the last minute could cost you a lot. Another important thing to consider when booking your flight is the selection of the right airline. You should always consider the levels of service, timeliness and comfort provided by different airlines. Nowadays, leading airlines are vying with each other to provide the best in-flight services to their customers. Many airlines also offer you the comfort and convenience to customize your experience to suit your liking and needs. Feel free to ask the airlines for any specific requirements you might need (e.g. wheelchairs) on the flight.

When traveling by air, it is beneficial for patients to buy a flexible ticket. This ticket might be a little more expensive, but it is well worth its cost, as you might have to extend your trip. In case any complications occur and you require more post-operative care, a flexible ticket will avoid you incurring any cancellation fees or non-reimbursable charges.

In case you do not want to spend time and effort in finding and booking the flight, you can always use a medical tourism facilitator to arrange this for you. Based on your budget and personal preferences, a facilitator will find the best accessible flights and will provide you with all the necessary information. After the patient has decided on the flight, the facilitator will take care of the booking process.

PASSPORT AND VISA

Besides the flight arrangements, you need to consider several other important things when booking your flight. Your passport needs to be valid and have enough pages for any visas that you might require for traveling overseas. At this point, one should keep in mind that some countries have stricter visa policies than others. Most of the countries with strict visa policies might require specific documents that prove the purpose of visit.

In the case of medical tourism, patients must provide the embassy with the necessary medical documents in order to explain the purpose of the trip. In addition to the valid documents, one may also have to attend face-to-face interviews. Such interviews involve questioning with respect to the identification of the purpose of visit. If you meet all the mandatory conditions, you may expect the visa within a specific span of time.

Nowadays, with the growth of medical tourism, many countries are offering a visa specifically for medical travel. Obtaining the medical tourism type of visa would be in the best interest of a medical traveler, as it allows for flexibility in case an extension is required due to unexpected complications. For example, India recently included easy visa extension for medical tourists, which offers multiple benefits for internationally traveling patients. It would be wise to enquire about this option, the benefits it offers and the costs involved from an embassy or your medical tourism facilitator.

It is also worth noting that there are laws and guidelines that deal with medical travel. Some nations will require that the medical tourists register before continuing their travel. WHO also has norms and guidelines related to medical travel. Be acquainted with these rules, or best, seek the services of a facilitator to take care of the documents and formalities for you.

TOURISM IN THE DESTINATION COUNTRY

Countries that have made a mark for themselves on the medical tourism map of the world, such as India, Thailand, and Singapore, also have beautiful tourism attractions that a medical tourist can visit. Indulging in tourism and participating in the country's rich cultural heritage can prove to be a wonderful experience, especially for people who usually do not get the time to travel often.

Most popular medical tourism destinations have a strong tourism sector and hence these places offer a plethora of good outdoor and indoor tourism activities for tourists, including sightseeing tours, sports, leisure activities, and more. An ideal activity for a medical tourist should be relaxing and enjoyable. Consult your doctor before indulging in sight-seeing or similar activities to ensure they have no negative impact on your health.

LEARNING ABOUT THE CULTURE

Your medical tourism journey can help you learn more about the culture of the country. It gives you the opportunity to immerse yourself in a completely different culture, which might be entirely unfamiliar to you. The fun of exploring a new region also includes the privilege to see local traditions and festivities. Apart from visiting the main tourist attractions, it is a good idea to visit some local spots, such as a market or a bazaar, to understand how the local people communicate with each other. You can also hire a local guide, who will be in a better position to tell you about the local people, their traditions and their culture in a much better way.

LANGUAGE

In addition to the information you get about a country's local culture, it is also important to learn a few sentences in the native language. You can easily purchase a pocket language guidebook of the region, or ask your tour guide to teach you a few important sentences in the local language. Know how to greet strangers, how to ask for food and water, and how to tell others that you are a medical tourist and visiting the country for treatment.

ACCOMMODATION CLOSE TO THE HOSPITAL

It is advisable that you make your lodging arrangements in a hotel or resort close to the healthcare facility. This will help you avoid long journeys to and from any consultations or for the procedure itself. If the patient has a serious medical condition, stay as close to the healthcare facility as possible, which will help you reach the hospital quickly in case immediate assistance is required.

SAFETY AND SECURITY

While most reputed medical tourism destinations in the world, such as Singapore, are safe for medical tourists, certain countries, such as Thailand, are not entirely politically stable. For your own safety, it is important to learn all safety precautions in your treating country to ensure that you select a hotel and a healthcare facility, which is located in a safe neighborhood.

FOOD AND LOCAL CUISINE

Getting a taste of local cuisine can be an important part of any tourist endeavor. Treat yourself to the best the region has to offer, and tickle your palate with the tastes and flavors of the region. Even if you regularly have foreign food in your own country, the authentic taste can create quite an impression. For example, Chinese food in China itself would be authentic, and likely very different from the "Chinese" food in your home country. The same is also true for other destinations, like Thailand and India.

In the comprehensive destination guide of this book, you will find a list detailing 70 medical tourism destinations ranked in terms of safety and security. This list will help you make a sound decision on where to get treatment.

CHAPTER 17

Travel Medicine

IN THIS CHAPTER

- Information on pre-travel considerations and preparations
- Protecting against infections
- Importance of immunization
- Essential items for a travel medicine kit

PRE-TRAVEL CONSIDERATIONS AND PREPARATION

More than 10 million patients travel abroad for various kinds of medical treatments. Since medical tourism involves patients crossing international boundaries frequently, it has become necessary for potential medical tourists to seek pre-travel advice in order to avoid problems. One important recommendation for potential medical travelers is to take precautionary measures to prevent themselves from contracting a disease or infection in a foreign country.

It is important for anyone traveling abroad for medical care to stay fit and healthy during the journey. There is a long list of travel-associated medical issues, making this section on travel medicine crucial for every medical tourist to read and understand thoroughly. The risk of contracting diseases varies, depending on geography, behavior of the traveler, accommodation and standards of sanitation in a particular region.

The concept of travel medicine includes pre-travel considerations, protecting against infections, and the prevention of foreign diseases. Studies suggest that a majority of patients going abroad for treatment suffer from some type of illness during their trip. Owing to the same reason, the concept of travel medicine holds an important significance in the field of medical tourism. Being knowledgeable about the travel medicine can greatly help patients to be prepared and avoid or minimize the chance of contracting any travel-related illnesses. More and more patients nowadays are traveling to foreign destinations to avail quality healthcare at reasonable cost, but a majority of the medical tourists does not even consider the possibility of contracting another disease when in a foreign country.

In this section, we will describe all the necessary preparations the potential medical tourists should have in place in order to prevent themselves from acquiring a potentially dangerous disease in a place unfamiliar to you. Proper packing of necessary first-aid medications can prove to be lifesaving.

Every country has different standards of healthcare and it is extremely important for the medical tourists to adhere to the guidelines set by professional practitioners in a medical tourism destination in order to stay healthy during the trip.

Some examples of common travel medicine practices are the prevention and treatment of malaria, traveler's diathermia, typhoid fever, influenza and various other viral and bacterial infections. These infectious diseases, wilderness diseases, tropical cures, immunization and public health are all a part of the complex nature and development of travel medicine.

TRAVEL MEDICINE PREPARATION

Considering all the international travel-related medical concerns, every patient traveling overseas for treatment should be knowledgeable about the importance of travel medicine. Over the years, travel medicine has become a multidisciplinary subject that includes various aspects, such as infectious diseases, tropical medicine and the need for proper immunization. When preparing for travel medicine, medical tourists should make themselves familiar with the pre-travel considerations for their chosen medical tourism destination. A patient should be familiar with the different conditions at a particular destination that could have an effect on his health, such as pollution levels, standards of healthcare services, necessary immunizations and the availability of medical supplies. Medical tourists should prepare a comprehensive travel medicine kit along with other essential travel-related things you intend to carry.

Combining travel medicine advice with preventive and curative measures is necessary as a safety measure. Living in a particular region or country helps us to develop immunity against various pathogens in the region. However, things are different when you travel to another country. When traveling to developing and third world countries, the chances are high that you could get sick because of several infections.

Proper travel medicine preparation can be useful in preventing many diseases in the foreign land. In-depth pre-travel knowledge can be a lifesaver in medical tourism. As a medical tourist traveling for treatment in a foreign country, you should always remember that you are first a patient and require extra protection. Do the necessary homework in order to keep yourself safe from various ailments that could invade you in a foreign country.

When you travel from one country to another or in some cases from one continent to another, the first thing that you need to do is to gather information about the kind of diseases that are predominant in the destination country. Your treating doctor can prescribe you the accurate and necessary medication. The CDC (Centers for Disease Control and Prevention) and WHO (World Health Organization) have a comprehensive database for all travel related medical considerations.

The ISTM (International Society for Travel Medicine) and ASTMH (American Society for Tropical Medicine and Hygiene) carry the latest knowledge on the safe practice of travel medicine. These organizations provide essential resources for tourists to get all the information regarding travel medicine.

Several public health organizations assess travel related medical issues and update the research findings on their official websites. Potential medical tourists can go through these findings anytime to know about various travel-related ailments. Travel medicine information provided in this chapter is only a part of the pre-travel considerations and preparation. The steps you take will be specific to your destination country. The process of proper medical preparation involves two distinct steps discussed below.

Step 1: The first step in the medical preparation involves the use of vaccinations and other drugs that prevent certain location-specific diseases. Ideally, the patients should consult their local physician at least six weeks before they embark on their journey to a foreign country. This will allow enough time for booster immunizations and evaluation of any unfavorable reactions of the vaccinations. Your local physician is the best person to determine the kind of vaccination you will require. Your local doctor will most possibly review your vaccination history and past medical history before prescribing the appropriate vaccines and medicines for your medical journey. Medical tourists should also check if they need any specific medical certificates for entering into a particular country.

Step 2: The second step in the process of medical preparation includes preparing a comprehensive list of preventive and curative medications that you must put in practice during your medical trip. Consult with your local or treating doctor for the right medicine prescription. You should also make sure that you carry sufficient medication for the duration of the trip. It is always better to maintain a list of routine prescriptions, complete with generic names and doses.

PROTECTION AGAINST INFECTIONS

One of the most common illnesses medical travelers face is the traveler's diarrhea and the major reasons for this ailment is the ingestion of certain organisms found in contaminated food or water. Anxiety, allergies and dietary changes could also be the reason for traveler's diarrhea. Other travel-related health issues include malaria, dengue, yellow fever, hepatitis A, hepatitis B, typhoid fever, and cholera.

In a foreign land, the infections can occur due to many reasons. Even a small allergy, if left ignored, could potentially trigger serious infections. The most common vector-borne diseases are the yellow fever and malaria. It is important to note that if you do not receive the right treatment for such diseases, they can turn fatal. If proper medication is on hand, you could avoid any further damage to the body.

In case of certain infections, the old adage "prevention is better than the cure" holds true. Prevention from infections is not easy. It is even more difficult for people who are already suffering from diseases. It is particularly important for patients who intend to undergo surgery in a foreign land to follow strict guidelines, as they are at an increased risk.

Medical tourists should have the necessary information on how to stay healthy and how to self-medicate or seek medical help in case they contract any disease in the foreign country. Medical preparation is even more important if you are traveling to a country where vector-borne diseases are widespread. When it comes to prioritizing travel-related health recommendations, a medical tourist should always keep in mind the risks of travel-related illness and the importance of vaccination and medicine.

HOW TO PROTECT AGAINST INFECTIONS

The first step towards protection against infections is to maintain hygiene. Medical tourists, as they are mostly unfamiliar with the climatic conditions and the region-specific ailments in a particular destination, are always at a greater risk of falling sick when compared with the natives of that particular country.

Usually the locally or internationally accredited medical facilities tend to follow strict hygiene and sanitary requirements. It is useful to determine whether the hospital or clinic where you are seeking care has received proper accreditation. Checking for the hospital's accreditation is an important step in determining the standards of hygiene and the healthcare services provided by the facility.

IMPORTANCE OF IMMUNIZATION

Before you embark on your medical trip, it is important to discuss your travel plans in detail with your local or treating doctor. The concerned doctor can then make recommendations, considering the patient's age, medical history, vaccine history, destination and the length of the trip. When it comes to medical tourism, proper vaccination plays an important role in protection against a number of infections in a foreign country. In some cases, your local physician might refer you to a travel medicine specialist for detailed information on travel medicine.

The process of vaccination usually consists of a few steps. Medical tourists should always undertake the entire immunization process prior to traveling, as it is important to ensure that the vaccine will work as desired. You must ask your travel medicine physician about the vaccination you will need for protection against food- and water-borne illnesses, and other travel-related illnesses. Although it is important for all medical tourists to consider the significance of vaccinations and medications, you should always rely on safe health practices, such as eating health food and drinking pure water, in order to prevent yourself from various infections.

Many of the diseases are water- and food-borne. Therefore, consciousness about the consumption of street food or tap water is very important in preventing certain diseases.

Some countries might ask for the proof of vaccination required to enter the country. For example, if you are traveling to sub-Saharan Africa or other yellow fever areas, you might need the proof of vaccination against yellow fever.

While contaminated water and food are the major sources of diseases overseas, a medical tourist should consider many other things for successful prevention of infectious diseases. Apart from food and water, you must also be cautious against insect bites. Mosquitoes can cause a number of life-threatening diseases. You should always carry mosquito repellent as a preventive step against mosquito bites.

Most internationally traveling patients visiting the tropical countries are concerned about the possibility of contracting malaria. Tropical countries have a relatively higher risk of mosquito borne illnesses. You can easily find various ointments, creams and pills that could protect you from the danger.

Certification and documents form a very important part of the medical endeavor. When going to a foreign country, carry all the records that certify the immunizations you have received in the past. This will enable the doctors at the medical tourism destination to have a proper knowledge about the kind of drugs and further treatment, so that they can attend to your case appropriately. If the documents are in a language that is not internationally recognized, then it is wise to translate this into a language that is acceptable at the destination.

The common vaccines you may need when going overseas include hepatitis A, hepatitis B, influenza, pneumococcal, polio, rabies, typhoid fever, yellow fever, tetanus and Japanese encephalitis.

Irrespective of the country you are visiting for your medical treatment, you should be up to date on all the routine immunizations you will require for effective prevention against infectious diseases in unfamiliar environments. Even if you have to embark on a medical journey in less than three to four weeks, you should consult with your local doctor to check if you need any vaccines or medicines. In nutshell, the recommendation of the right vaccinations is one of the major components of a pre-travel medical consultation.

ESSENTIAL ITEMS FOR A TRAVEL MEDICINE KIT

The things a medical tourist should include in his/her travel medications kit depends a lot on the destination and the region-specific infections. When preparing the medicine kit, you must make sure that it has enough medicinal supplies to prevent common infectious illnesses, handle minor injuries, and manage your current medical conditions during the entire trip. Having a few important medications at hand can help you greatly in unpleasant situations that might arise during your journey. Here is a list of the items that form an integral part of a complete medical kit.

Prescription medications – You should always include your prescription medicines in the kit, as it will help manage your pre-existing health condition. It should include the medicines your doctor has recommended in order to prevent various travel-related illnesses.

Thermometer - This is necessary to understand the degree of fever and the kind of medicine you will require in the foreign country. Digital thermometers are safer to carry than the glass mercury thermometers.

Over the counter medicine - There are certain medicines that fall under this category and can offer temporary relief from fever or acute pain. You should consult your physician who will then suggest the kind of medicine allowed in your particular condition. You can use over-the-counter medicines to treat common problems, such as headache, heartburn, mild diarrhea, cold and motion sickness, which people usually face while traveling.

Bandages - Adhesive bandages are the best option for treating minor cuts and injuries. They are handy to carry and offer protection against minor injuries. Gauze pads and first-aid tapes are also important and are easy to carry. You should always include adhesive bandages in different sizes.

Hand sanitizer gel - Sanitizer gel is particularly important for maintaining hygiene.

Antibiotic creams - These are important to treat cuts and many other infections. You can add ophthalmic creams your medicine kit in order to address eye infections. You should also include the creams that help in treating allergic rashes.

Antacid preparation - These are available in both tablet and liquid forms and you should select the variety that suits you the best. However, tablets may be more convenient to carry than liquids.

Sunscreen - It is vital because during traveling, the exposure to sun could be extensive and there are higher chances that you can suffer sunburn and other skin aliments caused by sun exposure.

Tweezers - It can serve a variety of purposes from removing splinters to opening caps on your medicine packs. Whether you have a basic medicine kit or a comprehensive one, the tweezers are a must-have tool.

You could include many other things in your travel medical kit, as suited to personal needs. You should take note of the fact that the list may vary in accordance to the destination and the kind of activities you intend to indulge in during the course of your journey.

Other vital additions to your travel medicine kit include safety pins, scissors, insect repellents creams, and diarrhea medicines such as Imodium, fluid and electrolyte replacement tablets or powders like gastrolyte, eye lubricant drops and earplugs. You should also consider adding condoms or other contraceptives, sterile needles and syringes, water purifying tablets and mosquito bed nets. Bear in mind that you should not change the containers of the medicines and check that the medicines carry clear labels.

It is mandatory that the names of the medicines match the prescription from a certified doctor. The prescription must contain the generic name of the medicines because the trade names may create problems in foreign lands. You can easily find travel-specific medicine kits and packages of over-the-counter medications at the pharmacies. If you have special medical needs, you should always consult your doctor before you finally prepare your travel medicine kit.

Points for your Companion

Why exactly do you need a medical companion and what does a medical companion actually mean? Well, a medical companion can be anybody – a comrade, a domestic partner, someone from your family or circle or friends – who will assist you, live with you and travel with you on your medical journey. A family member is generally preferred since they can handle documentation and formalities like signing the consent form.

Medical tourists must keep their general condition and health in mind. It is advised that you choose a suitable companion; one who has enough time to spend going along with you and is able to take care of all your medical needs in a foreign land.

Ideally, medical tourists should select someone who is physically and mentally strong, so that he/she can support you through all your good and difficult times. Your companion should have an emotional bond with you, so that you can ensure that he/she will not leave you midway through your medical journey. It is also beneficial if your medical companion has knowledge of your medical condition and of the destination to which you are traveling for treatment.

Your companion will be all you have when you are on your medical journey; apart from taking care of all your needs, he/she should be able to motivate you during difficult times. The companion should have a calm, fun-loving nature and should be able to interact with people. He/she should also be able to plan and execute things during times when you are hospitalized.

Your companion should have complete understanding of your requirements during your treatment phase, and should be able to communicate with your treating doctor effectively to know more about your condition. Moreover, your companion should be financially sound and able to take control over the expenses during testing times.

BASIC TIPS FOR A COMPANION

As a companion to a medical tourist, you too carry a load of responsibility. You not only have to take care of the medical traveler, but also handle the entire journey during times when the patient is hospitalized. Here are certain points that you must remember and adhere.

- As a medical tourist's companion, you should have complete information about the patient's medical condition, the procedure he/she will have to go through and the precautions that have to be taken prior to the treatment and afterwards. You also need to be familiar with all the medication necessary for the patient after the procedure. Make sure that you constantly remain in touch with the treating doctor so that you know about your companion's medical requirements. You might also have to do some post-operation duties such as pushing the patient in a wheelchair, as they might not be allowed to walk for a certain period. You should take it upon yourself to make sure that the patient is complying with the doctor's recommendations and not indulging in activities that are detrimental to his/her health.
- Remember to take notes, which should include information about important contacts including their phone numbers and email addresses. The contacts should

also include the name and number of doctors and surgeons and medical consultants. It would also be beneficial to keep phone numbers and other contact details of hospitals and clinics in the destination country, along with the numbers to reach emergency ambulance services in the region.

- In addition to preparing a list of important contact numbers, you should also remember to carry your own identity documents, including passport and driving license with you while you travel. Since, at times, the patient might not be in a position to drive a vehicle, carrying your own credentials will save you from any trouble, in case you need the assistance of a car.

- As a companion, you should have exceptional communicating skills, so that you can keep in touch with the healthcare providers at all times, before, during and even after the treatment. At times, a patient might feel uncomfortable or simply become nervous while asking certain questions, which is when you should come in handy.

- Since you will not be having any pre-procedure jitters, you are most likely to retain vital information about the patient's surgery and all pre- and post-treatment care that is required. Once the treatment is over, you should be in a position to communicate the success of the treatment to the eagerly waiting relatives and family members of the patient back home.

- Since a companion too is on a medical tourism journey, just like the medical traveler, you too should prepare for the journey. You might be required to arrange for special care for the medical traveler at the airport or departure from and arrival back into the home country. You should be prepared to ask for special care and make similar arrangements at the airports and after reaching the destination country.

- Besides providing physical support to the patient, you should be able to emotionally and mentally console the patient and prepare him/her well for the treatment. You have to make sure that your patient does not feel any pre-treatment jitters and he/she should be emotionally relaxed before the treatment commences. You should make sure that you are ready to do everything in your power to cheer up the medical traveler and keep him/her in good spirits, as this will aid in a speedy recovery.

- One thing that most companions to medical tourists often forget is that they too need to be financially sound when traveling to a foreign land. Although medical tourism is a cost-effective option for treatment, the medical bills that the patient receives at the end of his/her treatment might be more than what was planned. In such times, you should make sure that you have ample cash and credit available with you, with which you can pay the pending dues.

- Companions should also be careful about documentation and restrictions in the host country. Several destinations will allow a visa to the medical companion, but many countries also prohibit the companion from undergoing any major medical treatment.

CHAPTER 19

Expecting the Unexpected

IN THIS CHAPTER

- Potential unexpected events that could occur when abroad
- Developing comprehensive plans and preparations for unexpected events
- Ways to prepare yourself for the worst-case scenarios

EXPECTING THE UNEXPECTED

When preparing for the medical treatment overseas, one cannot overlook the possibilities of unexpected events during the stay in a foreign country. A medical tourist should always be ready for emergencies or worst-case scenarios that are an unavoidable part of travel, as no one can predict the future.

Various things to consider in an emergency depend a lot on the type of situation you might face during your medical journey. If it is a medical emergency and you are not near a hospital, you should immediately contact the local emergency services and arrange for an ambulance to reach the treating facility. The hotel you are staying at could also have medical facilities in-house that may be capable of handling emergencies, or at the very least, provide first aid. You must consider all the potential complications that could arise, and develop a comprehensive plan. One of the best ways to do this is by learning from the experiences of other internationally traveling patients. You can read about their experiences on many websites or online forums, or may ask directly from the patients if you get to know their contact details.

As a vacationing patient, you should be always ready to expect the unexpected during your medical journey. You should know the right persons to contact during the emergencies in the medical tourism destination. In case of any political or social emergencies, you could contact the local consulate office and seek assistance.

The main office is the embassy, which is usually located in the capital city. However, you may always get in touch with the smaller consulate centers that are generally located in other large cities. Before you embark on your medical journey, you must make yourself familiar with your rights in the foreign country and note down the details of the persons or organizations you might need to contact in case of emergencies.

PREPARE FOR THE WORST

For any patient traveling overseas for treatment, it is important to prepare in advance for all sorts of emergencies and worst-case scenarios. While you can choose the best treating facility abroad, which has a proven record of accomplishment of performing successful surgeries or special treatments, things can go wrong.

Carefully select your medical travel insurance to protect your finances. When choosing medical travel insurance, you must make sure that it covers the costs of medical errors and that of readmission post-operation for follow-up treatment. You should always keep your travel ticket as flexible as possible, so that you do not have to incur any cancellation fees in the event of having to extend your trip for further treatment. You also need to ensure that your passport and visa don't expire if you need to postpone your trip by a few days.

Since you are going out of the country for medical treatment, inform your family members about your medical tourism destination, and the name and location of the treating facility. Also talk to your local physician or surgeon and enquire about the possible complications that could arise overseas.

While a patient travels internationally to receive the best quality treatment in a good medical facility, we cannot overlook the importance of understanding the consequences pertaining to death. As a medical tourist, you need to have a fair understanding of all the matters. It is also very important to find out what will happen to the body in the event of death and who will be responsible for communicating the news to family and relatives. Also consider the recourse family members can take in terms of legal possibilities, and insurance cover, should a fatal experience happen.

LEARNING FROM OTHERS' EXPERIENCES

By checking the patient testimonials, you can get a clear idea of the services and facilities available in a particular medical tourism destination. It will help you know the complications and emergencies you might face during your medical journey. Another viable option is to ask your doctor to arrange a session with patients he/she may be acquainted with, who have traveled abroad for treatment. You can ask them to share their experience and get to know ways in which they managed situations when things went wrong. It is a better way of clearing all your doubts and fears before traveling abroad for medical treatment.

DEVELOPING A COMPREHENSIVE PLAN

Proper planning is the key to a successful. It is important for a medical tourist to develop a comprehensive plan to avoid any stressful situations in a foreign land. If you want to organize a safe, stress free trip, plan all the activities beforehand. However, we must not deny the fact that a medical tourist could face an unpredictable event that is simply out of his/her control. Nevertheless, if something goes wrong during your medical trip, it should have nothing to do with the lack of planning and preparation.

PROTECTION FROM THE UNEXPECTED

During the preparation phase of medical tourism, many patients only budget for the procedures that are sure to take place. Most medical tourists do not account for the unexpected events, and therefore find themselves cash strapped during emergencies. The worst part of such a situation is the fact that they are far away from their home country and family and friends.

You could purchase an insurance policy that will protect you against unexpected expenses during your stay overseas. Examples of these unexpected situations may include losing your luggage, developing complications that would require you to overstay your medical journey, facing legal problems, or other cases of emergencies.

It is important to ensure that you purchase the best type of cover for your individual needs. Moreover, you should always check for exclusions on your medical travel insurance policy, so you do not get a surprise when filing a claim. Choose a policy that protects you against financial loss in cases you find the need to cancel, delay or interrupt your medical trip.

CHAPTER 20

Post-Operative Care Preparation

IN THIS CHAPTER

- Distinguishing between post-operative care and continuity of care
- How to prepare for continuity of care before traveling
- Post-operative care tips when at destination
- Considerations when you are traveling back home
- Tips for continuity of care when you arrive home

The list of available options for a potential medical tourist is endless. While the reason for your travel might simply be a check-up, most medical tourists travel overseas for a surgical procedure, which requires careful planning for post-operative care arrangements. Those who are traveling for diagnostic procedures might not require any post-operative care arrangements; those who will be undergoing a surgery might have to stay in the destination country to receive post-operative care at the healthcare facility before they can return home. For such patients, we recommend going through this chapter in detail, as post-operative care is just as crucial as the treatment itself.

Before we begin highlighting the preparations that you should make before traveling, it is important to differentiate between post-operative care and continuity of care. Although patients often use both terms, not many understand the core difference between them. Post-operative requirements refer to the patient's need immediately after the treatment has been completed. These procedures are usually performed in the hospital and continue until the patient is discharged. Critical concerns during the post-operative phase are to ensure that the patient is breathing properly, pain is being managed, the mental status of the patient is good, and the wounds are healing as expected. Since medical tourists have to fly back home after the treatment is complete, physicians ensure that the patient has fully recovered and is fit for travel.

Continuity of care refers to the continuity of health services after the patient has returned home. For continuity of care, the patient has to immediately get in touch with his/her local doctor while seeking vital information from the overseas treating physician to ensure appropriate recuperation from the surgery. Continuity of care after returning home is essential for medical tourists, as only good care can guarantee the success of the treatment that has been performed overseas.

It is essential for medical tourists to prepare a plan for post-operative treatment. To ensure a successful treatment, it is vitally important for your post-operative plan to be ready before you commence your travel.

Comprehensive planning for post-operative care and continuity of care can be sub-divided into five major sections. These include continuity of care preparations prior to traveling, post-operative tips when you are at the destination, continuity of care requirements when at the destination, post-operative tips while you are traveling back home, and continuity of care arrangements after returning home.

This book tries to highlight the most important preparations that you will require after the treatment is complete. However, a different type of care is required for different conditions and getting in touch with your treating doctor to understand the intricacies of post-operative and continuity of care is recommended.

POST OPERATIVE PLANNING SUGGESTIONS AND TIPS

A. Continuity of care preparations before you travel

Before commencing the journey, it is extremely important to ensure that you will be able to gain access to healthcare services on your return. In most cases, the family doctor will play an important role in providing the required continuity of care. However, before you set out on your medical tourism journey, discuss the details and intricacies with your family doctor and make him/her aware of your requirements upon return.

In case your country has insufficient healthcare facilities, you must immediately coordinate with your treating doctor overseas and ask for recommendations. Usually reputed doctors who are members of globally renowned medical associations, have a large network of doctors in several parts of the world and they will be in a position to assist you in either finding a good physician or a healthcare facility that can handle your continuity of care requirements.

In an event, where your treating doctor is not in a position to provide sufficient recommendations, you can get in touch with a facilitator. The facilitator will make sure that you get appropriate medical care after you have returned from treatment. However, if none of the above works for you, you should get in touch with special healthcare organizations, which have primarily been set up just to ensure that medical tourists gain access to post-operative and continuity of care services.

These organizations have taken advantage of the niche market and have been helping patients with their post-operative and continuity of care needs. The internet can be helpful for finding and getting in touch with such an organization.

- **Digitizing medical documents**

Digitizing medical documents not only means that you can access the information in any country, but also ensures that you do not have to carry a file of documents and diagnostic reports whenever you visit a healthcare provider. By digitizing medical documents you can easily preserve and carry all your medical reports in a secure and convenient manner.

By digitizing medical information, a patient can be in charge of his/her own medical record, which he/she can carry to any part of the world in a portable format. Since portable media devices, such as USB thumb drives, are widely accepted in computers around the world, you can easily produce or refer to the relevant information at anytime you require. They not only help in augmenting the quality of healthcare that you receive, but also reduce cost of printing and sending documents to healthcare facilities in different parts of the world.

You can simply email your documents to all healthcare providers and await their response. In addition, you can also easily update your treating doctor and your local doctor about your progress during the post-operative recovery phase, in no time.

- **Make sure all preparations are made for when you return home**

After you return home from your medical journey, you should ensure that everything you need should readily be available at your home. Since you might not have completely recovered from your treatment after you have reached home, you will not always be in a position to arrange things that you require.

These things might include food that has been specified by your treating doctor, medication and other supplies, such as wheelchair or cane. You, or your companion, should be prepared to share all this information with your friends and family back home, so that they can make all necessary arrangements before you reach.

B. Plan for continuity of care while you are still at the treating facility

• Collection of post-operative instructions

Always keep in mind that while you are in your medical tourism destination, you should receive all necessary information and instructions of what you need after you reach home. This information will help you arrange for proper continuity of care procedures after return. During the time when you are in direct contact with your treating physician or doctor, make notes and write down important suggestions.

This will include the necessary post-operative instructions, details about the medication you require, things or activities you should avoid, and the right time to get back to your normal routine.

Do not hesitate in asking questions. If you are still drowsy or not in the best condition to understand the intricacies, your companion should take the required notes. If you do not have a companion with you, you can also request the physician to provide you with written notes that are clear enough for you to understand.

• Availability of medication prescribed by the doctor

One of the most important aspects of post-operative recovery is the medication that your treating physician has prescribed to you. For quick recovery, you (or your companion), have to ensure that you take the prescribed medicines at the scheduled time and do not miss on any dosage. While in your destination country, you will be easily able to buy your prescription drugs by showing the prescription letter given to you by your doctor.

Make sure that the same drugs will be available in your home country, if you have to remain on prescription for a longer period. Although certain medicines are prevalent in a particular region, the same drugs might be considered contraband in your home country. It is important to ask your physician or the pharmacist whether the medication, which you have been prescribed, is legal to be carried back home.

If the medication is legal in your country too, you can easily stock it up as it might be cheaper in your destination than in your home country. However, if the drugs are considered contraband in your home country, you will have to arrange a recommendation letter from your doctor that claims the importance of the drug for your case. You should get in touch with your local doctor who will be performing the necessary continuity of care procedures after your return. Try to get the name of an alternative drug for the same use, which you can legally purchase in your country.

• Gather medical documents, legal papers and bills

Before you start your journey back home, it is important to remember that all the documents you have received during your treatment are of vital importance and hence they should not be thrown in the bin of the hotel you are living in, but should be packed carefully. The documents might include your medical reports, notes and recommendations of the physician who treated you, lab test results and imaging reports. These will be important for the continuity of care procedures. Non-medical documents such as bills will be required for claim processing and tax deductions. In addition, the informed consent and other legal documents are something you should hold on to, in case a legal recourse is needed.

- **Traveling certificates, if required**

While you are traveling as a patient, you need special care from the airline staff, both prior to the treatment and afterwards. Many airlines have guidelines pertaining to such travelers, and they will only be in a position to help you and provide you with the required comfort after they check documents that prove your medical condition and get abreast of your requirements.

Sometimes, a patient might require a wheelchair to board a plane or possibly even require emergency services, in the case of a complicated condition. If you provide your traveling certificate, which carries important information about your medical condition and your care requirements, the airline staff will ensure that they provide all necessary services to you.

These services might include a roomier seat, food according to your doctor's recommendations and additional monitoring by the airline staff. Without the traveling certificates, airline staff cannot be held responsible for not making special provisions for you during your travel. Airline staff members work under set guidelines and these guidelines ask all patients to produce certificates which prove the medical condition.

C. Things to keep in mind while under post-operative care at your destination

- **Recovering once your procedure is completed**

After the treatment has been completed, you will need immediate post-operative care and your physician will usually shift you to a care ward where doctors and nurses will monitor your condition. It is essential at this phase for you to express your concerns, discomfort or pain that you might be feeling at that time. If you do not have a companion to aid you, you should take the help of the nursing staff to communicate with your family back home so that you can inform them about your current condition, and details regarding the surgery.

- **Recovering once you have been discharged**

Once you have completed the initial post-operative care procedures, you will be discharged from the healthcare facility. At this time, you and your companion will be on your own. You will still have to communicate with your treating doctor, while monitoring your own condition. You have to keep an eye on the healing process, while ensuring that you take the required prescription drugs at the right time. Book a hotel at a close distance to the treating facility, so that your companion does not have trouble shifting you to the healthcare facility if complications arise.

During this phase, you have to keep an eye out for any irregularities on your body or internally after the surgery. This has to be done by the patient himself/herself, as you will be the best judge in any discomfort or complications arise after the treatment. While pain is normal after a surgery, you should alert your companion if pain begins to increase for no reason, while you are still on medication.

Focus on the amount of pain you are experiencing, and communicate the same to your treating physician. After the surgery has been performed, your physician will also be focusing on ways to alleviate pain.

The post-operative care that a patient requires largely depends on the surgery that has been performed. Hence, the best advice to help you recover quickly will always come from your physician or healthcare provider. However, here are a few general post-operative care tips that you should follow:

- Make sure that your body is constantly hydrated. Since many medications make you sweat, your body loses a considerable amount of water, which if not taken care of, can lead to dehydration.
- You should try not to consume alcohol, quit smoking and avoid caffeinated beverages. Smoking and drinking can result in dehydration too.
- Make sure that your wound is properly treated and taken care of. Change the wound dressing as prescribed.
- While your diet should be according to the advice given by your treating physician, usually you should be consuming a bland, low fat and low sodium diet.
- Try to move around your room or hotel if you are able too. Walking will help you get back to a normal shape as quickly as possible.

D. Tips for continuity of care while you are traveling back home

• Flight back home

Since you have had treatment in a facility that is far from your home, you need to be extremely cautious about your post-operative flight back home. The flight back home needs even more attention if it is going to be a long one. Boarding a long flight post-surgery can result in complications if precautions are not taken.

It is essential for all medical tourists to consult their doctor before returning home, as they will be able to provide you with the best guidance and suggestions that ensure your safety. Ideally, you should be traveling back with a companion, who also knows everything about your medical condition and your specific in-flight requirements.

After your treating doctor has approved your flight back home, the flight itself can cause significant discomforts, especially if you have just undergone a surgery. Convey your requirements to the airline in advance. For example, after a surgery you might require a roomier seat or a certain diet that your doctor has recommended for you. If you have conveyed this in advance to the airline company, they will make sure that all your requirements are met and you get special attention from the airline staff.

Once onboard the flight, try to move around as much as possible so that you can avoid the risk of embolism or deep vein thrombosis. These conditions can significantly affect medical patients, as they arise due to the lack of blood circulation at high altitudes. Constantly drink fluids, such as fruit juices and water, to remain hydrated. Additionally, if it is possible, do a few in-flight exercises to improve your blood circulation.

E. Tips for continuity of care when you reach home

- **Stay connected with your treating doctor**

After your return, it becomes important for you to constantly remain in touch with your treating doctor. Only he/she knows the best about your medical condition and the specific requirements in the continuity of care procedures. Remaining in constant touch with your treating doctor is vital for your quick and easy recovery after the surgery. Talk to your treating doctor about the precautions you need to take, and the symptoms of complications that you need to keep an eye on.

- **Connecting with the local doctor**

Even with the use of telemedicine services, your treating doctor will not be able to provide all the help that you need after your return. Therefore, once you are back home and are able to move around, visit your local doctor. Give him/her all the details of your treatment, the procedure you went through and the type of medication that you are currently using.

In addition, share all the notes provided by your treating doctor to your local doctor, so that he/she can thoroughly understand your condition from a medical point of view. You should also share all your medical reports and lab test reports with your local doctor so that he/she can determine the progress.

If possible, share the contact number of your treating doctor with your local doctor, so that both of them can communicate and figure out the best course of treatment required for speedy recovery.

WHAT SHOULD YOU DO IF COMPLICATIONS DEVELOP?

If you had done ample research when planning and choosing a healthcare destination before you started your medical tourism journey, you will be satisfied with the experience and will even encourage other people to take advantage of this qualitative and economical alternative. However, just like any other medical procedure, there is definitely a certain element of risk associated with medical tourism. The patient needs to understand this risk and contemplate the probability of complications after return. Although all medical treatments have a certain risk involved, the complications can get worse after a medical tourism journey, as you will no longer be able to interact with your treating doctor physically.

If you see complications occurring after your return home, you should understand that not all complications mean a life-threatening condition. However, you should be wary about them so that you can receive timely medical attention. Some of the common complications that are likely to occur, especially after a surgical procedure, are risk of an infection, abnormal and continuous bleeding around the incision, high fever, migraine or shortness of breath.

If you are experiencing any of the above-mentioned symptoms, immediately consult your local doctor. Once your condition has improved, you should consult your treating doctor and get his advice on what exactly happened and how you can prevent any reoccurrence of the symptoms.

CHAPTER 21

Who to Seek Guidance From

IN THIS CHAPTER

- Pros and cons of seeking advice from a facilitator
- Using medical tourism association to seek information
- How friends and family at home and abroad could provide valuable information

FROM WHOM SHOULD YOU SEEK GUIDANCE WHEN PLANNING YOUR MEDICAL TRIP?

Facilitators or agencies:

In recent years, the concept of medical tourism has gained a lot of popularity, owing to which there has been a rise in the number of medical travel companies that work to make the complex process of obtaining medical care overseas easy for the patients. A medical tourism facilitator, also called a medical tourism provider, offers full support to the internationally traveling patients. A facilitator is familiar with the medical tourism industry and the process that a patient has to follow. A facilitator takes care of the travel arrangements, accommodation, medical services, pre- and post-operative care, tourism activities and much other facets. These professionals have a strong network of hospitals and physicians around the world that they represent.

Pros:

Since medical tourism facilitators are quite familiar with the tourism and medical sector, they are the best people to contact for making your medical journey smooth and comfortable. One of the major benefits of hiring a medical tourism facilitator is that you get to choose from a range of options and select the best course of treatment that suits your specific needs. A good medical travel facilitator will ensure patient safety guidelines by informing you of the agencies that provide the highest quality in hospitals, skilled staff and experienced doctors overseas.

Since the facilitators are familiar with medical travel and all its aspects, they can educate you on any potential problems you could face during your medical journey to a foreign country. A facilitator is of great help, especially for the first-time medical tourists, who will obviously have a lot of questions and concerns regarding their travel arrangements and treatment overseas.

Cons:

While using a medical tourism facilitator has a number of advantages, you should also take note of the disadvantages of working with a facilitator. Do not rely completely on the information the facilitators provide. It would not be wrong to say that most facilitators clearly do not have the time and resources to have complete information about every medical destination. Therefore, they may be inclined to promote every place as the best one.

In some cases, medical tour facilitators may recommend a particular institution or physician because they receive a commission, service charge or both from the hospital or doctor in question. Having an intermediary liaise between the patient and doctor can lead to serious confusion or miscommunication.

A medical tourist should always get all the terms in writing and crosscheck them for errors, so that you do not have to face any stressful situations during your medical trip owing to miscommunication.

A medical tourist should ask several questions from the facilitator, not only to clear your doubts, but also to have a clear idea about the facilitator's experience and any commission-based contract they may have with the hospitals in medical tourism destinations. Always bear in mind that it is not difficult for a facilitator to mislead patients and make good money by recommending some specific hospitals that give them great commissions. Having a fancy website does not indicate their experience or skill in the industry. It is better to source the necessary information from someone who has been on a similar medical tour. For this you can always read patient reviews and testimonials on different websites and online forums.

HOSPITALS

Pros:

Other than the medical tourism facilitator, the other best source of information is your treating facility. Seeking guidance from the treating facility could be very beneficial in the preparation phase of your medical trip. The hospital in which you will receive the medical treatment should have all the relevant medical information and documents you might require to accurately budget and plan your trip.

They also have specialized international patient representatives whose job is to assist foreign patients and communicate with them regarding the treatment process and other things related to their medical journey. After you have decided on the treating hospital, it is of the utmost importance to initiate the communication in order to get as many details as possible regarding your treatment and other important things. You can also enquire about probable outcomes, results and other relevant data directly from the source. The hospital should be able to provide you with detailed consent forms that demonstrate their legal structure.

Cons:

One of the biggest downsides to seeking information from your treatment facility regarding your medical procedure is that you might get a biased response. Many healthcare institutions might create fake testimonials and reports to increase inflow of patients. It is better to crosscheck all the information they are providing by contacting previous patients and checking patient testimonials at different websites.

MEDICAL TRAVEL ASSOCIATIONS

Due to the ever-increasing popularity of medical tourism, many associations are nowadays working specifically in the medical travel industry to support patients. A fine example of this is the Medical Tourism Association, a leading non-profit association for medical tourism industry. Many regional associations could provide essential information pertaining to that region. These associations promote as well as support the medical tourism industry, and can educate potential medical tourists about all the aspects of medical travel.

Pros:

A majority of people are nowadays using the internet to search for health related topics. The medical travel associations assist potential medical tourists by providing detailed information related to the medical tourism sector. These associations act as information portals for patients who wish to seek guidance related to the entire process of traveling overseas to receive medical or wellness care.

These tourism associations provide the information for patients about things the internationally traveling patients may need to know, such as the insurance companies, legal issues and top hospitals (about their quality of service and care). They also conduct informational sessions and programs to educate the internationally traveling patients about the advantages of medical tourism and the varying quality of treatment available in different medical tourism destinations.

Cons:

The only disadvantage of these organizations is that they offer general and wide-ranging advice for all medical tourists, which may not be applicable in your specific case. Since the individual needs of patients vary greatly, you will want to have specific information that benefits you during the preparation phase. You may find that you have particular requirements that you need to communicate with these associations, based specifically on your medical condition.

Some associations have social network platforms or community forums, which can provide you with more details about the type of support these associations provide to the patients. For example, the Medical Tourism Association's social network engine "Medical Tourism City" is a good platform where potential medical tourists can discuss the challenges and issues associated with medical tourism.

FRIENDS AND RELATIVES AT HOME AND ABROAD

Friends or relatives residing in the destination where you are seeking treatment can be of great help. They might have much more knowledge about the quality of treatment and healthcare services available in that particular country or area, they will be better able to guide you.

With the support of friends and family, a medical tourist can easily address a range of problems, such as accommodation and financial support. They can give you their honest opinion related to your decisions and can provide great emotional support during tough times. You can ensure that the advice they give you will only be in your best interests because they care about your wellbeing.

LOCAL DOCTORS

Your local doctor is the person who knows your medical history in detail. This makes your local doctor the ideal candidate to offer accurate information and guidance that you can use when considering treatment in a foreign country.

Their strong medical knowledge can help you understand the various aspects of your condition and any expectations you may have regarding the proposed treatment. Since they understand quality care practices better than you do, they can also differentiate between the standard of treatments available in different countries, and guide you accordingly. They can also help translate and decipher the complex medical jargon associated with the medical treatment you need. Furthermore, they could possibly have contacts with either physicians or individuals abroad that you may find useful during your medical journey.

TOURISM BOARDS

Many nations (rightly) consider medical tourism under the larger ambit of tourism. As such, they make information related to medical facilities freely available. Most of this information is generally sourced and provided by government bodies, so you can place a greater level of trust in the authenticity of the information. As a rule of thumb, tourism boards of nations will promote and provide information on only their medical facilities. Given this situation, the tourist might feel the need for contacting related boards and ministries of various countries.

EXHIBITIONS AND CONFERENCES

Interested organizations often hold exhibitions and conferences to educate people about the larger role of medical tourism. Such gatherings could be organized by individual facilities, medical travel facilitators, national boards, academicians, or organizations working within the ambit of medical tourism. In any case, such events can be excellent places for gaining knowledge and insights into the world of medical tourism.

CHAPTER 22

Gathering Authentic Information

IN THIS CHAPTER

- Tips on using various resources to get accurate information on medical tourism
- The Pros and Cons of using the internet to seek information
- Importance of double-checking and cross-referencing

There is no denying the fact that traveling abroad to seek healthcare services is a crucial decision to make, and hence it requires proper planning. For a thorough and accurate plan, you require accurate and credible information, which can be sourced from a variety of channels. Information sourced from the internet or television advertisements has a potential of being biased. This information, which an average medical tourist has to go through, makes it difficult for them to differentiate between credible and inaccurate information.

It is important for all potential medical tourists to understand the information they are receiving, and realize if the source of that information is reliable and believable. Further, this section will help you differentiate between channels covering inaccurate information from the channels where you can source accurate and verifiable information.

THE WORLD WIDE WEB

The growth in the number of internet users around the world means that the World Wide Web is the primary source of information for most people. However, one of the biggest drawbacks of using internet as a source of information is the fact that anybody can write and produce any type of content. This is the main reason many potential medical tourists are misled by false information and promises regarding medical tourism.

It is necessary that a potential medical tourist perform a thorough research to gather vital and credible information. This would involve surfing multiple websites for the same information and verifying the facts given by each. One should make smart use of the internet by reading and researching valuable material on websites that appear credible and accredited.

There are certain systems that tend to set up credibility, for example, the HONcode certification from the Health on Net organization, is given to websites that have authoritative content. Unfortunately, the system is not very popular, and the average user is very unlikely to be aware of the value of such measures.

By collecting similar data from similar websites, you can compare the gathered information. You can also visit government websites or other non-profit websites regulated by medical authorities, as their sole aim is to provide accurate information to all potential medical tourists.

DOUBLE CHECK, CROSS-REFERENCE AND TAKE SECOND OPINIONS

After you have thoroughly researched enough information from the internet, you should make it a point to consult everything that you have learned with your local doctor. If you have found out anything about the treatment alternatives, it is best if you share all this information with your trusted general physician, who is the best person to either confirm or clarify the knowledge you have gathered. Further, if you have done research about a medical facility or a hospital overseas, your general physician will still be able to identify if the claimed services are possible and if they will benefit your medical condition.

In addition, while doing internet research on a website, ensure that you investigate everything about the publisher of the information and verify that the information is not biased, but accurate and balanced. Further, you should make sure that the website is updated on a regular basis, so that you can ascertain that the information you are reading is accurate and updated. Most medical tourism websites display the names and specialization of doctors who work at a specific healthcare facility. You can validate the information by calling up the facility or writing a quick email.

As a rule of the thumb, you should go with a website that makes all attempts to communicate in a comprehensible language. If you feel that the website is simply advertising the services of a particular healthcare facility or a doctor, it is in your best interest to move to some other page.

PATIENT TESTIMONIALS

One way to get access to accurate and reliable information about a healthcare facility or treatment procedure is to go through patient testimonials. To access patient testimonials, the best you can do is to participate in medical tourism forums and discussions. Sometimes, you can find articles or real life experiences of medical tourists on reputed websites and newspapers.

It is more likely that you receive accurate information from such websites and forums, as the content is generated by medical travelers, who are not being paid to advertise services of a healthcare facility. On the other hand, you should not take patient testimonials and claims on websites, which promote medical tourism, for granted as here the website administrators could manipulate the feedback to attract more patients. You should try to find a website or a forum, where many patients participate to share their experiences, as this dynamic information is hard to manipulate.

MEDICAL TOURISM WEBSITES

With growth in the medical tourism sector, we now have several government and private websites that help potential medical tourists with their queries. These websites enable all potential medical tourists to access an enormous amount of impartial information related to the intricacies of their medical travel. These websites also provide important informative links, using which you can connect to reputed hospitals, clinics, doctors, surgeons, financing institutions, facilitators and related resources. Hence, you can gain access to testimonials of past patients, the different types of treatment alternatives available for your condition, and the best healthcare facilities in a reputed medical tourism destination. You can further use this information when making decisions for your medical travel.

INFORMATION FROM OTHER RESOURCES

In addition to using channels of technology, such as the internet, the potential medical tourist, can gather authentic and verifiable information from other resources as well. A good alternative to seeking testimonials online and verifying their accuracy would be to ask your local doctor to arrange an interactive session with his/her past patients who have traveled abroad to seek good quality healthcare services. Most reputed doctors know people who have traveled abroad for treatment and will be open for such discussions.

You can also speak out your mind with your friends and co-workers and ask them if they know anybody who has been a medical tourist in the past. On getting a reference, you can take out some time and seek an appointment with the patient. Once you have made contact, you can get all details about his/her medical tourism experience in the past and hence prepare accordingly. You can also raise your concerns or doubts regarding your potential medical tourism journey and take their advice on them.

Moreover, you can also contact an overseas medical facility directly and enquire about the details. Most reputed healthcare facilities that cater to foreign patients have an international patient department with dedicated representatives to help potential medical tourists. You can even seek help from a medical facilitator who is well versed with the medical tourism industry. They have connections with different healthcare facilities and hence can guide you on your journey. However, you as a potential medical tourist should make sure that the facilitator works for an independent agency and is not representing a certain hospital or doctor.

CHAPTER 23

Understanding Cultural Issues

IN THIS CHAPTER

- Cultural considerations to take into account
- Importance of having sanitary food and water when abroad
- Preparing for religious/national holidays in the foreign country

CONSIDER THE CULTURAL ISSUES

Researching the culture of the region you are visiting could be very useful, as you might encounter many differences between the cultures of the home country and the host. These cultural differences may or may not suit you. Let us discuss various factors a medical tourist needs to consider to get a general idea of another culture's predispositions.

When it comes to medical tourism, the understanding of cultural issues is a two-way process. Not only does the host country need to be aware of the patient's cultural beliefs, but the medical tourist must also understand the culture of the destination. Since patients are traveling across the borders to receive quality affordable medical or wellness care, there is a great need for bilateral cultural understanding.

A clear understanding of the cultural values and beliefs can help achieve higher levels of satisfaction. Since patients coming from different geographic areas may have diverse cultural beliefs, it is important for them to understand and value the cultural beliefs of their medical tourism destination.

RELIGIOUS AND NATIONAL HOLIDAYS

Every country has its own list of official, national and religious holidays. Therefore, it makes great sense to search for the list of national and religious holidays in the particular country you are visiting before you embark on your medical journey.

The celebrations in the country you are visiting could have an effect on your travel plans, as many hospitals, banks and stores will remain closed. In addition, it might be important to understand a few aspects of the host country's religion prior to traveling, so that you do not have to face any cultural shocks when you reach your destination.

More importantly, if you are not aware of the cultural matters of your medical tourism destination, you might get into trouble with the law. For example, during the period of Ramadan in Arab countries, it is not just disrespectful, but illegal to eat, drink or dress immoderately in public places.

CLOTHING

Clothing laws vary greatly around the world. While some countries have no clothing laws, others have strict laws governing what people can and cannot wear. You might be used to wearing anything that suits you in your home country, but do take into consideration that other countries may have a certain dress code and attire. In order to avoid offending the locals, do a quick search on how the local population dresses in that nation. It is essential to respect the traditional dress code of a particular country in order to create mutual respect and tolerance.

For example, certain Middle Eastern countries, such as Iran or Saudi Arabia, require visitors to be completely covered (including headscarves) in public locations. As a medical tourist, your focus is speedy recovery and you will not want to get into trouble by wearing anything that offends the residents of your medical tourism destination.

FOOD AND WATER AT THE DESTINATION

When traveling abroad, you should be very cautious about your food and drinking habits. Contaminated food and drink can lead to intestinal illnesses when you travel to some foreign country. Food and water safety is of the utmost importance when traveling overseas. A key benefit of traveling abroad is the fact that you get to enjoy the wide variety of cuisine a particular nation has to offer. While tasting new and local foods in a foreign country seems so inviting, it can also turn out to be a very bad experience if you consume contaminated food and water.

When you travel from one part of the world to another, you will notice a drastic change in food habits. Food is an integral part of any culture, and something that you cannot avoid while visiting any country across the globe. The food available abroad might be entirely different from what you get in your home country and it might be difficult to deny the appeal of the local cuisine. The delectableness of the local street food in a foreign land might be mouth-watering at first, but might cause harm to your stomach.

Some illnesses you can face during your international travel include diarrhea, hepatitis, Typhoid fever, and cholera. Therefore, you must only eat the foods that suit your health conditions. When in a foreign country, you must consider choosing a restaurant or hotel that serves high quality, contamination-free delicacies.

The same rule applies to water as well. Perhaps the rules are even stricter for water. Safe drinking water is the key to good health. If possible purify the drinking water by boiling it. To avoid any water-borne diseases, patients should opt for bottled drinking water, which is easily accessible at convenience stores and markets.

Although it might seem tempting to experiment with different cuisines while on your medical trip, it might be more beneficial to stick to food that is light and bland while recovering from your treatment. Physicians will recommend avoiding food that is high in sodium, fat and spice, and suggest you stick with foods that suit your body and assist in speedy recovery.

Before you begin your medical journey, you should spend some time online to learn about the different types of food available in the country you are visiting. Hospitals should be able to provide you with a menu from the food department, which you can access before you begin your journey to get an idea of the cuisine they serve.

CHAPTER 24

Understanding Ethical Issues

IN THIS CHAPTER

- Ethical considerations to take into account
- How some facilities servicing medical tourists engage in unethical practices
- Tips to avoid being duped by unethical medical organizations

Due to the growth of medical tourism industry, several facilities try to woo potential medical tourists using unethical, and sometimes even dangerous practices. The aim of this section is to highlight some of the main controversies that surround the medical tourism industry to allow all potential medical tourists to make a well-informed decision long before their journey commences.

Several medical tourists decide on medical tourism because they need organ or tissue transplants. In the developed world, the waiting list for organ or tissue transplant is large, and patients in a critical condition have no other option but to travel overseas for the procedure. However, there are several controversies surrounding transplants in the developing world, as the source of the organs or the tissues is usually a mystery for most patients.

There have been several issues in the past concerning the legality of organ and tissue transplants in many countries. There have been reports of organs being obtained without the consent of the donor, such as from prisoners or poor patients who have no knowledge of the kind of treatment they are receiving at a medical facility. It becomes essential for the medical tourist, to check with the treating facility and ascertain that the organs the facility transplants in patients are being sourced legally. You have to ensure that the healthcare facility that you have selected is not involved in unethical practices.

While an illegally obtained organ might put the donor at risk, it could even be dangerous and not a complete match for the receiver. This increases the chances of organ rejection, and might worsen your condition in the near future. Hence, before traveling to any healthcare facility in the world for organ or tissue transplant, you should ensure that the organ has been obtained with the consent of the donor and that it will be a complete match to your own medical profile. You can also try to personally get in touch with the donor, if possible, so that you know that the organ was obtained legally.

In addition to the controversies surrounding the source of transplant organs and tissues in some developing countries, doctors give more importance to medical tourists, obviously for financial gain and neglect the condition of the critical patients in their own country. This has created a dual level of healthcare, where medical tourists receive good treatment, while local residents have a hard time finding specialist care.

On the other hand, healthcare facilities in some countries also follow a dual-pricing system, where treatment for local residents is offered at a far lower price than foreign patients are charged. This however can be attributed to the special care and services demanded by, and offered to the medical tourists.

Certain unethical doctors try to cater to more foreign patients, as they usually can afford to pay more, while neglecting local patients. Foreign patients are mostly overcharged for services, and you might have to pay for services or tests that you do not require, or pay a large amount of money for a regular test.

Additionally, several medical tourism facilities provide documents in their regional language, which a foreign medical tourist cannot understand. These facilities also lack translation services and have no concept of cultural competency. You should try to avoid such healthcare facilities and clinics as you and your doctor will not be able to understand these documents after you return. It is therefore important for you to ascertain that the healthcare facility you have chosen will provide all documents in a common language or provide the services of an interpreter to ensure that you can understand all legal formalities.

Moreover, violation of ethics also entails providing insufficient legal documents to the patient, such as not providing a complete list of malpractice laws and consent forms to the patient, which leads to a lack of information for the medical tourist. You should hence ensure that the healthcare facility is working legally and is following all guidelines set up by the government and healthcare associations.

On the bright side, governments of medical tourism destinations are well aware of such problems and are moving aggressively to fix ethical issues in their medical facilities.

CHAPTER 25

Understanding Legal Issues

IN THIS CHAPTER

- Understanding factors of a legal system in a country
- Issues of legal recourse and malpractice
- Importance of searching for a legal representative in the foreign country to help with your legal concerns

LEGAL CONCERNS

Before you embark on your medical journey, you should take into consideration the legal issues associated with medical tourism. It is important for patients traveling from developed countries to third world regions for obtaining medical treatments to understand their rights in that particular destination before they enter into an agreement.

It is the responsibility of the treating facility overseas and the medical tourism facility, if you have hired one, to explain all the relevant legal matters to a patient in a language and manner the patient can understand. Before you sign the agreement, you should always check for the accuracy of details of the parties and persons entering the contract. Since what is legal in one country may not be legal in another, it is important for a medical tourist to have a fair understanding of all the legal concerns. While understanding the legalities involved in medical tourism and the legal system of the host countries, you must ensure that the treating region has the following guidelines in place.

Established laws: It is important for a medical tourist to be aware of the recognized rules of conduct accepted by an authority that regulate the working of the day-to-day affairs of any state, organization and undertaking. As a patient going abroad for treatment, you should make yourself familiar with the established laws related to medical practices in the particular country.

Evenness of enforcement: This refers to regularity in ensuring obedience to and observance of accepted laws or standards of behavior through force or other means.

Legal recourse: This refers to an action that an individual or an organization can take to sort out any legal matters. There are many examples where patients have died or suffered serious health issues owing to preventable medical errors. As a medical tourist, you should be aware of your rights to seek legal recourse in a foreign country.

Protection of patients: Healthcare professionals are becoming more and more conscious of the importance of acknowledging an active role for the patient. In defense of patient protection, public authorities need to recognize the patient's role and encourage their participation in the decision-making process.

Malpractice recognition: This refers to the identification or acknowledgement of a breach of duty by any professional who fails to follow accepted standards when undertaking his/her contractual obligations. Medical malpractice is professional negligence by a doctor, medical staff or provider. If the treatment provided is below the industry standards, it can cause harm, injury or death to a patient.

Accounting and financial disclosure: This refers to the requirement of revealing all information pertinent to any transaction involving the accounts and finances of any organization or undertaking.

Tax system: The country in which you will receive medical treatment should have properly established laws governing medical tourisms along with a legal body to enforce the laws. These rules and regulations must be in favor of the protection of the patient and a proper tax system. Prior to agreeing to any consent forms provided by the hospital abroad, ensure that you have all the terms and conditions in writing in order to avoid any complications later. If you have any doubts regarding the conditions, it is better to consult a specialist medical lawyer.

If you do not find the prescribed terms and conditions satisfactory, you should never sign the agreement. If you have selected a package deal through a facilitator, make sure to protect yourself by guaranteeing that the medical cost includes covering any expenses for medical complications that might arise. The consent form provided by the hospital should reflect the same. Ask about your rights regarding legal actions and make sure to check and read the agreement carefully before signing.

Humans can make mistakes. Since physicians or surgeons are still likely to make errors, the patients should be familiar with the legal remedies related to medical malpractice. It is also important for you to find out whether the legal body of your home country can take legitimate action against the healthcare provider of another country. Clear all your doubts regarding who will be liable or held responsible in case of any mishaps or the medical complications – the treating doctor or the hospital's medical staff.

Some clinics have jurisdiction clauses in their agreement to protect themselves from being sued by the internationally traveling patients or the local patients. You should inquire about the possibility of receiving a refund in case you plan to cancel the surgery or the doctor decides not to perform the treatment. Before you sign the agreement, you should follow certain steps to ensure the quality of service available at the treating facility.

- Inquire about the qualifications of the doctors/surgeons you are consulting and their experience.
- Read the terms and conditions of the medical insurance and the limits to the policy
- Find out what international standards the medical facility meets
- Ask to review any available records or reports of pending lawsuits against the medical staff
- Find out the liability that the medical staff will assume in case of malpractice or errors
- Ask for the average payout as compensation in case of any error

Receiving medical treatment in an unfamiliar country may subject an internationally traveling patient to different legal issues. Since it might be difficult for you to understand the legal system of a foreign country completely, you can always consider searching and hiring a legal representative from the host country.

A prospective medical tourist should also be aware of possible legal issues. There is presently no international legal regulation of medical tourism. All medical procedures have an element of risk. The issue of legal recourse for unsatisfactory treatment across international boundaries is a legally undefined issue at present.

CHAPTER 26

Understanding the Quality, Safety & Security of a Hospital and Patient Rights

IN THIS CHAPTER

- Understanding the importance and benefits of accreditation
- Accreditation examples from around the world
- The necessity of appropriate safety and security at a hospital or clinic
- Learning about the various patient rights you have at a medical facility

ACCREDITATION

According to the guidelines of the Joint Commission International, the term accreditation is "a process" through which an entity, separate and distinct from the healthcare organization, usually nongovernmental, assesses the healthcare organization to determine if it meets a set of requirements (standards), designed to improve the safety and quality of care.

Accreditation facilities need healthcare providers to go through rigorous tests and preparations in order to receive the stamp of accreditation. A healthcare facility with these credentials is definitely committed to patient safety and care. Such healthcare facilities try to do everything that they can to ensure a safe and caring environment for their patients.

The doctors here are highly qualified and the infrastructure is regularly updated with the latest in technology. Hospitals and clinics, which implement these high levels of quality and standards, continually strive to improve their facilities. Usually, these hospitals and healthcare facilities develop continuous improvement programs for their staff, and utilize all patient evaluation data, which can be used to improve their organization.

Benefits of an accredited hospital

- **Improving public trust**

Since potential medical tourists normally check the credentials of a healthcare facility before they choose it, a healthcare facility that clearly displays the accreditation certificate on their webpage demonstrates its quality. This certification displays the facility's willingness to implement standards that are based around patient safety and quality care, thus also helping patients in their decision making process.

- **Providing an environment that enhances the provider's satisfaction**

An accredited healthcare facility is not just beneficial for the patients and medical tourists, but also benefits the doctors. Good and experienced healthcare professionals want to work in a facility that they know is investing a lot of time and money in training and education. Moreover, in such facilities, healthcare professionals are able to use the latest equipment, while continuously updating their knowledge.

- **Providing clear and transparent data to patients**

During the selection phase of a healthcare facility, all potential medical tourists want to gain as much information about the facility as possible. Accredited healthcare facilities normally share data with the public, which can help patients differentiate between the best hospitals and the rest. Gaining access to information is a crucial factor in any potential medical tourist's decision of where to seek care, as this could easily affect his/her entire life.

- **Respecting the patient's opinions**

Accredited hospitals pay great attention to patient opinions and surveys, and try to implement all their suggestions for the betterment of the facility and all future patients.

• Creating a culture of learning and sharing

A better hospital is one that implements a culture of sharing and learning, has doctors and staff members who keep fewer secrets and surprises. As every error made is an opportunity to learn something new, steps can easily be taken to learn from past mistakes, promoting the growth of the hospital.

ACCREDITATION EXAMPLES FROM AROUND THE WORLD:

Since different healthcare facilities around the world have different criteria and guidelines to follow, accreditation processes differ as well. Here are some examples of accreditation in different countries.

- In the United States, healthcare facilities have to follow strict guidelines set up by an accreditation agency called Joint Commission on Accreditation of Healthcare Organizations. The JCAHO is a private, non-profit organization, which has accredited over 17,000 healthcare organizations and programs. This shows how committed these accredited facilities are in providing quality healthcare to their patients.
- The World Health Organization ranks France as having the best healthcare system in the world, and extremely high rates of patient satisfaction. In France, the "La Haute Autorite de Sante" gives accreditation, which is a local government accreditation body.
- In the United Kingdom, the Healthcare Accreditation and Quality Unit accredit healthcare facilities. The HAQU, which was previously known as the Health Quality Service, specializes in the administration of healthcare organizations and facilities, while making sure that all these facilities implement appropriate regulations for effective management.
- South Africa has contracted with the Council for Health Services Accreditation System of Southern Africa, a non-profit organization that implements the accreditation policies in the nation.
- Canada, along the lines of South Africa, has implemented a similar procedure whereby the government has contracted with Accreditation Canada, an independent body, which operates in a manner similar to JCI.
- In India, which is a growing medical tourism destination, healthcare facilities are accredited by a local institution called the National Accreditation Board for Hospitals (NABH). The organization works under the Quality Council of India (QCI), which works to ensure the quality of healthcare within the country.

HOW CAN A PATIENT EVALUATE THE QUALITY OF A HOSPITAL?

Although accreditation proves the quality of healthcare delivered to patients by the doctors of a hospital, patients can evaluate the quality of a hospital themselves. Even if any healthcare facility that you are planning to visit for your treatment has not been accredited by a renowned organization, there are certain criteria that can help a patient evaluate whether they demonstrate a high level of quality or not. Here we look at 10 such factors:

- Affiliation with an international organization, such as Johns Hopkins or Harvard Medical School
- The level of communication efforts the hospital invests for its patients.
- The healthcare provider's commitment to continuous improvement and culture of sharing
- How much they ask you to participate with their medical team to share feedback. Furthermore, how much they respect your opinions and take them seriously
- The level of personalized and individualized care offered
- The track record of infection control within the healthcare facility
- Outcomes and success rates of the treatments offered by the healthcare professionals in the facility
- The presence of a comprehensive system that deals with complaints and suggestions from the patients in an appropriate way
- A safe and secure location for the facility
- Encouragement of a healing atmosphere with the use of natural light and greenery

SAFETY AND SECURITY

Once patients enter the gate of a healthcare facility, they feel vulnerable, as their lives are in the hands of the healthcare professionals. Therefore, the only concern they should have in a hospital is how they are going to recover from their illness, without having to worry about their personal safety. The safety and security of all patients is the responsibility of the management of the facility, and they have to make sure that they implement proper protocols to ensure the protection and security of the patients. Although patients do not have to worry about their own safety in a healthcare facility, executives on duty should educate patients about the process of judging the level of security in the facility. As a patient, one of the first things you should do is to understand the entire facility management system of the hospital. The facility management system involves a number of factors, some of which are listed below:

THE HOSPITAL BUILDING

While inspecting the hospital building you should evaluate and rate the building on the following factors:

- Look for the presence of facilities for handicapped individuals, or for patients who are currently undergoing treatment and require additional assistance in physical activities.
- The level of hygiene that is maintained throughout the entire hospital premises.
- Check if the hospital has a good security system, which should include guards on duty and an electronic alarm and surveillance system. The presence of a good security system will ensure that the patients in the facility remain in a secure environment.

PATIENT IDENTIFICATION

You should ensure that the healthcare facility gives a unique patient identification card or number to all their patients. The importance of unique patient identification cannot be underestimated, as any error in identifying the patient and his or her requirements could prove to be life threatening.

COMMUNICATION

Communication between the doctor, staff members, and the patient plays an extremely important role in all steps of the treatment procedure. You must ensure that the hospital authorities provide you with information that is in a language you can clearly understand, failing which they should provide you with translator services.

In addition, there needs to be a healthy two-way communication between the patient and the doctor. While the doctor will instruct you on certain guidelines, it is your responsibility and the responsibility of your companion to make sure that you adhere to all these guidelines for the betterment of your health. Furthermore, you should ensure that all papers concerning the course of your treatment, billing and other consent letters are put down in writing and signed.

PRECAUTIONARY MEASURES AGAINST INFECTIONS

You must make sure that the healthcare facility meets international standards for precautionary measures against infectious diseases. Global organizations such as the World Health Organization and the CDC have clear-cut specifications regarding the hygiene and spread of infections in hospital premises. Patients should not go for hospitals that fail to meet the globally recognized standards.

LIFE SAFETY SYSTEMS

Natural disasters can strike at any place and at any time. Although nobody can prevent such disasters from occurring, nor can anybody forecast these disasters, you should choose a hospital or healthcare facility that is well equipped to handle both natural and manmade disasters. Some of the safety measures that you should look for in a hospital are adequate fire safety measures, protection against lightning, and other natural disasters.

SECURITY TIPS A PATIENT MUST TAKE NOTE OF

- When you enter the premises of the healthcare facility, you should always remember that you are solely responsible for your personal items. It is advisable that you either avoid carrying expensive items, which you will not need during hospitalization, or give them to your companion or family members for safekeeping.
- You should always be ready to cooperate with the doctors and the nursing staff.
- Always ensure that you do not roam around in the hospital at night, as it might be dangerous, especially if you are under medication that causes drowsiness.

SECURITY RESPONSIBILITIES THAT THE HOSPITAL AUTHORITIES MUST MAINTAIN

- The hospital must be under protection of security guards and each room well connected with a centralized emergency alert system.
- The hospital should be a completely no smoking zone.
- Although many hospitals attach telemetry transmitters to patients so that the hospital staff can easily track them, you should always remember that it is your responsibility to stay within the confines of the hospital.
- All reputed hospitals in renowned medical tourism destinations should regularly practice mock drills for handling disasters. Fire safety should also be given prime importance by the hospital staff.
- Both the patient and the hospital staff should ensure that you get only those drugs that are prescribed by the physician. Also check that nursing staff administers the correct doses at the right time and the drugs are procured from reliable sources.

PATIENT RIGHTS

Patients, including medical tourists, have certain rights when they are in the confines of the hospital. These rights highlight the quality of the healthcare facility and its essence and hence, both the patient and the healthcare provider should exercise these rights to ensure quality treatment and care.

You should check that the hospital should provide you with a document carrying the patient rights. You may even ask hospital authorities to paste the same document on the hospital walls.

GUIDELINES OF PATIENT RIGHTS AS DESCRIBED BY THE AMERICAN MEDICAL ASSOCIATION

- The right to receive information from physicians and doctors, and the right to discuss the benefits, risks and costs of the appropriate treatment alternatives
- The right to make decisions regarding the treatment options that the physician is recommending
- The right to courtesy, respect, dignity, responsiveness and timely attention of all healthcare needs
- The right to confidentiality
- The right to receive continuity of care
- The right to receive complete information regarding the cost of the entire treatment, without any hidden costs

SPEAKING UP

One of the biggest misconceptions that almost all patients have is that they believe that within the confines of the healthcare facility, their opinion does not count and they are completely in the control of the healthcare professionals in charge. However, the fact here is that the more you speak up with the healthcare professionals during consultation, the better it will be during the course of the treatment.

You should always remain honest during every interaction with the healthcare provider, which includes the doctors, nurses and lab technicians. The more you speak about your current condition, the better care will you be receiving. In addition to being honest, you should always try to clear your doubts regarding anything. Moreover, as physicians often use medical terms, which not many patients can understand, you have the right to ask questions until the time you are completely satisfied with the response.

Furthermore, the patient should also be in a position to speak his/her mind, during patient satisfaction surveys and customer feedback forms. You should try to find out ways by which your response and feedback can be utilized to improve facilities for all future patients. All reputed healthcare facilities should provide patients with some survey or feedback forms, where patients can document their stay at the hospital. It is your responsibility to fill out all details honestly. Try to ascertain that the hospital staff and management take notes of these surveys and forms, and are always open to make changes in their system for the benefit of all patients.

The patient's safety and the challenges of seeking care in another country are significant and require careful consideration. Although some medical tourism firms suggest relaxing destinations and amenities, high quality care and patient safety must always be top priorities. It is important to remember that despite medical breakthroughs and an ever-expanding knowledge base, providing safe, high quality care is a challenge for each and every health care organization around the world.

The measurement of customer satisfaction has become very important for the health care sector also. The concept of customer satisfaction has encouraged the adoption of a marketing culture in the health care sector in both developed and developing countries. As large numbers of hospitals are opening their doors, and people are becoming more aware and conscious of health, great competition has emerged in this industry.

Destination Guide

■ ARGENTINA

General	
Language	Spanish
Time Zone	GMT -3
Dialing Code	+54
Electricity	220V, 50Hz
Medical Tourism Status	Buenos Aires, Córdoba, Rosario
Currency	Peso
Clothing	Take lightweight clothes you can layer, a sweater and an all -weather coat.
Health Related	
Mortality Rate	7.4 deaths/ 1,000 live births
Life Expectancy	M 72.5/ F 79.1
Patient: Physician Ratio	330: 1
Hospitals JCI accredited	
Recommended Vaccinations	Hepatitis A, Typhoid, Hepatitis B, Rabies, Diphtheria-teta- nus, Measles, Varicella, Poliomyelitis, Yellow fever
Other Infections	Chagas disease, Argentine hemorrhagic fever, St. Louis en-cephalitis, West Nile virus infections, Tick-borne relapsing fever, Anthrax, HIV

Tourism Related			
Population	41,660,417	Reliability of Police Services	130/140
Global Competitiveness	3.87/7	Physician Density	3.2/140
Tourism Competitiveness	4.2/7	Hospital Beds	45/140
GDP/Capita	18,112	Quality of Air Transport Infrastructure	113/140
Health and Hygiene	5.8/7	International Air Transport Network	96/140
Safety and Security	4.5/7	Quality of Roads	104/140
Air Transport Infrastructure	3.1/7	Hotel Rooms	55/140
Tourism Infrastructure	4.3/7	Tourism Openness	108/140
Cultural Infrastructure	3.3/7	Attitude of Population Towards Foreign Visitors	113/140
Visa Requirements	27/140		

Argentina is a one-stop destination for those who wish to explore the ethnically rich Spanish culture, its various music forms, dance styles, architectural diversity and luscious food. Argentina's climatic conditions create a perfect background that urges adventure seekers to indulge in hiking in the rainforests, skiing and trekking in the glaciers. Further, visitors may enjoy the rich culture and history while participating in eco-tours, enjoying several delicacies, exploring amazing nightlife along with camping and diving.

Location

Argentina shares its borders with Uruguay, Brazil, Paraguay, Bolivia and Chile. The world's eighth largest country, Argentina provides shelter to no less than 41.6 million people. Lush rainforests, sweeping plains, white capped glaciers, underwater geography and a comprehensive portfolio of amazing tourist attractions make Argentina a perfect tourist destination. The country further offers itself as the gateway to one of the most scintillating yet uninhabited places on earth – Antarctica.

Tourism

The capital city Buenos Aires was the first city on the entire South American continent that ever surpassed one million inhabitants. Known as Tango and Paris of South America, the city enjoys the highest international repute among other South American cities. You would find quite a number of European immigrants here who have successfully survived several crises and managed to make Buenos Aires the cultural and political capital of the nation. The capital city flaunts exciting nightlife, and a wide range of tourism related amenities in tandem with a rich history to keep visitors interested through their explorative jaunts. Further, tourist friendly locals demonstrate unyielding spirit, energy and tenacious passion for life.

Thrill seekers will not find any other tourist destination more suitable than Argentina to soothe their fancies. The second largest city, Córdoba, the third largest city, Rosario and the fourth largest one, Mendoza, have tremendous scope for tourism.

Those who have that latent desire to explore flora and fauna would find the jungles of northern Iguazu Falls National Park and the wild terrains of Tierra del Fuego extremely soothing and indicative of pristine natural beauty. Both these attractions draw large crowds when compared to other parts of the country. Aside from touting an ethereal landscape of enchanting proportions, the Iguazu National Park also allows visitors to be conversant with diverse animal and plant life. Thanks to the free flowing Rio piranha that makes the Iguazu Falls four times wider and half the height of Niagara, it is now included in the UNESCO Heritage Sites' list.

Allowing visitors to travel around the immense eastern plains and explore the impressive Andes mountain range to the west that further has the highest peak in the Western Hemisphere at 6,959 meters; Argentina, undeniably, is a paradise on earth. Those who seek variety while traveling would feel more than pleased to visit Jujuy and Tierra del Fuego in the Andes, the Northwest plateaus, the lake region, the forests and glaciers in the Patagonia.

Climate

Climate always plays a vital role in sustaining tourism related activities. Argentina flaunts different climatic conditions like subtropical in the North, sub-Antarctic in the southern Patagonia and mild and humid in the Pampas plains. The median temperature from November to March is 23° C, which is quite suitable to embark on sightseeing spree. From June to September, the median temperature remains at 12° C.

Medical Tourism in Argentina

Notwithstanding the collapse of Peso in 2002, the medical tourism industry stayed unaffected and has been on the rise since then. Since US dollar grew stronger, the North Americans opted to travel to Argentina for cost-effective medical treatments. Similar to its other South American counterparts, clinics and hospitals in Buenos Aires offer excellent cosmetic and dental procedures without asking patients to shell out a fortune for it.

Exhibiting a definitive intent to break the language barrier, Buenos Aires has several English-speaking physicians and surgeons who can converse with medical tourists with no trouble. Thus, while receiving excellent yet affordable healthcare, medical travelers may also enjoy an unparalleled vacation in Argentina.

Healthcare System

The Ministry of Health and Social Action oversees the healthcare infrastructure in Argentina. Consisting of a three-tier system, i.e. the public sector, the private sector and the Obras Sociales, an organization representing the Argentina's work unions, the healthcare system promises to offer the best medical treatment to visitors.

While the public sector relies on taxes for financing, the private sector sustains its growth on its own. The private sector, which represents over 200 medical facilities across the nation, provides quality healthcare to about two million Argentines. The third component, i.e. Obras Sociales, counts on health insurance funds to offer quality healthcare to employees.

Quality of Healthcare

Owing to high quality medical facilities and foreign trained, highly qualified physicians, Buenos Aires outshines all other Argentine cities when it comes to offering the best medical care. Medical tourists can avail the finest, the most affordable and advanced surgical and wellness options in the capital city.

However, if you move out of the capital city, the quality of healthcare suffers a serious decline. Medical facilities, especially in rural areas, do not have the latest medical equipment available and hence, they do not offer equivalent, high quality healthcare services when compared to urban centers.

■ ARMENIA

General	
Language	Armenian
Time Zone	UTC (UTC+4)
Dialing Code	+374
Major Cities	Yerevan, Gyumri, Vagharshapat, Armavir, Ashtarak
Currency	Dram
Clothing	Summers are dry and sunny and Winters are quite cold with plenty of snow so warm and light clothes are recommended as per the season

Health Related	
Mortality Rate	8.49 deaths/ 1000 population
Life Expectancy	67.2M /75.1F
Patient: Physician Ratio	270:1
Recommended Vaccinations	Hepatitis A, Hepatitis B, Rabies
Other Infections	HIV

Tourism Related			
Population	3,262,200	Physician Density	12/140
Global Competitiveness	4.41/7	Hospital Beds	47/140
Tourism Competitiveness	4.0/7	Quality of Air Transport Infrastructure	69/140
GDP/Capita	$5,838	International Air Transport Network	92/140
Safety and Security	5.3 /7	Quality of Roads	79/140
Health and Hygiene	5.9/7	Hotel Rooms	111/140
Air Transport Infrastructure	2.7/7	Tourism Openness	26/140
Tourism Infrastructure	3.4/7	Attitude of Population Towards Foreign Visitors	95/140
Cultural Infrastructure	2.1/7		

Steeped in rich history and culture, the Republic of Armenia is a truly wondrous destination offering visitors the right blend of civilization and beautiful natural attractions. Located in Eurasia (the South Caucasus region), the country sits on mountainous terrain, and is bordered by Turkey, Georgia, Nagorno-Karabakh Republic, Azerbaijan, Iran and Nakhchivan (the Azerbaijani exclave).

In addition to the Armenians who make up most of the country's population, Armenia comprises several ethnic groups like Russians, Azerbaijanis, and Kurds. Although fiercely protective of their culture and traditions, the people of Armenia are a friendly lot who love everything about music. Though the country has become urban to an extent, the diverse cultural backgrounds provide a conservative streak that keeps the balance perfect.

The country enjoys a continental climate with sunny, dry summers (from June to September). However, the low humidity levels allow some freshness to enter the city in the form of cool breezes that blow in from the mountains. Otherwise, the springs are short, the autumns are pretty long and colorful and the winters are cold wherein temperatures fall up to -10 °C.

Events and festivals

A rich history and diverse cultural background enable Armenians to enjoy a wide variety of festivals throughout the year. Some of the more prominent festivals celebrated in the country include New Year, Independence Day, Christmas, Kids' Day, Remembrance Day, One Nation One Culture Day, Yerevan International Film Festival "Golden Aprico", Vartavar, Extreme Sports Festival, "High Fest" International Theater Festival, Bread in the Mountains, Tolma Festival, Barbeque Festival and the Areni Wine Festival.

Medical Tourism in Armenia

Armenia is home to more than 350 groups of natural mineral springs, the benefits of which are reaped by several spas, health resorts and sanatoriums located in these areas. These health resorts offer some of the best health care facilities in the country, including the best medical equipment, medical personnel and customer service.

Armenia has become a popular destination for dental tourism these days. Medical tourists can get the best dental treatment possible (including the latest medical technology and highly experienced doctors) at affordable prices, even if they do not have any dental insurance at all.

Healthcare System

Recent years have seen a dramatic increase in the quality of healthcare facilities and services in Armenia. For instance, The Yereavan State Medical University produces some of the finest doctors and nurses to practice in several hospitals in the country. The University Clinic Hospital N3 also happens to be one of the best healthcare facilities in Armenia. The hospital has tie ups with several smaller medical facilities like the Clinic of Children Surgery and the Pediatric Clinic.

■ AUSTRALIA

General	
Language	English
Time Zone	GMT(+8 to +10) summer(DST) (GMT+8 to +11)
Dialing Code	+61
Electricity	240V, 50Hz
Medical Tourism Status	Sydney, Melbourne, Brisbane
Currency	Australian dollar
Clothing	Due to Australia's warm climate, common summer clothing is often comprised of shorts, sleeveless shirts and thongs (footwear which is the equivalent of American flipflops)

Health Related	
Mortality Rate	5.8 deaths/ 1,000 live births
Life Expectancy	80M / 84.3F
Patient: Physician Ratio	400: 1
Hospitals JCI accredited	0
Recommended Vaccinations	Rabies, Yellow Fever, Japanese encephalitis, Diphtheria-tetanus, Measles and Varicella
Other Infections	Leptospirosis, Queensland tick typhus, Scrub typhus, Barmah Forest virus, Flinder's Island spotted fever, Jellyfish stings, HIV

Tourism Related			
Population	23,170,982	Reliability of Police Services	16/140
Global Competitiveness	5.11/7	Physician Density	32/140
Tourism Competitiveness	5.41/7	Hospital Beds	45/140
GDP/Capita	67,722	Quality of Air Transport Infrastructure	29/140
Health and Hygiene	5.9/7	International Air Transport Network	24/140
Safety and Security	6.0/7	Quality of Roads	36/140
Air Transport Infrastructure	5.9/7	Hotel Rooms	32/140
Tourism Infrastructure	5.9/7	Tourism Openness	80/140
Cultural Infrastructure	5.2/7	Attitude of Population Towards Foreign Visitors	27/140
Visa Requirements	112/140		

Australia, also known as the land of plenty, enjoys the dual status of being the world's smallest continent and the sixth largest country by area. Tourists love visiting this prime tourist destination that flaunts a plethora of natural and manmade attractions. Australia's most popular tourist destinations include Sydney Harbor Bridge, Fraser Island, Great Barrier Reef, Scenic World, Kakadu National Park, Sydney Opera House, Port Arthur and National Gallery of Australia. National parks, tropical rainforests, galleries and museums make Australia the perfect place to explore.

Aside from being one of the oldest cities of Australia, Sydney represents the Aussie lifestyle and culture. Undeniably, it is the economic powerhouse of the nation. Adorned with shady avenues, parks and skyscrapers, Melbourne is the second largest city of Australia.

Location

Australia is a unique destination for those who wish to explore its wilderness area, mountain ranges, waterways and dramatic landscape. Avid surfers feel like heaven as they hit the shores of one of the world's premier surfing destinations. Blessed with beaches, coral reefs and point breaks, Australia's 37,000 km shoreline has always attracted thrill seekers.

Speckled with a million and a half hectares of rocky landscape, which further includes national parks, protected areas and alpine environment, Australia is home to several, exceptional plant and animal species. Anyone, who loves reveling in the call of the wild, would love to see the marine environment, lush green forests, fertile terrains and rich wildlife thriving in Australia.

People

Aussies are friendly people who believe in having congenial relations with tourists. They have always welcomed visitors with open arms. Since they are jovial people, they love wearing relaxed and casual clothes. Unless it is highly required or the occasion demands it, you won't see them adorning their persona with formal attires. The people of Australia are primarily of Irish or British ethnic origin.

Events

The Australian events calendar includes several regional festivals and major sporting events as well, which allows a distinct blitheness and diversity to Australia's rich culture. December marks the official start of the Aussie summer and the festival season as well. If you are visiting or planning to visit Australia in December, you are most likely to see Aussies kicking off their shoes, kicking up their heels and toe tapping in various local and international festivals.

You cannot afford to miss the Tour Down Under, the Australian Open, Melbourne Food and Wine Festival, Sydney Royal Easter Show, Melbourne Cup Carnival, and the New Years Eve.

Weather

Covered by sand dunes, Australia's 40 percent landmass is desert or semi-arid. As you head towards southeastern or southwestern Australia, the desert makes way for a rather temperate climate and moderately fertile soil. The northern part of the country has a tropical climate, which further varies between tropical rainforests and grasslands; nonetheless, it's part desert as well. Rainfall is highly variable. Dust storms blanket a particular region or several states several times a year.

Medical Tourism in Australia

Australia ranks quite high among several major players of medical tourism industry. Thanks to beautiful locale, high quality healthcare infrastructure and excellent medical facilities, Australia has become one of the most preferred medial tourism destinations. With no language or cultural barriers to discourage visitors, Australia attracts medical tourists from countries around the world.

Considering all wellness tourists as medical tourists would be a gross injustice to the term Medical Tourism, Australia does not offer medical tourism in an organized way. Rather, people visiting Australia lay great emphasis on wellness tourism. Hence, the international inbound visitors who come to Australia to improve their health constitute a major chunk of medical tourists.

Healthcare System

Healthcare in Australia, better known as Medicare, is a combined responsibility of both the public and private sector. This mixed system gathers necessary finances mainly out of tax revenue, with the government contributing 70 percent, and the rest provided by private pay and insurance.

Medicare covers all Australians citizens who pay the entire cost of the treatment in a public hospital. It also reimburses the expenses toward visits to the doctors. The majority of healthcare facilities belong to the public sector (public hospitals have about 70 percent of beds and major teaching facilities). Those who prefer to choose private care gain access to private healthcare insurance; however, they are likely to pay more when compared to public sector.

Quality of Healthcare

A recent international comparison claims that the Australian healthcare system ranks either first or second on several health indicators. Australia further promotes healthy living. In general, the quality of healthcare in Australia in both public and private sectors is excellent when adjudged from the perspective of patients and providers.

The government-supported care provides their citizens with all-inclusive healthcare, while the private sector fills in the gap for any lacking facilities by providing an overall comprehensive care. The major Australian teaching hospitals have significant research profiles and the care is, undeniably, first-rate. Suburban and rural hospitals provide high-quality healthcare to medical tourists.

■ AUSTRIA

General	
Language	German
Time Zone	CET (UTC+01) CEST (UTC+02)
Dialing Code	+43
Electricity	220V-60Hz
Major Cities	Vienna, Salzburg, Leonding, Leoben
Currency	Euro
Clothing	Summers are warm and sunny, where as winters are very cold. Clothing should be kept accordingly.
Health Related	
Mortality Rate	10.23 deaths/ 1,000 population
Life Expectancy	78.3M /83F
Hospitals JCI accredited	2
Recommended Vaccinations	Hepatitis B
Other Infections	HIV

Tourism Related			
Population	8,414,638	Physician Density	2/140
Global Competitiveness	5.27/7	Hospital Beds	6/140
Tourism Competitiveness	5.4/7	Quality of Air Transport Infrastructure	31/140
GDP/Capita	$42,408	International Air Transport Network	27/140
Safety and Security	6.1/7	Quality of Roads	7/140
Health and Hygiene	7.0/7	Hotel Rooms	4/140
Air Transport Infrastructure	4.4/7	Tourism Openness	34/140
Tourism Infrastructure	7.0/7	Attitude of Population Towards Foreign Visitors	5/140
Cultural Infrastructure	5.9/7		

Located on alpine terrain in Central Europe, Austria is a federal republic situated along the Alpine mountain range. As such, only a small portion of the country lies below 500 meters while the highest point is located at 3,798 meters.

Austria enjoys a temperate, alpine climate throughout the year. The friendly locals speak Bavarian dialects pertaining to the country's official language, German. Other common languages spoken include Slovene, Hungarian, and Burgenland Croatian.

Events and Festivals

Austria celebrates more than 200 festivals every year, with most of them related to music and theater. Some of the more prominent festivals, apart from the public holidays like New Year, Christmas and Easter, include the New Year's Concert, Mozart Week, Johann Strauss Ball, Easter Music Festival, Arlberg Eagle, Wiener Festwochen, Vienna City Festival, Roman Week, Old Town Magic, Rupertikirday, Klangbogen Festival, Schlossberg Festival, International Ski Countdown, and Christmas Markets.

Medical Tourism in Austria

Austria happens to be one of the most popular medical tourism destinations in Europe, with health and wellness being its forte. The country has several world famous medical clinics, holistic wellness centers, rehabilitation centers and natural mineral spas that offer the best in terms of technology, services and customer care for patients arriving from Europe and beyond.

Healthcare System

Austria's healthcare system is state of the art, with several private clinics employing the best medical personnel in their respective fields. The clinics are also well maintained and hygienic, and house the best in infrastructure facilities and medical equipment.

Some of the more popular treatments that can be availed in Austria include cosmetic surgery (facial and body), elective surgery, cosmetic dentistry, obesity surgery, reconstructive surgery and cancer treatment. Most of the treatments for these procedures would only cost a fraction of what they cost in countries like the US or the UK. Austria's successful tryst with traditional preventive medications also helps reduce infection rates and quicken up the recovery process after a procedure.

Additional highlights that contribute to Austria's increasing popularity as a medical tourism destination include immediate surgery options, personal consultation with trained staff, short consultation periods, short waiting lists, quality post-operative care and excellent rehabilitation programs for quick recovery.

Couple all these factors with low healthcare costs and very promising results (very high success rates), and Austria would no doubt emerge as a clear frontrunner for most of the "Best Medical Tourism Destinations" polls and lists.

■ BAHRAIN

General	
Language	Arabic
Time Zone	AST (UTC+3)
Dialing Code	+973
Major Cities	Manama, Riffa, Muharraq, Hamad Town, A'ali, Isa Town
Currency	Bahraini dinar
Clothing	summers are very hot and dry with high humidity, Rainfalls mostly occur in winter

Health Related	
Mortality Rate	10.23 deaths/ 1,000 population
Life Expectancy	77.7M /80.1F
Hospitals JCI accredited	1
Recommended Vaccinations	Hepatitis A, Hepatitis B, Typhoid
Other Infections	HIV

Tourism Related			
Population	1,234,571	Physician Density	76/140
Global Competitiveness	4.63/7	Hospital Beds	87/140
Tourism Competitiveness	4.3/7	Quality of Air Transport Infrastructure	16/140
GDP/Capita	$27,556	International Air Transport Network	13/140
Safety and Security	5.2/7	Quality of Roads	18/140
Health and Hygiene	4.2/7	Hotel Rooms	46/140
Air Transport Infrastructure	4.2/7	Tourism Openness	38/140
Tourism Infrastructure	4.2/7	Attitude of Population Towards Foreign Visitors	20/140
Cultural Infrastructure	2.5/7		

Located quite close to the western shores of the Persian Gulf, Bahrain aka The Kingdom of Bahrain is an island country. The country is connected to Saudi Arabia in the west via the King Fahd Causeway. Bahrain is an Islamic country, with most of its residents being native Arabs. The country also has a small population of Christians, and a comparatively large population of South Asian expatriates.

Dust storms are common in Bahrain, with the northwesterly winds (called Shamal winds) bringing them from Saudi and Iraq. These winds would cause reduced visibility between

June and July. Summers in the country also tend to be very hot, dry and humid with very little rainfall, most of which occurs only in winter.

Events and festivals

Being an Islamic country, Bahrain follows all religious festivals pertaining to the Islamic lunar calendar. These include Muharram, Ashura, Milad Al Nabi, Ramadan, Eid Al Fitr, Eid Al Watani and Eid Al Adha. The country also celebrates other festivals like the Independence Day, National Day, Chinese Trade Fair Association Day, Jewelry Arabia Show and the Gulf Jazz Festival on an annual basis.

Medical Tourism in Bahrain

Of late, the government of Bahrain is taking measures to tap into the medical tourism market by establishing a dedicated medical tourism sector that would provide facilities, which cannot be availed anywhere else in the entire region. Land has been set aside for health care projects while international branches have been added to existing medical facilities. The government of Bahrain hopes that these measures would increase the influx of medical tourism patients to the country in the coming years.

Healthcare System

The quality of healthcare has increased substantially over the past few years in Bahrain, with many public and private healthcare facilities boasting of having standards at par with those available in hospitals in the US and UK.

Most of the highly skilled doctors practicing in Bahrain are not native citizens, but foreigners with several years of experience behind them. The quality of treatment and service is also high, with minimal waiting periods for consultations and procedures. Most of the hospitals catering to medical tourists also boast of having the best infrastructure and medical services, thereby increasing the success rates of medical treatments and procedures largely.

The national public health system present in Bahrain enables locals and expatriates to avail health care services/treatments free or for very low charges. Medical tourists arriving at the country for treatments can also access the services offered by the public health care system, even if they do not have medical insurance.

■ BARBADOS

General	
Language	English, Bajan
Time Zone	Eastern Caribbean (GMT-4)
Dialing Code	+1 -246
Electricity	115V, 50Hz
Major Cities	Bridgetown, Speightstwon, Oistins, Bathsheba
Currency	Barbadian Dollar
Clothing	Shorts, light clothing for the warm tropical island temperatures
Health Related	
Mortality Rate	11.63 deaths/ 1,000 live births
Life Expectancy	74.6M / 80.4F
Hospitals JCI accredited	1
Recommended Vaccinations	Hepatitis A, Yellow fever, Hepatitis B, MMR, Diphtheria-tet- anus
Other Infections	Dengue fever, Leptospirosis, HIV

Tourism Related			
Population	274,200	Reliability of Police Services	24/140
Global Competitiveness	5.09/7	Physician Density	65/140
Tourism Competitiveness	4.84/7	Hospital Beds	12/140
GDP/Capita	25,372	Quality of Air Transport Infrastructure	8/140
Health and Hygiene	6.0/7	International Air Transport Network	16/140
Safety and Security	5.5/7	Quality of Roads	33/140
Air Transport Infrastructure	4.4/7	Hotel Rooms	7/140
Tourism Infrastructure	5.6/7	Tourism Openness	4/140
Cultural Infrastructure	3.0/7	Attitude of Population Towards Foreign Visitors	11/140
Visa Requirements	6/140		

Despite its small size, Barbados offers plenty to travelers who love exploring frothy beachfronts, playing with sand and paragliding over the sea waves. In recent years, Barbados has emerged on the tourism scene as it successfully blended the tenets of medical tourism and wellness tourism with the niche travel business. The island country is an exciting place to be at, especially since a nice stay here combines vacations with several health benefits.

Thanks to white sand beaches and stunning blue waters, it won't be an exaggeration to call this destination a tiny paradise.

However, if you think Barbados simply offers just some beaches and beach activities, you definitely need a reality check. Aside from flaunting unbelievable beach beauty, the country also lures visitors with diverse flavors, cultures, tourist destinations and festivals. Also known as the Atlantic Island, Barbados is one of the Caribbean's leading tourist destinations and the most developed islands in the region.

Location

As mentioned earlier, Barbados is a small country with 431 sq km area. Strategically located to the east of the Caribbean Sea and the Windward Islands, and the west of the North Atlantic, the island country did not have to suffer the wrath of the principal Atlantic hurricanes even during the hyperactive period (1400 BCE to 1000 CE).

People

Barbados is home to around 300,000 people, who primarily are of Afro-bajan, Asian, multiracial or European origin. Ever since Barbados gained independence from the British rule in 1966, the lifestyle of native inhabitants has been on a constant rise. The post-independence era also led to better cultural changes within the country. Exhibiting the Caribbean way of life, Barbadian are jovial and fun loving people who enjoy gathering around to celebrate various occasions and festivities around the year.

Events

Rightly known as the Caribbean's cultural capital, Barbados is famous for hosting several events and festivals. Be it the annual Barbados Crop Over, the Barbados Jazz Festival, Holetown Festival, Holder's Season, Oistins Fish Festival or the Gospelfest, one cannot afford to miss any of these festivals and events. If you plan to travel Barbados in November, do not forget to be a part of the Barbados Independence Day festivities and the Barbados Food & Wine and Rum Festival. Therefore, you can expect parties or festive celebrations going on throughout the year.

Weather

Being outside the principal hurricane strike zone, the country is comparatively safer than the other Caribbean countries. The average temperature ranges from 21 to 31°C (70 to 88 °F) from December to May (the dry season); however, between June and November, i.e. the wet season, it ranges from 23 to 31 °C (73 to 88 °F). While Barbadians experience higher rainfall during the wet season, the dry season has comparatively less rainfall. The flowing trade winds bring steady breeze to the mainland, which helps in lowering the temperature to a considerable extent.

Medical Tourism in Barbados

Medical tourists from all over the world visit Barbados for medical procedures like dialysis and open-heart surgery. Aside from getting the desired medical treatment, medical tourists can have their opportunity to explore the natural wonders, miles of sandy beaches and breathtaking scenic views. Barbados has the most advanced medical facilities, thanks to the 600-bed government owned Queen Elizabeth Hospital, the Bayview hospital and numerous other nursing homes, health centers and polyclinics.

The Sandy Crest Clinic in St. James provides excellent accident and emergency medical services. A variety of wellness and health treatment options makes the small island of Barbados a popular medical tourism destination. Even though it is in its nascent stage, the medical tourism brings in loads of revenue and pushes the country forth to be a major player in the global healthcare sector.

Healthcare System

Barbados operates a system of nationalized healthcare, similar to other nations within the Commonwealth of Nations. Including the Queen Elizabeth Hospital aka General Hospital, Bridgetown, Barbados has more than 20 polyclinics that provide exceptional healthcare to millions of Barbadians.

Subsequent to the Memorandum of Understanding, which the Government of Barbados signed in 2011, now the Denver, Colorado based America World Clinics has acquired the 22-acre Saint Joseph Hospital. The deal further implies that the American leasers will explore the possibilities for medical tourism in Barbados.

The Government of Barbados also intends to replace the QEH with a new $800 million high-tech hospital. The new hospital would allow Barbadians and other medical travelers to access a superb healthcare system.

Quality of Healthcare

With over 20 polyclinics, a dialysis center, and high-tech medical facilities that can handle major surgery and the Queen Elizabeth Hospital, Barbados has appeared on the world map as a prime medical tourism destination within the Caribbean.

In order to demonstrate its ability to maneuver international standards of care and quality, Barbados already has its first accredited facility in the region. This is a stepping-stone in the right direction for the island country as it demonstrates the desire of Barbados to grow as a medical tourism destination offering high quality care to foreign patients.

■ BELGIUM

General	
Language	Dutch, French, German
Time Zone	CET(UTC+1) summer CEST(UTC+2)
Dialing Code	32
Electricity	230V, 50Hz
Medical Tourism Status	Brussels, Antwerp, Arlon, Waterloo
Currency	Euro
Clothing	Light to warm clothes throughout the year, supplemented by heavier wear for winter months, rainwear at any time.

Health Related	
Mortality Rate	10.64deaths/ 1,000 live births
Life Expectancy	M 77.8/ F 82.9
Patient: Physician Ratio	220: 1
Hospitals JCI accredited	1
Recommended Vaccinations	MMR, Tetanus-Diphtheria, Influenza
Other Infections	Lyme disease, Q fever, Brucellosis

Tourism Related			
Population	11,035,948	Reliability of Police Services	29/140
Global Competitiveness	5.52/7	Physician Density	30/140
Tourism Competitiveness	5.0/7	Hospital Beds	17/140
GDP/Capita	37,883	Quality of Air Transport Infrastructure	14/140
Health and Hygiene	6.4/7	International Air Transport Network	15/140
Safety and Security	5.9/7	Quality of Roads	26/140
Air Transport Infrastructure	4.2/7	Hotel Rooms	50/140
Tourism Infrastructure	5.5/7	Tourism Openness	40/140
Cultural Infrastructure	6.0/7	Attitude of Population Towards Foreign Visitors	19/140
Visa Requirements	40/140		

Belgium, officially known as the Kingdom of Belgium, is a country in Western Europe. The European country is home to various international organizations like NATO and headquarters of the European Union; in fact, it is one of the founding members of the European Union. In recent years, Belgium witnessed a sort of crises emanating from the rise of contrasts between the Francophones and the Flemish, which turned the unitary Belgian state into a federal one. The country owes its cultural origin to Germanic and Latin European influences. Characterized by two main linguistic groups, the Dutch speakers and the French speakers, Belgium has always shown great respect toward its bilingual people and their culture. Further, while the Dutch speaking Flanders dominate the northern part, the French-speaking people consider Wallonia as their rightful home.

Location

Spread across an area of 30,258 square kilometers, the country's population figures read 11 million inhabitants. Belgium shares its boundaries with France, Germany, Netherlands and Luxembourg. While you would find the coastal plain in the north-west of Belgium, the central plateau offers you a glimpse of the Anglo-Belgian Basin. The third main geographical region, i.e. the Hercynian orogenic belt has the Ardennes uplands as its inseparable part. We cannot ignore the Belgian Lorraine, which meets the Paris Basin at Belgium's southernmost tip.

Belgium undoubtedly is a historic, artistic and cultural destination, further blessed with some must-visit wild places, natural environment, Nature Reserves, Forest Reserves and Nature Parks. Aside from allowing visitors to see the European beaver, the country also brings them closer to a variety of flora and fauna. The beautiful country sustains wildlife, which includes buzzards, falcons, larks, gulls, terns, cormorants, storks, geese, divers, owls etc. The most famous wild reserves include the Blokkerdijk Nature Reserve and Kalmthoutse Heide.

People

Owing to their inherent nature, Belgians are friendly and helpful people who never mind going out of their way to accommodate strangers. When compared to other countries in Europe, Belgium is a peaceful country with lesser instances of violence. Well known for its dark chocolates and quality beer, Belgium has the most productive and hard working people in the world. Thanks to their sincere efforts, Belgium has successfully managed to have 20 percent higher industrial production when compared to other developed countries.

Events

The Belgian calendar is full of vibrant and colorful events like the Belgium Roller Parade, annual carnivals, the Heilig-Bloedprocessie, the Gentse Feesten, Bal Rat Mort, Bloesemfeesten, Jazz Marathon and others. Belgians actively participate in each of these events. It would not be an exaggeration to consider Skoda Jazz Festival as the national event of Belgium as 16 cities around the country host this event. People enjoy to their fullest in each of the 70 concerts that make this event the biggest event of Belgium.

Weather

Those who wish to experience moderately cold weather throughout the year would find Belgium as the best country to visit. However, you would be more than thrilled to witness a comparable difference between winter and summer temperatures. Belgium flaunts the lowest average temperature, i.e. 3 °C (37.4 °F), in the month of January and the highest in July at 18 °C (64.4 °F). Thanks to its maritime temperate climate, Belgium's average precipitation per month stays within tolerable limits.

Medical Tourism in Belgium

Belgium has become a prime European destination for tourists seeking medical care. Belgium offers its citizens and foreign patients high quality medical services at a much lower rate when compared to other European countries, which helps make Belgium medical tourists' favorite destination. Belgium garners over 50,000 medical travelers each year and the number just keeps growing for this bustling European country.

Most of the patients considering surgery or medical treatments in Belgium usually end up seeking care in the capital city of Brussels. The cosmopolitan city is ideal for patients who wish to combine their treatment with a holiday; Brussels is a modern, relaxing location for a holiday and the ideal destination for procuring medical treatment.

Healthcare System

Similar to other European countries, Belgium has a nationalized system of healthcare wherein all citizens get free or low cost medical services. The system is funded through the national sickness fund, which consists of four tiers of governmental operations. It is mandatory for employees and employers to participate in the national health insurance scheme through payroll deductions.

Quality of Healthcare

Belgium offers high quality healthcare to solidify its name as a notable medical tourism destination. The hospitals house the latest technology to allow the execution of complicated and specialized treatments with unparalleled ease. Belgium offers one JCI accredited hospital for tourists seeking healthcare that can assure international standards.

The Belgian doctors are usually foreign trained and go through strict requirements to practice medicine – it's compulsory for them to gather and utilize the latest medical information. Therefore, patients receive the best care from highly educated providers.

Belgium is also home to several innovative cancer research centers, making it a prime destination for those seeking care or new treatments in oncology. It is also interesting to note that the hospitals in Belgium have recorded less than 0.5 percent secondary infection rates.

■ BRAZIL

General	
Language	Portuguese and indigenous language
Time Zone	BRT (UTC -2 to -4) summer BRST (UCT -2 to -4)
Dialing Code	+55
Electricity	110V/ 220V, 60Hz
Medical Tourism Status	Sao Paula, Rio de Janeiro, Salvador, Fortaleza
Currency	Euro
Clothing	Take natural fabrics and lightweight clothing, cotton linen and silk are comfortable even in the heat and humidity.

Health Related	
Mortality Rate	6.35deaths/ 1,000 live births
Life Expectancy	M 71.0/ F 77.8
Patient: Physician Ratio	900: 1
Hospitals JCI accredited	13
Recommended Vaccinations	Hepatitis A, Typhoid, Hepatitis B, Rabies, Diphtheria-tetanus, Measles, Varicella, Poliomyelitis, Yellow Fever,
Other Infections	Plague, Brazilian purpuric fever, Lymphatic filariasis, Hepatits D, Brazilian spotted fever, HIV, Lyme Disease

Tourism Related			
Population	201,032,714	Reliability of Police Services	116/140
Global Competitiveness	4.49/7	Physician Density	70/140
Tourism Competitiveness	4.4/7	Hospital Beds	73/140
GDP/Capita	11,875	Quality of Air Transport Infrastructure	131/140
Health and Hygiene	4.7/7	International Air Transport Network	74/140
Safety and Security	4.7/7	Quality of Roads	121/140
Air Transport Infrastructure	3.8/7	Hotel Rooms	60/140
Tourism Infrastructure	4.4/7	Tourism Openness	133/140
Cultural Infrastructure	5.6/7	Attitude of Population Towards Foreign Visitors	43/140
Visa Requirements	67/140		

Known for its natural beauty and the famous Carnival, Brazil is one of the most popular tourist destinations that attract thousands of tourists throughout the year from all around the world. When talking about Brazil, few things that conjure your mind are the great Amazon forest, fantastic beaches, great soccer players and the annual lively Carnival. Officially known as the Federative Republic of Brazil, the South American nation is the biggest Lusophone, Portuguese speaking, country in the world, and the solitary one in the Americas. Brazil was a colony of Portugal from 1500 to 1815, which greatly influenced their culture as well as language.

Brazil is one of the fastest growing economies of the world and tourism plays an integral part to the economy of a number of regions of the nation. Attracting over five million foreign tourists annually, Brazil is the second major tourist hotspot in South America and the third in Latin America. Combining ecotourism with leisure and recreation, Brazil presents a wide range of option to both foreign and domestic tourists.

Travelers can visit various historical and cultural sites in Minas Gerais and it is an incredible place for adventure lovers. Tourists looking to explore Amazon Rainforest and dunes must visit Northeastern area, Rio de Janeiro and Santa Catarina. Wherever you travel in Brazil, you must hire a local guide to explore the natural beauty and untouched places to make your trip memorable.

Location

Brazil is the fifth largest country, both by area and by population, in the world and the largest in South America as well as the Latin American area. Other than Ecuador and Chile, Brazil shares its borders with every South American country.

Surrounded by Venezuela, Guyana and Suriname in the north, Colombia in the northwest, Bolivia and Peru in the west, Argentina and Paraguay in the southwest and Uruguay in the south, Brazil features a huge coastline of 7,491 km (4,655 m), which offers some of the most beautiful and exotic beaches to the travelers.

People

The new race of Brazilians is a successful amalgam of African, European and indigenous strains, as more than half of the population is of European descent, while 40 percent are a cross of African and European ancestry. The official language of Brazil is Portuguese that is spoken in different parts of the country, thanks to colonialism. English is used as second or business language in São Paulo and other commercial zones.

Events

The Carnival is the biggest annual event or festival celebrated throughout Brazil. This event takes place about a week before Ash Wednesday to mark the commencement of Lent, the forty-day long celebration period before Easter. The annual Carnival and the samba parades have become synonymous to fun and merrymaking in Brazil, as people from different sects of society wearing unique dresses participates in these parades. Other popular events of Brazil include the football league, which is the most popular sports in the nation, Christmas celebrations and Rio Fashion Week.

Weather

Brazil offers a wide range of weather patterns, together with an awesome mixture of cultures and races. Brazil is essentially a tropical country, but it has a wide range of weather conditions in different parts, thanks to a varied topography of the nation. Different regions in Brazil have diverse microclimates that can be categorized into five climatic subtypes, i.e. equatorial, tropical, semiarid, highland tropical, temperate, and subtropical. Visitors can enjoy diverse climate conditions of equatorial rainforests in the north and semiarid deserts in the northeast, temperate coniferous forests in the south and tropical savannas in the central part of Brazil.

In addition, Brazil has the longest tropical beach coast of the world with some incredible tropical beach resorts, and the most secret rain forests around the Amazon River. Flaunting hot and humid summers from December to February, Brazil's tropical climate props up frequent rain showers throughout the year, but there are some dry interiors with scant rainfall as well. Winters in Brazil lasts from June to August with temperatures between 13 °C and 18 °C, but the weather gets colder south of Rio.

Medical Tourism in Brazil:

Brazil boasts some of the leading hospitals in the world, especially in the growing private sector. Offering the best facilities in cosmetic surgery, Brazil has become a prime medical tourism destination for people looking to enhance their looks and body shape. Aside from featuring high quality, accredited hospitals and state-of-the-art clinics, Brazilian healthcare system also flaunts low treatment costs, almost half when compared to other developed countries like the UK and US. Many of the hospitals offer bilingual staff and translator options to attend or manage international patients.

Often dubbed the international hub of cosmetic and plastic surgeries, Brazil is the second largest destination for tourists seeking plastic surgery in the world, after the US. Medical treatment in Brazil is not only cheap but of the highest quality, thanks to highly qualified medical professionals.

Healthcare system at a glance

Quality of healthcare services varies from region to region in Brazil. The ratio of doctors per 1000 patients is 3.28 in the urban areas but it is only 0.63 in rural areas. Private surgeons or owners own approximately 60% hospitals in Brazil. Around 80% of urban inpatients as well as foreign patients use privately owned health facilities.

Quality of Healthcare

There are 13 JCI accredited hospitals in Brazil, which assure quality healthcare services to medical travelers from all across the world. Usually, cosmetic surgeons practicing in Brazil get training in the US. Therefore, the American Board of Plastic Surgery certifies most of the surgeons while a few of them are associated with the American Society of Plastic and Reconstructive Surgeons.

■ CAYMAN ISLANDS

General	
Language	English
Time Zone	UTC -5
Dialing Code	+1-345
Major Cities	George Town, West Bay, Bodden Town, East End
Currency	Cayman Islands Dollar
Clothing	Warm, loose clothing
Population	56,732
GDP/Capita	43,800
Health Related	
Mortality Rate	6.35deaths/ 1,000 live births
Life Expectancy	M 77/ F 83
Hospitals JCI accredited	0
Recommended Vaccinations	Hepatitis A, Diphtheria-tetanus, MMR, Typhoid, Hepatitis B, Poliomyelitis
Other Infections	West Nile Virus, HIV

Encompassing three islands, including Grand Cayman with an area of 76 sq miles, Cayman Brac with an area of 15 sq miles and Little Cayman with an area of 11.0 sq miles, the Cayman Islands is a British Overseas Territory situated in the western Caribbean Sea. Among the three, the Grand Cayman is the most developed island with a population of more than 35,000 people.

Surrounded by the sea, these islands are home to some of the most beautiful and exotic beaches in the world. The serenity, charm and peacefulness of the islands provide tourists with much-needed rest and relaxation. These islands provide a relaxing escape for beach lovers, where they can enjoy the coastal life as well as water sports to the fullest. Shaped by large coral heads lying on top of the underwater peaks of the extended Cuban Sierra Maestra range, the Cayman Islands are generally flat, with the exception of The Bluff, which rises 43m above sea level and is located on the Cayman Brac.

Location

Located in the Caribbean Sea, with Cuba on the south and Jamaica on the northwest, the Cayman Islands are an extension of the peaks of an enormous underwater ridge called the Cayman Ridge. Essentially a part of the geographic Western Caribbean Zone and the Greater Antilles, the Cayman Islands have emerged as a chief world offshore financial centre, as these islands are situated in the middle of the trade route which connects Europe and Americas to Africa, Asia and Australia. Sited about 430 miles (700 km) south of Miami, 227 miles (366 km) south of Cuba and 310 miles (500 km) northwest of Jamaica, the Cayman Islands are characterized a low-lying limestone, enclosed by coral reefs, terrain.

People

The total population of Cayman Islands is around 60,000, which includes a mix of more than 100 nationalities. Out of the total population, 40% people are of mixed race or ethnic group, 20% black, 20% white and rest 20% are emigrants of various ethnic groups. Be they Anglicans or Presbyterians, most of the people in this island are Christians or follow Christianity. Majority of population of the Cayman Islands is of Cayman descent, which lives on the island of Grand Cayman.

Events

Cayman Islands host a number of events throughout the year, which not only entertain the residents but also attract tourists from different parts of the world. Annual fishing tournament is the main event among locals as well as tourists, which invariably attracts a lot of fishing enthusiasts. Taste of Cayman Food & Wine Festival is another major event, which is organized annually in the Cayman Islands. This festival is popular among both local residents as well as tourists, who participate in various social events and become an integral part of the local community. During these celebrations, locals put on colorful costumes and dance to soulful music.

Weather

Cayman Islands feature a typical tropical marine weather, wherein summers are warm, wet and rainy and winters are relatively dry and cool. Summers in Cayman Islands last from the month of May to October, while winters stretch from November to April. Temperature in Cayman Islands is very high during daytime when compared to nights. The coastal country is known for tropical cyclones between June and November during the Atlantic hurricane season. The month of December is the perfect time to visit the Cayman Islands.

Medical Tourism in Cayman Islands

Cayman Islands provide tourists with a tranquil atmosphere so that they can enjoy a relaxing vacation, while availing the medical services. Even though medical tourism industry in the Cayman Islands is currently at a developing stage, the coastal country still shows the potential of providing good medical facilities as other developed countries offer in different parts of the world. Other than peaceful white beaches, the Cayman Islands promise a high quality healthcare in the days to come.

Healthcare System

According to a law that came into effect in 1997, health insurance or cover is compulsory for all citizens living in the Cayman Islands. The law requires all residents to purchase health insurance that other than providing life insurance also covers basic medical care. Employers and residents share the premium of the health insurance in equal proportions. There is a great disparity in healthcare services provided by private and public hospitals and healthcare clinics.

Quality of Healthcare

Offering diverse healthcare services, the Cayman Islands house three major hospitals, i.e. the Chrissie Tomlinson Memorial Hospital - a private hospital in Grand Cayman, the public Cayman Islands Hospital and the Faith Hospital in Cayman Brac. Apart from these hospitals, several polyclinics and private physicians provide healthcare services to domestic as well as foreign patients visiting the Cayman Islands. The Cayman Island is planning to bring the medical institutes or facilities under the accreditation policy to ensure safe and quality healthcare, while making them more accountable.

■ CHILE

General	
Language	Spanish
Time Zone	CLT and EASTd (UTC–4 and –6) CLST and EASST (UTC–3 and –5)
Dialing Code	+56
Major Cities	Santiago, Puente Alto, Vina Del Mar, Valparaiso
Currency	Peso
Clothing	The climate in Northern Chile is desert temperatures. In the central region of Chile is Mediterranean and in the South it is cool and damp.

Health Related	
Mortality Rate	5.8 deaths/ 1,000 population
Life Expectancy	76.2M /82.3F
Hospitals JCI accredited	2
Recommended Vaccinations	Hepatitis A, Hepatitis B, Typhoid
Other Infections	HIV

Tourism Related			
Population	17,402,630	Physician Density	88/140
Global Competitiveness	4.65/7	Hospital Beds	77/140
Tourism Competitiveness	4.3/7	Quality of Air Transport Infrastructure	39/140
GDP/Capita	$19,475	International Air Transport Network	33/140
Safety and Security	5.5/7	Quality of Roads	23/140
Health and Hygiene	4.6/7	Hotel Rooms	62/140
Air Transport Infrastructure	3.4/7	Tourism Openness	129/140
Tourism Infrastructure	4.7/7	Attitude of Population Towards Foreign Visitors	84/140
Cultural Infrastructure	2.9/7		

The Republic of Chile is a small country in South America, located right in between the Andes mountain range and the Pacific Ocean. The country's territory extends to the islands of Salas y Gomez, Juan Fernandez, Easter Island and Desventuradas in the Pacific Ocean. Recognized as a prominent middle power, Chile is one of the most stable and economically prosperous nations in South America.

Chile's climate has several extremes, including a very dry desert like climate up north. Moving further down south, one would start to experience a sub-tropical climate, which would soon give way to oceanic climate complete with glaciers and alpine tundra.

The fun loving people of Chile come from different ethnic backgrounds. While Spanish influences dominate the country, one could find other European influences pertaining to the German, French and English languages.

Events and festivals

Chileans love to celebrate; hence, the country allows residents to enjoy several festivals the year around. Some of the more prominent ones include the Vina del Mar Music Festival, Carnival Andino Con la Fuerza del Sol, Patrias Festival de la Tirana, Santiago a Mil, We Tripantu, Festival Costumbrista Chilote, Festival of Song, Semana Valdiviana, Fiesta del Cuasimodo, Pedro Pablo, Columbus Day, All Saints Day and the Fiesta de la Virgin del Rosario.

Medical Tourism in Chile

When compared to other countries in South America, Chile offers excellent medical facilities and services at affordable costs (just a fraction of what you pay in the US). Some of the medical services offered by the country include oncology, internal medicine, cosmetic procedures, ophthalmology, neurology, urology, dental treatments, psychiatry, dermatology and physical therapy etc.

Healthcare System

The quality of healthcare in Chile is relatively advanced than other Latin American countries. The hospitals catering to medical tourists are accredited by the JCI (Joint Commission International), which offer the best in terms of infrastructure, facilities and medical services.

Highly skilled and experienced doctors in Chile conform to the highest standards of medical care. The country's exemplary medical services also allow it to set international benchmarks on factors like birth rates, life expectancy and infant mortality.

Chile has a national health care system called FONASA, which offers basic medical services and insurance coverage for people belonging to different sections of the society. The quality of services would be better in private hospitals when compared to public hospitals. That does not need to be a deterrent though as even expensive private hospitals would be affordable for medical tourists (when compared to hospitals in the US and the UK).

■ CHINA

General	
Language	Standard Mandarin
Time Zone	China Standard Time (UTC+8)
Dialing Code	+86
Electricity	220V, 50Hz
Major Cities	Shanghai, Zhumadian, Beijing, Nanchong, Guangzhou
Currency	Renminbi (yuan)
Clothing	Summers are warm, humid and rainy, whereas winters are mild.

Health Related	
Mortality Rate	15.6 deaths/ 1,000 live births
Life Expectancy	M 74.1/ F 77.2
Patient: Physician Ratio	950: 1
Hospitals JCI accredited	10
Recommended Vaccinations	Hepatitis A, Typhoid, Hepatitis B, Rabies, Diphtheria-tetanus, Measles, Varicella, Japanese encephalitis, Poliomyelitis and Yellow fever.
Other Infections	Cutaneous leishmaniasis, Scrub typhus, Hemorrhagic fever with renal syndrome, Hepatitis E, Trachoma, Brucellosis, Murine typhus, Anthrax, North Asian tick, Q fever, Lyme disease, Lung fluke, Oriental liver fluke, Tapeworm (fish & pork), HIV

Tourism Related			
Population	1,353,821,000	Reliability of Police Services	50/140
Global Competitiveness	5.25/7	Physician Density	78/140
Tourism Competitiveness	4.5/7	Hospital Beds	43/140
GDP/Capita	9,233	Quality of Air Transport Infrastructure	70/140
Health and Hygiene	4.2/7	International Air Transport Network	69/140
Safety and Security	4.8/7	Quality of Roads	54/140
Air Transport Infrastructure	4.3/7	Hotel Rooms	109/140
Tourism Infrastructure	2.5/7	Tourism Openness	123/140
Cultural Infrastructure	5.5/7	Attitude of Population Towards Foreign Visitors	130/140
Visa Requirements	128/140		

Flaunting one of the oldest cultures and civilizations in the world, China is a great contributor to some of the basic essentials of day-to-day life. China faced a lot of turbulence due to civil war that lasted until 1864, foreign interference and Japanese invasion. After long turmoil, China finally became the People's Republic of China on October 1, 1949, when the Communist Party took control of the nation.

Location

Located in the eastern part of Asia, the People's Republic of China is surrounded by Pacific Ocean in the east. Surrounded by Vietnam, Laos and Burma in Southeast Asia, India, Bhutan, Nepal and Pakistan in South Asia, China shares its borders with Afghanistan, Tajikistan, Kyrgyzstan and Kazakhstan in Central Asia, Russian Altai and Mongolia in Inner Asia and North Korea in Northeast Asia.

Featuring the longest combined land border in the world, which measures 22,117 km (13,743 miles), China shares its border with 14 countries. With an area of 9.6 million square kilometers, China covers almost one-fifteenth of the world's land mass and is the third largest country (area wise) in the world after Canada and Russia.

People

With a population of over 1.35 billion, China is the most populous country in the world. Due to the cheap labor in China, the economy of the nation is growing rapidly, as many hardworking individuals work in several industries while contributing in the rapidly increasing economy.

China revolutionized its education system in 1980s, as it started following the western standards of education to increase the number of skilled employees or laborers in their offices and industries. Furthermore, Chinese people are very friendly and pay a lot of respect to their rich culture and heritage.

Events

Like most other Asian countries, Chinese people cherish their traditional and cultural values and participate actively in their time-honored festivals. A number of old and modern fairs and events, based on both lunar and solar calendar, take place in China throughout the year. These festivals and events bring people of different sects and societies together, while propagating the rich cultural heritage and old traditions that prevail in China from ages.

Weather

Weather or climate in China is either dry (especially in winters) or wet in summers or monsoons. Lying between latitudes 18° and 54° N and longitudes 73° and 135° E, the landscape and climate in China differ from region to region due to highly complex topography of the country. The southern part of China lies in the tropical and sub-tropical zones, while the northern part lies in the frigid zones, causing huge difference in winter and summer temperatures across the nation.

The northern part of Heilongjiang province has long winters but no summers. On the other hand, the Hainan Island has long summers without winters. Tourists can enjoy spring all round the year in the southern part of the Yunnan-Guizhou Plateau. The temperature in tundra zones like Qinghai and Tibet remains very low all through the year.

Medical Tourism in China

China has been a prime destination for travelers seeking alternative, traditional Chinese medicines and therapies for years now. A number of private institutes in China employ traditional methods of treatment, which are very popular among foreign tourists. In addition, special departments in several public hospitals in China are designed to cater foreign tourists. China is investing heavily in its hospitals and medical industry to promote medical tourism and attract foreign tourists seeking treatment.

Combining wellness and medical trip with excellent medical facilities and traditional medicine therapies, China is attracting a huge number of medical tourists from different parts of the world. Moreover, China has emerged as a prime destination for travelers seeking stem cell therapies. Medical tourists need to understand that stem cell research is banned in several countries; hence, they should consider China for doing it legally.

Healthcare System

The communist government of China provides funds and healthcare facilities. The healthcare system is divided in various sub-systems, such as medical services, preventive care, primary/public health, drugs and medical equipment, to promote better health services in the country.

As China is becoming a capitalistic market, several private clinics and hospitals provide medical facilities for domestic and foreign patients who are willing to pay more. China may lack an official private healthcare system, but you can find a number of private doctors or practitioners who provide exclusive healthcare services.

Quality of Healthcare

Almost all the healthcare facilities in China are under government control; therefore, local and state authorities ensure that the hospitals and clinics are in good shape and offer quality services. You would find physicians with years of experience and the latest medical equipments installed in Chinese hospitals.

Seven JCI accredited hospitals in China provide high quality medical facilities to both domestic and foreign patients. In fact, the 2008 Beijing Olympics brought about a revolution in the Chinese healthcare system, as the country provided healthcare facilities to a vast number of foreign travelers who visited China to support their country in the mega sporting event.

■ COLOMBIA

General	
Language	Spanish
Time Zone	COT (UTC–5b)
Dialing Code	+57
Electricity	110V, 60Hz
Major Cities	Bogota, Cali, Medellin, Barranguilla
Currency	Peso
Clothing	Important and popular clothes are trousers, shirts, skirts, t-shirts, swim trunks and such like.

Health Related	
Mortality Rate	5.24 deaths/ 1,000 population
Life Expectancy	M 74.5/ F 80.5
Patient: Physician Ratio	750: 1
Hospitals JCI accredited	2
Recommended Vaccinations	Hepatitis A, Typhoid, Hepatitis B, Rabies, Diphtheriatetanus, Measles, Varicella, Poliomyelitis, Yellow fever
Other Infections	Anthrax, Murine typhus, Oroya fever, Tick-borne relapsing fever, Rocky Mountain spotted fever, Mayaro virus disease

Tourism Related			
Population	47,072,915	Reliability of Police Services	78/140
Global Competitiveness	4.14/7	Physician Density	119/140
Tourism Competitiveness	3.9/7	Hospital Beds	114/140
GDP/Capita	7,854	Quality of Air Transport Infrastructure	105/140
Health and Hygiene	3.6/7	International Air Transport Network	79/140
Safety and Security	3.8/7	Quality of Roads	124/140
Air Transport Infrastructure	2.9/7	Hotel Rooms	70/140
Tourism Infrastructure	2.8/7	Tourism Openness	130/140
Cultural Infrastructure	3.5/7	Attitude of Population Towards Foreign Visitors	88/140
Visa Requirements	16/140		

Colombia is a vibrant country that attracts tourists from all over the world. Essentially a country of growing middle class that plays a significant role in economic as well as cultural development of the nation, Colombia is a mix of old-world charm and the urban modernization, which makes it one of the most sought after tourist destination in the world. Featuring exotic landscape and lively cultural values in different parts, Colombia can easily be distinguished in one way or the other from its South American counterparts.

Location

Situated in northwestern South America, Colombia is surrounded by Panama in the northwest, the Caribbean Sea in the north, the Pacific Ocean in the west, Ecuador and Peru in the south and Venezuela and Brazil in the east. Covering an area of about 440,000 square miles (around 1.14 million square kilometers), Colombia also shares its coast with the Atlantic Ocean. Characterized by rain forests, inland plains and the Andes mountain range, Colombia also comprises a number of small and medium sized islands, including San Andrea, Providencia, Malpelo and Gorgona. Some of these islands have been converted into national parks or reserves to protect the wildlife in and around the coastal area. Colombia is an ultimate tourist destination for nature lovers who simply love to spend holidays in tranquil beaches.

People

Known for their vibrant lifestyle, Colombian people work hard to maintain their high standard of living. They actively participate in their religious festivals and other social or public gatherings and welcome tourists with a warm heart. And why not, as tourism is one of the most growing sectors in the nation that provide livelihood to a large number of people. Usually, Colombian people are friendly and respect their guests, which make it a safe and popular tourist destination.

Events

Colombia is known for its traditional music, dance and art forms, and theater lies in the heart of Colombians. The Colombian calendar is full of events and festivals that range from New Year celebrations to theater festivals and other social or religious gatherings. Considered one of the biggest theater festivals in the world, the Ibero-American Theater Festival of Bogotá is an important cultural event in Colombia.

While other important theater events include the Festival of Puppet The Fanfare, Manizales Theater Festival, Caribbean Theatre Festival and The Art Festival of Popular Culture. No matter what the event is, people simply love to enjoy each festival to the fullest and that too with active participation.

Weather

To describe the regional weather, Colombians segregate the country in different climate zones, i.e. tierra caliente (the hot land), tierra templada (the temperate land) and tierra fría (the cold land). The hot land is the area below 900 meters where temperature ranges between 24°C and 38 °C. This zone comprises about 86 percent of the total area of the country. On the other hand, the temperate land covers the area between 900 and 1,980 meters that provides suitable conditions to cultivate coffee. The cold land lie between 1,980 and 3,500 meters where temperatures vary between 10 and 19 °C, which is appropriate for wheat and potato cultivation. There are few more zones like the forested zone, the grasslands and freezing zone above 3,500 meters.

Medical Tourism in Colombia

Like most other South American countries, Colombia is investing massively in its healthcare industry to attract medical tourists from different parts of the world. Colombian government is promoting the medical tourism aggressively and setting new standards to improve the healthcare facility in the country. Offering excellent cosmetic surgical procedures like Brazil, Colombia is right on the track to become a leading medical services provider in the region.

Other then cosmetic surgery, the South American nation is also becoming a prime destination for the ophthalmology, orthopedics and vascular surgeries. Featuring state-of-the-art hospitals and clinics with certified plastic surgeons, Colombia is growing as an exotic destination to avail healthcare services. Moreover, healthcare cost in Colombia is very low if compared to North American and European countries. According to the government statistics, over 27,000 tourists from different regions, especially the US, Mexico, Spain and Panama, visited Colombia in 2008 to benefit from the cost-effective medical services.

Healthcare System

The Colombian healthcare system is segregated in three different sectors, i.e. public, private and Social Security Institutes, which provide healthcare facilities to over 80% citizens (in one way or the other) of the country. Among these three systems, the private sector seems to dominate the medical industry, as it provide medical services to maximum number of domestic as well as foreign clients or patients in the country. Apart from healthcare reforms, Colombian authorities pay special attention on preventive measures to eradicate diseases from the nation.

Quality of Healthcare

Despite the disparity in healthcare facilities in the nation, medical tourists or foreign patients can enjoy state-of-the-art clinics and medical services in cities or urban areas of Colombia. If compared to developed countries, Colombia offer cheap medical services but without compromising the quality to attract medical tourism.

To strengthen its healthcare system, Colombia is implementing accreditation policy to classify hospitals, clinics or medical institutes according to their services. Currently, two accredited hospitals in the country are providing excellent health care services to domestic as well as foreign patients. Of course, the number of accredited medical organization is bound to increase in the near future.

■ COSTA RICA

General	
Language	Spanish, English
Time Zone	CTZ(UTC -6)
Dialing Code	+506
Electricity	120V, 60Hz
Major Cities	San Jose, Puerto Limon, San Francisco, Alajuela
Currency	Costa Rican colon
Clothing	Away from the touristy beaches, clothing is generally conservative.
Health Related	
Mortality Rate	4.29 deaths/ 1,000 population
Life Expectancy	M 77.0/ F 81.3
Hospitals JCI accredited	3
Recommended Vaccinations	Hepatitis A, Typhoid, Hepatitis B, Diphtheria-tetanus, Measles, Varicella
Other Infections	Chagas disease, Rocky Mountain spotted fever, Tick-borne relapsing fever, HIV

Tourism Related			
Population	4.586.353	Reliability of Police Services	84/140
Global Competitiveness	4.04/7	Physician Density	79/140
Tourism Competitiveness	4.4/7	Hospital Beds	107/140
GDP/Capita	12,606	Quality of Air Transport Infrastructure	60/140
Health and Hygiene	4.5/7	International Air Transport Network	43/140
Safety and Security	4.8/7	Quality of Roads	129/140
Air Transport Infrastructure	3.9/7	Hotel Rooms	35/140
Tourism Infrastructure	5.1/7	Tourism Openness	44/140
Cultural Infrastructure	1.9/7	Attitude of Population Towards Foreign Visitors	41/140
Visa Requirements	12/140		

Located in Central America, Costa Rica is one of the prime destinations for eco tourists and medical tourists. Surrounded by the Caribbean Sea in the east, the Pacific Ocean in the west, Nicaragua in the north and Panama in the southeast, Costa Rica has always been among the top Latin American nations in the Human Development Index (HDI) since it become a democracy in 1950. When it comes to the Environmental Performance Index, Costa Rica is at the top in both the Americas and third in the world.

Eco-Tourism

Officially known as the Republic of Costa Rica, the Central American nation is all set to become the first carbon neutral country by 2021. According to the New Economics Foundation, Costa Rica ranks first in the Happy Planet Index and is the "greenest" country in the world. People of Costa Rica are friendly, peaceful and progressive, which makes the country one of the world's top eco-tourism destinations.

Almost a quarter of the country's total area comes under either national parks or protected areas; allowing vast opportunities to explore its rich natural life to the visitors from all over the world. Presenting splendid beaches at Tamarindo where tourists can enjoy surfing and various other water sports, Costa Rica's active Arenal volcano also attracts the attention of the domestic as well as foreign travelers.

Language

There are a number of native or regional languages prevalent in the Central American nation, but Spanish, rather Costa Rican Spanish, is the primary language spoken throughout the country for regular communication. With growing tourism industry, English is emerging as a business language, as around 11% of Costa Rica's adult population speaks the universal language to communicate with foreign travelers in hotels, airports and other popular public places. French, Portuguese and German are the second languages in some parts of the country.

Weather

Due to its close proximity to the Equator, Costa Rica largely features a tropical climate. However, Costa Rica's weather can be segregated into various microclimates according to the elevation, rainfall and topography of different regions or areas. There are mainly two seasons in the country, i.e. the dry season or summers and that stretches from the month of December to April and the rainy season or winters that extends from the month of May to November.

Coastal regions, especially the Caribbean slopes of the Central Cordillera Mountains, of Costa Rica experience frequent showers throughout the year, which makes them more humid when compared to the Pacific side of country. The average annual temperature on the coastal areas remains between 20 °C and 27 °C, which is just ideal to spend holidays.

Events

A number of festivals and various other cultural events take place in Costa Rica all through the year. Limon Carnival is one of the liveliest events in Costa Rica that takes place on or around the Columbus Day in the month of October. During this colorful event, people enjoy traditional dancing, music and Caribbean food. Costa Rican people take pride in their culture and Caribbean roots and enjoy the festive season by actively participating in various events and gatherings.

The Virgin of the Angels is another major event held in the month of August to commemorate Costa Rica's patron saint. Thousands of Costa Ricans as well as foreign tourists take part in a long walk and gather in Basilica de Los Angeles in Cartago city.

Medical Tourism in Costa Rica

Costa Rica has not only won accolades as an eco tourism destination, but it has also emerged as a medical tourism destination in past few years on the world map. Tourists seeking medical assistance keep flocking to the Latin American nation from all over the world. Costa Rica simply becomes an ideal destination for medical tourists from United States and Canada due to the shorter travel time, quality medical services and cheap healthcare cost. All these factors make the Latin American country a popular destination for medical tourism. Moreover, growing eco tourism allows a great opportunity to foreign tourists to explore and enjoy the natural life as well as exotic beaches of the country.

Healthcare System

Costa Rica has shown a great commitment to healthcare and social reforms that can be seen in their current health care system, which is ranked higher than that of the developed countries with higher GDP. Based on the principles of universal coverage and equality, Costa Rica features a comprehensive, publicly funded health care system to ensure quality medical services to all domestic as well as foreign recipients.

Primarily the public sector dominates the healthcare services in Costa Rica, but a number of clinics and surgeons provide personal medical services to encourage private health sector in the country.

Quality of Healthcare

With three JCI accredited hospitals under its belt, Costa Rica is slowly emerging as one the finest medical tourism destinations in the region. Foreign medical tourists keep flocking to Costa Rica as they get an opportunity to combine an eco-friendly vacation with top quality medical care. Costa Rica has modern hospitals and state-of-the-art clinics that utilize the latest medical technologies and employ surgeons trained and certified by North American or European organizations. Quality of Costa Rica's healthcare system can be gauged with its rank that is higher than that of the United States and many other developed countries.

■ CROATIA

General	
Language	Croatian
Time Zone	CET(UTC+1) summer CEST(UTC+2)
Dialing Code	+385
Electricity	230V, 50Hz
Major Cities	Zagreb-Centar, Zagreb, Split, Rijeka
Currency	Kuna (HRK)
Clothing	Lightweights with rainwear for summers, medium weights for winter with heavier clothing for inland areas.
Health Related	
Mortality Rate	11.38 deaths/ 1,000 population
Life Expectancy	M 74.0/ F 80.3
Hospitals JCI accredited	0
Recommended Vaccinations	Hepatitis A, Typhoid, Hepatitis B, Influenza, Tickborne encephalitis, Diphtheria-tetanus, MMR, Varicella
Other Infections	Brucellosis, HIV

Tourism Related			
Population	4,284,889	Reliability of Police Services	53/140
Global Competitiveness	3.39/7	Physician Density	44/140
Tourism Competitiveness	4.6/7	Hospital Beds	28/140
GDP/Capita	18,191	Quality of Air Transport Infrastructure	79/140
Health and Hygiene	6.0/7	International Air Transport Network	99/140
Safety and Security	5.3/7	Quality of Roads	29/140
Air Transport Infrastructure	3.0/7	Hotel Rooms	13/140
Tourism Infrastructure	6.7/7	Tourism Openness	11/140
Cultural Infrastructure	3.9/7	Attitude of Population Towards Foreign Visitors	65/140
Visa Requirements	37/140		

Croatia, officially known as The Republic of Croatia, is a unitary democratic parliamentary republic that lies in the southeastern part of Europe. It forms a long maritime border with Italy in the Adriatic Sea, which stretches up to 2028 kilometer. Another feature of this country is its unique shape, which is very uncommon. This uncommon shape was a result of the expansion by the Ottoman Empire towards the central part of the Europe.

Location

Located at the crossroads of Central Europe, Southern Europe and the Mediterranean, Croatia is surrounded by Hungary in the northeast, Serbia in the east, Bosnia and Herzegovina in the southeast, Montenegro in the southeast, the Adriatic Sea in the southwest and Slovenia in the northwest.

People

The people of Croatia are very friendly, hospitable and are proud of their culture and national identity. They welcome guests and foreign travelers with open heart. Croatians are open-minded and fun-loving people who enjoy music and good food with their family and friends. Offering a safe and healthy environment to foreign tourists, Croatia is fast becoming a popular tourist destination in Europe.

Events

Croatia hosts a number of colorful festivals and events throughout the year in various towns and cities. Rijeka Carnival is one of the largest events not only in the Croatia but also in Europe, which starts in mid-January and lasts until mid-February. People enjoy the festive season by actively participating in different parades, concerts, exhibitions and balls. Rijeka Carnival attracts over 100,000 domestic as well as foreign spectators.

Croatia also hosts an international documentary film festival, the Zagreb Dox, which takes place at the MoviePlex cinema in the Kaptol Center. This event organizes a number of themed programs, together with a contest for the best documentary. Held in the month of October, the Zagreb International Chamber Music Festival attracts a number of domestic as well as foreign artists from different parts of the world.

Weather

Presenting diverse climate conditions, largely continental and Mediterranean, the weather in most parts of Croatia is moderately warm and rainy. The average monthly temperature of Croatia ranges between –3 °C in the month of January and 18 °C in the month of July. The inland of Croatia is characterized by a very harsh continental climate with extreme differences in summer and winter temperatures. Lika and Gorski Kotar flaunting a frosty climate at elevations over 1,200 meters are the coldest parts of the nation, while the areas around the Adriatic coast presenting the Mediterranean climate are the warmest areas of Croatia where the temperature mounts up to 40 °C in summers.

Medical Tourism in Croatia

Croatia is a new entrant in the medical tourism industry where medical tourism is growing slowly and steadily. The country assures quality health care services not only to locals but also to the foreign patients coming to the nation from different parts of the world. Offering specialized health services to domestic as well as foreign medical tourists, the

Central European nation is attracting more and more individuals seeking quality health care. Providing a universal health care system and free primary and secondary education to its citizens, Croatia also supports its culture through several public institutions and corporate investments.

The medical tourism or healthcare services in Croatia revolve around dental care, plastic surgical procedures and spinal surgery. Offering a number of medical as well as wellness facilities, Croatia has the potential to become a leading healthcare service provider in Europe.

Healthcare System

Based on the concept of accessibility and continuity of care, the healthcare system in Croatia is characterized by a very dominant public sector with a large number of state owned hospitals and government undertaking medical centers. Croatia also spends a high percentage of its GDP on healthcare facilities.

The public sector of the healthcare system in Croatia is funded through the mandatory health insurance of the citizen, which ensures the access to healthcare services to all its citizens. General taxes gathered from the public also contribute to the public healthcare system in the country.

Quality of Healthcare

Majority of the people receive quality healthcare services in Croatia, as the life expectancy, which currently is just three years below the EU average, is growing steadily throughout the nation. The private healthcare sector, together with a few public hospitals or clinics, offer as good medical service as you get in other European and American countries. However, the healthcare or wellness cost is far less in Croatia if compared to its European and American counterparts.

Since Croatia is still a newcomer in the medical tourism market, there are no officially accredited hospitals in the nation. However, Croatia is committed to offer quality healthcare services to both domestic and foreign patients, turning it into a popular destination for medical tourists seeking economical yet satisfactory medical services.

Croatia has signed a contract with the Canadian Society of International Health to implement a national accreditation program that will monitor and improve the quality of healthcare services in the country.

▪ CUBA

General	
Language	Spanish, English, French
Time Zone	UTC-5 summer UTC-4
Dialing Code	+53
Electricity	110V and 220V
Major Cities	Havana, Santiago de Cuba, Camaguey, Holguin
Currency	Cuban peso
Clothing	Due to warm weather pack shorts, t-shirts and such like Clothing.
Health Related	
Mortality Rate	6.1 deaths/ 1,000 population
Life Expectancy	M 76.4/F 80.3
Patient: Physician Ratio	170: 1
Hospitals JCI accredited	0
Recommended Vaccinations	Hepatitis A, Typhoid, Hepatitis B, Rabies, Diphtheriatetanus, Measles, Varicella, Poliomyelitis
Other Infections	West Nile virus, HIV, Leptospirosis

Tourism Related	
Population	11,163,934
GDP/Capita	$6,106

Comprising the central island of Cuba, the Isla de la Juventud and a number of archipelagos, the Republic of Cuba is an island nation in the Caribbean. Havana is the capital and the largest city of Cuba. Surrounded by the United States in the north, Bahamas, Mexico in the west, the Cayman Islands and Jamaica in the south and Haiti and the Dominican Republic in the southeast, Cuba is the biggest island in the Caribbean with a total population of more than 11 million people.

Offering some of the finest beaches of the world, Cuba has emerged as one of the prime tourist destinations in the region. Furthermore, in the last decade, Cuba has managed to triple its market share of Caribbean tourism.

Location

Located at the north of Caribbean Sea at the merging point of the Gulf of Mexico and the Atlantic Ocean, Cuba lies between latitudes 19° and 24°N and longitudes 74° and 85°W. The main island of Cuba together with four small groups of island makes the

Republic of Cuba. Featuring the Colorado Archipelago on the northwestern coast and the Sabana-Camagüey Archipelago on the north-central Atlantic coast, the main island of Cuba covers the major part of the nation's land area, which is further surrounded by the Jardines de la Reina on the south-central coast and the Canarreos Archipelago on the southwestern coast.

People

Cuban people like most other Caribbean inhabitants are very friendly and lively. Old traditions and culture, including music and dance, are one of the most important aspects of Cuban life, as people love to take part in different social or cultural events throughout the year and live a happy life. Spanish is the official language of Cuba and its culture is a mix of old African and Spanish traditions. Cubans are generally enthusiastic about sports and other activities. Baseball and basketball are some of the main sporting activities in Cuba.

Events

Cuba is a lively place to visit, as a number of traditional as well as modern festivals and carnivals take place on the island nation throughout the year. The carnival at Santiago de Cuba, held annually from July 18 to 27, is one of the major events in Cuba. Essentially a religious event, this carnival incorporates various elements of African, Spanish, French and communist Cuban tradition and culture. Not only locals enjoy the music, dance and colorful parade of the Santiago festival, but it also attracts fun lovers from different parts of the world.

The carnival de la Habana, held in late July and early August in the capital city, Havana, is the second biggest Cuban festival. Bringing top bands and dancers from across the island together to perform, the carnival de la Habana features dazzling parades wherein local as well as foreign tourists march down the historic El Malecon walkway.

Weather

Located close to the Tropic of Cancer, Cuba features a tropical weather, which is influenced with northeasterly trade winds that remain active throughout the year. Caribbean current that draws warm water from the equator to the coastal areas largely controls the temperature in and around the island nation. Cuba has a rainy season from the month of May to October and dry season from the month of November to April with an average temperature of 21 °C in the month of January and 27 °C in the month of July. Sitting along the entrance to the Gulf of Mexico, Cuba is prone to frequent hurricanes and thunderstorms, especially in the months of September and October, thanks to warm temperatures of the Caribbean Sea that attract powerful winds towards its coasts.

Medical Tourism in Cuba

The concept of medical tourism is not new to the island nation, as Cuba has been one of the prime healthcare destinations for over 40 years now. Combining the quality healthcare system with an unrivaled holiday destination, Cuba offers an alluring package, which is difficult to resist for an avid traveler. The Cuban Medical tourism sector attracts thousands of European, Latin American, Canadian and American clients every year.

Offering economical healthcare facilities in comparison to the Americas and Europe, Cuba is making big splashes in medical tourism industry. Tourists not only receive quality healthcare facilities in Cuba, but they can also enjoy some of the most alluring beaches to soothe their body as well as mind. Cuba is investing heavily in its tourism and healthcare industry to attract more and more foreign tourists from all over the world.

Healthcare System

Despite being a developing nation, Cuba has both a high life expectancy and literacy rate, and the infant death rate in the island nation is less than some developed countries. Featuring a national health system that works under the socialist government who takes the healthcare responsibility of all its citizens, Cuba touts the average life expectancy rate of 78 years. Regardless of the monopoly of public sector on the healthcare system, Cuba provides some of the best healthcare facilities in the region to domestic as well as foreign patients, which is quite evident in its high life expectancy rate.

Quality of Healthcare

To make medical tourism industry better than before, Cuba is making conscious efforts to keep the standard of medical facilities as high as possible in the country. Cuba may not have any JCI accredited hospital or medical institute at this point in time, but most of the medical organization in the country have set up quality-check standards to provide patients with the best possible treatments. Medical tourists from different parts of the world are flocking to the island nation to avail unique treatment of common diseases like Retina Pigmentosa (night blindness) and that too for a low price.

■ CYPRUS

General	
Language	Greek, Turkish
Time Zone	EET(UTC+2) summer EEST(UTC+3)
Dialing Code	+357
Electricity	230V, 50Hz
Major Cities	Nicosia, Limassol, Larnaca, Famagusta
Currency	Euro
Clothing	In summers, lightweight fabrics and light-colored clothing are the best to beat the heat. As for winters warm clothes such as jacket or sweater are appropriate.

Health Related	
Mortality Rate	6.48 deaths/ 1,000 live births
Life Expectancy	M 79.4/ F 83.7
Hospitals JCI accredited	1
Recommended Vaccinations	Hepatitis A, Typhoid, Hepatitis B, Rabies, Diphtheriatetanus, Measles, Varicella and Poliomyelitis.
Other Infections	HIV, Tick-borne relapsing fever, Brucellosis

Tourism Related			
Population	1,117,000	Reliability of Police Services	30/140
Global Competitiveness	3.77/7	Physician Density	45/140
Tourism Competitiveness	4.8/7	Hospital Beds	45/140
GDP/Capita	$27,085	Quality of Air Transport Infrastructure	43/140
Health and Hygiene	5.7/7	International Air Transport Network	55/140
Safety and Security	5.6/7	Quality of Roads	22/140
Air Transport Infrastructure	4.3/7	Hotel Rooms	2/140
Tourism Infrastructure	6.7/7	Tourism Openness	12/140
Cultural Infrastructure	3.1/7	Attitude of Population Towards Foreign Visitors	26/140
Visa Requirements	41/140		

Situated in the Eastern Mediterranean Sea, Cyprus is an island nation that combines different traditions and cultures, which makes it one of the unique tourist destinations in the world. Cyprus is located closer to Asia and Africa, which makes it a unique blend of the East and the West. Known as the "Island of Aprhodite," the island nation attracts beach lovers from different parts of the world who love to soak up the sun and sand. The rich history of Cyprus coupled up with contemporary infrastructure makes it a must visit place for travelers.

Location

Lying amid latitudes 34° and 36° N and longitudes 32° and 35° E, Cyprus is a well-oriented island in the Mediterranean. Surrounded by Turkey in the north, Syria and Lebanon in the east, Israel in the southeast, Egypt in the south and Greece in the northwest, Syria after the islands of Sicily and Sardinia is the third largest island in both area and population. Featuring two mountain ranges, i.e. the Troodos Mountains and the Kyrenia Range, Cyprus is separated in four major geographic sections, which includes the Republic of Cyprus that covers the two-third area of the island in the southern part and the Turkish Republic of Northern Cyprus that covers around 34.85% area.

The third section comprises the United Nations-controlled Green Line that covers 2.67% area in the middle of above two sections and works as a buffer zone between the two. Two British bases, Akrotiri and Dhekelia, which cover the remaining 2.74% area, comprise the fourth section of the island.

People

The people of Cyprus are friendly and they usually are very enthusiastic about their cultural beliefs and festivals. The people of Cyprus have excelled in different fields and they represent their country on several intercontinental fronts successfully. Due to their hard work and natural ability, the people of island nation play an important role in both domestic and international circuits.

There are two official languages, Greek and Turkish. While 76% of the population can converse in English, 12% of the whole population communicates in French and 5% in German, which makes it an ideal destination not only for European travelers but also for the people travelling from different parts of the world. Even though Russian is not an official language of Cyprus, but minorities and migrants of post-Soviet nations use and speak it widely.

Events

A number of annual events and festivals take place in Cyprus in various locations throughout the year. The Limassol Carnival is an important event for not only the citizens of Limassol but also the whole nation and tourists that visit the island nation. Held in late February and early March, the Limassol Carnival is a colorful festival that lasts for ten days. People take part in fancy dress parades and music and dance parties to enjoy the festive atmosphere.

The Greek Drama Festival is another cultural event held in late July and early August in the ancient Theatre of Citrium. Organized by the Cyprus Tourism Organization in collaboration with the Cyprus Theatre Organization, the festival hosts a number of ancient Greek dramas and comedies and attracts wide audiences from different parts of the country. The music events, including Bellapais Music Festival, held between the months of May and June bring world-renowned musicians together at one place.

Weather

Flaunting a subtropical climate, Cyprus has the warmest weather in the Mediterranean side of the European Union. Summer in Cyprus lasts for eight months, which begins in the month of April and ends in November. The average annual temperature on the coastal areas of Cyprus remains around 24 °C during the day and 14 °C at night. Cyprus receives brilliant sunshine more than 320 days a year. Usually, summers in Cyprus are dry and warm, which provides excellent conditions for water sports. During winters, the climatic conditions are very gentle in the country.

Medical Tourism in Cyprus

Over the period, Cyprus has become one of the leading destinations for wellness and medical tourism. Combining the tourism industry and health services sectors together, Cyprus attracts medical tourists from all around the world. Here they can avail quality medical care while enjoying beautiful and tranquil beaches. When compared to other developed countries, healthcare services are far economical in Cyprus.

The past few years have seen the health service in Cyprus gain a reputation at least equal to that of developed European countries. There is a large and growing private health sector. Currently, more than 80 private hospitals and clinics with 2,500 beds, 2,250 doctors and 720 dentists in Cyprus attract medical tourists from different parts of the world.

Healthcare System

The healthcare services in Cyprus are divided into the public and private sectors, which are responsible for the healthcare services in the region. The public sector provides free or nominal healthcare for those who fall under a certain category, while patients availing the services of the private healthcare sector have to pay for their treatment.

Quality of Healthcare

The private sector offers quality healthcare services in Cyprus, as private hospitals and clinics hire specialized physicians trained in the UK and other English speaking countries to provide excellent healthcare to domestic and foreign patients.

■ CZECH REPUBLIC

General	
Language	Czech, Slovak, Bulgarian, Croatian, German, Greek, Hungary, Polish, Romani, Russian, Serbian, Slovak, Ukrainian
Time Zone	CET(UTC+1) CEST(UTC+2)
Dialing Code	+420
Electricity	230V, 50Hz
Medical Tourism Status	Praha, Brno, Ostrava, Plzen
Currency	Czech koruna
Clothing	strappy vest, warm scarf, scarves, pashmina, jeans, long skirts, casual dress

Health Related	
Mortality Rate	10.94 deaths/ 1,000 population
Life Expectancy	75.0M / 81.1F
Patient: Physician Ratio	325: 1
Hospitals JCI accredited	5
Recommended Vaccinations	Hepatitis A, Typhoid, Hepatitis B, Rabies, Influenza, Tickborne encephalitis, Diphtheria-tetanus, Measles, Varicella
Other Infections	Hemorrhagic fever, Lyme disease, HIV

Tourism Related			
Population	10,513,209	Reliability of Police Services	91/140
Global Competitiveness	4.51/7	Physician Density	16/140
Tourism Competitiveness	4.8/7	Hospital Beds	9/140
GDP/Capita	$18,579	Quality of Air Transport Infrastructure	21/140
Health and Hygiene	6.8/7	International Air Transport Network	32/140
Safety and Security	5.3/7	Quality of Roads	76/140
Air Transport Infrastructure	3.7/7	Hotel Rooms	32/140
Tourism Infrastructure	5.1/7	Tourism Openness	52/140
Cultural Infrastructure	5.4/7	Attitude of Population Towards Foreign Visitors	66/140
Visa Requirements	40/140		

Situated in central Europe, Czech Republic is a landlocked country that supports liberalization in most sectors of the economy, including banks and telecommunications. Previously known as Czechoslovakia, the central European nation peacefully separated from

Slovakia on January 1, 1993. Czech Republic joined NATO in 1999 and the EU in 2004, and enjoyed the Presidency of the European Union in the early half of 2009. Ranked 30th in the 2012 Index of Economic Freedom, Czech Republic enjoys a high GDP rate even when most of the American and European nations are facing the economic slowdown. Comprising the historical regions of Bohemia and Moravia and a small part of Silesia, the landlocked nation attracts tourists from different parts of the world.

Location

Lying between latitudes 48° and 51° N and longitudes 12° and 19° E, Czech Republic is surrounded by Germany in the west, Austria in the south, Slovakia in the east and Poland in the north. Czech Republic Presenting a varied terrain, which can be divided into four sub-regions, i.e. the Carpathian montane conifer forests, Pannonian mixed forests, Central European mixed forests and Western European broadleaf forests. Rising 3000 feet above the sea level, the Bohemian Massif dominates this region and encircles a large elevated basin that in turn forms the Bohemian Plateau. The Elbe and Vltava are two main rivers of this region.

People

Usually, people of Czech Republic are very warm and friendly, but when it comes to traditional customs and family values, they become very conservative. Divided in small families, the Czech Republican society cherishes its old values and traditions. Maintaining a close coordination between relations and privacy, people of this country are very polite in nature. Strangers or tourists may find difficulty in jelling up with the locals, but they get very well along with the people they know.

Events

The Czech Republic has a number of major events, ranging from festive holidays to blow-out dance parties, throughout the year, wherein majority of local people as well as foreign tourists take part to enjoy the lively atmosphere.

The CzechTek is possibly the most popular festival that generally takes place on the last weekend in the month of July in the Czech Republic. This festival attracts thousands of dancers and party freaks from Europe and different other parts of the world. The Brno International Music Festival in late September and early October, the Agharta Jazz Festival, Easter celebrations in springs, the Night of Witches in April, Moto Grand Prix races and winter sports are some other major events that attract large audiences.

Apart from religious and cultural festivals, there are a number of beer festivals, including the Czech Beer Festival that is biggest Czech beer festival held every year in Prague in the month of May and lasts for 17 days, which attract a large number of people from different parts of nation as well as the rest of the world.

Weather

The weather conditions in Czech Republic are very mild, with warm and wet summers and cold winters. The average summer temperature ranges between 26.7 and 32.2 °C, while it mounts up to 43 °C on the coastal areas of the Red Sea. On the other hand, the average winter temperature in Czech Republic ranges between 13 and 21 °C, thanks to the northwestern wind that reduces the temperature around the coastal areas of the Mediterranean Sea. Spring season in Czech Republic is generally sunny and the period between May to August are the wettest months of the year.

Medical Tourism in Czech Republic

Offering quality medical services at an affordable price, Czech Republic is in the process of developing its medical tourism sector and looks set to rub the shoulders with the best in the business. Apart from focusing only on medical services like several other European countries, Czech Republic is strongly promoting spa and other wellness sectors to enhance medical tourism industry in the nation. Therefore, the future of medical tourism in this country looks very bright.

The abundance of natural resources in Czech Republic has made it a popular tourist destination since the 16th century, and the nation continues to grow as a therapeutic place for many domestic as well as foreign patients. Czech Republic has created the Natural Health and Therapeutic Spa, which displays the abundance of mineral sources in the country that can do wonders for the people seeking therapeutic treatment.

Healthcare System

The context of healthcare in Czech Republic has changed rapidly since its separation from Slovakia in January 1993. Czech Republic provides free healthcare services, including all medical and dental treatments, to all its citizens through compulsory contributions to a state insurance provider known as General Health Insurance Company. Offering high quality healthcare services and that too at a low price in comparison to its neighboring as well as other developed countries; Czech Republic is focusing on preventive care and therapeutic treatments.

Along with the strong public healthcare sector, the government is also promoting private medical sector to ensure quality medical services and attract more medical tourists from different parts of the world.

Quality of Healthcare

Featuring five JCI accredited medical facilities, Czech Republic emphasizes on the quality of healthcare system to ensure the wellbeing of all its citizens. In addition, the Central European nation has pioneered a number of groundbreaking procedures, including first ever robot-assisted surgery and a three-organ transplant from a single donor, to set new trends in the field of medical science. Moreover, Czech Republic was the first country to use the Ampli Chip device, which determines whether a drug is suitable for a patient.

■ ECUADOR

General	
Language	Spanish
Time Zone	ECT / GALT (UTC-5 / -6)
Dialing Code	+593
Currency	United States Dollar
Health Related	
Mortality Rate	5.03 deaths/ 1,000 population
Life Expectancy	73.2M /78.8F
Hospitals JCI accredited	1
Recommended Vaccinations	Hepatitis A, Hepatitis B, Typhoid, Yellow Fever , Rabies
Other Infections	HIV
Clothing	tropical along coast, becoming cooler inland at higher elevations; tropical in Amazonian jungle lowlands

Tourism Related			
Population	15,223,680	Physician Density	80/140
Global Competitiveness	4.42/7	Hospital Beds	99/140
Tourism Competitiveness	3.9/7	Quality of Air Transport Infrastructure	80/140
GDP/Capita	$10,055	International Air Transport Network	84/140
Safety and Security	4.0/7	Quality of Roads	53/140
Health and Hygiene	4.6/7	Hotel Rooms	66/140
Air Transport Infrastructure	2.7/7	Tourism Openness	113/140
Tourism Infrastructure	3.2/7	Attitude of Population Towards Foreign Visitors	119/140
Cultural Infrastructure	2.2/7		

Located in South America, Ecuador, or the Republic of Ecuador is a small democratic republic bordered by Peru, Columbia and the Pacific Ocean. Considered one of the mega-diverse countries in the world, Ecuador is home to countless numbers of endemic species of plants and wildlife.

Ecuador has a varied climatic pattern, ranging from mild, temperate weather in the Andean Highlands, rainforest in the lowlands, including the Amazon basin and subtropical in the Pacific coastal area. The mountain valleys enjoy a mild climate throughout the year.

The people of Ecuador are ethnically diverse, but live in harmony with each other, often marrying into different groups. It is possible to find several influences pertaining to the Spanish colonists, Amerindians, Pardo, Afro Ecuadorians, Latin Americans, Palestinians, Lebanese and even Jews.

Events and festivals

Ecuador celebrates several interesting festivals throughout the year. People of Ecuador actively take part in different festivals and events, and welcome foreign tourists with warm hearts. They love to share their traditional values with outsiders traveling to their country. In addition to the national holidays like Independence Day and Christmas, some of the other festivals celebrated in the country include Carnival, Peach Festival, Holy Week, Battle of Tapi, Labor Day, IntiRaymi, Corpus Christi Festival of Saint, Fiestas de Guayaquil, Primer Grito de Independencia, Fiestas de Mama Negra, Day of the Dead, Fiestas de Quito and Old Years etc.

Medical Tourism in Ecuador

Dental tourism has become a major part of the Ecuador's economy, with the country's medical facilities are considered as some of the best in the world. In fact, Ecuador is considered as one of the best places in South America for a variety of medical procedures, thanks to its JCI accredited hospitals, excellent infrastructure and healthcare facilities, skilled and experienced doctors, and low medical costs. Many people have claimed that the healthcare facilities in Ecuador cost much less than those in other medical tourism destinations like Thailand.

Healthcare System

It is possible to find several standard medical centers or healthcare facilities in Ecuador. The country's health care system is divided into public and private practices. And while doctors working in the country need to work in public hospitals, they can set up private clinics as well. Private healthcare is definitely better in terms of quality, and surprisingly, does not cost much. Insurance plans can cover almost 100% of the healthcare and medication costs (provided the medications are generic).

■ EGYPT

General	
Language	Arabic
Time Zone	EET(UTC+2) summer EEST(UTC+3)
Dialing Code	+20
Electricity	220V, 50Hz
Medical Tourism Status	Cairo, Alexandria, Al Jizah, Port Said, Aswan
Currency	Egyptian pound
Clothing	Summers are unbearably hot so cotton clothing should be taken, whereas winters are pleasant so a light coat and jacket will suffice.

Health Related	
Mortality Rate	4.85 deaths/ 1,000 population
Life Expectancy	71.4M /75.4F
Patient: Physician Ratio	1900: 1
Hospitals JCI accredited	3
Recommended Vaccinations	Hepatitis A, Typhoid, Hepatitis B, Rabies, Diphtheria-tetanus, Measles, Varicella, Poliomyelitis, Yellow fever
Other Infections	Dengue fever, Lymphatic filariasis, Tick-borne relapsing fever, Hepatitis E, Brucellosis, HIV

Tourism Related			
Population	84,550,000	Reliability of Police Services	52/140
Global Competitiveness	3.73/7	Physician Density	36/140
Tourism Competitiveness	3.9/7	Hospital Beds	92/140
GDP/Capita	$6,652	Quality of Air Transport Infrastructure	54/140
Health and Hygiene	5.3/7	International Air Transport Network	66/140
Safety and Security	2.7/7	Quality of Roads	107/140
Air Transport Infrastructure	3.4/7	Hotel Rooms	81/140
Tourism Infrastructure	2.9/7	Tourism Openness	69/140
Cultural Infrastructure	2.6/7	Attitude of Population Towards Foreign Visitors	61/140
Visa Requirements	38/140		

Famous for its ancient culture and civilization, Egypt is one of the prime tourist destinations that attract a large number to tourists from different parts of the world. The pyramid at Giza and the Great Sphinx are important tourist sites in the country. Egypt has emerged as one of the fastest growing and developed economies in the Middle East, thanks to the tourism, agriculture and industry sectors that contribute a major portion of its economical expansion.

Location

Lying lies between latitudes 22° and 32°N and longitudes 25° and 35°E, Egypt is located in the northern part of Africa adjoining the Mediterranean Sea. Being a transcontinental country, Egypt has emerged as a major economic and cultural force in Africa, Middle East and the Mediterranean. Surrounded by the Gaza Strip and Israel in the northeast, the Gulf of Aqaba in the east, the Red Sea in the east and south, the Mediterranean Sea in the north, Sudan in the south and Libya to the west, Egypt's major territory falls in northern part of Africa. The Sahara Desert covers a large portion of the country, which is thinly populated.

People

Egypt's people are urbanized, as half of the total population lives in urban areas. The population is largely Muslim, but several minority religions and ethnic groups also exist. People take pride in their traditional values and participate in different religious and cultural events.

Events

Egypt hosts a number of religious and cultural festivals and prominent events throughout the year, which not only attract locals but also foreign tourists from different parts of the world. Most of the religious carnivals in Egypt are linked with a specific Coptic or saint, but a majority of population irrespective of creed or religion takes part in these festivals. Ramadan, the Islamic month of fasting, is a major festival celebrated with sounds and lights in Egypt, which attracts many Muslim tourists. The Sham en Nisim is another ancient spring festival, held between the months of April and May, celebrated by Egyptians.

The Cairo International Film Festival that lasts over ten days in the month of November is another major event, which features several films by world-renowned directors and attracts tourists to the capital city. The Sphinx Festival at Le Meridien Pyramids in December lets the visitors experience the traditional music, dance and art forms of the nation.

Weather

Due to its diverse terrain and geographical conditions, the weather condition in Egypt varies from one place to the other. Usually, summers in the transcontinental country are hot and dry, whereas winters remain moderate, as most of the rain falls in the winter months. The average summer temperature in Egypt fluctuates between 26.7°C and 32.2°C that increase up to 43°C on coastal areas of the Red Sea, while the winter temperatures average between 13°C and 21°C. The cold winds from the northwest control temperatures in and around the Mediterranean coast, which makes it an ideal tourist destination.

Medical Tourism in Egypt

Egypt has been attracting foreign tourists, thanks to rich history and world-renowned attractions in the country. In the recent past, it has managed to make a significant mark in the field of medical tourism that is growing slowly yet steadily in various parts of the nation. A number of foreign tourists visit Egypt to avail medical services, particularly cosmetic surgery.

The medical services are not only cheap in the country but medical institutes and surgeons also maintain high standards of treatment to attract foreign patients. Combining quality healthcare services with tourism, Egypt is on the way to become a popular medical tourism destination, where people can visit places of historic significance while curing their diseases.

Healthcare System

Both the public and private sectors currently control the healthcare services in Egypt. While majority of population (about 56%) use private hospitals or clinics for treatment, only 36% of the population utilizes government healthcare services. Despite the facility of free healthcare in public hospitals in their locality, many Egyptians prefer to visit private clinics or physicians for their treatment.

Quality of Healthcare

Among 22 Middle East North Africa (MENA) countries, Egypt is ranked at 12th place as far as quality of the healthcare is concerned. Like many other Middle Eastern countries, the health system in Egypt is based more on curative approach than preventive; therefore, many people suffer from various chronic diseases, which are common in most of the Arab countries. There are two JCI accredited hospitals in the country, which provide quality medical services to both domestic as well as foreign patients. The Private sector is fast growing and offers quality healthcare by appointing trained and experienced physicians.

■ EL SALVADOR

General	
Language	Castilian
Time Zone	CST (UTC-6)
Dialing Code	+503
Electricity	115V, 60Hz
Medical Tourism Status	San Salvador, Soyapango, Santa Ana, San Miquel
Currency	U.S. dollar
Clothing	Due to the climate, the most recommended clothing is light, thin, usually made of cotton.

Health Related	
Mortality Rate	5.61 deaths/ 1,000 population
Life Expectancy	67.6M /75.7F
Hospitals JCI accredited	0
Recommended Vaccinations	Hepatitis A, Typhoid, Hepatitis B, Rabies, Tetanus-Diphtheria, MMR, Yellow fever, Poliomyelitis
Other Infections	Venezuelan equine encephalitis, Chagas disease, Visceral and cutaneous leishmaniasis, Tick-borne relapsing fever, Brucellosis, HIV

Tourism Related			
Population	6,134,000	Reliability of Police Services	96/140
Global Competitiveness	3.80/7	Physician Density	72/140
Tourism Competitiveness	3.6/7	Hospital Beds	114/140
GDP/Capita	$3,855	Quality of Air Transport Infrastructure	42/140
Health and Hygiene	4.2/7	International Air Transport Network	39/140
Safety and Security	3.6/7	Quality of Roads	52/140
Air Transport Infrastructure	2.8/7	Hotel Rooms	103/140
Tourism Infrastructure	3.3/7	Tourism Openness	106/140
Cultural Infrastructure	1.5/7	Attitude of Population Towards Foreign Visitors	90/140
Visa Requirements	23/140		

One of the smallest and most densely populated countries in Central America, El Salvador is a mix of different ethnic groups, which is mainly dominated by the Spanish and expatriate refugees. These diverse factors contribute toward the rich and unique cultural heritage of the nation. When it comes to the Human Development Index, El Salvador finds a place in the top 10 Latin American countries and in the top 3 in Central America countries in terms of industrial growth.

El Salvador's tourism industry has seen a rapid growth in past few years, thanks to the conscious efforts of the government. Since it is one of the major cultural and commercial centers of Central America, El Salvador now attracts a number of travelers from different parts of the world.

Location

Located in the western coast of Central America, El Salvador is surrounded by the Pacific Ocean in the south, Guatemala in the west, the Gulf of Fonseca in the east and Honduras in the northeast. With a total area of 8,123 miles, the Central American nation can be categorized in three sub-regions. Lying between latitudes 13° and 15°N and longitudes 87° and 91°W in the isthmus of Central America, El Salvador stretches 88 miles from north to south and 168 miles from east to west. Featuring over 300 rivers and several lakes enclosed by volcanic craters, El Salvador is the only Central American country without Caribbean coastline.

People

With a total population of around 7.2 million, El Salvador is the most densely populated nation in the region. Most of the Salvadoran people (around 86 per cent) are of mixed ancestry, largely indigenous Native American and European descent, and just one percent population is purely indigenous, which finds its roots in native Mayan, Pipil, Lenca and Kakawira lineage. Due to racial intermixing during colonial period, El Salvador has no evident African population at present.

Events

A number of festivals and other social and cultural events take place in El Salvador throughout the year. These festivals and events are not only important for local people, but foreign travelers also enjoy the lively atmosphere during the festive time in the country. El Salvador Independence Day, held on September 15 each year, is an important event that exhibits national heritage and culture of the country.

The "Balls of Fire Festival" is another major event that takes place in the city of Nejapa on August 31 and lets people experience the culture of El Salvador. People come to streets with painted faces and fireballs to entertain spectators.

The "Fiestas Agostinas" held in the month of August is one of the most popular El Salvador festivals, which is characterized by a range of sports events, art exhibitions, theater performances, food fairs and many other events that take place in various parts of the nation. People actively take part in various events and enjoy the festive time.

Weather

Featuring a tropical climate characterized by wet and dry seasons, El Salvador's weather remains constant throughout the year, with minor changes in hilly regions. The temperature in the mountain areas and Central Plateau remains moderate, while the Pacific lowlands with average temperature ranging between 25°C and 29°C becomes hot in summers.

The summers in El Salvador extend from the month of November to April, when northeast trade winds influence the weather patterns in the country. On the other hand, the rainy season (also referred as winters) stretches from the month of May to October with heavy rainfall on southern-facing mountain slopes. The start or end of the dry season, flaunting moderate weather conditions, is possibly the best time to visit El Salvador.

Medical Tourism in El Salvador

Due to its close proximity to North American countries like the US and Canada and low cost of medical services, El Salvador is emerging as one of the biggest medical tourism hubs in the region. Offering personalize care without compromising the quality, the Central American nation is attracting a large number of medical tourists not only from the Americas but also from different parts of the world.

Featuring several state-of-the-art hospitals and clinics equipped with high tech equipments and technologies in different parts, El Salvador provides quality healthcare for both domestic as well as foreign patients. Known for cosmetic treatments and pre and post-operative services, El Salvador also offers rehabilitative care, which is becoming popular among medical tourists worldwide.

Healthcare System

The healthcare in El Salvador operates as a two-tiered system, i.e. public and private. The former sector is responsible for delivering and managing the healthcare for the deprived people who cannot afford the expensive healthcare services on their own. In this sector, the physicians are usually overburdened, as they have to attend to or treat a large number of patients in public hospitals.

The private healthcare system is on the rise because of economic growth and the high living standard of people in the country. Private hospitals and clinics provide high quality healthcare to domestic as well as foreign patients, of course for a price.

Quality of Healthcare

Offering superior healthcare, El Salvador is emerging as a new medical and wellness tourism destination in Central America. Private clinics and hospitals appoint well-trained, experienced physicians, who usually get training in North America and Europe, to treat medical tourists visiting the nation from different parts of the world.

Most of the medical institutes in the country are equipped with the latest equipment to provide the best possible care to local patients as well as medical tourists. At present, there are no JCI accredited hospitals in El Salvador, but the standard of care is on the rise in both public and private healthcare sectors.

■ ESTONIA

General	
Language	Estonian, Voro, Setu
Time Zone	EET (UTC+2) EEST (UTC+3)
Dialing Code	+ 372
Major Cities	Tallinn, Tallinn, Maardu, Maardu
Currency	Euro
Clothing	Warm, dry summers and fairly severe winters with Heavy snowfall or even snowstorms.

Health Related	
Mortality Rate	13.6 deaths/ 1,000 population
Life Expectancy	71.1M /81.3F
Hospitals JCI accredited	0
Recommended Vaccinations	Hepatitis A, Hepatitis B,
Other Infections	HIV

Tourism Related			
Population	1,286,540	Physician Density	24/140
Global Competitiveness	4.64/7	Hospital Beds	28/140
Tourism Competitiveness	4.8/7	Quality of Air Transport Infrastructure	73/140
GDP/Capita	$21,713	International Air Transport Network	102/140
Safety and Security	5.6/7	Quality of Roads	61/140
Health and Hygiene	6.2/7	Hotel Rooms	25/140
Air Transport Infrastructure	3.1/7	Tourism Openness	25/140
Tourism Infrastructure	6.1/7	Attitude of Population Towards Foreign Visitors	50/140
Cultural Infrastructure	2.5/7		

The Republic of Estonia, more commonly known as Estonia, is a North European state in the Baltic region. It is surrounded by Gulf of Finland in the north, Latvia in the south, Baltic Sea in the west and Russia in the east. As of now, the total population of Estonia is nearly 1.3 million. The climate of the country varies between oceanic and continental. The mild weather of this place is ideal for medical tourists. February is the coldest and July is the warmest month in Estonia. From the midweek of December to later half of March, heavy snowfall can be expected.

Events and Festivals

One can experience the true essence of Estonia in terms of art and culture by participating in local festivals. Music is an important part of almost every event. Special festivals dedicated to different types of music are organized at various time of the year. Some of them include Jazzkaar and Pärnu Jazz Festival, dedicated to Jazz music; Õllesummer Festival dedicated to jazz, rock, reggae and conventional Estonian music. Other events that are popular among the Estonians include Beach Party Festival, Street Theatre Festival, Tallinn Baroque Music Festival, Independence Day, Evgeny Mravinsky Festival, Midsummer (St John's Day), Black Nights Film Festival, Harpsichord Days, and so on.

Medical Tourism in Estonia

Medical tourism is one of the most rapidly growing industries in Estonia. Renowned medical professionals and the ease of getting treatment are two most important factors that make this place ideal for medical tourists. Estonian hospitals offer varied types of treatment to international as well as the local patients. Some of them include dental facilities, hair transplantations, cancer treatment, aesthetic surgeries, fertility treatments, rehabilitation and wellness therapies and many more. The healing qualities of mud baths available in Estonia are quite famous all across the world. The cost of treatment is low as compared to the United States. Tallinn with its breathtaking beauty is a perfect place, which ensures speedy recovery to tourists.

Healthcare System

The healthcare system in Estonia has seen a lot of improvement since the year 1990. Public health insurance is the main source of finance for the healthcare system. Estonian Health Insurance Fund (EHIF) takes care of the health insurance of the patients. Those who are insured with this organization have family practitioners, who refer patients to specialists when need arises.

Medical tourists can also seek medical advice from their own family practitioners. For consultation with dermatologists, gynecologists, pulmonologists, dentists, ophthalmologists, orthopedics, and surgeons or in time of emergencies, one does not require any sort of recommendation or referral from a practitioner. However, measures are being taken to deal with the recent shortage of doctors and nurses around the country.

■ FRANCE

General	
Language	French
Time Zone	CET(UTC+1) summer CEST(UTC+2)
Dialing Code	+33
Electricity	230V, 50Hz
Medical Tourism Status	Paris, Marseille, Lyon, Toulouse
Currency	Euro
Clothing	Summers are warm and sunny, where as winters have Heavy snowfall.

Health Related	
Mortality Rate	8.65 deaths/ 1,000 population
Life Expectancy	78.5M /85.F
Patient: Physician Ratio	300:1
Hospitals JCI accredited	0
Recommended Vaccinations	Influenza, Diphtheria-tetanus, Measles, Varicella
Other Infections	Toxoplasmosis, Leptospirosis, Cutaneous leishmaniasis, tick-borne encephalitis, Mediterranean spotted fever, Lyme disease, West Nile Virus, Malaria, Hepatitis E, HIV

Tourism Related			
Population	65,350,000	Reliability of Police Services	19/140
Global Competitiveness	5.52/7	Physician Density	22/140
Tourism Competitiveness	5.3/7	Hospital Beds	11/140
GDP/Capita	$41,141	Quality of Air Transport Infrastructure	10/140
Health and Hygiene	6.7/7	International Air Transport Network	9/140
Safety and Security	5.5/7	Quality of Roads	5/140
Air Transport Infrastructure	5.4/7	Hotel Rooms	36/140
Tourism Infrastructure	6.1/7	Tourism Openness	87/140
Cultural Infrastructure	6.0/7	Attitude of Population Towards Foreign Visitors	80/140
Visa Requirements	40/140		

France is one of the largest nations in Europe and is quite famous for its rich traditions and cultural heritage. This nation has been a dominating force in the region that supports the traditional values of Western Europe, especially in the field of art and literature. A unique blend of traditional and modern values, France is essentially a unitary semi-presidential republic. Boasting the second largest exclusive economic zone worldwide, the France Republic also exerts strapping cultural, military and political authority, which makes it major power not only in Europe, but also in the world. France is a very popular tourist destination and receives over 79 million foreign tourists in a year from different parts of the world.

Location

Stretching from the Mediterranean Sea to the English Channel and the North Sea, France holds a strategic position in Western Europe. Lying between latitudes 41° and 51° N and longitudes 6° W and 10° E, France is surrounded by Germany, Luxembourg, Spain, Andorra, Monaco, Belgium, Switzerland and Italy. In addition, France borders Suriname in the west and Brazil in the east and south. With total land area, including overseas territories, of 246,201 square miles, France is the largest EU state by area.

People

France is an urbanized nation, where over 75% of the population lives in cities or urban areas. The French people are known for their exclusive taste for culture and fashion, and they take pride in their cultural and social values. France has been a popular tourist destination for centuries, and the people welcome foreign tourists with open heart and share their cultural values with them. People of France preserve their cultural heritage and love to share it with foreign tourists. Artists and fashion enthusiasts from different part of the world keep gathering in France throughout the year to enrich themselves with the affluent cultural and artistic legacy of the nation.

Events

The French calendar is full of numerous social, cultural and sports events, which are not only popular among locals but also attracts foreign tourists in bulk. Tour de France in the month of July, Paris Marathon in April and French Open in late May and early June are some of the most popular sporting events that attract a number of local as well as foreign supporters. In addition, Great Wines Fair held in the month of February and Paris Fashion Week in March, together with Paris Film Festival in late March and early April and the Vintage Car Rally in May are some other important events that capture larger audiences from various parts of the world.

Weather

Featuring a wide array of landscapes, which ranges from coastal plains in the northwest to Alps mountain ranges in the southeast, and the Massif Central in the south central to Pyrenees in the southwest, the climate in France varies from one place to the other. Weather in France remains cool during the winters and gentle during summer, while the inland climate becomes more continental with hot, stormy summers and scant rain.

Medical Tourism in France

Offering quality healthcare, France has been one of the prime medical tourism destinations that attract people seeking the best medical facilities from Europe and different other parts of the world. Despite expensive healthcare services, France attracts a large number of medical tourists, as tourists can enjoy rich cultural heritage and visit famous tourist destinations, while availing some of the best medical facilities or services in the country.

Healthcare System

Touting one of the highest life expectancy rates of the European Union, France offers free healthcare facilities for people suffering from chronic diseases like cancer, AIDS, Cystic Fibrosis and so on. Like many other European countries, France also presents a nationalized, universal health care system, which is funded through various taxes and revenues. The public sector owns and manages the majority of hospitals and medical institutes (approximately 62 percent) in France, while remaining 32 percent health facilities are managed by the private sector, which comprises both non-profit and profitable organizations. With 3.22 physicians for every 1000 residents, France ensures the wellbeing of all its citizens.

Quality of Healthcare

According to the World Health Organization, France is the "best overall health care" provider in the world, as most of the healthcare institutes or hospitals in the country are equipped with latest medical equipment and technologies, ensuring the best possible health care for both domestic as well as foreign patients. Most of the hospitals and clinics in the country appoint highly qualified and professionally trained surgeons to provide the best medical services in the world.

Offering customized treatments to suit the individual needs of different patients, France is one of the most popular medical tourism destinations in the world.

■ GERMANY

General	
Language	Germany
Time Zone	CET(UTC +1) summer CEST(UTC+2)
Dialing Code	+49
Electricity	220-240V
Medical Tourism Status	Berlin, Hamburg, Munchen, Koln, Munich
Currency	Euro
Clothing	Summers are warm and sunny, where as winters have Heavy snowfall.
Health Related	
Mortality Rate	11 deaths/ 1,000 population
Life Expectancy	78.3M /83F
Patient: Physician Ratio	300:1
Hospitals JCI accredited	5
Recommended Vaccinations	Influenza, Tickborne encephalitis, Diphtheria-tetanus, Measles, Varicella
Other Infections	Lyme Disease, Cowpox Infections, HIV

Tourism Related			
Population	80,399,300	Reliability of Police Services	4/140
Global Competitiveness	5.48/7	Physician Density	19/140
Tourism Competitiveness	5.4/7	Hospital Beds	5/140
GDP/Capita	$41,513	Quality of Air Transport Infrastructure	7/140
Health and Hygiene	6.8/7	International Air Transport Network	5/140
Safety and Security	6.0/7	Quality of Roads	10/140
Air Transport Infrastructure	5.4/7	Hotel Rooms	24/140
Tourism Infrastructure	5.7/7	Tourism Openness	89/140
Cultural Infrastructure	6.3/7	Attitude of Population Towards Foreign Visitors	83/140
Visa Requirements	40/140		

Situated in western-central Europe, Germany is a global economic and political power. Divided into three major geographical regions, the European nation offers a variety of attractions to visitors from different parts of the world. Featuring vibrant cities with amazing architecture and fabulous shopping malls, Germany offers a pulsating nightlife for party freaks.

On the other, enchanting medieval villages and traditional wine villages, picturesque countryside, castles, palaces and abbeys epitomize the German romanticism. Visitors can enjoy the natural landscape, ranging from high Alps to dramatic gorges and huge silent forests to rugged coastline.

Cherishing 33 UNESCO listed sites, Germany has many major cities, each presenting a unique character with rich history and mesmerizing surroundings. Not only the art and architecture of various cities differ from each other, but they also present a very distinctive lifestyle. Local traditions and values of the country simply reflect in its art forms, celebrations or events and the way people live and work.

Tourist Attractions

Characterized by a variety of landscapes from north to south, Germany offers some of the most magnificent sights and locations in the world that invariably attract tourists. If you are a nature lover and enjoy a peaceful life, the Federal Republic of Germany offers an assortment of natural places like the Rhine and Moselle valleys, the Bavarian Alps and Lakelands, the Baltic coast and the Harz Mountains, together with Lake Constance, Saxon Switzerland, the Black Forest, the Bavarian Forest and the volcanic Eifel region.

Germany may appear an industrial, modern and technologically developed nation from the outskirt, but it also touts a rich cultural heritage, which is visible in many towns and villages across the country. Bamberg, Goslar and Lübeck are some of the famous heritage sites in the country, which enjoy the UNESCO World Heritage Site status as well.

The road and railway infrastructure in Germany is possibly the best in Europe, which makes the journey across the country easy and pleasant. In addition, there are some famous tourist paths, including Romantic Road, Castle Road and Fairy Tale Road, inviting visitors to enjoy a refreshing walk.

Events

No matter, if you visit Germany in springs, summers, autumns or winters, you will find an exciting festival or event going on in the country. Apart from religious and cultural festivals, a number of wine and beer festivals take place from spring through autumn all over the country. The "Oktoberfest" beer festival in Munich is the largest international festival of its kind, which attracts wine lovers from various parts of the world. The Berlin Film Festival (held in the month of February), Bach Fest and Rose Monday Parade are some other popular German festivals that attract larger audiences.

Weather

Weather in Germany is temperate, though it varies from place to place. Winters in Germany can be extremely cold as the temperature come close to or even below freezing point in some parts, while the summers are hot. The temperature in summer remains between 20°C and 30°C, which is characterized by frequent showers. Combine the continental Eastern European and the oceanic Western European climate, Germany provides ideal condition for great biodiversity that attracts nature lovers from all parts of the world.

Medical Tourism in Germany

Offering some of the best healthcare services, Germany is a prime medical tourism destination. Touting the world's oldest universal health care system, Germany has been attracting medical travelers from different parts of the world for centuries and continues to lead the industry even today.

The best part of the German medical sector is that the patients need not to wait for long durations to seek the care even for complicated diseases, which is very common in most of the developed nations, including the United Kingdom, Canada and Ireland. Many medical tourists from the Gulf and Arab nations travel to Germany to avail quality health services.

Healthcare System

Segregated in two parts, i.e. public and private, Germany's health care system provides the best services to both foreign and domestic patients. Around 75 percent health care institutes in the country are managed by public sector, while remaining 25 percent hospitals and clinics are owned by private sector. About 85 percent of the total population is covered under a basic health insurance plan that ensures vital healthcare services, while the remaining inhabitants choose private insurance, which offers additional benefits to the policyholders.

Since majority of the Germans enjoy the health cover in one form or the other, the country has a huge number of per capita hospitals, which is almost double than that in the US. The high number of hospital cut down the waiting list of patients, while ensuring better medical facilities and treatment.

Quality of Healthcare

German hospitals follow strict international standards and are equipped with the latest medical equipments and technologies. As legislated by German law, almost all the hospitals in the country undergo quality surveillance programs under the supervision of government. Additionally, physicians have to qualify a number of tests and training programs before practicing in their specific fields.

Currently, there are four JCI accredited hospitals in Germany. German hospitals are known for their exceptional services in the field of oncology. Germany is one of the top medical tourism destinations for cancer patients, owing to its revolutionary procedures and alternative treatments.

■ GREECE

General	
Language	Greek, English
Time Zone	EET (UTC-2)
Dialing Code	+30
Electricity	220V, 50Hz
Medical Tourism Status	Athens, Thessaloniki, Piraeus, Patrai
Currency	Euro
Clothing	Summers are warm and sunny, where as winters have Heavy snowfall.

Health Related	
Mortality Rate	10.61 deaths/ 1,000 population
Life Expectancy	78.3M /83.6F
Patient: Physician Ratio	230:1
Hospitals JCI accredited	1
Recommended Vaccinations	Hepatitis A, MMR, Diphtheria-tetanus, Influenza, Yellow feve
Other Infections	Crimean-Congo hemorrhagic fever, tick-borne encephalitis, Leishmaniasis, HIV

Tourism Related			
Population	10,815,197	Reliability of Police Services	63/140
Global Competitiveness	4.13/7	Physician Density	1/140
Tourism Competitiveness	4.8/7	Hospital Beds	36/140
GDP/Capita	$22,055	Quality of Air Transport Infrastructure	45/140
Health and Hygiene	6.4/7	International Air Transport Network	58/140
Safety and Security	4.7/7	Quality of Roads	71/140
Air Transport Infrastructure	4.7/7	Hotel Rooms	3/140
Tourism Infrastructure	6.8/7	Tourism Openness	48/140
Cultural Infrastructure	4.3/7	Attitude of Population Towards Foreign Visitors	37/140
Visa Requirements	40/140		

Greece is one of the urns of human civilization, which makes this country a tourist hot spot as it offers a number of ancient sites and historical attractions to tourists from different regions of the world. Greece has long been a tourist attraction for individuals interested in exploring the ancient culture and traditions. However, Greece in recent times has also become an attraction for travelers looking for exquisite cuisine, bustling city life and beautiful islands. Tourism is an important part of Greece's national income, as it funds approximately 16 percent of the gross domestic products of the country.

Location

Situated at the crossroads of Asia, Europe, Africa and the Middle East, Greece is surrounded by the Mediterranean Sea in the south, the Ionian Sea in the west and the Aegean Sea lies in the east. Lying between latitudes 34° and 42° N and longitudes 19° and 30° E, Greece shares its borders with Albania in the northwest, Bulgaria and the Republic of Macedonia in the north and Turkey in the northeast. Greece is popular for its beaches and beautiful coastline, which measures 14,880 km and features over 1,400 islands that become a centre of attraction among tourists.

People

People in Greece are very passionate about their rich past and culture. They greet foreign tourists with a warm heart and love to explain their cultural values and historical facts to the visitors that keep flocking the mystic country from different parts of the world. Greeks are very friendly and hospitable to the tourists. Though the official language of Greece is Greek, which is spoken by 99 percent of the population but majority of individuals speak English as well.

Events

Greece celebrates a number of festivals and events throughout the year. These festivals are not only important for local people, but they also attract a large number of tourists from Europe and various parts of the world. Usually, festivals in Greece are based around spiritual or religious beliefs and are celebrated according to the Greek Orthodox calendar.

The Carnival or Apokries, which takes place from 31 January to 22 February every year, is one of the major events in Greece that bring people to streets dancing on traditional music. Characterized by chariot parade and costume parties, the Carnival gives the glimpse of traditional Greek culture as people dress themselves in traditional costumes to enjoy the parade. Besides the religious celebrations, several cultural, sporting, theatrical and musical events take place, mainly during summers, in the country.

Weather

With nine geographic regions, including Thrace, Crete and the Ionian Islands, Thessaly and Epirus, together with the Aegean Islands, Macedonia, Central Greece and the Peloponnese, Greece can be categorized in three climate zones, i.e. Mediterranean, Alpine and Temperate. While the Mediterranean climate is usually mild, wet in winters and hot, dry in summers and the temperate climate features colder winters and hot summers with frequent thunderstorms, on the other hand, the Alpine climate is visible in the mountainous regions. The capital city, Athens, which is also the largest city in the country features both Mediterranean and Temperate weather patterns.

Medical Tourism in Greece

If compared to other European nations, the medical tourism industry in Greece is very new and still looking to make a mark in the region. However, Greece has an edge over other neighboring countries in the region, as it is already a established tourist destination, attracting the tourist from various parts of the world. Million of travelers visit or travel Greece every year in order to get a glimpse of its famous ruins and other historical attractions.

If Greece manages to develop the healthcare industry or the standard of the medical facilities in the country, it has the potential to attract the medical tourism and become a leader in the region. Greece could be an ideal medical tourism destination for tourists, as they can combine a fine vacation with quality health services.

Healthcare System

Since 1983, Greece opted for a nationalized healthcare system where medical services are provided free or at a nominal cost to all the citizens. This ensures that all Greeks have access to healthcare, no matter, whether they belong to a particular socio-economic class or are affected by a chronic or fatal disease. Rural health centers and clinics provide primary care around the nation, while the secondary or advanced care is delivered through the public hospitals and private facilities.

Greece is reforming its healthcare system in order to improve the health services for their citizens and foreign patients. Through additional funds received from the EU and other world bodies, Greece is focusing more on quality care practices, building new facilities and installing more high-tech equipment and machines.

Quality of Healthcare

The public hospitals provide adequate care to its citizens; however, the private facilities provide excellent quality care but for those who can afford it. The private sector provides personalized care by appointing skilled surgeons who utilizes the latest technology for the treatment of a patient.

■ GUATEMALA

General	
Language	Spanish
Time Zone	CST (UTC-6)
Dialing Code	+502
Major Cities	Guatemala City, Mixco, Villa Nueva, San Juan Sacatepéquez
Currency	Quetzal
Health Related	
Mortality Rate	4.92 deaths/ 1,000 population
Life Expectancy	65.8M /72.8F
Hospitals JCI accredited	0
Recommended Vaccinations	Hepatitis A, Hepatitis B, Typhoid, Rabies
Other Infections	HIV
Clothing	Tropical, hot, humid in lowlands, cooler in highlands

Tourism Related			
Population	15,438,384	Physician Density	92/140
Global Competitiveness	4.65/7	Hospital Beds	124/140
Tourism Competitiveness	3.56/7	Quality of Air Transport Infrastructure	58/140
GDP/Capita	$5,208	International Air Transport Network	57/140
Safety and Security	3.5/7	Quality of Roads	90/140
Health and Hygiene	3.8/7	Hotel Rooms	64/140
Air Transport Infrastructure	2.5/7	Tourism Openness	76/140
Tourism Infrastructure	2.6/7	Attitude of Population Towards Foreign Visitors	97/140
Cultural Infrastructure	2.0/7		

Guatemala, officially known as the Republic of Guatemala, is located in Central America and is flanked by Mexico in the north and west, Honduras and Caribbean in the east, Belize in the northeast, El Salvador in the southeast and Pacific Ocean in the southwest. It has a population of around 14 million. Guatemala has a varied climate, which ranges from tropical to temperate. The entire country can be divided into three climatic zones - hot, pleasant and cool. The coastal plains have a hot climate, whereas most of the tourist destinations like Antigua are pleasant enough. The mountainous regions of Guatemala fall under the cool zone.

Events and Festivals

Mayan history and culture plays an important role in the celebrations of different festivals in Guatemala. The Mayan New Year varies every year as the Mayan calendar is of 260 days only. Other festivals that are celebrated as Mayan only festivals include the Coban Folklore Festival. Since Guatemala is a Roman Catholic country, many carnivals here are related to this specific religion. Some of the popular events and festivals include Semana Santa, Dia de la Asuncion, The Pilgrimage of the Black Christ of Esquipulas, Revolution Day, The Day of the Dead Kite Festival, Coffee Harvest Celebration, Burning the Devil Celebrations (La Quema del Diablo), etc.

Medical Tourism in Guatemala

Medical tourism in Guatemala is relatively new as compared to other countries in Latin America. However, with the use of modern technology and the finest medical services, this country has become a favorable destination for medical tourists. The cost of treatment is also a fraction of what people have to spend in the United States of America. There are first-rate hospitals and clinics to cater to patients coming from outside the country. The doctors are well trained and highly skilled. Dermatology, bariatric, oncology, dental, orthopedic, fertility, ophthalmology, urology, cosmetic surgery, etc. are some of the vital medical procedures that have made the country one of the hottest medical tourism destination.

Healthcare System

Though Guatemala is flourishing as a medical tourism hub, the healthcare system in the country still requires lots of improvement. There are three sectors in the entire healthcare system including private-profit, private-nonprofit and public. Doctors, nurses and other medical professionals volunteer to support various local healthcare providers. However, the quality is yet to be up to the mark. Those living in the rural areas even lack the basic medical facilities. However, steps are being taken to eliminate all these issues and improve the condition significantly. Mobile Medical Groups have been launched for providing essential primary health care facilities to people. Different volunteer organizations are also trying to make the medical system better for the patients.

■ HUNGARY

General	
Language	Hungarian
Time Zone	CET(UTC+1) CEST(UTC+2)
Dialing Code	+36
Electricity	220V,50Hz
Medical Tourism Status	Budapest, Debrecan, Nagyvarad
Currency	Forint
Clothing	Light clothes in the summer with a jacket for cool evenings. In winter you should put on a warm coat and boots. It is very useful if you have raincoat in autumn and spring.

Health Related	
Mortality Rate	12.67 deaths/ 1,000 population
Life Expectancy	71.3M /78.8F
Patient: Physician Ratio	300:1
Hospitals JCI accredited	0
Recommended Vaccinations	Hepatitis A, Typhoid, Hepatitis B, Rabies, Influenza, Tickborne encephalitis, Diphtheria-tetanus, MMR (Measles-Mumps-Rubella), Varicella
Other Infections	bacterial diarrhea and hepatitis A , Yellow fever, Plague, HIV

Tourism Related				
Population	9,942,000	Reliability of Police Services	46/140
Global Competitiveness	4.78/7	Physician Density	29/140
Tourism Competitiveness	4.5/7	Hospital Beds	9/140
GDP/Capita	$12,735	Quality of Air Transport Infrastructure	91/140
Health and Hygiene	6.6/7	International Air Transport Network	107/140
Safety and Security	5.3/7	Quality of Roads	69/140
Air Transport Infrastructure	2.9/7	Hotel Rooms	44/140
Tourism Infrastructure	5.2/7	Tourism Openness	50/140
Cultural Infrastructure	4.1/7	Attitude of Population Towards Foreign Visitors	116/140
Visa Requirements	40/140		

Located in the Carpathian Basin, Hungary is a landlocked country that comprises of many vibrant locations that are very different from each other. Featuring low mountains in the northwest and the plains in the east, Hungary houses many small, beautiful villages that add to the natural beauty of the nation. Hungary is one of the eminent members of European Union and Schengen Agreement that led to the formation of borderless Europe.

Hungarian, also called Magyar, is the official language of the nation, which is widely spoken throughout the country, and the capital city Budapest is the largest city in Hungary. The Central European country has switched from textile and food industry to renewable energy systems and high-end tourism, which makes it one of the most popular destinations not only in the continent but also in the world.

Location

Situated in Central Europe, Hungary is surrounded by Austria in the west, Slovenia in the southwest, Slovakia in the north, Serbia and Croatia in the south and Ukraine and Romania in the east. Lying between latitudes 45° and 49° N, and longitudes 16° and 23° E, Hungary stretches around 93,030 square kilometers, out of which 690 square kilometers lie under water, Hungary is a small country, which is roofed by Carpathian Mountains, the Alps and the Dinaric Alps. More than half of the area in Hungary is covered by plains, which comprises the Great Hungarian Plain in the southeast and the Little Hungarian Plain in the west. While the hilly regions comprise the Transdanubian Mountains in the central part of Transdanubia and eastern part of the Alps, together with Alpokalja in the west and the Mecsek Mountains and Villány Mountains in the southern part of the country.

People

Apart from the art of hospitality, Hungarians have a great flair for cuisine, which is an important part of their culture. They actively take part in various cultural or/and social events and enjoy the festive period. Being a land of thermal water, Hungary and its people have a passion for spa culture, which combine Roman, Greek, Turkish, and northern country architectural elements to woo tourists from different parts of the world.

Events

With more than 200 events taking place throughout the year, Hungary is known as a "Festival City" that attracts a large number of tourists from Europe and other parts of the world. The Budapest Spring Festival, which starts in March, is one of most prestigious cultural events in the whole country, wherein a large number of national and international performers entertain people with their performances.

The Formula 1 Hungarian Grand Prix in the month of August, the European Wine Song Festival in September and Danube Carnival and the Miskolc Opera Festival (or the International Opera Festival of Miskolc) in June are some other major events that invite worldwide visitors to the nation.

Weather

Influenced by the Mediterranean and Atlantic Ocean, the climate of Hungary is generally continental, with a variation in hilly regions. The weather varies from place to place in the country according to the location or altitude. While winters are cold, cloudy and damp or windy with average low temperature ranging between –3 °C and –7 °C, on the other, summers are warm with average high temperature ranging between 23 °C and 28 °C. Hungary receives heavy rainfall (around 600 mm), especially the western and southwestern parts, in the months of May, June and November.

Medical Tourism in Hungary

Hungary is emerging as a popular medical tourism destination for European travelers, especially from UK, Germany and Austria, seeking cost-effective healthcare. Hungry provides some of the best medical service in cosmetic surgery and dentistry. Treatment costs in Hungary are comparatively lower than that in Western European countries. Featuring around 1,300 thermal springs across the country, some of which are being used as spas, Hungary has a great potential to become a wellness tourism hub in the region. In addition, Hungary is actively promoting their physical and mental wellbeing service all over the world to attract medical tourists. Even though the tourist season in Hungary stretches from April to October, but July and August are the peak months when tourists enter the nation in bulk.

Healthcare System

Based on the nationalized medical system of the Great Britain, the healthcare system in Hungary is largely controlled by the public sector. The Hungarian National Healthcare fund was created in 1993, which controls or manages the health care in the country. The major part of the healthcare system (around 83 percent) is generated through general taxes and revenues, which is mandatory for all working individuals. On the other hand, the private medical sector in Hungary provides personalize care, of course, for a price.

Quality of Healthcare

Most of the private medical institutes are equipped with the latest technology and facilities, which offer high quality medical and dental facilities to domestic as well as foreign patients. Under the influence of German patients, who have been visiting the country for decades to take advantage of affordable dental and surgical treatments, the quality of healthcare in Hungary has been on the rise.

The medical facilities in Hungary might lack international accreditations like JCI, but the Hungarian Ministry of Health certifies and licenses the hospitals and clinics to ensure the quality of care in the country. Most of the healthcare institutes appoint well-qualified surgeons who use latest medical equipments and technologies for treatment.

■ INDIA

General	
Language	English, Hindi
Time Zone	IST (UTC+05:30)
Dialing Code	+91
Electricity	240V,50Hz
Medical Tourism Status	Mumbai, Delhi, Bangalore, Calcutta, Chennai, Ahmadabad
Currency	Indian Rupee (NIR)
Clothing	In Summers T-shirts and baggy pants. Whereas in Winters pack woolen clothes. When visiting places of worship you should be fully clothed.

Health Related	
Mortality Rate	Male: 44.71 deaths/1,000 live births; Female: 47.59/1,000 live births
Life Expectancy	63.8M /67.3F
Patient: Physician Ratio	1750:1
Hospitals JCI accredited	21
Recommended Vaccinations	Hepatitis A, Typhoid, Hepatitis B, Rabies, Diphtheria-tetanus, Measles, Varicella, Yellow Fever and Japanese encephalitis
Other Infections	African trypanosomiasis, Cutaneous leishmaniasis, Vibrio parahemolyticus, Brucellosis, Anthrax, Typhus, Tick-borne relapsing fever, Lymphatic filariasis, West Nile virus, HIV

Tourism Related			
Population	1,210,193,422	Reliability of Police Services	62/140
Global Competitiveness	4.26/7	Physician Density	97/140
Tourism Competitiveness	4.1/7	Hospital Beds	116/140
GDP/Capita	$3,851	Quality of Air Transport Infrastructure	68/140
Health and Hygiene	3.0/7	International Air Transport Network	52/140
Safety and Security	4.7/7	Quality of Roads	85/140
Air Transport Infrastructure	4.2/7	Hotel Rooms	136/140
Tourism Infrastructure	2.6/7	Tourism Openness	120/140
Cultural Infrastructure	4.7/7	Attitude of Population Towards Foreign Visitors	60/140
Visa Requirements	127/140		

India is the seventh biggest country in area and the second most populous nation after China in the world, which is admired for its historic trade routes and royal kingdoms. Comprising the larger part of the Indian subcontinent, India is the origin place to the first urban culture in South Asia, the Indus Valley Civilization, which incorporated ancient cities like Harappa and Mohenjo-daro. These sites make India a mystic nation and attract a vast number of tourists from all over the world. Hospitality runs deep down in the tradition values and culture of India. The Republic of India is also a fascinating kaleidoscope of races, languages, religions, customs and festivals, making it an all-appealing, year-round tourist destination.

Location

Situated in the north of the equator, India lies between 6° 44' and 35° 30' north latitude and 68° 7' and 97° 25' east longitude. Sharing its eastern border with Burma and Bangladesh; northeastern border with Nepal, Bhutan and China western border with Pakistan; India presents enormous diversity in topography, natural resources and climate. Surrounded by the Indian Ocean, the Bay of Bengal and the Arabian Sea, on the south, southeast and southwest respectively, India offers a mesmerizing marine life to magnetize both domestic as well as foreign tourists. India presents a great diversity in topography, natural resources and climate, which makes it one of the most fascinating tourist destinations in the world.

Tourism

Vast geographical diversity in India provides a wide range of outdoor adventures. The major adventure activities in India comprise trekking and skiing in Himalayas, river rafting in Ganges and other major rivers, water skiing in Goa, trout fishing in Himachal Pradesh and Uttarakhand, Heli-skiing in Himachal Pradesh and wind surfing, scuba diving and yachting in Andaman & Lakshadweep islands.

India abounds in attractive and well-preserved historical sites and ancient monuments of architecture grandeur like Taj Mahal, which is one of the Seven Wonders of the World. India is home to several architecturally and historically rich Hindu temples, churches and mosques.

India has several beaches, hill stations, wildlife sanctuaries, pilgrimage places, temples, forts and palaces, which make it a perfect tourist destination for all. The South Asian nation is well connected by road, rail and air, allowing tourists to move freely throughout the nation.

People

India is a great example of unity in diversity, as people of different communities and religions live in harmony in different parts of the nation. Indian people are very warm and hospitable, as they consider their guests as God and treat them likewise. Indians are very passionate about cultural and religious beliefs and actively take part in various social events. They love to share their cultural heritage with foreign travelers.

Events

India is a spiritual country, which turns the nation into a land of festivals and celebrations. The Indian calendar is full of festivals and events, which bring the people of different religions and cultures together. The range and diversity of Indian festivals that are held throughout the year attract a large number of foreign travelers. Characterized by color, cheerfulness, passion, prayers, and customs, Indian festivals create a lively atmosphere across the nation. Festivals in India range from Diwali (the festival of lights) and Holi (the festival of colors) to Eid-ul-Fitar (celebrated by Muslims), Gurpurb (celebrated by Sikh community) and Christmas.

Medical Tourism in India

Offering healthcare facilities at third world prices, India is one of the world's leading medical tourism destinations. Economical and reliable healthcare facilities attract a vast number of medical tourists from all around the world. The number of foreign medical tourists visiting the country is growing at a rapid pace every year. According to the International Business Times report, around 500,000 medical tourists are expected to travel to India this year, which is very high if compared to 150,000 foreign patients in 2002. Due to the increasing number of foreign patients, India is investing heavily in its medical industry and developing the state-of-the-art healthcare institutes across the nation.

Healthcare System

Segregated in two sectors, public and private, Indian health system offers medical services to both domestic and foreign patients. In addition, a number of Ayurvedic hospitals that practice traditional Indian system of alternative medicine also offer conventional healthcare to a large number of patients in the country. The public hospitals provide basic care to a large population in the country but they usually are understaffed and lack infrastructure and facilities; therefore, a family member is required with the patient during his/her stay in the hospital. Although these hospitals charge very less, but the standard of care is also low in comparison to private hospitals.

On the other hand, the private hospitals and clinics offer quality care that you can compare with the western standards of healthcare. These hospitals hire highly qualified surgeons, usually trained abroad, and use latest equipments and technology to provide best medical services to their clients.

Quality of Healthcare

India witnesses a big disparity in the quality of healthcare in the public hospitals used by locals and the private hospitals and clinics that attend affluent local clients and medical tourists. Private healthcare in India is as good as you find in any other developed nation. Featuring 13 Joint Commission International (JCI) accredited hospitals, India is becoming one of the biggest medical tourism hubs in the world, thanks to inexpensive services and quality care.

■ IRAN

General	
Language	Persian
Time Zone	IRST (UTC +3.30)
Dialing Code	+98
Electricity	220V-240V
Medical Tourism Status	Tehran, Mashhad, Esfahan, Karaj
Currency	Rial
Clothing	The style of dressing in Iran is very conservative—especially for women. It is usually necessary to cover the head with an Arabic scarf. For men, it is prohibited to wear shorts and short-sleeved shirts.

Health Related	
Mortality Rate	5.94/1,000 population
Life Expectancy	M71.8/75.2F
Patient: Physician Ratio	2200:1
Hospitals JCI accredited	0
Recommended Vaccinations	Hepatitis A, Typhoid, Hepatitis B, Rabies, Diphtheriatetanus, Measles, Varicella, Yellow fever and Poliomyelitis.
Other Infections	Tularemia, Tick-borne relapsing fever, Leptospirosis

Tourism Related			
Population	77,176,930	Reliability of Police Services	62/140
Global Competitiveness	4.69/7	Physician Density	93/140
Tourism Competitiveness	3.6/7	Hospital Beds	92/140
GDP/Capita	$13,127	Quality of Air Transport Infrastructure	129/140
Health and Hygiene	4.5/7	International Air Transport Network	124/140
Safety and Security	4.0/7	Quality of Roads	76/140
Air Transport Infrastructure	2.5/7	Hotel Rooms	110/140
Tourism Infrastructure	1.4/7	Tourism Openness	79/140
Cultural Infrastructure	3.2/7	Attitude of Population Towards Foreign Visitors	135/140

Meant for explorers and travelers, Iran opens itself layer by layer. While the cities of Esfahan, Tabriz and Kerman offer beauty and insight into the real culture and living in Iran, the city of Tehran provides travelers with a chance to explore its ancient society amalgamated with present day sophistication. Islamic Republic of Iran offers priceless experiences, thanks to significant development in medicine, mathematics and astronomy. Currently, it is slowly but steadily contributing toward world economy and medicine.

Location

Located in the South West region of Asia, Iran extends up to 1,648,000 square kilometers and is just slightly larger than Alaska. Bounded by Azerbaijan, Armenia, Turkmenistan and the Caspian Sea, this country has strong Islamic influences and continues to command a strong authority and stance in the Islam community, which includes countries like Afghanistan and Pakistan.

People

Around 90 percent of the population in Iran comprises of Islamists. Introduced during the 7th century, Islam is the official religion of this country while Kurds and Arabs or Sunni Muslims are a minority. Persian or the Farsi language is major mode of communication and writings in Arabic are common.

Events

Iran's Islamic calendar is full of festivities, including Moharam. Grape harvest festival is one of the prime harvesting festivals in the country. One of the major events in this country is victory of Revolution, which is celebrated to commemorate the anniversary of Islamic revolution of Iran, wherein Ayatollah Ruhollah Khomeini (known for issuing fatwa against prominent writer Salman Rushdie) overthrew the government of Shah. Islamic Republic Day closely follows this event in April. Then Eid- Ul Fitr is celebrated to marks the end of festive month of Ramadan.

Apart from these festivities, a number of events are celebrated in the field of science and technology, particularly medicine, which is one of the developing fields in Iran. The country witnesses a number of camps, researches and medical experiments every year in the field of medicine, which has been growing slowly but steadily in the country.

Weather

The climate of Iran is extreme, with heat waves during summer and harsh cold weather during winters. In steep desert regions, the precipitation level is below 300/12in. In the central areas, the precipitation is higher than other areas of the country. Summers in Iran are warm with heat waves and constant sunshine, while winters are quite unpredictable. Due to cold winds flowing from Siberia, travelers can expect extreme colds in some regions.

Medical tourism in Iran

For the slowly developing economy of Iran, medical tourism is relatively new as the health care sector is quite underdeveloped. Although there is huge demand for public health care services, yet the services are not quite up to the mark. World Health Organization ranks Iran 58th in heath care and 93 in health care performance. However, death rates have fallen significantly over the years.

With intent to engage more foreign tourists and to develop its medical tourism, the country has developed a health tourism office to boost the levels of health care system in the country. According to the head of Majlis Health Commission, the country has witnessed a number of medical advancements because of which medical tourism has received a kick-start.

One such area of medical tourism is their stem cell researches and cloning. The country has collaborated with a number of scientists and Nobel Laureates, including Stephen Hawking, to continue their researches in the field of science and technology. The Annual Razi Medical Sciences Research Festival is one of their attractions in terms of medical tourism, which promotes medicines in Iran.

Iran is one of the major destinations for health care, with medical tourism specifically targeted towards lung transplants. The country has been one of first nations to do artificial lung transplant in 2009, which makes it one of the five countries in the world to have such technologies. Currently, medical developments in the country are increasing by 344 percent every year, giving a much-needed boost to medical tourism in the country.

Health Care Systems

The country has over 400 medical research facilities along with 76 magazine indexes. Iran is currently ranked 19th in medical research. Still, the country's health care system is underdeveloped, especially public sector undertakings. The market for medical sector was 24 billion dollars in 2002 and has crossed 32 billion dollars in a decade. Public health care infrastructures have increased over the years and 73 percent of the total population has health care coverage. Consequently, the medical education system has also noticed a rise and more scientists and doctors are coming up with innovations and new techniques.

Quality of Health Care Services

As mentioned before, the disparity between public and private health care services is glaring. The private healthcare sector has been keen on taking up organ transplants and several doctors have developed newer ways of dealing with medical emergencies, particularly in neuroscience. On the other hand, there is a huge scope for improvement in public healthcare sector.

Despite its political instability as a country, Iran still manages to offer affordable health care to foreign tourists, which makes it an attractive destination for medical tourism.

■ ISRAEL

General	
Language	Hebrew, Arabic
Time Zone	IST(UTC+2) summer IDT(UTC+3)
Dialing Code	+972
Electricity	230V, 50Hz
Medical Tourism Status	Jerusalem, West Jerusalem, Haifa, Tel Aviv
Currency	New shekel
Clothing	Cotton clothing for dry and warm summers, and in winters it would be advisable to take rainwear and warm clothing.
Health Related	
Mortality Rate	5.45 deaths/ 1,000 population
Life Expectancy	80.2M /83.8F
Hospitals JCI accredited	6
Recommended Vaccinations	Measles and Varicella.
Other Infections	Tick- borne relapsing fever, Brucellosis, Leptospirosis, Cutaneous leishmaniasis, Visceral Leishmaniasis, Murine Typhus, Israeli tick Typhus, Human monocytic ehrlichiosis, Q Fever and Rabies.

Tourism Related			
Population	8,051,200	Reliability of Police Services	76/140
Global Competitiveness	5.10/7	Physician Density	17/140
Tourism Competitiveness	4.3/7	Hospital Beds	50/140
GDP/Capita	$32,312	Quality of Air Transport Infrastructure	48/140
Health and Hygiene	6.1/7	International Air Transport Network	40/140
Safety and Security	4.6/7	Quality of Roads	46/140
Air Transport Infrastructure	3.6/7	Hotel Rooms	49/140
Tourism Infrastructure	4.6/7	Tourism Openness	90/140
Cultural Infrastructure	2.6/7	Attitude of Population Towards Foreign Visitors	68/140
Visa Requirements	24/140		

Israel takes immense pride in its history and present colorful culture that attracts tourists from different parts of the world. The country itself has myriad flavors and places of interest to offer to its travelers. Its historical sites have made it one of the countries with a large list of UNESCO World Heritage sites. However, the country is not just for vacationing and traveling, but it is also about medical advancements and medical tourism.

Location

Israel is not a large country by any standards. Smaller than the US state of New Jersey, the country covers a total area of 8,630 square miles. It is bordered by Mediterranean Sea, Gulf of Aqaba and Sinai Peninsula. Located in the Middle Eastern Region, the country shares its boundaries with war torn Syria, Jordan, Egypt as well as Lebanon in the northeast, east, southwest and north respectively. Mediterranean Sea to the west offers it an incredible coastline, which is just perfect for a great vacation.

People

Israel is largely Jewish, though it does has a notable Muslim and Christian population.

Events

Although a number of medical events are celebrated in this country every year, it does not have a large number of festivals in its calendar year. Most popular festivals that attract foreign tourists from all over the world include Jerusalem Film Festival, Wine tasting festivals and special events such as the Israel Festival, which is an extravaganza of dance, music and theatre. The Taste of City is a culinary event that is a heaven for epicureans who love to try different dishes and drinks. One of the largest food festivals in the world, this event sees over 400,000 visitors a year.

Several events related to medical research are also held every year. This includes events for studies on stem cell research, which draws medical tourists from all over the world, along with regenerative study events and medical marijuana study events held from time to time.

Weather

The temperate to tropical climate of this country is what makes it perfect for vacationing and medical tourism. Two seasons, mainly rainy winters from November to May and dry summer for the rest of year, mark the climate of Israel. The northern and central regions of the country receive heavy rainfall, while Southern areas have ample sunshine.

Medical tourism in Israel

In the last decade, medical tourism in Israel has become one of prime sectors for Israel's national income. Thanks to a wide variety of researches, along with health care benefits and affordable treatments, Israel has become a hub for medical tourism. Every year, thousands of travelers visit the country for treatment.

In 2010, over 30000 tourists, especially from Russia and other nearby regions arrived here for treatment. This led to generation of over 75 million dollars in revenue. Quality healthcare for surgeries and in-vitro fertilization makes it one of the prime contenders for those seeking treatment. Dead Sea, a therapeutic resort is one of the regions that get ample revenue through medical tourism.

Palestinian Medical tourism is also popular, as people from these territories do not receive the same kind of treatment and facilities as they do in Israel. Currently, Israel has also been offering treatment to Syrian citizens who have been hurt in Syrian Civil war. As a part of its humanitarian aid, it also offers quality and cheaper services to military officers from all over the world.

Health Care System

What makes health care more affordable and accessible for foreign tourists as well as nationals is the fact that health insurances are mandatory for all, which are provided to all citizens irrespective of their religion, financial status or gender. The health care system has been designed to be effective and safety. Israel has one of the most advanced systems for health care worldwide and has a ratio of 3.36 doctors for every 1000 people, which is one of the highest ratios in the world. The doctors in the country are trained in accordance to 6-year training plan that has been modeled after European doctor training programs.

Quality of health care

There is no doubt about the fact that the quality of healthcare in Israel is at par with the world standards. Its emergency services are one of the swiftest emergency services in world and humanitarian aid is what gives it an edge in medical tourism sector. Stem cell research, along with biotechnology and neurosciences, increases health care quality up a notch. With most of its doctors interning in foreign countries, the level of healthcare services has increased.

Technologically innovative diagnostic procedures, along with latest instruments, techniques and monitoring system, makes healthcare affordable, efficient and highly effective.

■ ITALY

General	
Language	Italian
Time Zone	CET(UTC+1) summer CEST(UTC+2)
Dialing Code	+39
Electricity	230V, 50Hz
Medical Tourism Status	Rome, Venice, Florence, Milan, Napoli
Currency	Euro
Clothing	Light or medium weight clothing is recommended in summer. In winter take a raincoat and an overcoat or heavy jacket.
Health Related	
Mortality Rate	10.83 deaths/ 1000 population
Life Expectancy	79.8M /84.7F
Patient: Physician Ratio	240:1
Hospitals JCI accredited	21
Recommended Vaccinations	Influenza, Diphtheria-tetanus, Measles, Varicella
Other Infections	Anthrax, HIV, Scorpion stings, Black widow spider bites

Tourism Related			
Population	59,685,227	Reliability of Police Services	54/140
Global Competitiveness	4.81/7	Physician Density	21/140
Tourism Competitiveness	4.9/7	Hospital Beds	48/140
GDP/Capita	$30,136	Quality of Air Transport Infrastructure	67/140
Health and Hygiene	6.0/7	International Air Transport Network	81/140
Safety and Security	5.3/7	Quality of Roads	57/140
Air Transport Infrastructure	4.6/7	Hotel Rooms	11/140
Tourism Infrastructure	7.0/7	Tourism Openness	93/140
Cultural Infrastructure	6.1/7	Attitude of Population Towards Foreign Visitors	79/140
Visa Requirements	40/140		

Italy is a delightful destination that attracts travelers not only from Europe but also from various parts of the world. Whether you are a traveler, an epicurean, an explorer, a medical tourist or a lover, Italy is one of those beautiful and medically developed countries that one must visit at least once in a lifetime. The beauty of Italy is never overrated and that is what makes it praise worthy. This is one of the few places where art and life intermingle with technology in such effortless manner that you would be bound to appreciate. With a feast of endless courses, along with alluring arts, architecture, landscapes and developments, Italy leaves indelible experience in the heart of visitors.

Location

Located in Southern part of Europe, Italy's geographical structure appears to be shaped like a high-heeled booth kicking a triangle. Sharing its boundaries with France, the country draws its cultural influences from Austria as well as Switzerland, along with a blend of Slovenia's cultures and France's art. Extending to the central Mediterranean Sea, this country has its own unique culture that blends with the best from all over the world.

People

Italy is known for its gregarious and friendly people who have a smile that can light up one's day. Passionate about their food and language, people from Italy have a rhythmic tone of speaking, which makes conversations quite flowery and long-winded. Apart from that, Christianity is one of the prime religions in the country and most people here have a strong reverence for Vatican City, which shares its borders with Italy.

Events

Italy's calendar year is full of a number of events, including Catholic Church festivities that see a wide number of tourists enjoying a vacation in Italy before they visit the main church in Vatican City. The country is also known for being a host to a number of small village festivals, especially food festivals, involving travelers from all over the world. Changing seasons and harvests are also one of the main reasons behind celebrations.

Weather

The climate of Italy varies from north to south. Therefore, the northern areas witness Alpine climate, which is known for its cold winds as well as average rainfall. The plains in Padana region have a sub tropical climate with hot summers and harsh winters. The diverse range of climates in different regions makes it possible for travelers to visit a region with climate of their choice.

Medical tourism in Italy

Over the last few years, medical tourism in Italy has been quite average. Mostly, it is limited to doctors from around the world who visit the country to know and learn more about their healthcare facilities. Apart from this, the country attracts medical tourists only from neighboring countries. This is despite the fact that Italy has one of the best health care systems in the world.

Italy has its own National Health Service, which is called as the SSN or the Servizio Sanitario Nazionale. This service organizes a number of events in private hospitals and public undertakings, which include research experimentations, special events for doctors and scientists from all over the world, which encourages medical tourism in the country.

The reason behind declining popularity of Italy as a medical tourism destination is that healthcare facilities are costlier than most of other countries in the world. Although, the services are quite affordable for nationals, these can be quite expensive for foreign tourists, who could rather get the same kind of services in other European countries. The medical tourism has received a little boost due to its popularity as a vacationing destination. Medical tourism here is mostly popular for procedures such as cosmetic surgery, dentistry, hair transplant and alternative cancer therapies.

Health Care System

In 2000, the healthcare system of Italy was ranked second in Europe, just below France. The country provides nationalized health care services to its nationals who receive equal access to patient care and medications. The healthcare system is mostly limited to public sector and National Health Service has its own plan of working. Emergency medicines services are offered free to patients, even in the case of undocumented patients. The specialist diagnostic tests are offered free to the poor and family doctors only charge Co-pay of $40 for visit and medicines.

■ JAMAICA

General	
Language	English (Jamaican English)
Time Zone	(UTC-5)
Dialing Code	+1-876
Electricity	110V, 50Hz
Medical Tourism Status	Kingston, New Kingston, Spanish Town
Currency	Jamaican dollar
Clothing	All informal clothing such as t-shirts, shorts and swimsuits.

Health Related	
Mortality Rate	6.48 deaths/ 1000 population
Life Expectancy	71.5M /78.2F
Patient: Physician Ratio	1200:1
Hospitals JCI accredited	0
Recommended Vaccinations	Hepatitis A, Yellow fever, Hepatitis B, MMR, Diphtheria-tetanus
Other Infections	HIV

Tourism Related			
Population	2,889,187	Reliability of Police Services	102/140
Global Competitiveness	3.82/7	Physician Density	92/140
Tourism Competitiveness	4.1/7	Hospital Beds	84/140
GDP/Capita	$9,029	Quality of Air Transport Infrastructure	37/140
Health and Hygiene	4.1/7	International Air Transport Network	41/140
Safety and Security	4.3/7	Quality of Roads	82/140
Air Transport Infrastructure	3.2/7	Hotel Rooms	28/140
Tourism Infrastructure	4.4/7	Tourism Openness	13/140
Cultural Infrastructure	1.6/7	Attitude of Population Towards Foreign Visitors	81/140
Visa Requirements	8/140		

Jamaica is one of the prime destinations in the Caribbean, where sunrays are addictive, the sands are nothing less than crystallized sugar and the resort life can revitalize the mind, body and soul of the travelers. That is why Jamaica, one of the largest islands on the Caribbean, is a destination, which stands out from the rest for its unique history, enchanting landscapes and colorful culture. The island's unique character, along with its places of interest and variety of offerings, makes it exploratory enough for any curious or weary traveler. Health care in this country is quite adequate for locals and the steadily growing medical facilities make it a place for curious medical tourism explorers.

Location

Located in the Caribbean Sea, Jamaica is the fifth-largest island country in the region and is surrounded by Cuba in the north and Hispaniola, the island containing the nation-states of Haiti and the Dominican Republic, in the east. Occupying an area of around 4400 square miles, Jamaica is one of the largest English speaking islands of the Caribbean region. The country flaunts beaches and endless range of water activities. Scuba diving, wind surfing and horse riding are some of the activities that any visitor would definitely enjoy in the island nation.

People

Jamaica boasts of a strong African lineage, with most of its population coming from the African descent. The ancient culture and civilization has played a vital role in developing this country's unique way of life. The people here are warm and friendly, with most of them thriving on country's tourism. Apart from that, individuals are mostly conservative and have respect for their culture. They participate in their respective religious events and gatherings.

Events

Apart from religious events and other festivities, the country takes pride in organizing a wide range of entertainment events, including special music reggae festivals like Sum fest and Sun Splash. Jamaican festivals are marked with music, dance, drama and various folk forms. The celebrations start from Accompong Maroon Festival, which is held in January every year and ends with Howzzat, a theater movement festival that is celebrated in December. All over the year, more than 24 festivals and events are celebrated with vigor and zest.

Weather

The climate of Jamaica is tropical in nature, with hot and humid weather throughout the year. The higher inland regions have temperate climate, but Pedro Plains generally have dry areas. Jamaica is prone to damages from storm, as it is located in the hurricane belt of the Atlantic Ocean; however, the country is well equipped to deal with storm related adversities.

Medical Tourism in Jamaica

Medical tourism in Jamaica is all about exploration and trying varied alternative ways of treatment. The treatments offered here combine conventional medical ways with alternative ways such as acupuncture, massages and spa therapies.

The country is all about soaking up the sun and the sea for treatment. For medical tourists who seek surgeries and organ transplants, Jamaica might not be the best destination. However, Jamaica offers alternative treatments for those who want some peace of mind and want to connect with their inner self, and rejuvenate their body and get rid of common and recurring ailments. For instance, the relaxation and spa spots help medical tourists improve their health. A large number of cancer survivors and patients visit the country to find solace for their bodies as well as mind and to overcome the after effects of chemotherapy.

In terms of conventional treatment and health care facilities, the country is not at par with developed nations and therefore, not a prime choice for medical tourism for individuals who seek conventional treatments for different medical conditions. However, its mineral springs and therapeutic waters draw medical tourists from all over the world.

Health care System

The Island of Jamaica has nationalized healthcare systems and policies for their citizens and legal residents. The Ministry of Health is responsible for controlling public hospitals and clinics with special emphasis on providing affordable or free health care services. The promotion of healthcare and prevention of morbidity has resulted in development of its infrastructure. Currently, the country has 23 hospitals as well as 350 health care centers and clinics.

Quality of Health care

The quality of health care services in Jamaica is quite average. One of the biggest issues that this country faces in terms of health care is that patients have to wait in long queues at government hospitals. On the other hand, the private sector has exorbitant rates that work well only for rich citizens and foreign nationals. The discrepancy between private and public sector hospitals in Jamaica is quite glaring, but the government is trying to bridge the gap.

Therefore, Jamaica is one of the countries that have the potential to become one of the leaders in medical tourism for alternative treatment strategies. Its spas and therapeutic centers offer a lot to tourists who seek invigoration.

■ JAPAN

General	
Language	Aynu itak, Japanese, Ryukyuan
Time Zone	JST(UTC+9)
Dialing Code	+81
Electricity	100V, 50Hz
Medical Tourism Status	Tokyo, Yokohama-shi, Ōsaka-shi
Currency	Yen
Clothing	Light jackets, light sweaters and other similar kinds of tops.

Health Related	
Mortality Rate	9.83 deaths/ 1000 population
Life Expectancy	79.5M /85.8F
Patient: Physician Ratio	500:1
Hospitals JCI accredited	1
Recommended Vaccinations	Hepatitis A, Typhoid, Hepatitis B, Rabies, Diphtheria-tetanus, Measles, Varicella, Japanese encephalitis, Poliomyelitis, Yellow fever
Other Infections	Leptospirosis, Hepatitis E, Lung fluke, Oriental liver fluke, Fish tapeworm, Giant intestinal fluke, Japanese spotted fever

Tourism Related			
Population	126,659,683	Reliability of Police Services	22/140
Global Competitiveness	5.30/7	Physician Density	53/140
Tourism Competitiveness	5.1/7	Hospital Beds	1/140
GDP/Capita	$36,266	Quality of Air Transport Infrastructure	46/140
Health and Hygiene	6.3/7	International Air Transport Network	46/140
Safety and Security	5.7/7	Quality of Roads	7/140
Air Transport Infrastructure	4.5/7	Hotel Rooms	28/140
Tourism Infrastructure	4.6/7	Tourism Openness	137/140
Cultural Infrastructure	5.9/7	Attitude of Population Towards Foreign Visitors	74/140
Visa Requirements	37/140		

Once a country that was horrified by the after effects of a war, Japan has now become one of the leading tourist destinations in the world. Japan is traditional as well as modern, where tourists can experience conventional as well as contemporary lifestyle. The country has blossomed, seen some of the best technological developments and is certainly a pioneer for medical tourism. Japan is a joy that is open for all types of tourists and all kinds of travel.

Location

Located in East Asia, Japan is an island country that has over three thousands islands grouped together. It covers an area of 377,835 kilometers and is smaller than the state of California. Surrounded by Pacific in the north and Philippine Sea and East China Sea on the south, Japan is one of those places that attract beach lovers from various parts of the world. Its capital, Tokyo, is a perfect amalgamation of traditional styles and modern development. Main Island of Honshu is one of the major tourist attractions in the island nation.

People of Japan

The life expectancy rate in Japan is quite high, which is indicative of its quality health care systems. More than 17 percent of the total population in the country is recognized as old and the numbers are rising. The community here is quite friendly, calm and welcoming, with most of the people enjoying their lives with high earning capacities. Japan is known for its creative pursuits and its high regard of traditional art as well.

Events

Almost all events and festivals celebrated in Japan reflect its rich cultural heritage. There are a number of local shrines dedicated to different deities, which people carry in palanquins during these festivities. The country has a range of events, including the most popular Sapporo Yuki Matsuri event, which has spectacular shows of ice and snow sculptures. Drawing two million visitors from all over the world, this is definitely the biggest winter festivals in the country. Apart from this Omizutori, a religious Buddhist ceremony takes place in the beginning of March every year.

Weather

The climate of Japan varies from one region to the other. Tourists can experience temperate to sub tropic climate in the country, along with four different seasons. Hokkaido and Sea of Japan are colder locations marked with heavy snowfall, while Okinawa remains relatively warm in the month of January.

Medical Tourism in Japan

For long, Japan was not considered a popular destination for Medical Tourism, primarily because of the language barriers. However, medical tourism has developed over the years and those who want the best health care services and have money to spend on it choose Japan for medical tourism purposes. High quality and specialized procedures are popular in this country, as most of the hospitals use several innovative surgical techniques to treat domestic as well as foreign patients.

The country mainly targets wealthier foreign tourists from developed countries, such as Russia and China. Advanced imaging and radiology techniques give Japan an edge over other countries. Medical travelers visit Japan in search of efficient and effective screening examinations and contemporary treatment strategies.

The fact that people of Japan have better life expectancy than those all around the world is what gives this country an edge in medical tourism. The only problem with medical tourism here is that the health care services are costly for foreign nationals or medical tourists.

Health care system

The health care system of Japan is dominated by the universal health care insurance system, which dictates that patient covers 30 percent of the costs while the government covers 70 percent of the cost of any medical procedures. Patients in Japan have the option to select their own physicians as well as facilities and no one can deny them coverage. Hospitals in this country work on nonprofit basis and the laws state that physicians must manage these hospitals and clinics.

This plan has been running for over five decades and has offered accessible services through regional or national level public hospitals. Still, some regions in the country have shortage of medical resources as a number of patients force themselves into hospitals for minor diseases. In fact, the MRIs in the island nation have eight times more per capita income than in Britain.

Quality of Health Care

The quality of health care in Japan is quite high, which is reflected by its life expectancy rates. The country has higher number of practicing nurses that are specifically trained for different ailments. The only problem that the health care system in this country faces is that people come to hospital for minor problems, which affects certain cases of major ailments. However, the Japanese government is trying to implement universal health care systems to ensure that these services become more affordable and effective.

■ JORDAN

General	
Language	Arabic
Time Zone	UTC+3
Dialing Code	+962
Electricity	230V, 50Hz
Medical Tourism Status	Amman, Az Zarqā', Irbid, wadī as Sīr
Currency	Jordanian dinar
Clothing	It is warm year round, take light weight, long, loose pants/skirts shorts and long sleeve tops. Dress modestly. Wear sunglasses and use sunhats or scarves to prevent sun stroke.

Health Related	
Mortality Rate	2.66 deaths/ 1000 population
Life Expectancy	72.2M /74.9F
Patient: Physician Ratio	490:1
Hospitals JCI accredited	9
Recommended Vaccinations	Hepatitis A, Typhoid, Hepatitis B, Rabies, Diphtheria-tetanus, Measles, Varicella, Poliomyelitis and Yellow fever
Other Infections	Hepatitis E, Brucellosis, Cutaneous leishmaniasis, Tick-borne relapsing fever

Tourism Related			
Population	6,508,887	Reliability of Police Services	20/140
Global Competitiveness	4.61/7	Physician Density	48/140
Tourism Competitiveness	4.2/7	Hospital Beds	87/140
GDP/Capita	$5,899	Quality of Air Transport Infrastructure	38/140
Health and Hygiene	5.1 /7	International Air Transport Network	36/140
Safety and Security	4.7/7	Quality of Roads	45/140
Air Transport Infrastructure	3.2/7	Hotel Rooms	69/140
Tourism Infrastructure	3.5/7	Tourism Openness	17/140
Cultural Infrastructure	1.9/7	Attitude of Population Towards Foreign Visitors	52/140
Visa Requirements	35/140		

Enchantingly beautiful deserts, citadel and enthralling edifices define the small country of Jordan. With its history entwined in destroyed Roman cities, Biblical sites and castle, Jordan is one of those countries that boast of a strong cultural lineage along with medical tourism and advancements. A trip to this country is not only pleasurable but medically relevant as well. With thousands of tourists visiting the country for medical procedures, Jordan has by far established itself as a premier medical tourism destination in the region.

Location

Situated in the South West part of Asia, Jordon is surrounded by the Mediterranean Sea in the south east coast, Syria in the north, Saudi Arabia and Gulf of Aqaba in the South, Palestine and Israel in the West and war torn Syria in the north.

People

Lovingly referred to as Jordanians, the people of Jordan are amiable and passionate about their culture. Offering warm welcome to tourists of all religions, regions and cultures, Jordanians have established themselves as one of the friendliest communities in the world. The country is one of the best tourism destinations in the world, which offers affordability in terms of traveling and effective medical treatments for medical tourists. Despite trapped between war torn regions like Syria and Iraq, Jordan is still stable and offers best hospitality to the tourists from different parts of the world.

Events

Jordan has a strong ethnic lineage and diversity because of which a number of annual festivities and events take place in the country. At least one major event takes place each month in the country. However, the most popular events include, Muharram, which marks the beginning of Muslim year and King Abdullah Birthday celebrated in January. In February, a popular event called the Aqaba Traditional Arts Festival is held annually which endeavors to bring forward the best traditional crafts of this country. April marks the commencement of Amman International Theatre Festival, which is known for bringing the Middle Eastern and North African communities together. This is also the time when most medical tourists visit the country, as the weather remain warm and people have a pleasurable trip to compliment medical procedures. Independence Day in Jordon is celebrated in the month of May. Rest of the year is marked with a number of festivals and events that bring people from different countries together.

Weather

While the regions of Jordan Valley and Gulf of Aqaba are known for extreme heat and humidity, the Northern regions and higher altitude areas experience average cold during winters. Rest of the year in Jordon is characterized by a temperate climate with warm weather conditions and frequent rain showers in different parts of the country.

Medical tourism in Jordan

Despite the fact that Jordan is a hidden nation in the deserts of Middle East, it still ranks high when it comes to providing affordable medical facilities to foreign tourists. Over the years, Jordan has established itself as one of the premier medical tourism destinations in the region, as it offers advanced medical facilities at more affordable costs than other neighboring countries.

To ensure that the country gets more medical tourisms and boosts up the tourism sector, the government of Jordan invests large amounts to develop its health care infrastructure. The increase in medical tourism is quite visible in numbers itself. For instance, while 190,000 tourists came to Jordan seeking healthcare in 2007, the number rose to 220,000 in 2009. The medical sector now fetches at least a billion dollars annual revenue for the government.

A majority of medical tourists arrives here from neighboring war torn countries and regions, such as Iraq and Syria; however, a large section of tourists from other parts of the world visit the nation in search of quality healthcare at an affordable price as well. Currently, the country offers special guest suites to their tourists and has special recovery resorts for patients undergoing rigorous treatments, such as chemotherapy. To remove language barriers, most of the hospitals in the country hire nurses and doctors that can communicate in English, together with Arabic and Russian, fluently.

Healthcare System

Jordan's advanced health care system is mostly concentrated in Amman, but most of the other cities and regions are also picking up. According to the World Bank, the health care system of Jordan is one of the best in the world, which makes it a prime medical tourism destination for Middle East and North Africa. The country's health care system has been divided into public and private sectors. Housing 1245 primary health care centers, along with 27 hospitals managed by Ministry of Health and several other by private sector, Jordon promises to provide quality healthcare to domestic as well as foreign patients.

Quality of Healthcare

Jordan is an emerging medical tourism destination in the region. Therefore, the country is investing profoundly in its medical sector to provide quality care and attract more medical tourists. The popularity of Jordan as a medical tourist destination can be gauged with the fact that over 250,000 patients from 84 countries visited Jordan in 2008. Around 70 percent of the total population enjoys health insurance in one form or the other. Jordan is truly one of the best destinations for those seeking affordable medical treatments.

■ KENYA

General	
Language	Kiswahili, English
Time Zone	EAT (UTC+3)
Dialing Code	+ 254
Major Cities	Nairobi, Mombasa, Nakuru, Eldoret
Currency	Kenyan shilling
Health Related	
Mortality Rate	7.26 deaths/ 1,000 population
Life Expectancy	58.1M /61.4F
Hospitals JCI accredited	1
Recommended Vaccinations	Hepatitis A, Hepatitis B, Meningitis, Polio, Rabies, Yellow Fever, Typhoid
Other Infections	HIV

Tourism Related			
Population	44,354,000	Physician Density	121/140
Global Competitiveness	3.62/7	Hospital Beds	101/140
Tourism Competitiveness	3.7/7	Quality of Air Transport Infrastructure	65/140
GDP/Capita	$1,802	International Air Transport Network	54/140
Safety and Security	3.2/7	Quality of Roads	72/140
Health and Hygiene	1.9/7	Hotel Rooms	122/140
Air Transport Infrastructure	2.8/7	Tourism Openness	64/140
Tourism Infrastructure	2.4/7	Attitude of Population Towards Foreign Visitors	51/140
Cultural Infrastructure	1.8/7		

Kenya or the Republic of Kenya is a self-governing country positioned on the equator in the eastern part of Africa. The total population of the country is approximately 44 million. It is surrounded by Ethiopia in the north, Tanzania in the south, Somalia in the northeast, Uganda in the west and the Indian Ocean in the southeast. Due to the presence of the Indian Ocean as well as a part of the rolling grassland Savannah, the southeast region of Kenya is quite temperate and humid. As we go inside and reach the region around the Mount Kenya, the weather becomes colder.

Events and Festivals

From regional events to national festivals, Kenya has no dearth of reasons for celebration. Most of them are based on the diversity in community and unity in family, and are related to the African religions, arts, culture, foods, music and dance. Some of the notable events and festivals that are famous among international medical tourists are Mombasa Carnival, International Camel Derby and Festival, Kenya Tourism Week, East African Art Festival, Blankets & Wine Festival, Kenyan Safari Rally, Easter, Good Friday, Eid-al-Fitr, Jamhuri Day (or 'republic' day), Christmas, New Year, etc.

Medical Tourism in Kenya

Kenya has become a popular medical tourism destination in both east and central Africa. The country is known to offer quality medical care and a range of services to its medical tourists. Be it general surgery, cardiac surgery, spinal surgery, dentistry or orthopedic surgery, Kenya has proved its efficiency as a major healthcare hub for foreign patients in every sector.

As the health care costs are rising rapidly in Europe and the US, scores of regular as well as high profile patients are choosing Kenya as their medical alternative. The three biggest factors present behind this trend are quality of health care, excellent services and cost-effective treatment. Moreover, the Government of Kenya is putting efforts in establishing the country as a high-potential destination for health tourism.

Healthcare System

There is a robust network of around 4,700 medical facilities across the nation and most of them provide basic diagnostic, remedial and rehabilitative services. Kenyatta National Hospital, Karen Hospital, Aga Khan University Hospital, Mater Hospital, Nairobi Hospital, M P Shah Hospital, etc. are some of the largest as well as well-known health care facilities of the country that boast of having competent staff and state-of-the-art equipment. The Ministry of Health of Kenya is also about to launch a social insurance scheme named 'National Social Health Insurance Fund' (NSHIF) to enhance healthcare funding, as well as give better access to healthcare for international patients.

■ KUWAIT

General	
Language	Arabic
Time Zone	AST / KSA (UTC+3)
Dialing Code	+965
Major Cities	Kuwait City, Hawalli, Al Farwaniyah, Doha, Bayan, Kayfan, Al Jahrah
Currency	Kuwaiti dinar
Health Related	
Mortality Rate	2.13 deaths/ 1,000 population
Life Expectancy	79.5M /80.4F
Hospitals JCI accredited	2
Recommended Vaccinations	Hepatitis A, Hepatitis B, Typhoid
Other Infections	HIV

Tourism Related			
Population	2,646,314	Physician Density	66/140
Global Competitiveness	5.21/7	Hospital Beds	81/140
Tourism Competitiveness	3.6/7	Quality of Air Transport Infrastructure	87/140
GDP/Capita	$58,080	International Air Transport Network	68/140
Safety and Security	5.2/7	Quality of Roads	44/140
Health and Hygiene	5.0/7	Hotel Rooms	77/140
Air Transport Infrastructure	2.9/7	Tourism Openness	60/140
Tourism Infrastructure	4.1/7	Attitude of Population Towards Foreign Visitors	137/140
Cultural Infrastructure	1.9/7		

Kuwait, officially known as the State of Kuwait, is located in Western Asia and lies northeast to the Arabian Peninsula. It is flanked by Iraq in the north and Saudi Arabia in the south. The population of this Arab country is approximately 2.7 million. Spring is the most pleasant time in Kuwait, which is also considered as the ideal time to visit for the medical tourists. July and October is the time for southeasterly winds, which make the weather hot and humid. Sandstorms may occur during June and July, which is caused by northwesterly winds. Hot, dry winds can be expected during early summer and spring.

Events and Festivals

Kuwait celebrates a number of religious events and national holidays all year round. The most popular among them are Eid el-Fitr and National Day. Ramadan is a special occasion, which is celebrated throughout the country. Some other events include Kuwait Jazz Festival, Liberation Day, Hala Festival, Film Festival, Eid el-Adha, Islamic New Year, and many more. The Hala festival is celebrated to usher in the spring season. The Islamic New year is celebrated on the first day of Muharram and can fall on October, November or December, as per the Islamic calendar. Medical tourists can have a good time during these festivals.

Medical Tourism in Kuwait

Medical tourism in Kuwait is catching up really well. The Clover Medical Centre is one of the well-known hospitals, which is giving medical tourism a much-needed boost in Kuwait. Physicians are skilled and have years of experience. Patients can get themselves treated for sleep disorders, breathing related problems, obesity, aging issues, and many more. Rehabilitation is another significant part of the health tourism offered in this Arabian country. Quality treatment along with affordability is what makes Kuwait a good location for medical tourism.

Healthcare System

The healthcare system of Kuwait is state funded. People having valid passports can avail medical benefits free of cost. The quality of healthcare is good and almost all kinds of medical treatment are available here, except a few complicated surgeries. The standards are at par with the USA and Western Europe. Apart from the local nurses and doctors, foreign physicians are also a part of the medical teams. Medical tourists can avail many facilities at affordable costs. The effectiveness of the healthcare system is a major attraction for medical tourism in the country.

■ LEBANON

General	
Language	Arabic
Time Zone	EET (UST +2) Summer (UTC+3)
Dialing Code	+961
Electricity	230V, 50Hz
Medical Tourism Status	Beirut, Ra's Bayrūt, Tripoli, Sidon
Currency	Lebanese pound
Clothing	The summers get very hot in Lebanon, so shorts and breezy clothes will be helpful. However, when visiting in winter, pack warm clothes as it gets very chilly—especially in the mountainous areas.

Health Related	
Mortality Rate	6.46 deaths/ 1000 population
Life Expectancy	71.8M /75.7F
Patient: Physician Ratio	403:1
Hospitals JCI accredited	2
Recommended Vaccinations	Hepatitis A, Typhoid, Hepatitis B, Rabies, Diphtheriatetanus, Measles, Varicella and Yellow fever.
Other Infections	Hepatitis E, HIV, Tick-borne relapsing fever, Brucellosis.

Tourism Related			
Population	4,822,000	Reliability of Police Services	20/140
Global Competitiveness	3.79/7	Physician Density	48/140
Tourism Competitiveness	4.0/7	Hospital Beds	87/140
GDP/Capita	$15,522	Quality of Air Transport Infrastructure	51/140
Health and Hygiene	6.0 /7	International Air Transport Network	49/140
Safety and Security	3.8/7	Quality of Roads	113/140
Air Transport Infrastructure	3.0/7	Hotel Rooms	43/140
Tourism Infrastructure	5.5/7	Tourism Openness	2/140
Cultural Infrastructure	1.9/7	Attitude of Population Towards Foreign Visitors	22/140

An amalgamation of ultra modern and ancient styles, Lebanon is one of the most enthralling destinations in the world. Known as the "Hospital of the Middle East," this country is emerging in medical tourism sector. Apart from its beautiful landscapes, edifying mountains, beaches and steady economy, the growing medical sector gives this country an edge over the other neighboring countries. People can get affordable cosmetic procedures in this country, while enjoying Roman ruins, stunning Islamic architecture and healing resorts.

Location

Situated in the eastern shore of the Mediterranean Sea, the Republic of Lebanon is bordered by Israel and Syria on south and north respectively. Lebanon also shares its borders with the Mediterranean as well as Arabian Sea. Because of its strategic location, Lebanon has witnessed several developments and boasts of a strong heritage that has shaped its unique cultural identity.

People

Lebanese people are popular for their friendliness and they welcome foreign tourists with a warm heart. The hospitable nature of the Lebanese people makes medical tourism more effective in the country, as tourists can expect better healthcare facilities. The community here loves to enjoy traditional and modern art, with cultural playing a major role in different spheres of life. Despite the ongoing political instability in certain regions, most of the Lebanese destinations, particularly cosmopolitan regions are safe to travel.

Events

The vibrant hues of Lebanese culture are best reflected in its festivities and events, which showcases the nation's strong cultural influences. The country is a proud host to a number of fashion shows, film and theater festivals, along with art, dances and music festivals. Food festivals here draw thousands of epicureans from all over the world. Beirut, its capital is perhaps best known for being a fashion capital where people can socialize with latest trends in fashion industry. The country celebrates all the popular Islamic festivals. It also hosts Middle East's most prestigious and oldest Baalbek International Festival that displays various dance, music, theater and jazz performances. Feast of the Assumption is another major event that the Christian minority celebrates in the country.

Weather

Lebanon's Mediterranean climate offers this country a variety of seasons. Those who seek to enjoy the warmth of beaches should visit here in summer from June to September. The temperature during this period ranges from 20 to 32 degree Celsius. Rainfall is scanty and does not affect travelling plans during this season. Winters in Lebanon are for those who love to enjoy the cold and can opt for a period from December to Mid March, when temperature drops to 0 degree Celsius at night.

Medical Tourism in Lebanon

What gave Lebanon limelight in global medical arena are its surgical procedures, particularly several kinds of cosmetic surgeries, which are performed by skillful and experienced surgeons across the nation. The country attracts a number of celebrities seeking cosmetic procedures such as facelift, Botox injections, Nose jobs, surgical enhancement or reduction of body parts as well as removal of cellulite and reducing years from the skin. The best part is that they can evade the prying eyes of media and enjoy the medical trip without being noticed. This is what has given medical tourism a kick-start in this country.

Several other Middle Eastern countries, including Israel and Jordan are far more successful in the field of medical tourism, but Lebanon is slowly following them. It has labeled itself as the "Hospital of the East" to brand its warm hospitality and efficient healthcare services. The country, which is now using aggressive marketing approaches to attract medical tourism, is slowly becoming a competitor for other Middle Eastern nations that thrive on medical tourism. In fact, the government, hotels, clinics, hospitals and even tour organizers now provide comprehensive and customizable tour packages to encourage medical tourism in the country.

Healthcare System

The healthcare system in Lebanon was in a good shape as the medical facilities were available to most of the local as well as foreign patients. However, the overall healthcare sector has witnessed a decline in past few years due to the war and political instability in the country. Because most of the post war healthcare centers were mainly catered to treat wounded soldiers and trauma or emergency cases.

However, this has also paved the way for private healthcare sector in the nation. The country now provides a universal healthcare system that covers all nationals and provides basic coverage to every citizen. Although, people cannot choose their own physician, yet they can expect better healthcare services.

Quality of Health care

The quality of health care in Lebanon has deteriorated in the past few years, as the country is going through political instability and facing guerilla wars that keep medical tourists away from the war struck nation. However, the situation is changing swiftly with the emergence of private sectors. Currently, the country has two JCI accredited hospitals that are located in Beirut. Some of the best hospitals provide costlier cosmetic surgeries at more affordable costs to boost medical tourism in the country.

Therefore, despite the fact that Lebanon still has to improve their healthcare facilities rapidly, it still offers some of the best medical services, if compared to other neighboring countries. This is what makes Lebanon an emerging destination for medical tourism.

■ LITHUANIA

General	
Language	Lithuanian
Time Zone	EET (UTC+2) EEST (UTC+3)
Dialing Code	+370
Major Cities	Vilnius, Alytus, Jonava, Visaginas, Kretinga, Palanga
Currency	Lithuanian litas
Health Related	
Mortality Rate	11.4 deaths/ 1,000 population
Life Expectancy	68.2M /79.1F
Hospitals JCI accredited	0
Recommended Vaccinations	Hepatitis A, Hepatitis B
Other Infections	HIV

Tourism Related			
Population	2,955,986	Physician Density	18/140
Global Competitiveness	4.41/7	Hospital Beds	12/140
Tourism Competitiveness	4.4/7	Quality of Air Transport Infrastructure	86/140
GDP/Capita	$21,615	International Air Transport Network	108/140
Safety and Security	4.9/7	Quality of Roads	32/140
Health and Hygiene	6.2/7	Hotel Rooms	67/140
Air Transport Infrastructure	2.6/7	Tourism Openness	61/140
Tourism Infrastructure	4.3/7	Attitude of Population Towards Foreign Visitors	112/140
Cultural Infrastructure	3.0/7		

The Republic of Lithuania, more commonly known as Lithuania, is a North European country. It is located in the southeastern coast of Baltic Sea and is surrounded by Latvia in the north, Poland in the south and Belarus in the west. As per the records, in 2012, the total population of the country was approximately 3 million. The weather here is mild which makes it an ideal location for medical tourism. The climate varies between continental and oceanic. October to April is the time when snowfall occurs. Winters can be very cold and storms may occur in coastal areas.

Events and festivals

Different events and festivals are an important part of Lithuania. All throughout the year, the local people take part in diverse celebrations. Starting from the Republic Winter Festival in January, the celebrations end with Christmas in December. All the communities in this location get together to celebrate their Independence Day in February. Medical tourists visiting this place can enjoy various festivals and events irrespective of the time they visit. Some of the popular events and festivals that are celebrated in various cities at different time of the year include Vilnius festival, Kaziukas Fair, Ice Cream Festival, International Children's and Youth Theatre Festival, Street Musician Day, Folklore Festival, Summer Festival, Mardi Gras, etc.

Medical Tourism in Lithuania

Lithuania, with its reasonably priced healthcare facilities, is an ideal location for medical tourists. The medical services are up to date and accomplished doctors are always there for treating the patients. The medical care provided to medical tourists is similar to that of the standards of USA and Western Europe. The environment of this place is another important factor, which makes it an ideal location for medical tourism. Dazzling white sand beaches, majestic hills, attractive cities and towns all provide the perfect setting for relaxation after any medical treatment. There are even special amenities, which are provided to medical tourists exclusively.

Healthcare System

Though investment is needed to make the quality of healthcare even better, the medical professionals here are highly qualified. Cardiologists of this country are quite in demand. The Ministry of Health manages the State Patient Fund (SPF) and the Territorial Patient Funds (TPF). The public healthcare system is state funded mainly through taxes from employees and employers. Private healthcare system is also there. Those who do not have state health insurance can also avail free medical services in case of emergency. There are around 169 hospitals, 149 primary healthcare centers, 868 medical stations and 1489 pharmacies in Lithuania.

■ MALAYSIA

General	
Language	Malaysian
Time Zone	MST(UTC +8)
Dialing Code	+60
Electricity	240V, 50Hz
Medical Tourism Status	Kuala Lumpur, Klang, Kampung Baru Subang, Johor Bahru
Currency	Ringgit
Clothing	Considering the climatic conditions wear comfortable clothes like t-shirts, pants, jean, long shirts and khakhi shorts.

Health Related	
Mortality Rate	4.92 deaths/ 1000 population
Life Expectancy	71.7M /76.4F
Patient: Physician Ratio	1400:1
Hospitals JCI accredited	6
Recommended Vaccinations	Hepatitis A, Typhoid, Hepatitis B, Rabies, Diphtheria-tetanus, Measles, Varicella, Japanese encephalitis and Yellow fever.
Other Infections	Scrub typhus, Hepatitis E, Lung fluke, Sea snakes HIV, Giant intestinal fluke, Melioidosis

Tourism Related			
Population	28,334,135	Reliability of Police Services	37/140
Global Competitiveness	5.38/7	Physician Density	89/140
Tourism Competitiveness	4.7/7	Hospital Beds	87/140
GDP/Capita	$17,675	Quality of Air Transport Infrastructure	24/140
Health and Hygiene	4.6 /7	International Air Transport Network	23/140
Safety and Security	4.8/7	Quality of Roads	27/140
Air Transport Infrastructure	4.5/7	Hotel Rooms	47/140
Tourism Infrastructure	3.8/7	Tourism Openness	21/140
Cultural Infrastructure	3.9/7	Attitude of Population Towards Foreign Visitors	56/140
Visa Requirements	1/140		

Enchanting beaches, sparkly sands, beautiful cities and a blend of different cultures is what makes Malaysia reflect the entire Asia. This country is one of the fastest growing economies in the world. Thriving on different sectors of tourism, Malaysia boasts of comprehensive medical healthcare system, alternative treatment plans and an array of places of interests, which lead to the rejuvenation of mind, body and spirit. It is because of these reasons that Malaysia has become a popular destination for medical tourism.

Language

Being a multiethnic and multicultural society, Malaysia is one of those countries where several languages are spoken widely. Malay is language that majority of people use for day-to-day communication. At the same time, English is a language that most of the people can speak and comprehend. It is widely spoken in cosmopolitan regions. Individuals who can speak English as their first or second language dominate the medical sector.

Sites to See

Malaysia houses a number of places or sites in that attract tourists from different parts of the world. Some of the most visited places in the country include the Sunway Lagoon Theme Park, the Batu Cabes, Thean Hou Buddhist Temple and Sungeo Tua Waterfall. The capital city, Kuala Lumpur, is one of those destinations that have something for everyone, as it includes various edifices, architectural marvels, natural beauty and colonial buildings. PETRONAS Towers are a prime attraction in the capital city. Numerous beaches, along with the Langkawi Island and Geopark Borneo Rainforest, attract a large number of tourists. Taman Negara National Park, which is one of the oldest jungles in the world covers 443 square kilometers of jungle, is the largest protected evergreen lowland rainforest cover in the country.

Weather

Malaysia has a climate that would suit all kinds of tourists. The climate is generally humid and tropical in nature, with average temperatures being 30 degree Celsius. The highland areas in the country are relatively colder than coastal areas. Malaysia experiences heavy monsoon in October and February, while the weather remain pleasant between the months of April and October, which is the best time to visit the country.

Events

Being a multicultural society, Malaysia celebrates a wide range of events and festivities throughout the year. Chinese New Year and Thaipusam, celebrated by the Tamil community, are popular festivals here. To encourage tourism and water based sports, the country hosts Malaysia Water Festival every year that attracts thousands of tourists from all over the world. Dragon boat festival is also popular, which is followed by Independence Day and Hungry Ghost Festival in the month of August. Malaysia Day is another popular event that is celebrated on September 16 every year. Malaysian people celebrate Hindu festival of Diwali as well as Christmas with great enthusiasm.

Medical Tourism in Malaysia

Because of its two tier health care system, which comprises of parallel working public and private sector undertakings, Malaysia has become one of the hotspots for medical tourists in Asia. The country is a one-stop destination for tourists who seek treatment for various kinds of ailments. Malaysia is ranked only next to Japan for its effective yet affordable healthcare systems in the region.

What gives medical tourism in Malaysia a further boost is the fact that apart from conventional medical treatments, the country also offers a wide range of alternative treatment procedures. These procedures include acupuncture therapy, massages and spa therapies, together with customized body massage therapies, Ayurveda treatments and other types of procedures that can help in overall healing of the body.

Medical tourism in Malaysia also gets encouragement from these types of alternative treatments that rejuvenate mind, body and spirit. Therefore, several tourists who suffer from chronic ailments visit this country for a comprehensive treatment and reduce side effects of medicines. For regular healthcare infrastructure, the country mostly thrives on patients and tourists who visit the country for cardiology and ophthalmology treatments.

Health Care System

Ministry of Health in Malaysia generally provides widespread healthcare system in the country, with universal healthcare program run by the government. This program co-exists with private healthcare programs, which have helped in reducing infant mortality rate to 10, which is favorable when compared to Western countries. The country has undergone radical transformations with 5 percent of development budget of the government going straight into the public healthcare systems. While rural areas may still need some development, urban areas have plethora of options. The country also provides medicine via post facilities for those suffering from chronic diseases.

Quality of Healthcare System

Due to two-tier system of healthcare system, the overall quality of healthcare has improved in the country. The country is known for making innovative plans and technologies for dealing with medical tourists as well as locales. For instance, it has medicine via post and tele-health programs to help people receive better medical care.

Therefore, the quality of Malaysian health care services is quite high. Still, the country needs to work a little for its rural areas to ensure better services.

■ MALTA

General	
Language	Maltese, English
Time Zone	CET(UTC+1) CEST(UTC+2)
Dialing Code	+356
Electricity	220V, 50Hz
Medical Tourism Status	Birkirkara, Qormi, Mosta, Żabbar
Currency	Euro
Clothing	During summer months, lightweight clothing typical of any European summer including shorts, t-shirts and hat. Whereas, in winter month, lightweight clothing but with something a little warmer for cooler evenings.

Health Related	
Mortality Rate	8.49 deaths/ 1000 population
Life Expectancy	78.8M /82.0F
Hospitals JCI accredited	0
Recommended Vaccinations	Hepatitis B, Yellow fever, Diphtheria-tetanus, MMR
Other Infections	Brucellosis

Tourism Related			
Population	452,515	Reliability of Police Services	29/140
Global Competitiveness	5.12/7	Physician Density	28/140
Tourism Competitiveness	4.9/7	Hospital Beds	39/140
GDP/Capita	$27,022	Quality of Air Transport Infrastructure	25/140
Health and Hygiene	6.1 /7	International Air Transport Network	32/140
Safety and Security	5.9/7	Quality of Roads	103/140
Air Transport Infrastructure	4.8/7	Hotel Rooms	1/140
Tourism Infrastructure	6.3/7	Tourism Openness	9/140
Cultural Infrastructure	3.1/7	Attitude of Population Towards Foreign Visitors	17/140
Visa Requirements	40/140		

Situated in southern European, Malta is an island nation that is proud of its history of more than 7000 years. The historic nation embraces rich culture, which the tourists can experience across the island. Featuring many historical sites, including palaces, caves and museums, Malta also has numerous sunny beaches, which attract tourists from different parts of the world. Housing three UNESCO World Heritage Sites, including the Megalithic Temples that comprise some ancient freestanding structures, the southern European nation also holds a strategic position and becomes an important state not only for tourists but also for commercial purposes, in the region.

Location

Located in the middle of the Mediterranean Sea, Malta is essentially an archipelago that is comprised of three islands, i.e. Malta, Gozo and Comino, and a number of small-inhabited islands, together with Cominotto and Filfla. Lying between the Eurasian and African tectonic plates, the island nation has few neighbors, which include Sicily in the north, Tunisia in the west and Libya in the south, in the Mediterranean. Stretched in 122 sq miles area, Malta is one of the smallest nations in the world.

People

With total population of around 408,000, Malta is one of the most densely populated countries not only in the EU but also in the world. A larger part (about 97 percent) of the total population of Malta is comprised of native Maltese people, while the minorities include Brits and so on, who have retired to the island nation. The people of Malta are very hospitable who welcome tourists with a warm heart. There are two official languages in Malta, Maltese and English, while the former is the constitutional national language; the latter is spoken by around 88 percent of the total population in the country.

Events

The Maltese calendar is full of religious festivities and cultural events, which are celebrated by both young and old throughout the year. For long, the Maltese Islands have been considered as a destination for families and older couples; however, with the addition of the Isle of MTV in recent years, the island nation has managed to shed off its conventional reputation and since then, it has emerged as a vibrant place.

Offering an array of events, the small yet lively nation has something for everyone. Apart from religious and cultural events, Malta also hosts a number of intercontinental invents, including International Spring Orchestra Festival, Malta International Jazz Festival and Isle of MTV and Malta Music Week which are becoming popular among foreign tourists.

Weather

The weather conditions in Malta are largely influenced by the Mediterranean Sea. Featuring a subtropical climate, winters in the island nation are usually mild with frequent rain showers while summers are warm/ hot and dry. August is the warmest month in Malta and the temperature during this period ranges between 28°C and 34°C during the day and 19°C and 24 °C at night, while January remains the coldest month with temperature raining between 12°C and 20°C during the day and 7°C and 12 °C at night. Unlike most other European nations, the Maltese Islands remain "green" throughout the year, which makes it a popular tourist destination.

Medical Tourism in Malta

The beautiful weather and sandy beaches of Malta bring in tourists all year round. Tourists from Europe and other parts of the world flock the nation to relax in utmost comfort while enjoying the natural beauty and coastal life of the surrounding islands. Known as the "Nurse of the Mediterranean" in the 16th century, Malta has successfully carried forward its legacy of being a quality healthcare provider to the present day in the region.

The Maltese government is investing heavily in the niche healthcare and medical sectors across the nation to attract medical tourists. Combining the private healthcare sector with the public tourism industry, Malta has become one of the most popular medical tourism destinations in the region. Most of the medical professionals practicing in Malta get training in Europe and are well versed in English to ensure quality healthcare to domestic as well as foreign patients.

Healthcare System

Malta presents a nationalized or public healthcare system under the Ministry of Health, which is funded through general taxation and employer/employee monthly contribution. The public healthcare system covers the cost of treatment to ensure free medical care for all its citizens. The nationalized healthcare system provides free care, which include diagnosis, treatment and medication, for patients suffering from chronic diseases.

On the other hand, the private healthcare sector is growing rapidly across the nation to provide personalized and specialized treatment for domestic as well as foreign patients. The healthcare services in both the public and private sectors are of high quality, which allows the Maltese people to lead a healthy life, while attracting medical tourists as well.

Quality of Healthcare

Maintaining a very high standard of healthcare, Maltese people are proud of their state-of-the-art hospitals and well-qualified physicians. The medical staff is well versed in English, which removes the language barriers with the foreign patients. Physicians practicing in the public sector handle more common procedures and treatments, while the private surgeons provide care for the more complicated cases.

Despite no international (JCI) accreditations, most of the Maltese medical centers provide quality healthcare for domestic as well as foreign clients. According to a recent survey conducted across the EU regarding the healthcare services in Malta, around 81 percent of the medical tourists are fully satisfied with the quality of healthcare in the country.

▪ MAURITIUS

General	
Language	French, English
Time Zone	MUT (UTC+4)
Dialing Code	+230
Major Cities	Vilnius, Alytus, Jonava, Visaginas, Kretinga, Palanga
Currency	Lithuanian litas
Health Related	
Mortality Rate	6.73 deaths/ 1,000 population
Life Expectancy	70.1M /77.8F
Hospitals JCI accredited	1
Recommended Vaccinations	Hepatitis A, Hepatitis B, Typhoid
Other Infections	HIV

Tourism Related			
Population	1,291,456	Physician Density	87/140
Global Competitiveness	4.35/7	Hospital Beds	53/140
Tourism Competitiveness	4.3/7	Quality of Air Transport Infrastructure	49/140
GDP/Capita	$15,591	International Air Transport Network	56/140
Safety and Security	5.3/7	Quality of Roads	58/140
Health and Hygiene	4.8/7	Hotel Rooms	38/140
Air Transport Infrastructure	3.3/7	Tourism Openness	10/140
Tourism Infrastructure	4.7/7	Attitude of Population Towards Foreign Visitors	28/140
Cultural Infrastructure	1.6/7		

Mauritius aka the Republic of Mauritius is an island country located in the Indian Ocean, which includes the individual islands of Rodrigues, Saint Brandon, Agalega and Port Louis. The country enjoys a tropical climate for the most part of the year. The summer seasons are warm and stretch from November to April, with the warmest months being January and February, while the winters are cool and dry, and stretch from June to September, with the coolest months being July and August.

Mauritius has a multi-ethnic population, with several of its inhabitants being of African, Chinese, French and Indian descent. The locals for the most part, are bilingual, and can speak a variety of languages like Chinese, English, Cerole and French etc. proficiently.

Events and festivals

The multi-ethnic populace of Mauritius celebrates several festivals in the country throughout the year. Some of the more prominent ones include New Year, Chinese Spring Festival, Abolition of Slavery Day, Thaipoosam, Cavadee, Maha Shivratri, National Day, Ugadi, Easter and Assumption of the Blessed Virgin Mary Day, together with Labor Day, Ganesh Chathurthi, Diwali, Eid-Ul-Firt, Arrival of Indentured Laborers Day and Christmas.

Medical Tourism in Mauritius

Mauritius offers its medical tourists a unique opportunity to combine their healthcare needs with leisure and wellness in the same trip. Mauritius provides the best healthcare facilities and services when it comes to medical procedures like dentistry and cosmetic surgery. The country also offers other benefits like highly skilled medical personnel, training and education, specialization, wellness treatments and cost savings that are highly appreciated by medical tourists.

Healthcare System

The doctor to patient ratio is Mauritius is considered the best in the African region. The country has two healthcare systems: the private healthcare system and the public healthcare system. Private healthcare is further divided into two categories, i.e. private clinics with inpatient, diagnostic and research facilities, and private practice (by medical care practitioners).

The public health care system, on the other hand, is divided into the primary, district/regional, and hi-tech/quarterly healthcare services. The primary service deals with general clinics, health centers and outpatient hospitals, which can be easily reached by 100 percent of the island's population. The District/Regional Service deals with district and regional hospitals that offer inpatient, outpatient and emergency medical services to targeted individuals in a specific region or district. In addition, the Hi-tech/Quaternary Service deals with hospitals that offer state of the art infrastructure and facilities in the form of specialized cardiac and psychiatric centers, and services pertaining to cardiac surgery, neurosurgery and cardiology.

■ MEXICO

General	
Language	Spanish
Time Zone	CET(UTC +1) summer CEST(UTC+2)
Dialing Code	+52
Electricity	127V-60Hz
Major Cities	Mexico City, Iztapalapa, Ecatepec, Guadalajara
Currency	Peso
Clothing	cotton shirts, or pants with leather sandals, long skirts, shawls
Health Related	
Mortality Rate	4.83 deaths/ 1,000 population
Life Expectancy	72.3M /77.7F
Patient: Physician Ratio	500:1
Hospitals JCI accredited	9
Recommended Vaccinations	Hepatitis A, Typhoid, Hepatitis B, Rabies, Diphtheriatetanus, Measles, Varicella, Poliomyelitis, Yellow Fever
Other Infections	Hepatitis E, Trench Fever, Tick-borne relapsing fever, Anthrax, Rocky Mountain spotted fever, Encephalitis

Tourism Related				
Population	118,395,054	Reliability of Police Services		123/140
Global Competitiveness	4.64/7	Physician Density		59/140
Tourism Competitiveness	4.5/7	Hospital Beds		96/140
GDP/Capita	$15,312	Quality of Air Transport Infrastructure		64/140
Health and Hygiene	4.7/7	International Air Transport Network		48/140
Safety and Security	3.7/7	Quality of Roads		50/140
Air Transport Infrastructure	3.8/7	Hotel Rooms		57/140
Tourism Infrastructure	4.4/7	Tourism Openness		121/140
Cultural Infrastructure	5.1/7	Attitude of Population Towards Foreign Visitors		45/140
Visa Requirements	82/140			

Mexico is the second most visited country in the Americas, after the United States, and the tenth most-visited tourist destination in the world. The North American nation is a unique blend of modernism and traditional values, as there is a profound contrast in the traditional cathedrals, futuristic buildings and fully equipped beach resorts across the country. You can easily find the elements of the ancient and colonial cultures in rural life of Mexico. The diversity in Mexico offers some exciting tourist destinations to travelers from around the world.

Location

Situated in the southern part of North America, Mexico is surrounded by the Gulf of Mexico in the east, the United States in the north, the Pacific Ocean in the south and west and Guatemala, Belize and the Caribbean Sea in the southeast. Lying between latitudes 14° and 33°N and longitudes 86° and 119°W, Mexico comprises 31 states, each offering numerous tourist destinations to attract foreign travelers. Toluca, Greater Mexico City and Puebla are three major cities, which over the period have become a center of trade and commerce.

Events

Mexican culture is a mix of indigenous cultures and the culture of Spain, which makes it a vibrant place, with a number of festivals and events taking place across the nation. The events in Mexico range from soccer games to the religious festivals and art & music festivals to social gatherings, wherein all the Mexicans take part actively and enjoy the festive season. People are enthusiastic about fêtes and festivals and the markets in towns and villages become lively throughout the country. Mexico hosts a number of carnivals every year characterized by colorful parades, dance performances, live music and grand celebrations. The Son Jarocho Music Festival celebrated in the month of February, Festival de México in March, Morelia International Film Festival in October and Guelaguetza Festival in May are some other major events that take place in Mexico and attract a large number of tourists not only from the Americas and Europe but also from different other parts of the world.

Weather

The Tropic of Cancer divides Mexico into two zones, i.e. temperate and tropical, which forms the world's most diverse weather systems in the country. The temperature in the north of the twenty-fourth parallel usually remains cool in winters, while it remains constant year round to the south and ranges between 24°C and 28°C in the coastal plains. Other than south coast of the Bay of Campeche and northern Baja, the Mexican coasts are prone to severe hurricane, which become more active in summers.

Sites to See

The Meso-American ruins, colonial cities and beach resorts are some of the major attractions for tourists in the country. The nation's temperate climate and unique culture, which is a fusion of the European, particularly Spanish and the Meso- American cultures, also make Mexico an attractive destination.

Mexico City, which is the capital of the nation, is popular with tourists as an ancient Meso-American city and offers many popular tourist attractions, such as the Pyramid of the Sun and the Pyramid of the Moon. The La Zona Rosa or Shopping District and El Palenque and El Zócalo, which is one of the largest public plazas in the world, are some other manmade tourist zones that attract worldwide travelers.

The city also houses the Plaza de toros México, the world's largest bullring, the Mexican National Palace, and the huge Metropolitan Cathedral built over the even greater Temple of Teocalli, which is the largest place of worship in the Western Hemisphere. The National Museum of Anthropology and History located in Mexico City is one of the finest museums in the world.

Guadalajara, Jalisco, the second most densely populated city in the Republic, preserves some of the best-known traditions like tequila, mariachi music and Mexican cowboys. This city combines traditional values with modern architecture that makes it a major tourist attraction. Moreover, a number of archeological and ecotourism sites make Mexico a prime destination for foreign tourists.

Medical Tourism in Mexico

The high cost of healthcare in the US, coupled with the escalating number of uninsured individuals, forces several Americans to cross the border and receive medical services in Mexico. Known for its dentistry and cosmetic surgery, Mexico is fast becoming a popular medical tourism destination for patients seeking orthopedic procedures.

Offering several state-of-the-art institutes and facilities, comparable to American hospitals, Mexico has become one of the leading destinations for the US medical tourists. The cheaper cost of healthcare, including prescription drugs and physician's fees, and shorter or no waiting lists, also makes it a prime medical tourism destination in the region.

Healthcare System

The healthcare system in Mexico is a combination of public and private sectors. The country spends around seven percent of its GDP on healthcare and provides health insurance to only 40 percent of the population. Mexico provides highly rated medical infrastructure in major cities; however, the rural areas and small towns still lack infrastructure for advanced medical procedures, and people have to travel urban areas for specialized treatment. Private healthcare organizations deliver quality medical services, of course, for a price in the country.

Quality of Healthcare

Healthcare services in Mexican private hospitals are as good as one can find in the developed countries, including the US. These hospitals offer healthcare packages, which include accommodation, treatment and aftercare, to attract domestic as well as foreign medical tourists. Mexico's best hospitals and clinics operate from Mexico City, Guadalajara and Monterrey. There are many private clinics across the US border in cities like Tijuana, Mexicali and Laredo that cater to Americans. Featuring six JCI accredited hospitals, Mexico ensures international medical facilities to the medical tourists and that too at a reasonable cost.

■ MOROCCO

General	
Language	Arabic, Tamazight
Time Zone	WET(UTC+0) summer WEST(UTC+1)
Dialing Code	+212
Electricity	220V-50Hz
Major Cities	Casablanca, Marrakech, Rabat, Fez
Currency	Moroccan dirham
Clothing	It is warm all year round, although temperatures differ depending on where you stay. As Morocco is an Islamic country, choose your clothes modestly.

Health Related	
Mortality Rate	4.74 deaths/ 1,000 population
Life Expectancy	70.2M /74.4F
Patient: Physician Ratio	2000:1
Hospitals JCI accredited	0
Recommended Vaccinations	Hepatitis A, Typhoid, Hepatitis B, Rabies, Diphtheriatetanus, Measles, Varicella, Poliomyelitis, Yellow fever
Other Infections	Schistosomiasis, Lymphatic filariasis, Tick-borne relapsing fever, West Nile virus, HIV

Tourism Related			
Population	32,878,400	Reliability of Police Services	47/140
Global Competitiveness	4.60/7	Physician Density	98/140
Tourism Competitiveness	4.0/7	Hospital Beds	110/140
GDP/Capita	$5,537	Quality of Air Transport Infrastructure	52/140
Health and Hygiene	3.4/7	International Air Transport Network	53/140
Safety and Security	4.5/7	Quality of Roads	70/140
Air Transport Infrastructure	3.1/7	Hotel Rooms	84/140
Tourism Infrastructure	3.8/7	Tourism Openness	27/140
Cultural Infrastructure	3.1/7	Attitude of Population Towards Foreign Visitors	3/140
Visa Requirements	32/140		

Characterized by different forms of beliefs, ranging from paganism to Judaism and Christianity to Islam, Morocco is an ethnically diverse country in Northern Africa. The social structure of the African nation is greatly influenced by the French, Spanish and An-glo-American lifestyles that separate it from other neighboring countries in the region. Various art forms, including painting, sculpture, music, amateur theatre and filmmaking, flourished in the country after independence. Moroccans are proud of their diverse legacy and cultural heritage, which also attract tourists from different parts of the world. Morocco's centuries-long interaction with the outside world has not only influenced its culture but also cuisine, which is considered as one of the most diversified cuisines in the world.

Location

Located in the in the extreme northwestern part of Africa, Morocco is one of the few countries that have both Atlantic and Mediterranean coastlines, other two are Spain and France. Lying between latitudes 27° and 36°N and longitudes 1° and 14°W, the North African nation is surrounded by Spain in the north, Algeria in the east and Western Sahara in the south. The topography of Morocco ranges from the Atlantic Ocean to the Sahara desert and mountainous areas to coastal plains, which offers diversified tourist locations to attract tourism across the nation. The capital of Morocco is Rabat and Casablanca is its largest city, both of them attract a large number of visitors.

People

A large part of the Moroccan population is a mix of Arab, Berber and Niger-Congo races, and among them Arab and Berber ethnic groups comprise about 99 percent of the total population in the country. While Berbers are the indigenous people, on the other, other groups like Arab, sub-Saharan African immigrants and Jews settled in the country during the colonial period. Moroccan people by nature are very friendly and hospitable, which is an essential element of Moroccan culture.

Events

Morocco is an ethnically diversified country, which contributes to a number of festivals and events that take place in different parts of the nation throughout the year. Held in the month of February, Eid Al Adha or Eid El Khebir is one of the major festivals in Morocco, which is celebrated across the nation to honor the sacrifice of Abraham. During this festival, a commemoration feast is organized across the nation. Considered as an Islamic New Year, the Fatih Mouharam is another major festival that is celebrated in the month of March.

A number of art and music festivals, including the World Sacred Music Festival held an-nually in Fes and the Essaouira Gnawa and World Music Festival, also take place in the country during the summers that attract prominent musicians as well as music lovers from various parts of the world.

Weather

The climate of Morocco varies according to the season and region. The northern part of the nation is characterized by Mediterranean climate, which become extreme towards the interior regions of the country. The inland areas have more of a continental climate, which remain hot and dry throughout the year. The coastal plains are ideal for agriculture, which is the backbone of Morocco's economy. The climate in the Atlas range between Mediterranean and Maritime, which provide perfect conditions for the growth of allow different species of oaks, moss carpets, junipers, Atlantic cedars and various other plants and forests. The temperature in the lowlands and on the valleys facing the Sahara becomes extremely dry and hot during the summers.

Medical Tourism in Morocco

Morocco has long been known for its diverse culture, cuisine and tourist destinations, but the medical tourism is a new addition that is strengthening its roots though slowly in the country. In recent times, Morocco has seen a surge in cosmetic surgery clinics that are offering reasonable care for domestic as wells foreign patients. The affordable rate of these surgeries coupled up with the beautiful vacation is attracting a number of patients from Europe and the Middle East to the African nation.

Since medical tourism is not a defined sector of Moroccan healthcare industry, international standards of healthcare and quality regulations are missing in medical institutes in the country. Therefore, patients need to be a bit cautious and must do some research or perform checks on the facilities before choosing a clinic for their treatment in the country.

Healthcare System

The healthcare system in Morocco consists of three sectors - public (which includes Ministry of Public Health and the Armed Forces Health Services), semi-public and private sector. The developments in the healthcare structure has led to a dramatic decrease in mortality rate and improved health of the majority of individuals.

The number of hospitals and clinics are rising to provide basic health services, including primary, preventive and special care, to common people. The healthcare system is on the rise in the country to offer highest quality of healthcare to the Moroccans.

Quality of Healthcare

Like most other Northern African countries, the quality of healthcare in Morocco has certainly improved in the last decade; still there is a great scope for improvement in its healthcare system as well as services. Moreover, the handsome revenue generated through medical tourism has prompted the nation to improve medical facilities and attract more and more medical tourists from various parts of the world.

■ NEW ZEALAND

General	
Language	English, Maori
Time Zone	NZST(UTC+12) summer NZDT(UTC+13)
Dialing Code	+64
Electricity	230V-50Hz
Major Cities	Auckland, Wellington, Christchurch, Manukau City
Currency	New Zealand dollar
Clothing	In summer a jacket should be included in your luggage, whereas in winters pact warm garments and layer your clothing.

Health Related	
Mortality Rate	7.54 deaths/ 1,000 population
Life Expectancy	79.4M /83.1F
Patient: Physician Ratio	420:1
Hospitals JCI accredited	0
Recommended Vaccinations	Diphtheria-tetanus, Measles and Varicella
Other Infections	HIV

Tourism Related			
Population	32,878,400	Reliability of Police Services	23/140
Global Competitiveness	5.65/7	Physician Density	20/140
Tourism Competitiveness	5.2/7	Hospital Beds	23/140
GDP/Capita	$30,804	Quality of Air Transport Infrastructure	12/140
Health and Hygiene	6.3/7	International Air Transport Network	10/140
Safety and Security	6.1/7	Quality of Roads	41/140
Air Transport Infrastructure	5.2/7	Hotel Rooms	9/140
Tourism Infrastructure	6.3/7	Tourism Openness	51/140
Cultural Infrastructure	3.0/7	Attitude of Population Towards Foreign Visitors	2/140
Visa Requirements	68/140		

New Zealand, officially known as "The Dominion of New Zealand," is an island nation in the Pacific Ocean. The country consists of two main islands, i.e. the North and South Islands that are separated by the Cook Strait, and several small islands. Touting rich and diverse cultural heritage, New Zealand is one of the most recent lands to be habited by human beings because of its aloofness from the rest of the world.

English is the main language in New Zealand, which is spoken by about 98 percent of the total population. Known for extreme sports, adventure tourism and mountaineering, New Zealand also offers some of the most beautiful sites to attract the tourists from all over the world. With total population of around 4 million, New Zealand is essentially an urban country, wherein 72 percent of the population lives in cities or urban areas, including Auckland, Christchurch, Wellington and Hamilton.

Location

Located in the southwestern Pacific Ocean, New Zealand is surrounded by Australia in the west and the Pacific island nations of New Caledonia, Fiji and Tonga in the north. Lying between latitudes 29° and 53°S and longitudes 165° and 176°E, New Zealand covers a total land area of 2,68,670 square kilometers and Mount Cook is the highest point of the country, which is 3,764 meters above sea level. Apart from the North and South Islands, the major inhabited islands that comprise the island nation are Stewart Island, the Chatham Islands, Great Barrier Island, d'Urville Island and Waiheke Island.

People

Majority of the population, around 67 percent, in the island nation is of European descent. The indigenous Māori (around 14 percent) are the largest minority in New Zealand, while the Asian (around 9 percent) and Pacific people (around 6 percent) are other major ethnic groups. Most of the people in the country are highly sophisticated and educated, and enjoy the modern lifestyle in terms of technology as well as way of life. Usually, people in New Zealand are not as outspoken as you come across in other parts of the world, but they are passionate hosts and tourists can rely on them. They feel pride in sharing their culture and tradition with the visitors.

Events

New Zealand is a diverse country that presents unique cultural and natural beauty. The annual calendar of the country is full of local and international festivals and events that attract a large number of tourists from different parts of the world. Serving the best of natural local foods, Māori kai food festivals are an integral part of New Zealand's culture that attracts both domestic and international tourists. Apart from food and wine festivals, the island nation also hosts various dance exhibitions and shows, flower shows, music events and sports events throughout the year.

Weather

New Zealand has a temperate climate, which varies from region to region. The average temperature in the country ranges between 10 °C in the south and 16 °C in the north. Weather conditions become extremely wet on the West Coast of the South Island, subtropical in

Northland and semi-arid in Central Otago and the Mackenzie Basin of inland Canterbury. New Zealand has a large coastline (approximately 15,000 km), and features coastal weather characterized by mild temperature, moderate rainfall and abundant sunshine.

Medical Tourism in New Zealand

Even though New Zealand is a newcomer in the medical tourism industry, the country is attracting a number of patients from all around the world. New Zealand has all the key aspects to become a prime destination for patients seeking a vacation and medical services. Being a first world country, New Zealand has a well-developed, stable economy and boasts of a comprehensive medical system. All the medical providers are well versed in English, which makes it an ideal destination for North American and European medical tourists.

Known for orthopedic procedures, especially hip and knee replacement surgeries, New Zealand provide healthcare at a much lower cost if compared to the US or other medically developed countries.

Healthcare System

New Zealand was one of the few countries in the world to offer universal healthcare to all its citizens, as the government used to fund the medical sector and was responsible for delivering the majority of medical services. However, like most other countries providing free healthcare, New Zealand succumbed to the idea of a free-market, which led to two-tier healthcare system, public and private, in the country. The private system offers specialized treatments and mainly caters to foreigners and wealthy citizens, while the mass population utilizes public healthcare facilities.

Quality of Healthcare

Presenting a fully developed healthcare system, with well-equipped hospitals and clinics across the nation, New Zealand offers quality healthcare to domestic as well as foreign patients. Many of the private hospitals in the country maintain international standards and offer specialized medical services, of course for a price. The surgeons are trained in both New Zealand and abroad, and they spend years on training in either North America or Western Europe.

Even though the private hospitals lack JCI accreditation, many medical facilities in New Zealand are accredited by the national accreditation agency, the Quality Health New Zealand (QHNZ). The QHNZ, like JCI, is a member of the International Society for Quality in Healthcare.

▪ NICARAGUA

General	
Language	Spanish
Time Zone	CST (UTC-6)
Dialing Code	+502
Major Cities	Guatemala City, Mixco, Villa Nueva, San Juan Sacatepéquez
Currency	Quetzal
Health Related	
Mortality Rate	4.92 deaths/ 1,000 population
Life Expectancy	65.8M /72.8F
Hospitals JCI accredited	0
Recommended Vaccinations	Hepatitis A, Hepatitis B, Typhoid, Rabies
Other Infections	HIV
Clothing	Tropical, hot, humid in lowlands, cooler in highlands

Tourism Related			
Population	15,438,384	Physician Density	92/140
Global Competitiveness	4.65/7	Hospital Beds	124/140
Tourism Competitiveness	3.56/7	Quality of Air Transport Infrastructure	58/140
GDP/Capita	$5,208	International Air Transport Network	57/140
Safety and Security	3.5/7	Quality of Roads	90/140
Health and Hygiene	3.8/7	Hotel Rooms	64/140
Air Transport Infrastructure	2.5/7	Tourism Openness	76/140
Tourism Infrastructure	2.6/7	Attitude of Population Towards Foreign Visitors	97/140
Cultural Infrastructure	2.0/7		

The Republic of Nicaragua shares its borders with countries of Costa Rica and Honduras. It is the largest country in all of Central America. Its capital Managua is the third biggest city in Central America as well. The country is biologically diverse, and enjoys a warm tropical climate throughout the year.

The population of Nicaragua is largely multi-ethnic, with several indigenous tribes showing influences pertaining to Europeans, Asians, Africans, Middle East and even the Mosquito Coast. The main language of the country is Spanish, with several native tribes speaking their own local languages like Rama, English Creole, Sumo and Miskito etc.

Events and festivals

In addition to Christmas and New Year, Nicaragua celebrates several interesting festivals throughout the year. Some of the more popular ones include Diriamba, Palo de Mayo, Crab Soup Festival, Fiesta del Toro Venado and Purisima/Grieria.

Medical Tourism in Nicaragua

Compared to other Central American countries, Nicaragua enjoys a higher economic growth. The recent years have seen the government taking efforts to tap into the medical tourism industry by offering medical procedures like gastric surgery and hip replacement at just a fraction of the original cost in the USA. Medical tourism in the country has also opened the doors for medical tourists and accompanying guests to stay longer in the country than normal tourists do. Moreover, hotels are trying to cash in on these benefits by tying up with some of the best healthcare services in the country.

Healthcare System

Not many know that Nicaragua has an impressive, high quality health care system. One of the most common issues in medical tourism; the language barrier, is nearly negligible here, thanks to the bilingual, well qualified and highly experienced medical personnel who practice here (most of the doctors who practice in Nicaragua get trained in foreign destinations like America, Europe, Caribbean, Mexico and Cuba).

The urban areas have a larger influx of patients and medical facilities while those living in the rural areas would need to travel a bit on order to get access to specialized medical services. The urban areas have specialized centers for personalized medical services as well, with two of the most renowned hospitals in the entire country located in the Managua area.

The healthcare system in the country is divided into different departments (like provinces and states). And every department has its own dedicated public hospital. The medical costs in these hospitals are very affordable for medical tourists who can also choose between a large range of insurance coverage choices offering coverage for different treatments or procedures, including life-threatening ailments.

■ NIGERIA

General	
Language	English, Hausa, Igbo, Yoruba
Time Zone	WAT (UTC+1)
Dialing Code	+234
Major Cities	Lagos, Kano, Kaduna, Benin City, Maiduguri
Currency	Naira
Health Related	
Mortality Rate	13.48 deaths/ 1,000 population
Life Expectancy	52.3M /54.1F
Hospitals JCI accredited	1
Recommended Vaccinations	Hepatitis A, Hepatitis B, Typhoid, Meningitis, Polio, Rabies, Yellow Fever
Other Infections	HIV

Tourism Related			
Population	170,123,740	Physician Density	104/140
Global Competitiveness	3.52/7	Hospital Beds	127/140
Tourism Competitiveness	3.1/7	Quality of Air Transport Infrastructure	99/140
GDP/Capita	$2,866	International Air Transport Network	73/140
Safety and Security	3.2/7	Quality of Roads	112/140
Health and Hygiene	1.7/7	Hotel Rooms	117/140
Air Transport Infrastructure	2.5/7	Tourism Openness	99/140
Tourism Infrastructure	2.4/7	Attitude of Population Towards Foreign Visitors	110/140
Cultural Infrastructure	1.8/7		

Nigeria aka the Federal Republic of Nigeria is located in West Africa, and is bordered by the countries Niger, Cameroon, Chad and Republic of Benin. The country's coastline is flanked by the Gulf of Guinea in the Atlantic Ocean. The varied landscape of the country enables it to enjoy a tropical rainforest climate for the most part of the year.

Also called the Giant of Africa, Nigeria is the most populous nation in all of Africa, and is also the 7th most populous nation in the entire world. The population of Nigeria is divided between Muslims who live in the northern part of the country, and Christians who live in central and southern part of the country. One can see small traces of local religions like Yoruba and Igbo in the country.

Events and festivals

Nigeria celebrates a range of festivals throughout the year, with importance given to Muslim and Christian festivals. These include Christmas Day, Eid Al Maulad, Easter, Eid Al Fitri and Eid Al Kabir. The country also celebrates other national holidays like the Osun Festival, Argungu Fishing Festival and Calabar Carnival.

Medical Tourism in Nigeria

Even though Nigeria's population opts to travel abroad for medical treatments, the government is making plans to improve the country's healthcare system, including setting up excellent clinics and medical facilities that would provide those healthcare options, which were previously not available at home. Nigeria is also in talks with India to collaborate with its medical tourism industry in order to boost its own prospects in the related field.

Healthcare System

The Federal Government, State Government and the Local Government currently manage the healthcare facilities and services in Nigeria. While the Federal Government deals with tertiary health care and hospitals, state governments take care of general hospitals related to secondary health care. The local governments deal with primary healthcare services via local dispensaries. The quality of healthcare varies between three levels, with the tertiary health care service offering the best services in the form of excellent hospitals and highly experienced doctors. There would be a decline in the quality of the medical services offered in secondary and primary health care systems.

The Government of Nigeria also provides free health care services to all of its citizens. While the government individually manages the health insurance schemes for government employees, private firms are hired to contract special health insurance programs for those working in the private sector.

■ OMAN

General	
Language	Arabic, Omani
Time Zone	GST (UTC+4), (UTC+4)
Dialing Code	+968
Major Cities	Muscat, Seeb, Salalah, Sohar, Suwayq
Currency	Rial
Health Related	
Mortality Rate	3.4 deaths/ 1,000 population
Life Expectancy	70.4M /75.6F
Hospitals JCI accredited	2
Recommended Vaccinations	Hepatitis A, Hepatitis B, Typhoid
Other Infections	HIV
Clothing	Dry desert, hot, humid along coast, hot, dry interior, strong southwest summer monsoon. A simple, ankle-length, collar-less gown with long sleeve

Tourism Related				
Population	3,869,873	Physician Density	62/140
Global Competitiveness	4.65/7	Hospital Beds	87/140
Tourism Competitiveness	4.3/7	Quality of Air Transport Infrastructure	40/140
GDP/Capita	$29,166	International Air Transport Network	45/140
Safety and Security	5.6/7	Quality of Roads	5/140
Health and Hygiene	4.7/7	Hotel Rooms	64/140
Air Transport Infrastructure	3.5/7	Tourism Openness	101/140
Tourism Infrastructure	4.5/7	Attitude of Population Towards Foreign Visitors	35/140
Cultural Infrastructure	2.2/7		

The Sultanate of Oman is a predominant Arab state that is located on the southeastern coast of the Arabian Peninsula in southwest Asia. The nation is surrounded by the countries of Saudi Arabia, UAE, Yemen and Iran (a marine border). The Gulf of Oman and the Arabian Sea flank the nation's coastline.

The climate of Oman is very hot, with very little rainfall experienced throughout the year. Temperatures can easily reach 50 degrees Celsius during the summer season, which falls between the months of May and September.

Oman's population consists of locals as well as people who migrated from Baluchistan or East Africa. The country also has over 600,000 immigrants as guest workers from countries like Egypt, India, Bangladesh, Pakistan and the Philippines. The predominant religion is Islam.

Events and festivals

Most of Oman's festivals pertain to the Islamic calendar. As such, the country celebrates festivals like Ramadan, Eid Al Firt, Eid Al Adha, Al Hijra, Mouloud and Leilat Al Meiraj etc. apart from other festivals like New Year's Day.

Medical Tourism in Oman

Oman has recently signed a land acquisition deal to set up a large, excellent medical tourism facility in Salalah in a bid to attract medical tourists to the nation on a grand scale. Touted to cost over $1bn, the complex will feature the best in infrastructure and healthcare facilities, including a diagnostic & medical prevention center, an organ transplant & rehabilitation center, a healthcare education complex and a healthcare resort. Highly skilled doctors from around the world would serve medical tourists in the facility to offer tertiary level care for its patients.

Healthcare System

Most of the hospitals in Oman offer quality medical and healthcare services for patients. The most prominent and advanced healthcare centers are located in Muscat. Most of Oman's population includes middle-income members who opt for the medical services offered by private hospitals and medical clinics.

In spite of the nation's healthcare services being the best in the region, many claim that they are not in par with those found in western countries or other medical tourism destinations. The government has taken this factor into consideration, and has started taking measures to improve the quality of the healthcare facilities and services offered, starting with the accreditation of several hospitals, healthcare facilities, medical universities and doctors. Many doctors practicing here have in fact, obtained their accreditation from countries like the UK, US, Australia and Canada.

The government's Omanization policy has also started to shift the balance of the healthcare workforce towards local facilities (most of the workforce in the nation was foreign born before).

■ PANAMA

General	
Language	Spanish, English
Time Zone	UTC-5
Dialing Code	+507
Electricity	110V-60Hz
Major Cities	Panamá, San Miguelito, Tocumen, David
Currency	Balboa, U.S. dollar
Clothing	Depends on the region and time you will be visiting. But generally lightweight cottons and linens are worn, with rainwear advisable. Warmer clothes are needed in the highlands.
Health Related	
Mortality Rate	4.62 deaths/ 1,000 population
Life Expectancy	74.0M /79.7F
Patient: Physician Ratio	700:1
Hospitals JCI accredited	0
Recommended Vaccinations	Hepatitis A, Typhoid, Hepatitis B, Rabies, Diphtheriatetanus, Poliomyelitis, Varicella, Yellow fever, Measles
Other Infections	Chagas disease, Amebiasis, Rocky Mountain spotted fever, Tick-borne relapsing fever, Mayaro virus disease, HIV

Tourism Related				
Population	3,661,868	Reliability of Police Services	99/140
Global Competitiveness	4.83/7	Physician Density	20/140
Tourism Competitiveness	4.5/7	Hospital Beds	23/140
GDP/Capita	$15,616	Quality of Air Transport Infrastructure	6/140
Health and Hygiene	4.2/7	International Air Transport Network	11/140
Safety and Security	4.7/7	Quality of Roads	47/140
Air Transport Infrastructure	4.8/7	Hotel Rooms	54/140
Tourism Infrastructure	4.8/7	Tourism Openness	31/140
Cultural Infrastructure	2.2/7	Attitude of Population Towards Foreign Visitors	111/140
Visa Requirements	29/140		

Situated in Central America, Panama is a small country that features natural beauty and fascinating culture to attract visitors from different parts of the world. Presenting an incredible rang of biodiversity, Panama, which means "abundance of fish, trees and butter-flies" in an indigenous language, houses about 10,000 varieties of plants and more than 1,000 species of birds, offering a grand treat for nature lovers. Panama City, which is the capital of the nation, is the only major city in Latin America with a rainforest nearby.

Location

Located on the southern end of the Central American isthmus that connects North and South America, Panama is surrounded by the Caribbean in the north and the Pacific Ocean in the south, Costa Rica in the west and Colombia in the southeast. Lying between latitudes 7° and 10°N and longitudes 77° and 83°W, the Central American nation holds a strategic position as it enjoys complete control over the Panama Canal, connecting the Atlantic Ocean and the Caribbean Sea to the Pacific Ocean, until 2000.

People

With a total population of over 3.5 million, Panama is a nation of mixed ethnicity, where-in 70 percent people are mestizo, 14 percent West Indian, 10 percent white and 6 percent Amerindian. The Caribbean and Spanish lineages have a great influence on the culture, customs and language of Panama. The official language of Panama is Spanish, which is spoken by around 93 percent of the population, while English is used as a business language and largely spoken by the people of West Indian descent.

Events

A number of events and festivals, which become a center of attraction among foreign travelers, take place in Panama through the year. Held in the month of March for four days before Ash Wednesday, Carnival is one of the biggest festivals in Panama that includes Carrabin flavor and hosts colorful parades, fireworks, and music and dance parties. However, the carnival is celebrated across the nation, but Panama City and Las Tablas are the hot spots where major carnival celebrations take place. People actively take part in different events and enjoy the festive time.

The Boquete Fair of Flowers and Coffee is another international event that takes place in the Chiriqui Highlands and is marked by competitive coffee tastings and stunning flower exhibitions. The Feria del Mar held in Playa El Ismito in the month of September is a four-day fair of the Sea that commemorates local fishing traditions and is very popular among the native people of the country.

Weather

Blessed with wonderful and pleasant tropical climate, which remain constant all round the year, Panama usually has two seasons rainy and dry. The average temperature in the capital city ranges between 24 °C and 30 °C, which provides perfect conditions for both domestic as well as foreign tourists. The rainy seasons range from May to December and despite of heavy rainfall, it is rare to find a day without the Sun. Summer season in

Panama usually remains dry with trade winds blowing constantly across the nation. If compared to the Caribbean side, the temperature on the Pacific side of the isthmus is fairly lower and pleasant, attracting a large number of tourists.

Medical Tourism in Panama

Panama has long been a destination for beautiful vacations, but the government is looking forward to combine the medical sector to the tourism sector to generate additional income. The heavy marketing and promotion of Panama as a tourist destination combined with high quality medical services has brought the Central American nation to the forefront as a key medical tourism destination.

Offering quality healthcare at a low price, Panama is growing as a one of the most prime medical tourism destinations in the region. Moreover, Panama's close proximity to the United States and other developed countries, where people have to pay heavily to avail medical services, makes it an attractive destination for medical tourists. The growth of foreign travelers seeking healthcare might be slow, but Panama is certainly making a name for itself as a notable vacation to seek healthcare.

Healthcare System

Both the private and public sector offer healthcare with foreign aid providing assistance to further develop the system. The healthcare system in Panama is composed of a network of hospitals, clinics, emergency and preventive services.

The Ministry of Health that provides key health-related facilities, including health education, check-ups and basic primary care to its citizens directs the healthcare, while the specialized and complicated procedures are provided through the medical facilities owned by private sector.

Quality of Healthcare

Featuring modern hospitals in metropolitan cities, Panama offers quality medical care to both domestic as well as foreign patients. Most of the surgeons and support staff have been trained abroad and are well versed with English, eliminating language barriers that medical tourists often face in developing and underdeveloped destinations.

Providing patients with customized and personalized care at reasonable or low price, Panama is fast becoming an ideal place to receive medical care. Since Panama is relatively new to the global healthcare sector, hospitals in the country have yet to acquire JCI accreditation. However, the promising growth of medical tourism has pushed them to seek international benchmark for their facilities.

■ PERU

General	
Language	Castilian
Time Zone	PET (UTC-5)
Dialing Code	+51
Major Cities	Arequipa, La Libertad, Piura, Ancash
Currency	Nuevo sol
Health Related	
Mortality Rate	5.97 deaths/ 1,000 population
Life Expectancy	75.1M /78.3F
Hospitals JCI accredited	1
Recommended Vaccinations	Hepatitis A, Hepatitis B, Typhoid, Rabies, Yellow Fever
Other Infections	HIV
Clothing	varies from tropical in east to dry desert in west; temperate to frigid in Andes

Tourism Related			
Population	30,475,144	Physician Density	91/140
Global Competitiveness	4.28/7	Hospital Beds	99/140
Tourism Competitiveness	4.0/7	Quality of Air Transport Infrastructure	74/140
GDP/Capita	$220.825	International Air Transport Network	59/140
Safety and Security	3.8/7	Quality of Roads	99/140
Health and Hygiene	3.7/7	Hotel Rooms	45/140
Air Transport Infrastructure	2.9/7	Tourism Openness	114/140
Tourism Infrastructure	4.2/7	Attitude of Population Towards Foreign Visitors	96/140
Cultural Infrastructure	3.3/7		

The republic of Peru is located in the western part of South America, and is bordered by the countries of Colombia, Ecuador, Brazil, Bolivia and Chile while its coastline is flanked by the Pacific Ocean.

Peru enjoys a varied climatic pattern throughout the year. While the Costa is characterized by moderate temperatures, high humidity and low precipitation, the Sierra enjoys frequent rainfall in the summer. Low temperatures and humidity levels characterize the Andes peaks, while the Selva experiences high temperatures and heavy rainfall, with the winters in the region being extremely cold.

Peru's population is multi-ethnic for the most part. It is possible to find traces relating to the Europeans, Amerindians, Asians and Africans. The most common language of the nation happens to be Spanish while local languages like Quechua are used sparingly.

This mixture of cultural traditions has resulted in a wide diversity of expressions in fields such as art, cuisine, literature, and music.

Events and festivals

Peru's diverse cultural background enables it to enjoy several festivals throughout the year. Some of the more common festivals celebrated in the country include the Marinera Festival, Virgen de la Candelaria, Carnival in Cajamarca, Easter Week in Ayacucho, Caballos de Paso, Festival of the Crosses, San Juan and Feast of the Virgen del Carmen. People also celebrate Festivity of the Virgin of Cocharcas, The Lord of Miracles Procession, All Saints Day, Day of the Dead and Santuranticuy Holiday.

Medical Tourism in Peru

Peru offers some of the most sought after medical services in the world for just a fraction of the cost when compared to countries like the UK and US. These include cosmetic procedures, dentistry and even certain life-saving medical procedures. Many individuals also opt for Peru for long term treatments in order to benefit from the low costs, high quality medical care and services, and the chance to couple their medical treatment with a holiday in one of the most enchanted destinations on earth.

Healthcare System

Healthcare insurance in Peru is divided into two individual sectors, the private and public sectors. The Public Healthcare system is further divided into two sectors, the SIS (Seguor Integral de Salud) which is mandated by the MINSA (Ministerio de Salud), the Peruvian Ministry of Health; and the EsSalud.

The SIS resembles the standard medical aid or Medicaid that is available in countries like the US. The EsSalud on the other hand, is insurance coverage that is given for working individuals and families in the form of employment based plans.

MINSA also makes it a mandate for certain public hospitals to provide advanced healthcare services for uninsured individuals for a variable fee, which depends on the type of treatment given.

■ PHILIPPINES

General	
Language	Filipino, English
Time Zone	PST(UTC+8)
Dialing Code	+63
Electricity	220V-60Hz
Major Cities	Manila, Davao, Cebu City, Antipolo
Currency	Peso(Filipino: piso)
Clothing	June to November the weather is rainy, whereas December to February are dry months. Dressing should be decent.
Health Related	
Mortality Rate	5.06 deaths/ 1,000 population
Life Expectancy	66.4M /72.5F
Patient: Physician Ratio	1800:1
Hospitals JCI accredited	3
Recommended Vaccinations	Hepatitis A, Typhoid, Hepatitis B, Rabies, Poliomyelitis, Diphtheria-tetanus, Measles, Varicella, Japanese encephalitis, Yellow fever and Meningococcal
Other Infections	Schistosomiasis, Anthrax, Hepatitis E, Scrub typhus, Murine typhus, Chikungunya fever, Capillariasis, Lymphatic filariasis, Lung fluke, Giant intestinal fluke,HIV

Tourism Related			
Population	98,215,000	Reliability of Police Services	98/140
Global Competitiveness	4.35/7	Physician Density	84/140
Tourism Competitiveness	3.9/7	Hospital Beds	128/140
GDP/Capita	$4,691	Quality of Air Transport Infrastructure	110/140
Health and Hygiene	3.8/7	International Air Transport Network	88/140
Safety and Security	4.1/7	Quality of Roads	86/140
Air Transport Infrastructure	3.0/7	Hotel Rooms	132/140
Tourism Infrastructure	2.9/7	Tourism Openness	97/140
Cultural Infrastructure	2.1/7	Attitude of Population Towards Foreign Visitors	26/140
Visa Requirements	3/140		

Situated in the western Pacific Ocean, Philippines is a sovereign island country that comprises around 7,100 islands. Known for its seabeds and vibrant marine life, the Southeast Asian country is also very rich in natural resources like warm tropical waters and coral gardens, which attract a number of tourists from different parts of the world. Philippines has two official languages, Filipino and English, prevalent in the country. Stretching approximately 300,000 square kilometers, the archipelago has 36,289 kilometers of coastline, which is the fifth longest coastline in the world.

Location

Lying between longitudes 116° 40' and 126° 34' E and latitudes 4° 40' and 21° 10' N, the Republic of the Philippines is surrounded by Taiwan in the north, Vietnam in the west, the island of Borneo in the southwest and Indonesia in the south. Being an island nation, Philippines is covered by a number of water bodies, including the Philippines Sea in the east, the South China Sea in the west, the Luzon Strait and the Celebs Sea in the north and south respectively.

People

Commonly known as Filipinos, the people of Philippines belong to several Asian ethnic groups, Tagalog, Cebuano, Ilocano, Bisaya/Binisaya, Hiligaynon, Bikol, Waray, and other non-tribal groups. There are more than 100 cultures growing throughout Philippines, mostly influenced by the countries like Spain and America, which makes the country an ideal destination for Western tourists. People in Philippines mainly speak English and Filipino; however, currently 80 other local languages are spoken in the country as well.

Events

Considering the fact that Philippines comprise over 7,000 Islands, there are hundreds of municipalities, towns and provinces in the country that have their own festivals and events that are celebrated to honor a Saint or place and commemorate a harvest or seasonal change, together with religious or social gatherings.

Held in the month of January, the "Fiesta of the Black Nazarene" is a popular festival, wherein thousands of devotees, men only, parade an image of the Black Nazarene, which was transported from Mexico to Manila in the 17th century, throughout the streets of Quiapo. People in the streets strive to touch the statue, as it is believed to have supernatural healing powers. The "Feast of Lady of Candles" and "Likhang Kamay" in the month of February, the "Bailes de los Arcos" in June and the "Grand Marian Procession" in December are some other major festivals celebrated in Philippines.

Weather

Being an island nation, Philippines features a tropical maritime weather, which remain hot and humid throughout the year. Usually there are three seasons in Philippines, the summer season from March to May that remain hot and dry, the rainy season from June to November and the winter season from December to February, which remain cold and dry. January is the coolest month in Philippines, while May is the warmest month. However, the temperature in the country ranges between 21 °C and 32 °C but it gets cooler or hotter according to the season. The temperature in Philippines varies according to the altitude, and drops up to six degrees in high altitude areas of the country.

Medical Tourism in Philippines

Offering high quality healthcare at an affordable price, Philippines is trying to compete with other Asian countries, including India, China, Japan and Singapore, dominating the Medical Tourism in the region. The American colonization of Philippines has influenced its culture and language, therefore, communication is not a problem for tourists as most of the people in the country are well versed with English. This attracts several foreign tourists seeking medical care without any language and cultural barriers.

Around 150,000 medical tourists from different parts of the world visit the island nation every year to seek different medical services, especially aesthetic and dental treatments, and enjoy the natural beauty. However, most of the medical tourists that visit the country are Filipino expatriates, but Philippines is also gaining popularity among the American and Arab communities as a medical tourist destination.

Healthcare System

There is a great disparity in the healthcare system of Philippines, as many rural areas in the country are still striving to get basic medical services, while urban areas or cities like Manila feature latest medical technologies and state-of-the art hospitals that ensure quality care to the patients. Private sector is responsible for most of the healthcare services in the country, while the public sector only comprise 36 percent of the total hospitals.

The Filipino government covers all the citizens of the country, whether employed or unemployed, under the PhilHealth program. The members of this insurance scheme are required to pay through salary deductions or premium, so they could receive reimbursements for healthcare.

Quality of Healthcare

The privately owned medical facilities in the capital city of Manila offer best healthcare services and accommodations to ensure quick recovery of the patients, which makes Philippines an upcoming medical tourism destination.

There is a vital difference between the public and private health institutions. Hence, medical tourist should opt for a private hospital or clinic while seeking healthcare in Philippines. Two JCI-accredited hospitals in Manila cater to domestic as well as foreign patients. The physicians in most of the private hospital are highly professional, as they usually get training in abroad, which help them eliminate certain cultural barriers while attending foreign patients.

■ POLAND

General	
Language	Polish
Time Zone	CET(UTC +1) summer(DST) CEST(UTC +2)
Dialing Code	48
Electricity	230V-50Hz
Major Cities	Warsaw, Lodz, Kraków, Wrocław
Currency	Zloty
Clothing	It is not too hot in summers but winters get really cold.

Health Related	
Mortality Rate	6.66 deaths/ 1,000 population
Life Expectancy	72.2M /80.5F
Patient: Physician Ratio	400:1
Hospitals JCI accredited	0
Recommended Vaccinations	Hepatitis A, Typhoid, Hepatitis B, Rabies, Influenza, Tick-borne encephalitis, Diphtheria-tetanus, MMR (Measles-Mumps-Rubella), Varicella
Other Infections	Lyme disease, Diphtheria, Brucellosis, HIV

Tourism Related			
Population	38,186,860	Reliability of Police Services	86/140
Global Competitiveness	4.66/7	Physician Density	52/140
Tourism Competitiveness	4.5/7	Hospital Beds	14/140
GDP/Capita	$13,540	Quality of Air Transport Infrastructure	91/140
Health and Hygiene	6.0/7	International Air Transport Network	104/140
Safety and Security	5.2/7	Quality of Roads	122/140
Air Transport Infrastructure	2.7/7	Hotel Rooms	73/140
Tourism Infrastructure	4.7/7	Tourism Openness	84/140
Cultural Infrastructure	5.4/7	Attitude of Population Towards Foreign Visitors	118/140
Visa Requirements	40/140		

Poland, edged by Baltic Sea in the north, is a popular tourist destination in central Europe that offers visitors from all over the world an opportunity to explore its rich history, culture and natural beauty. Labeled as an indestructible nation, Poland has risen majestically to modernity after remaining under communism for years. The attractions include more than 100 ancient castles, countless timber-built churches, medieval villages and towns and dense forests.

With a population of over 38 million, Poland that once was a hub for Nazi forces during the World War II has now become as one of Europe's most modern countries. Poland is regarded as a safe, friendly country that welcomes tourists warmly and shares it rich ancient legacy.

Tourism

After joining the European Union, Poland has witnessed a surge in its tourism industry, as Tourism contributes a major fraction to the overall economy of the country. According to World Tourism Organization, Poland is the 17th most visited country in the world. There are a number of tourist attractions in the central European country, but Wieliczka Salt Mine is one major destination that one would not want to miss while traveling Poland. Measuring over 300 kilometers in length, the salt mine reaches a depth of 327 meters and features an underground lake, together with extraordinary chambers, chandeliers and a chapel sculpted in salt.

The Old Town construction of the capital city, Warsaw, which entered the UNESCO World Heritage List in 1980, also offers a variety of attractions to lure tourists. Poland's fourth-biggest city, Wroclaw, comprises a series of islands that boasts around 100 bridges. The major tourist attractions in the Central European country revolve around city-sight-seeing, qualified tourism, agro-tourism, mountain hiking and climbing. In addition, Poland also attracts a large number of business travelers from all across the world.

Food and Accommodation

Known for its traditional dishes that are usually served during the festive season in the country, Poland is rich in meat, particularly pork, chicken and beef, winter vegetables and spices. Poles use traditional methods of cooking to prepare and enjoy their festive meals. Inspired by European traditions, Polish national cuisine is not only rich in nutrition but also great in taste, and has influenced the cooking and food habits of its neighboring countries. Tourists can have a variety of soups and potato dishes, together with traditional desserts and fermented dairy products to enjoy the traditional flavor of Polish cuisine during their stay in the country.

Poland houses most of the international hotel chains in major cities to accommodate tourists in utmost comfort. In addition, Poland offers over 200 campsites where tourists can enjoy the natural beauty. Agricultural tourism is a recent and evolving form of tourism in the country that encourages the concept of living closer to the land.

Weather

Featuring temperate weather in most areas, which become oceanic towards the north and west and continental (warmer) in the south and east, Poland provides pleasant conditions to enjoy its natural beauty and cultural heritage. Summer temperatures in Poland range between 18 °C and 30 °C according to the altitude of the region, while winters are relatively cold with temperature ranging between 3 °C and –6 °C in the northwest and the northeast respectively. Tourist season in Poland stretches from the month of May to September. The Central European country experiences rainfall throughout the year, while tourists can enjoy snow and winter sports from mid December to April in the southern part of the nation.

Medical Tourism in Poland

After Poland's induction and acceptance to the European Union, Poland has gradually been growing as a top medical tourism destination in Europe. Now a large number of European tourists travel to Poland and become aware of the country's ability to provide excellent healthcare at an affordable price. In addition, it provides first-rate leisure holidays, so medical travelers can enjoy their vacation while accessing healthcare in the country. Known for its cheap and effective dental treatments, Poland is attracting a large number of patients seeking dental treatment from the UK and other neighboring countries.

Healthcare System

Featuring a publicly funded health care system, Poland provides subsidized (rather free) health care in publicly funded hospitals to all its citizens, especially children, pregnant women, physically challenged and elderly people. However, a recent study shows that around 91% of pregnant women and 65% of citizens in Poland visit private healthcare centers, which clearly indicates the difference in the quality of healthcare in public and private hospitals. Polish government also provides pre-hospital emergency medical services, including first aid and ambulance service, through local, publicly operated hospital.

Quality of Healthcare

When we talk about the medical tourism, Poland is not lagging behind either. Even though there is a lack of JCI accredited facilities throughout Poland, hospitals catering to the medical tourists have other international accreditations like the ISO, Trent and the European Society for Quality in Healthcare to name a few. The medical services provided through clinics and hospitals are world-class supported by modern equipments and technology which is equivalent to the standards of Western European countries. Most of these medical facilities are government provided or aided in some way or the other. However, some leading private institutions also cater well to the needs of foreign medical patients.

■ PORTUGAL

General	
Language	Portuguese, Mirandese
Time Zone	WET(UTC0) summer (UTC+1)
Dialing Code	+351
Electricity	230V-50Hz
Major Cities	Lisbon, Porto, Amador, Braga
Currency	Euro
Clothing	Light clothing is recommended, accompanied by some warmer clothes for days when the weather may fall.
Health Related	
Mortality Rate	10.74 deaths/ 1,000 population
Life Expectancy	77.0M /83.1F
Patient: Physician Ratio	290:1
Hospitals JCI accredited	4
Recommended Vaccinations	Hepatitis A, Typhoid, Hepatitis B, Rabies, Influenza, Yellow fever, Diphtheria-tetanus, Measles, Varicella
Other Infections	Toscana virus, West Nile virus, Mediterranean spotted fever, Israeli spotted fever, Tick-borne relapsing fever, HIV

Tourism Related			
Population	10,487,289	Reliability of Police Services	34/140
Global Competitiveness	4.40/7	Physician Density	9/140
Tourism Competitiveness	5.0/7	Hospital Beds	55/140
GDP/Capita	$25,411	Quality of Air Transport Infrastructure	35/140
Health and Hygiene	6.1/7	International Air Transport Network	38/140
Safety and Security	5.8/7	Quality of Roads	4/140
Air Transport Infrastructure	4.3/7	Hotel Rooms	21/140
Tourism Infrastructure	6.1/7	Tourism Openness	42/140
Cultural Infrastructure	5.7/7	Attitude of Population Towards Foreign Visitors	7/140
Visa Requirements	40/140		

Considering Portugal has a fascinating history, tourists are likely to find classical attractions in this European country. From the medieval castles in the villages of Portugal to the sun kissed beaches, Portugal offers visitors unique attractions. The capital city of Lisbon has wonderful views of the river and cobble-stoned pathways to take you back into time. Along with the hustle and bustle of city life, tourists can truly feel the dichotomy of old and new in this region.

Location

Portugal is located in southwestern Europe on the Iberian Peninsula. Portugal is on the west-most side of Europe, borders Spain to the north and east and lies next to the Atlantic Ocean. The region of Portugal contains a total area of 92,212 sq km with a population of over 11 million inhabitants.

People

Even though Portugal has embraced a more informal way of life, polite terms of address are still in use with people in the country. Educated individuals are addressed as Senhor Doutor (Mr. Dr.) and upper class women are referred to as Dona. It is said that the high level of politeness in Portugal is seen as a reflection of respect. People, overall, are easy going and mild mannered.

Events

Despite the small size of the region of Portugal, it is filled with festivals and celebrations. The months of February and March are livened up with the onset of the Carnival (that takes place during the last few days before Lent). This festival is all about outrageous costumes, parades and fairs. Besides that, several sporting, cultural and musical events take place during the course of the year that simply makes Poland as a country of festivities and great culture.

Weather

Portugal has a typical Mediterranean climate and is known to be one of the warmest regions in Europe. The temperatures in the summer are above 30°C. However, during the winter months, the temperatures do fall and a high level of rain and wetness fills up the region.

Medical Tourism in Portugal

Portugal is gradually rising in the world of medical tourism and is to continue growing to new levels within the next few years.

Offering a considerably cheaper price of health services in comparison to other European countries, the region is drawing in travelers from the continent, from other countries close by or for that matter, from other developed countries of the world.

The WHO bestowed Portugal with a rank of 12 out of 191 countries as the world's best healthcare system. This high ranking, which demonstrates the good healthcare facilities coupled with its beautiful scenery, makes it a perfect spot for medical vacation that any tourist would love to visit anytime.

Healthcare System

Through extensive reforms in the healthcare system in 2002, Portugal is now able to boast an internationally recognized healthcare system that focuses on efficient and effective healthcare. There are three main arms that make up the healthcare system — the National Health Service (providing nationalized care to its residents), a specialized social health insurance scheme and the voluntary private health insurance.

In order to access the public hospitals, residents must contribute to the social security system on a weekly basis. However, those that are not interested or do not qualify for the public sector can seek healthcare in a private facility that have excellent specialists and utilize the latest advancements in technology and medicine.

Quality of Healthcare

The healthcare facilities in Portugal operate on a considerably high level of quality. Although the quality of care may vary from region to region, but it does not deteriorate to deter any medical tourist from visiting the country. There have been substantial improvements in the public sector and overall medical facilities in the region that have increased the standard of quality within the region and thereby increasing the number of foreign healthcare seekers.

Even though the quality might not be at the level of other European countries, Portugal is making great strides and efforts by having four of their medical facilities accredited by the esteemed Joint Commission International (a renowned international accrediting body). This demonstrates their ability to provide quality medical services on a global standard to individuals visiting the hospitals and clinics.

■ PUERTO RICO

General	
Language	Spanish, English
Time Zone	AST (UTC–4) No DST (UTC–4)
Dialing Code	+1 787 / 939
Major Cities	San Juan, Bayamón, Carolina, Ponce, Trujillo Alto
Currency	United States dollar
Health Related	
Mortality Rate	8 deaths/ 1,000 population
Hospitals JCI accredited	0
Recommended Vaccinations	Hepatitis A, Hepatitis B, Typhoid
Other Infections	HIV
Clothing	tropical marine, mild, little seasonal temperature variation

Tourism Related			
Population	3,667,084	Physician Density	47/140
Global Competitiveness	4.86/7	Hospital Beds	74/140
Tourism Competitiveness	4.4/7	Quality of Air Transport Infrastructure	28/140
GDP/Capita	$ 16,300	International Air Transport Network	44/140
Safety and Security	4.9/7	Quality of Roads	37/140
Health and Hygiene	4.7/7	Hotel Rooms	68/140
Air Transport Infrastructure	4.1/7	Tourism Openness	74/140
Tourism Infrastructure	4.9/7	Attitude of Population Towards Foreign Visitors	38/140
Cultural Infrastructure	1.9/7		

Puerto Rico, formally known as the Commonwealth of Puerto Rico, is situated in the northeast part of the Caribbean. It is an "unincorporated territory" of the United States of America. Bordered by the Dominican Republic in the east and the British Virgin Islands and the United States Virgin Islands in the west, Puerto Rico has the total population of around 3.6 million, as per records of 2012. The average temperature of Puerto Rico remains 28 degree Celsius all through the year. Drastic seasonal temperature fluctuation is not that common here. The weather in the northern region is cooler than that in the southern one. Similarly, the mountains have a low temperature as compared to the rest of the island.

Events and Festivals

Tourists, whether regular or medical, can enjoy and have fun in different festivals and events that are held in San Juan and other parts of this country. The Carnival is one of the most popular events of this place, which is held annually. Masked dances, parades, and many other events represent the culture of Puerto Rico with its vibrancy. Other popular festivals and events include Fiestas de la Calle San Sebastian, Saborea Culinary Festival, Heineken JazzFest, Puerto Rico Open, Emancipation Day, Independence Day, Columbus Day, Discovery of Puerto Rico, Rincón International Film Festival, Puerto Rico Symphony Orchestra, Aibonito Flower Festival and many more.

Medical Tourism in Puerto Rico

Puerto Rico is rapidly turning into a prime destination of medical tourism. Medical tourists, especially Americans visit this place for their treatment in large numbers. The cost of treatment is around 80 percent lesser than what one has to spend in the United States. Being a US territory, the quality of the services is almost similar to the US standards. Some of the medical services that are provided to the tourists include treatment of cardiovascular problems, orthopedic surgery, neurology, oncology, etc. The doctors and other medical professionals are certified and highly skilled. Hospitals are equipped with modern equipment for providing better treatment. The wonderful weather and the scenic beauty of the place help patients in their relaxation and recovery greatly.

Healthcare System

Puerto Rico has a reliable healthcare system. There are around 66 hospitals in this region, which are owned by either private or public sector. Most of the hospitals and medical centers are situated in Ponce, Mayaguez metropolitan and San Juan metropolitan. There are around 26 hospitals in San Juan metropolitan region. Puerto Rico also boasts of having quite a few medical research centers. Some of which include the Cardiovascular Center of Puerto Rico, the Caribbean and the Comprehensive Cancer Center, and so on. With such a good healthcare system, it has truly become an ideal location for medical tourism.

■ SAUDI ARABIA

General	
Language	Arabic
Time Zone	AST(UTC +3)
Dialing Code	+966
Electricity	127/220V-60Hz
Major Cities	Riyadh, Jiddah, Mecca, Medina
Currency	Saudi Riyal
Clothing	Very conservative dressing; women have to wear an Abaya in public places, whereas men should not wear shorts in public.
Health Related	
Mortality Rate	3.34 deaths/ 1,000 population
Life Expectancy	73.7M /77.3F
Patient: Physician Ratio	750:1
Hospitals JCI accredited	34
Recommended Vaccinations	Hepatitis A, Influenza, Typhoid, Hepatitis B, Rabies, Diphtheri-atetanus, Poliomyelitis, Varicella, Measles, Meningococcal and Yellow fever.
Other Infections	Respiratory Infections, Brucellosis, Onchocerciasis, Crime-an-Congo hemorrhagic fever, Plague, Foot-and-mouth dis-ease, HIV

Tourism Related			
Population	29,195,895	Reliability of Police Services	45/140
Global Competitiveness	5.19/7	Physician Density	90/140
Tourism Competitiveness	4.2/7	Hospital Beds	75/140
GDP/Capita	$25,085	Quality of Air Transport Infrastructure	34/140
Safety and Security	5.3/7	International Air Transport Network	19/140
Health and Hygiene	3.6/7	Quality of Roads	12/140
Air Transport Infrastructure	4.0/7	Hotel Rooms	39/140
Tourism Infrastructure	4.7/7	Tourism Openness	77/140
Cultural Infrastructure	1.8/7	Attitude of Population Towards Foreign Visitors	128/140
Visa Requirements	125/140		

Home to Islam's holiest cities of Makkah and Medina, Saudi Arabia offers a unique opportunity to visitors to explore the ethnic traditions and culture of Arabia. Home to more than 29 million (2012 estimates) people with a presence of expatriates from various nationalities, the Islamic country offers sunshine all the year round, places of natural beauty and a rich mix of history and culture dating back to thousands of years.

Visa Restrictions

Comparatively, the authorities maintain a conservative policy in allowing foreigners, including Muslims to explore the vast country. Muslim pilgrims and residents have to follow certain conditions for travelling within the country. The country issues tourist visas rarely. The best way to get into the Islamic country is by invitation of a Saudi national or company or if you are a Muslim, on a pilgrimage to one of the holy cities.

Saudi Arabia, however, allows the Gulf Nationals to enter the country without a visa. The kingdom is working on a new program called "Umra Plus" tourism that will allow pilgrims to extend their stay in the kingdom to visit certain areas that were previously inaccessible to them.

Cultural Do's and Don't

The holy country of Saudi Arabia has several restrictions for the foreigners as it practices Islamic principle strongly. There are other social and cultural restrictions - no short dresses, no mixing up with unrelated men and women. For the time being, the experience of visiting Saudi Arabia includes conforming to its norms. The country prohibits the use of alcohol, pornography and the entry of proselytizing materials into the country.

Saudi Arabia follows an austere version of Sunni Islam and religious police patrol the streets to ensure adherence to Islamic Shariah law, including a total ban on alcohol and certain types of music, books, literature, films, videos and photographs that it deems as vulgar and provocative. Men have to dress modestly and women have to cover their clothing with a loose black garment, called 'Abaya'. In restaurants and public places, the authorities observe strict privacy policy, segregating single men and families into separate sections.

The world's leading oil exporter has many tourist destinations. The country's capital, Riyadh, is a modern oil booming city with lot of high rising buildings. Makkah and Madina cities are strictly off limits to non-Muslims. Nearby Jeddah, the major Red Sea port city, gives a unique insight of culture and history of the West of Saudi Arabia.

If there is one highlight to be visited in the Kingdom, it is Mada'in Saleh, about 400 km North of Medina towards Jordanian border. It is the home of approximately 140 magnificent tombs of Nabataean origin, compared to Petra in Jordan, yet located in a different type of setting.

Terrain and Climate

About half of the Middle East's largest country consists of uninhabitable desert. There are no permanent rivers or lakes whatsoever and the average temperature in July is about 40°C.

The whole of the Middle East is tilted, so the southwest of Saudi Arabia has mountains as high as 3000 meters while the east has lowlands. The mountain area has the greenest and fresh climate especially compared to the deserts of the east.

Medical Tourism in Saudi Arabia

As compared to other Mideast countries, the medical tourism sector in Saudi Arabia is not highly developed or well promoted. However, with the abundance of wealth and luxury that this oil-rich country boasts, the medical facilities are an accurate reflection of high quality and class.

Even though Saudi Arabia remains in the shadows of other Arab countries like Jordan that actively market their medical services, there has been a rise in foreign patients seeking healthcare in the Kingdom.

There is a lack of marketing strategies in the medical tourism sector but has not deterred government officials from pushing tourists seek healthcare in Saudi Arabia. They are planning strategic developments to build medical cities in Jeddah that should attract private corporations and medical travelers.

Healthcare System

The government in Saudi Arabia offers its citizens healthcare with universal coverage in the public and private sector. The healthcare infrastructure is divided into two levels: the lower network is of primary healthcare facilities to provide preventive, emergency and basic healthcare. The upper tier of healthcare is more for specialized and complicated cases with the majority of clinics and hospitals in the urbanized areas of the Kingdom.

The Ministry of Health controls approximately 62 per cent of the hospitals in Saudi Arabia, with the remaining being part under the responsibility of other governmental agencies like Ministry of Defense, National Guard and other ministries.

Quality of Healthcare

The healthcare system in Saudi Arabia offers its residents excellent healthcare to mirror their luxurious lifestyle. The Kingdom boasts of an above average physician to patient ratio, and a hospital bed to population ratio in comparison to other MENA (Middle East North Africa) regions.

The hospitals and clinics in both the public and private sector demonstrate the superior quality with the latest technology and experienced providers. The Kingdom has over 30 JCI accredited hospitals highlighting its drive and ability to upkeep the international standards and regulations of high quality healthcare.

■ SINGAPORE

General	
Language	English, Malay, Mandarin Chinese, Tamil
Time Zone	SST (UCT+8)
Dialing Code	+65
Electricity	230V-50Hz
Major Cities	Singapore (Geyland & Katong, Chinatown, Toa Payoh, Holland Village, Little India)
Currency	Singapore dollar
Clothing	Take light weight cotton clothing; take plenty of rainwear as rains can occur at any season.

Health Related	
Mortality Rate	4.8 deaths/ 1,000 population
Life Expectancy	80.1M /84.6F
Patient: Physician Ratio	800:1
Hospitals JCI accredited	18
Recommended Vaccinations	Hepatitis A, Typhoid, Hepatitis B, Rabies, Diphtheriatetanus, Measles, Varicella, Japanese encephalitis, Poliomyelitis and Yellow fever.
Other Infections	Marine hazards in unmarked & unpatrolled beaches, HIV, Leptospirosis

Tourism Related			
Population	5,312,400	Reliability of Police Services	6/140
Global Competitiveness	5.72/7	Physician Density	64/140
Tourism Competitiveness	5.2/7	Hospital Beds	60/140
GDP/Capita	$50,323	Quality of Air Transport Infrastructure	1/140
Safety and Security	6.1/7	International Air Transport Network	1/140
Health and Hygiene	5.3/7	Quality of Roads	3/140
Air Transport Infrastructure	5.1/7	Hotel Rooms	37/140
Tourism Infrastructure	5.0/7	Tourism Openness	14/140
Cultural Infrastructure	3.6/7	Attitude of Population Towards Foreign Visitors	16/140
Visa Requirements	2/140		

Singapore is a bustling cosmopolitan city-state populated by high rising buildings and landscape gardens. Brimming with a harmonious blend of culture, cuisine, arts and architecture, Singapore is a dynamic city rich in contrast and color. Singapore embodies the finest of both – the East and the West.

Located in Southeast Asia, Singapore has a land area of about 710 square kilometers, making it the smallest country in the world. However, despite its size, Singapore commands an enormous presence in the world today with its free trade economy and highly efficient workforce.

People of Singapore

Singapore has a population well over five million people, with English as the main language of instruction and the country also accepts Malay, Chinese, and Tamil as the official languages. Coming together as a society and living in harmony, there are four major races – Chinese (majority), Malay, Indian and Eurasian. Each community offers a different perspective of life in Singapore in regard of culture, religion, food and language and creates the coherent whole of this beautiful yet progressive Southeast Asian sovereign city-state.

Tourism

Beyond the history, culture, people, shopping and food, there are many more facets of Singapore's thriving cityscape to discover. One can only experience these while exploring this once fishing village turned into cosmopolitan state. Singapore has a thriving ecosystem of nature and wildlife nestled within, which makes it perfect place for nature lovers to live in and tourists to visit. Nature lovers can look ahead to explore the rainforests and wetlands for an undisturbed as well as unparallel experience.

Singapore is a haven for culture vultures and a paradise for brand loyalists and hagglers as it brings different cultures and ethnicities together. While one can see Arab Street bringing alive the essence of Islam with many Mosques, shops and cuisines, the Orchard Street could easily merge into the Las Vegas landscape. If Little India strives to offer a comprehensive taste of the Indian culture, the Colonial Singapore keeps intact the city blueprint that has made Singapore what it is today – a lively and fast-paced business leader in the whole world.

Language

Almost everyone in Singapore speaks more than one language. The majority of the literate population is bilingual with English and Mandarin most commonly used in day-to-day life. However, it also has a considerable number of people speaking Malay and Tamil.

Weather

Singapore has equatorial climate (aka tropical rainforest climate) with no distinct seasons. Owing to its geographical location and maritime exposure, its climate is characterized by uniform temperature and pressure, high humidity and abundant rainfall. The temperature usually fall between 22 to 35 °C and the relative humidity averages around 79% and 73% in the morning and afternoon respectively. April and May are the hottest moths and has a monsoon season starting from November all the way to January.

Medical Tourism in Singapore

Singapore has long been a premier destination for healthcare attracting patients not only from Asia, but also from all over the world. Singapore's investments in State of the art, advanced medical technologies help achieve cost efficiency when large numbers of patients are served, thereby offering the medical tourists cost effective healthcare without compromising on quality.

International patients come to Singapore every year to seek a whole range of medical care from basic health screening and wellness services to high-end specialist care and surgical procedures like cardiology, neurology, ophthalmology, oncology and many more.

Healthcare System

Healthcare in Singapore is mainly under the responsibility of the Singapore Government's Ministry of Health. Singapore adopts a nationalized healthcare system where government ensures affordability, largely through compulsory savings (from payroll deductions) and price controls, while the private sector provides most of the medical care.

Patients are free to choose the providers within the government or private healthcare delivery system and can walk in for a consultation at any private clinic or any government polyclinic. In comparison to other medical tourism destinations, Singapore serves the international patient in order to provide quality care to local patients making it a win-win situation for all parties involved.

Quality of Healthcare

The World Health Organization ranked Singapore sixth in the list of best healthcare system in the world, which is much higher than the United States and Canada. The clinical services in Singapore emphasize excellence, safety and trustworthy. Singapore has internationally accredited facilities and renowned physicians trained in the best health centers of the world. The patients in Singapore are assured of quality treatment and high clinical outcome, similar to those in the United States and Europe.

Beyond international certifications, the quality of healthcare is also evident in published clinical indicators in measuring and sharing these performance standards publicly. Singapore encourages patients to make informed decisions regarding their treatment and institution of choice.

Thirteen hospitals and medical centers in Singapore have obtained Joint Commission International (JCI) accreditation and eleven hospitals have certification from the International Organization for Standardization (ISO).

■ SOUTH AFRICA

General	
Language	Afrikaans, English, Ndebele, Pedi, Sotho, Swazi, Tsonga, Tswana, Venda, Xhosa, Zulu
Time Zone	SAST (UTC +2)
Dialing Code	+27
Electricity	220V-50Hz
Major Cities	Cape Town, Durban, Johannesburg, Soweto
Currency	South African rand
Clothing	Depending on your activities pack your things accordingly, is planning a safari trip pack non-synthetic clothes. Temperature drops at night so also pack a jacket.

Health Related	
Mortality Rate	42.5 deaths/ 1,000 population
Life Expectancy	56.7M /59.6F
Patient: Physician Ratio	1300:1
Hospitals JCI accredited	0
Recommended Vaccinations	Hepatitis A, Typhoid, Hepatitis B, Rabies, Diphtheriatetanus, Poliomyelitis, Varicella, Yellow fever, Measles
Other Infections	Schistosomiasis (snail fever), Marburg fever, Tick-borne relapsing fever, African tick bite fever, West Nile fever, Anthrax, Plague, HIV

Tourism Related			
Population	5,312,400	Reliability of Police Services	108/140
Global Competitiveness	4.37/7	Physician Density	96/140
Tourism Competitiveness	4.1/7	Hospital Beds	65/140
GDP/Capita	$50,323	Quality of Air Transport Infrastructure	15/140
Safety and Security	3.8/7	International Air Transport Network	14/140
Health and Hygiene	4.3/7	Quality of Roads	42/140
Air Transport Infrastructure	4.0/7	Hotel Rooms	102/140
Tourism Infrastructure	4.5/7	Tourism Openness	85/140
Cultural Infrastructure	2.7/7	Attitude of Population Towards Foreign Visitors	42/140
Visa Requirements	28/140		

Often described as 'a world in one country', South Africa is one of the world's greatest tourist destinations. An excellent climate, natural beauty, first-rate infrastructure and welcoming people make this country one of the world's fastest growing tourism destinations. Added to these attractions is the fascinating story, accessible through ordinary people and historical monuments, of the transition from apartheid to democracy.

South Africa offers the visitors a multitude of destinations. Cape Town, considered as one of the top 10 destination in the world, the Kruger Park, the Garden Route and the pleasure resort of Sun City are among the few of the much sought after stops on any itinerary.

Tourism

South African tourist destinations would captivate the mind of travelers of all age groups. The fastest growing segment of tourism in South Africa is ecological tourism (aka ecotourism), which includes nature photography, bird watching, botanical studies, snorkelling, hiking and mountaineering. The national and provincial parks in South Africa, as well as private game reserves, involve local communities in the conservation and management of natural resources. Briefly, South Africa has varied spots serving people of different age groups and tastes.

Community tourism is becoming increasingly popular, with tourists showing keen interests to experience visiting many rural villages and townships across the country. Whether foreign tourists crave for endless beaches, birding, sports tours, the Big Five, historic battlefields, hunting, mountains, bush or forests, millions of people are discovering South Africa as an exceptional holiday destination and the numbers are to increase with each passing day

Among the attractions are breathtaking Cape Town nestling at the foot of Table Mountain, Cape Point, where two oceans meet, Cape Town's laid-back, welcoming attitude and fabulous nightlife. Along with Robben Island, the prison in Cape Town's Table Bay where Nelson Mandela was incarcerated, the delights of Sun City and many first rate casino resorts, walking in the spectacular Drakensberg Mountains. Johannesburg's moving, state-of-the-art new Apartheid Museum, the Big Hole in Kimberley, the world's biggest man-made hole and fly fishing in stunning scenery are few amongst all.

Language

South Africa is not called the rainbow nation for nothing. South Africa has 11 official languages and scores of unofficial ones. English is the most commonly spoken language in official and commercial life.

Weather

South Africa is a year round destination. Summers are hot but one can visit the cities located on the higher altitudes during the season. However, the best time for visit is spring.

South Africa has the seasons atypical for the southern hemisphere, with the coldest days starts from July till August. In winter, also due to altitude, temperatures drop to the freezing point, and in some places, even lower. Rare snowfall stunned the residents of Johannesburg in August 2012. During winter, it is warmest in the coastal regions, especially on the east of Indian Ocean coast.

Medical Tourism in South Africa

Even though South Africa might not be the first obvious choice for a potential medical tourist, yet it is slowly becoming a contender in the global healthcare. The reason being, more tourists are beginning to recognize the cost effective medical services that South Africa offers. In fact, South Africa is the leading medical tourism destination in Africa, having the best healthcare system found in south of the Sahara. It attracts patients from other African countries like Zambia, Zimbabwe, Botswana and Tanzania and a handful of them from America and Europe as well.

The country is already famous as a land of cultural diversity and natural attractions worldwide. This is an extra bonus for medical tourists who can recuperate while enjoying all that South Africa has to offer, right after checking out of their excellent medical institution.

Healthcare System

South Africa's healthcare system consists of a large public sector and a smaller but escalating private sector. Medical services in the country vary from basic primary healthcare offered free of cost by the government to highly specialized, technologically advanced health services available in the private sector for those who can afford to pay for the treatments on their own. Unfortunately, the public sector is under-resourced and overused. On the other hand, the fast developing private sector caters to middle and high-income groups and to the foreigners looking for top-quality surgical procedures at relatively affordable prices.

Quality of Healthcare

South Africa has been a world leader in medicine for long. In 1967, Dr Christiaan Barnard performed the world's first successful heart transplant, which boosted South Africa's reputation as being a pioneer in medical advances. Since then, the country has remained at the forefront of medical innovation and today can boast of significant achievements like successful separation of Siamese twins and the African developed HIV vaccine, which is the first one ever developed in a third world country.

To eliminate language barriers, the country has also an added advantage of English being one of the main languages for the medical tourists.

■ SOUTH KOREA

General	
Language	Korean
Time Zone	Korea Standard Time (UTC +9)
Dialing Code	+82
Major Cities	Seoul, Pusan, Inchon, Taegu
Currency	South Korean won
Clothing	Lightweight cottons and linens clothing are worn during summer, With light- to medium weights in spring and autumn. Medium to heavy weights are advised during the winter.
Health Related	
Mortality Rate	6.15 deaths/ 1,000 population
Life Expectancy	77.4M /83.9F
Patient: Physician Ratio	300:1
Hospitals JCI accredited	8
Recommended Vaccinations	Hepatitis a, Typhoid, Hepatitis B, Rabies, Diphtheria-tetanus, Measles, Varicella, Japenese encephalitis, Poliomyelitis, Yellow fever
Other Infections	Hemorrhagic fever with renal syndrome, Tick-borne encephalitis, Leptospirosis, Brucellosis, Scrub typhus, Murine typhus, Lung fluke, Fish tapeworm, HIV

South Korea, also known as the "Land of the Morning Calm," is a land of dualities that combines ancient traditions with modern infrastructure to present the best to whosoever visit it due to his/her own reasons – be as a tourist or as a healthcare seeker. Although infamous for being a key news topic due to unstable socio-political scenario, yet tourists can actually find South Korea to be a wonderful travel destination. Seoul, the capital and the largest city, highlights traces of ancient historical attractions of temples and places in conjunction with contemporary buildings and technological advancements.

Location

The lower part of the Korean peninsula is occupied by South Korea, which is about 1000 kilometers to the southwards, from the Eurasian landmass and it lies between Soviet Siberia lying in the northeast and Chinese Manchuria. Another interesting fact about South Korea is that it consists of around three thousand islands, which include the Province of Cheju Island being the largest of them all. The peninsula including the island covers an area up to 85000 square miles, out of which 100,210 square kilometer remains the territory of South Korea.

People

South Korea is a collection of vibrant cultures and traditions, which is why the people here are proud of their culture and nationality. Korean people tend to be very friendly and warm natured. They also pay a lot of attention and importance to their family, interpersonal relationships and ancestors. They also obey and respect elderly people.

Events

The events and festivals associated with South Korea are as vibrant as its culture is. The festivals celebrated over here are very colorful and beautiful like its landscape. These colorful festivals add a new life to spirits of people who celebrate them with great enthusiasm and joy.

Weather

Weather of South Korea keeps varying between seasons, especially between summers and mid-winters. The months of December to January are quite cold and freezing. The areas of south are much cooler in the winters compared to north, whereas the month of August is usually hot and sticky. One can find heavy rainfall here in the summer monsoon season, which usually arrives in July to mid august.

Culture

There are striking similarities between South and North Korea has if we talk about traditional culture. However, after division in 1945, two Koreas have developed different contemporary forms of culture to create their own, separate identities.

Although there is a tremendous influence of Chinese culture, yet South Korea has successfully created and managed is own distinct cultural identity which is considerably different from its larger neighbor. The ministry of culture in South Korea encourages traditional art together with modern forms to alive its tradition as well as create the best of two.

Medical Tourism in South Korea

South Korea is increasingly becoming popular as a medical tourist destination with unrivaled healthcare facilities by utilizing some of the latest technology in the world. Even though South Korea faces tremendous competition with other established medical tourism destinations in Asia, such as Thailand, India and Singapore, more medical tourists now know the benefits of traveling to South Korea and gradually, the medical tourists are increasing in the country.

Recent reports claim that in 2008, the country received around 25,000 foreign medical tourists, a striking increase of more than 56% from previous year. Along with a strong healthcare system and advanced technology, the plastic surgery industry is one of the main segments of medical tourism in South Korea attracting more and more medical tourists.

Owing to this popularity, nearly 10,000 people landed in South Korea in 2008 to obtain a cosmetic surgical procedure.

Healthcare System

The government of South Korea prioritized healthcare for all of its citizens. By 1988, around 79 per cent of the population had access to some form of healthcare or the other in the form of medical insurance benefits. Even though there is no official national insurance scheme in the country, the Ministry of Health has relentlessly worked with employers and private insurance corporations to make this happen.

The basic health plan covers a variety of health related services including hospital visits, physician fees, maternity health, and prescription drugs. Fees charged by physicians and hospitals are set by government, and medical fees are limited to economic growth.

Quality of Healthcare

Providers who boast international certifications and high qualifications staff most of the private medical facilities and especially those catering to foreign medical patients. The hospitals meet the world-class standards and are equipped with the latest technology and medical equipments to serve the foreign patients better.

Unlike other Asian countries where language barriers seem to possess a problem for medical travelers, South Korea assures foreigners the presence of language translator's available at most healthcare facilities.

■ SPAIN

General	
Language	Spanish
Time Zone	CET(UTC+4) summer CEST(UTC+2)
Dialing Code	+34
Electricity	220V-50Hz
Major Cities	Madrid, Barcelona, Valencia, Sevilla
Currency	Euro
Clothing	Light-to medium weights and rainwear, according to the season

Health Related	
Mortality Rate	8.72 deaths/ 1,000 population
Life Expectancy	79.0M /85.2F
Patient: Physician Ratio	300:1
Hospitals JCI accredited	18
Recommended Vaccinations	Influenza, Measles
Other Infections	Trichinellosis, Anthrax, Q fever, Mediterranean spotted fever, Tick-borne relapsing fever, Rabies, Scorpion stings, Black widow spider bites

Tourism Related			
Population	46,704,314	Reliability of Police Services	26/140
Global Competitiveness	4.60/7	Physician Density	8/140
Tourism Competitiveness	5.3/7	Hospital Beds	58/140
GDP/Capita	$30,557	Quality of Air Transport Infrastructure	17/140
Safety and Security	5.7/7	International Air Transport Network	28/140
Health and Hygiene	6.1/7	Quality of Roads	13/140
Air Transport Infrastructure	5.3/7	Hotel Rooms	10/140
Tourism Infrastructure	5.9/7	Tourism Openness	59/140
Cultural Infrastructure	6.6/7	Attitude of Population Towards Foreign Visitors	57/140
Visa Requirements	40/140		

Spain, officially the 'Kingdom of Spain' and a member of European Union, is a wonderful European destination that offers a lot more than bull fighting and Sangria. One of the unique features of Spain is the number of kingdoms present together to make up a complete nation. Along with the differences in region, there is diversity in culture and art that make it a favored destination of many tourists from all over the world.

Location

Located on the Iberian Peninsula, Spain is the largest among the three sovereign nations present. The total area of land area covered under Spain is 505,992 square kilometer. Officially known as the Kingdom of Spain, it touches Portugal, Morocco, France, Andorra, and Gibraltar from their borders. There are five mountain ranges in all that cross the country and two islands present are, Balearic Islands in the Mediterranean Sea and Canary Islands lying in the Atlantic Ocean.

Languages

Spain became the global empire in the early modern period and one of the first countries to colonize the new world. It left a wonderful legacy of 500 million people who has Spanish as a first language making it the second most spoken language in the world. Spanish is the official language, recognized in the constitution as Castilian, of Spain. Not only is Spanish but the country recognizes Basque, Catalan, Galician and Occitan as regional languages.

People

The total population of Spain, as per 2013 estimates, is 46,704,314 and the people are quite fun loving by nature, with a laid-back kind of attitude. Apparently, they seem to be serious in nature, but after conversing for a while, they appear to be very friendly and helpful.

Events

Spain celebrates a variety of different events symbolizing their diverse culture. Bull fighting is the most popular event held in Madrid in May and hundreds of thousands of visitors from Spain and all over the world throng to watch it. One can find multiple influences of Iberian, Latin, Roman Catholicism and Moorish Islam present in their culture.

People are also excessively in love with music and dance. Spain is famous world over for summer music festival named Sonar and Benicàssim. Sonar is a three-day electronic and advanced music festival that features the top up and coming pop and techno acts, whereas the latter one features alternative rock and dance acts.

Weather

Spain is blessed with generous amount of sunshine and has very diverse climates depending on different locations within the country. With the variation in latitudes, the climate changes from north to the south, while the Mediterranean and Atlantic Ocean influence the east and west regions. The weather condition in Spain is very different from the rest of the Europe and this is due to its position and natural land mass.

Medical Tourism in Spain

Even though the Spanish government has not yet actively marketed medical tourism in Spain, yet it has the potential to attract medical travelers from across the world.

With the high quality of Spanish healthcare system, cutting-edge equipment and medical facilities that offer cost effective services, there is a gradually increase in number of medical travelers mainly from Europe, Middle East and North Africa who are discovering the benefits seeking healthcare in this popular European country.

Spain offers varied treatments to visiting foreign patients. However, popular medical treatments sought in Spain include cosmetic surgery, dentistry, eye surgery, obesity surgery and orthopedic surgery to name a few.

Healthcare System

Spain was ranked seventh on the World Health Organization's international comparative list of the world's best health systems. The report also claimed that the Spanish people ranked second in Europe for the quality of healthcare they receive.

The Spanish healthcare system is a combination of both public and private involvement. The public sector provides free or cost effective healthcare to those who contribute to the Spanish social security. Spain has more than 750 hospitals served by 450,000 doctors and nurses. Spanish Ministry of Health recognizes and supervises all of the hospitals in currently functioning in Spain.

Spain's resilient economy has also helped to boost their healthcare system by creating leading medical facilities with qualified physicians providing healthcare to their citizens and foreign patients.

Quality of Healthcare

There are varieties of healthcare organizations in Spain, both private and government owned that have specialized departments catering exclusively for medical tourists. International patients can avail the services of English speaking doctors and medical staff that have to meet stringent requirements and undergo various tough procedures to practice medicine in Spain.

To ensure patients and medical tourists to get the high quality healthcare in the country, Spain boasts 17 medical facilities accredited by the JCI and Fundacion Avedis Donabedian (FAD), an accreditation partner of JCI.

■ SWITZERLAND

General	
Language	Germany, French, Italian, Romansh
Time Zone	CET(UTC +1) summer(DST) CEST (UTC +2)
Dialing Code	+41
Electricity	220/240V
Major Cities	Zürich, Genève, Basel, Bern
Currency	Swiss franc
Clothing	Depending on the season, summers are pleasant yet winters are really cold.

Health Related	
Mortality Rate	8.65 deaths/ 1,000 population
Life Expectancy	80.3M /84.7F
Patient: Physician Ratio	280:1
Hospitals JCI accredited	1
Recommended Vaccinations	Influenza, Tickborne encephalitis, Diphtheria-tetanus, Measles, Varicella
Other Infections	Alveolar echinococcosis, Lyme disease, HIV

Tourism Related			
Population	8,014,000	Reliability of Police Services	3/140
Global Competitiveness	5.72/7	Physician Density	7/140
Tourism Competitiveness	5.7/7	Hospital Beds	31/140
GDP/Capita	$79,033	Quality of Air Transport Infrastructure	5/140
Safety and Security	6.3/7	International Air Transport Network	6/140
Health and Hygiene	6.5/7	Quality of Roads	6/140
Air Transport Infrastructure	5.4/7	Hotel Rooms	12/140
Tourism Infrastructure	6.7/7	Tourism Openness	67/140
Cultural Infrastructure	6.2/7	Attitude of Population Towards Foreign Visitors	23/140
Visa Requirements	39/140		

Switzerland borders France in the West, Germany in the north, Austria and the principality of Liechtenstein in the east and Italy in the south. Switzerland was discovered more than 700 years ago. Long years of peace have their mark on its heritage, history and culture. The diversity of the landlocked, mountainous country is the essence of Switzerland that gives the European country its unique identity.

Apart from this, Switzerland is famous world over for its financial institutions, fine cheeses and chocolate, for watch industry that manufacture some of the best watches in the world, for its spectacular scenery and much more. The total area under Swiss Confederation is 41,285 square kilometers and over 8 million (as per 2012 estimates) people reside the country with population density of 188 people/ per square kilometers.

People of Switzerland

The Swiss are friendly and hospitable people, though somewhat reserved at times. Life in Swiss towns and cities is secured. The Swiss people share an independent spirit, a respect for tradition and no less than four languages, dozens of dialects make it a multilingual, and multi cultured country.

Languages

Switzerland's is multi ethnic society and has four official languages: German spoken by 65 percent populace, French by 22 percent people, Italian by 8 percent people and locally spoken Romansh, which is a romance language. Romansh is designated the by the federal constitution as the national language.

Events

Every major Swiss city honors its own symphony, opera or theatre, where acclaimed international artists appear. The Bern, Willisau and Montreux Jazz Festivals rival in recognition with the classical music events of Lucerne and Gstaad to name just a few.

About 700 museums round out a rich cultural life. An outstanding, internationally acclaimed art collections and specialized museums for every interest are established. Today scores of medieval castles and venerable mansions are open for a look around. Some house superb museums, other wonderful restaurants. Churches, monasteries and abbey libraries hold precious legacies of the ages.

Weather

From July to August the daytime temperature range is 18 to 28 °C (65° - 82° F) and from January to February the range is -2 to 7 °C (28° - 45° F). In spring and autumn, the daytime temperature range is 8 to 15 °C (46° - 59° F). Depending on the altitude, the temperature range may vary. It is highly recommended to visitors to pack a sweater, good walking shoes, sunscreen, sunglasses, a compact umbrella and/or a light raincoat.

Medical Tourism in Switzerland

Switzerland was one of the first health tourism destinations where wealthy travelers came for spas and saunas in early 19th century. Prior to medical tourism became a fully-fledged industry, local hospitals and clinics have treated well off people seeking specialist and discreet attention.

The majority of medical travelers come from Europe, Middle East or Russia to seek excellent health services at two of the most popular cities of this popular growing European country, Geneva and Zurich.

The Swiss hospitals do not compromise with quality when providing excellent healthcare services. The medical facilities within the country utilize advanced technology and latest medical equipment. Switzerland's popularity as medical tourism destination is as high as people seeking specialized or complicated procedures from the renowned physicians are ready to pay any price to receive the greatest healthcare.

Healthcare System

The Federal Health Insurance Act of 1994 ensures healthcare to citizens of Switzerland. The Swiss healthcare infrastructure is more successful than other failed systems as it involves people to participate in their healthcare.

The government does not 'ration' care but keeps down the high cost of healthcare through regulations of medications and laboratory fees.

Quality of Healthcare

Medical services in Switzerland flaunt high quality clinics, state-of-the-art technology, advanced equipments and well-trained doctors. It offers medical travelers a wide range of procedures ranging from medical treatments to spa and wellness clinics.

The Swiss treatment is by no means cost effective as it is in other popular medical tourism destinations like India and Thailand offer. The reason being, its high quality of care and dedication to medicine is unrivaled. Swiss surgeons have been regarded as 'artists' due to their skills in cosmetic surgery and they provide customized treatments for all patients.

For the last ten years, the Swiss Leading Hospitals (SLH), a federation of 18 hospitals in Switzerland, have been offering excellent medical treatments and five-star hotel accommodations, which is at par or for that matter, even above the healthcare that any medical tourism facility or health centers in developed countries offer.

■ TAIWAN

General	
Language	Mandarin, Taiwanese
Time Zone	CST (UTC+8)
Dialing Code	+886
Electricity	220V, 50Hz
Major Cities	Taipei, Kaohsiung, Taichung, Tainan City
Currency	New Taiwan Dollar
Clothing	Depending on the season, summers are mild t-shirt and short sleeve shirts should be packed, whereas in winter overcoat and woolen jackets should be taken.
Health Related	
Mortality Rate	8.87 deaths/ 1,000 population
Life Expectancy	73 M /79 F
Hospitals JCI accredited	12
Recommended Vaccinations	Hepatitis A, Typhoid, Hepatitis B, Rabies, Diphtheriatetanus, Measles, Varicella, Japanese encephalitis, Yellow fever and Poliomyelitis.
Other Infections	HIV, Hemorrhagic fever with renal syndrome

Tourism Related			
Population	23,340,136	Reliability of Police Services	40/140
Global Competitiveness	5.28/7	Physician Density	70/140
Tourism Competitiveness	4.7/7	Hospital Beds	24/140
GDP/Capita	$20,328	Quality of Air Transport Infrastructure	44/140
Safety and Security	5.8/7	International Air Transport Network	37/140
Health and Hygiene	5.8/7	Quality of Roads	21/140
Air Transport Infrastructure	3.7/7	Hotel Rooms	53/140
Tourism Infrastructure	3.8/7	Tourism Openness	72/140
Cultural Infrastructure	3.6/7	Attitude of Population Towards Foreign Visitors	78/140
Visa Requirements	93/140		

The first westerners to get a glimpse of Taiwan claimed to be enthralled with its beauty. In more modern times you can still find the beauty in the mountainous country side of Wulai, or engage in the hustle and the bustle of city life in Taipei; Taiwan has come to represent one of Asia's most diverse and unique regions. From travelers seeking to get a taste of the delicious cuisine or those looking to embrace their spiritual side, more and more individuals are beginning to realize the variety of attractions and activities this small country has to offer.

Coming to its demographics, officially the Republic of China has a total area of 36,193 square kilometers. The total number of inhabitants in the country, as per 2013 estimates, is well over 23 million with population density at 644 people/square kilometer.

Location

Taiwan is located in the Pacific Ocean and is about 100 miles away from the southeast part of the mainland China. It also acts as a natural gateway for travelers, who want to explore Asian subcontinent. It is situated in between Korea and Japan to the northern side and in the midway between Hong Kong and Philippines in the south.

Taiwan consists of 14 different islands, the main island being 240 miles in length and 90 miles in width. The entire Island is covered by mountain ranges and the highest mountain range is Yu Shan with a height of 13,113 feet. Out of the total area of Taiwan, two third of the region is mountainous. The largest city of Taiwan is Taipei, which is also the capital of Taiwan.

People

The majority of individuals that live in Taiwan are offspring of people that migrated from mainland China, particularly from the coastal provinces of Guangdong and Fujian. Over the years, the differences between various groups and people here have vanished and the economies have gradually integrated for the better progress.

Language

The official language of Taiwan is Mandarin and is also spoken by majority of Taiwanese people. It is also the primary language of instruction in schools. Other officially accepted languages include Hokkien, Hakka, Formosan and Fuzhou dialect.

Events

The traditional and ethnic Chinese festivals mostly dominate the event calendar of Taiwan. One of the most popularly celebrated is the Chinese New Year.

The liveliness of the events creates a jovial mood among all to celebrate each and every event with equal enthusiasm and with eagerness.

Weather

The weather in Taiwan is tropical and mostly warm throughout the year. The climate is quite unpredictable during spring and winter, while it is stable during summer and autumn in most of the conditions. It receives rain during the monsoon from June to August. Another unique thing about climate of Taiwan is the sky, which remains cloudy all round the year.

Medical Tourism in Taiwan

Reporters have given Taiwan the title of "sleeping giant" in the Asian Medical Tourism industry. The country has so much to offer, yet has not marketed itself as a prime health-care destination in comparison to its Asian counterparts that include India, Thailand and Singapore. However, it is said that this 'giant' is about to wake up from its slumber and embrace its potential as a major medical tourism destination.

Undoubtedly, medical tourism presents a profitable opportunity to boost the economic development of any country and Taiwan is no exception. It has the potential to position the country as a key player amongst the neighboring and competing nations in the medical tourism industry.

Healthcare System

The healthcare system in Taiwan is referred to as the National Health Insurance (NHI) and is administered by the Department of Health of the Executive of Yuan. The NHI is a government initiated social insurance plan that centralizes the funding of healthcare services. The system ensures all the citizens to have coverage and hence access to Taiwan's leading medical services.

Quality of Healthcare

Taiwan's single payer insurer monitors standards, usage and quality of treatment for diagnosis by requiring the providers to submit a full report every 24 hours. This improves the quality of treatment for patients and eliminates long waiting queues for them.

Taiwan's medical sector also boasts of a wide range of diagnostic technologies like world-class MRI, PET and CT machinery and can generally be considered as of higher quality than several of its Asian equivalents.

The future of medical tourism in Taiwan looks bright as it offers excellent physicians, state-of-the-art health service equipment, top-rankings in health infrastructure and low treatment costs. Currently, Taiwan has 10 JCI accredited facilities to demonstrate their ability to keep up with international accreditation standards.

■ THAILAND

General	
Language	Thai
Time Zone	UTC+7
Dialing Code	+66
Electricity	120V, 50Hz
Major Cities	Bangkok, Samut Prakan, Mueang Nonthaburi, Udon Thani
Currency	Baht
Clothing	Short sleeve shirts are acceptable in most dining venues. Adventure travelers will be more prone to walking shorts and pullover cotton shirts.
Health Related	
Mortality Rate	6.47 deaths/ 1,000 population
Life Expectancy	70.7 M /77.4 F
Patient: Physician Ratio	2700:1
Hospitals JCI accredited	13
Recommended Vaccinations	Hepatitis A, Typhoid, Hepatitis B, Rabies, Diphtheria-tetanus, Measles, Varicella, Japanese encephalitis and Yellow fever.
Other Infections	Scrub Typhus, Spotted fever rickettsoioses, Hepatitis E, Chikungunya fever

Tourism Related			
Population	66,720,153	Reliability of Police Services	71/140
Global Competitiveness	4.52/7	Physician Density	109/140
Tourism Competitiveness	4.5/7	Hospital Beds	77/140
GDP/Capita	$10,849	Quality of Air Transport Infrastructure	33/140
Safety and Security	4.4/7	International Air Transport Network	31/140
Health and Hygiene	4.3/7	Quality of Roads	39/140
Air Transport Infrastructure	4.6/7	Hotel Rooms	41/140
Tourism Infrastructure	5.2/7	Tourism Openness	24/140
Cultural Infrastructure	3.6/7	Attitude of Population Towards Foreign Visitors	13/140
Visa Requirements	75/140		

Located in the centre of Southeast Asia, Thailand is a fascinating and exotic country to explore. Thailand embraces a rich diversity of cultures and traditions. With its proud history, tropical climate and renowned hospitality, the 'Land of Smiles' is a never-ending source of fascination and pleasure for visitors. The Thai economy is largely export driven and strong being the second largest in Southeast Asia.

Its capital, Bangkok, offers incredibly varied attractions. Gleaming skyscrapers, glittering temples, colorful street markets, sophisticated shopping malls, bustling nightlife, and an energy that reflects the incredible economic growth. The scenery and seascapes makes Phuket, Thailand's biggest island, a dream destination.

The total area under Thailand, officially the Kingdom of Thailand, 513,120 square kilometers and a population of over 66 million (as per 2011 estimates) lives in the country with a density of 132.1 people/per square kilometer.

Religion

Thailand is one of the most strongly Buddhist countries in the world. The national religion is Theravada Buddhism, a branch of Hinayana Buddhism, practiced by more than 90 per cent of all Thais. The remaining population adheres to Islam, Christianity, Hinduism and other faiths. Thailand offers all the religions a freedom of expression. However, Buddhism continues to cast strong influence on daily life.

Language

Thai is the official language, but people also widely speak and understand English. English and other European languages are spoken in most of the hotels, shops, restaurants and in other major tourist places. Thai-English road and street signs are common sight across the country.

Weather

Thailand can be best described as tropical and humid for the majority of the country during most of the year. The area north of Bangkok has a climate determined by three seasons while the southern peninsular region of Thailand has only two.

The seasons of north of Thailand are clearly defined. The weather is mostly dry in between November and May. The other season is from May to November, dominated by southwest monsoon the time when rainfall in the north is the heaviest.

Overall, the south of Thailand gets most of the rainfall with around 2,400 millimeters every year, compared to the central and northern regions, both of which get around 1,400 millimeters.

Medical Tourism in Thailand

Thailand is leading Asia as the prime medical tourism destination. The number of medical tourists that come in Thailand has been steadily increasing since early 2000. This has resulted in the country taking its place on top of the global medical tourism market with over a million tourists visiting this exotic destination seeking affordable medical services.

Thailand is expected to continue dominating this market because of its ability to offer low cost medical treatment, excellent quality provided by experienced physicians and doctors at medical tourism destinations, in all the general government hospitals as well as in private clinics.

Thailand is home to some of the most renowned international hospitals in the world that acts as a benchmark for what medical facilities in Asia should strive like. From the level of customer service through international patient departments, to the emphasis on quality care, medical tourists visiting Thailand are assured excellent care.

Healthcare System

Thailand's health service infrastructure consists of government provided health services, non-profit health organizations (NGOs) and the burgeoning private medical sector. Thailand has introduced universal coverage reforms in 2001, becoming one of only handful of lower-middle income countries to do so.

Statistics from the WHO say 65 per cent of Thailand's health care expenditures in 2004 was from the government, while 35 per cent was from private sources. However, Thailand's medical tourism industry is largely driven by private hospitals. Thai doctors are attracted to the international hospitals as they can earn as much as 70 per cent more than in the public hospitals.

Quality of Healthcare

In recent years, Thailand's private sector has established a growing number of medical facilities that can match leading hospitals worldwide. The country has over 30 hospitals that cater to medical tourists, as well as numerous dental and cosmetic clinics and other medical and alternative medicine centers. Thailand boasts of the first hospital in Asia to receive JCI accreditation, Bumrungrad International, the world's most recognized facility catering to medical tourists.

Following suit, 11 more hospitals in Thailand have been prestige with JCI accreditation. The UK Foreign and Commonwealth Office states that Bangkok has "excellent international hospitals." Similarly, the US State Department states that in Bangkok offers "excellent facilities exist for routine, long-term and emergency health care"

■ TRINIDAD TOBAGO

General	
Language	English
Time Zone	(UTC-4)
Dialing Code	+1
Currency	Trinidad and Tobago dollar
Health Related	
Mortality Rate	5.97 deaths/ 1,000 population
Life Expectancy	66.5M /75.2F
Hospitals JCI accredited	0
Recommended Vaccinations	Hepatitis A, Hepatitis B, Typhoid, Yellow Fever
Other Infections	HIV
Clothing	Tropical, rainy season (June to December)

Tourism Related			
Population	1,346,350	Physician Density	83/140
Global Competitiveness	4.95/7	Hospital Beds	69/140
Tourism Competitiveness	3.9/7	Quality of Air Transport Infrastructure	56/140
GDP/Capita	$21,287	International Air Transport Network	63/140
Safety and Security	4.0/7	Quality of Roads	74/140
Health and Hygiene	4.6/7	Hotel Rooms	77/140
Air Transport Infrastructure	3.4/7	Tourism Openness	107/140
Tourism Infrastructure	3.6/7	Attitude of Population Towards Foreign Visitors	126/140
Cultural Infrastructure	2.4/7		

Trinidad and Tobago, officially known as the Republic of Trinidad and Tobago, is an island country, which is located on the northern side of South America. The country lies to the south of Grenada and off the seashore of the northeastern part of Venezuela. It has maritime boundaries with Grenada in the northwest, Barbados in the northeast, Venezuela in the south and west and Guyana in the southeast. As per records of 2011, the population was around 1.3 million here. It is a country with a tropical climate. There are mainly two seasons - the first six months are dry season, whereas the next six months are called the rainy season.

Events and Festivals

The festivals and events celebrated in Trinidad and Tobago are largely based on religious, sporting and cultural factors. Celebrated in February, the Carnival is the most important festival of Trinidad and Tobago. There is a festival almost every month in this country, which tourists can enjoy. Some of the popular events include Tobago's Heritage Festival, Diwali, Emancipation Celebrations, San Fernando Jazz Festival, Independence Day, Panyard Sensations, Santa Rosa Festival, etc. Some of the sports events that are organized throughout the year include Carib Great Race, Tobago International Game Fishing Tournament, Angostura Tobago Sail Week, Buccoo Goat and Crab Race Festival.

Medical Tourism in Trinidad and Tobago

Over the past few years, there has been a noteworthy growth in the medical tourism industry in Trinidad and Tobago. However, there is potential for more growth, provided the Ministry of Health and Tourism employs proper measures. Both private as well as public hospitals are present in the country. Unlike other popular medical tourism destinations, dentistry is completely a private sector here. As per the records of the Ministry of Health, three medical areas namely dentistry, cardiac surgery and joint replacements have proved to be great for medical tourists in Trinidad and Tobago.

Healthcare System

Both private and public sectors fund healthcare system in Trinidad and Tobago. There are a number of private as well as public hospitals. Public healthcare is free for residents as well as non-residents. The taxpayers and the Government pay for this system. Therefore, medical tourists can get their treatment done without spending money if they opt for public healthcare. The health sector is controlled by the Ministry of Health, which has been putting continuous efforts to improve the entire system for the overall benefits of the sufferers. The Government has launched the Chronic Disease Assistance Program (CDAP) to provide free treatment to the patients suffering from certain diseases like Cardiac Diseases, Mental Depression, Asthma, High Blood Pressure, Arthritis, etc.

■ TUNISIA

General	
Language	Literary Arabic
Time Zone	CET(UTC+1)
Dialing Code	+216
Electricity	230V, 50Hz
Major Cities	Tunis, Sfax, Sousse, Midoun
Currency	Tunisian dinar
Clothing	Cotton or other natural fibre shirts or t-shirts, teamed with cotton trousers or ankle length shirts are good and remember to cover your shoulders or you will be looked at!

Health Related	
Mortality Rate	5.24 deaths/ 1,000 population
Life Expectancy	73 M /77 F
Patient: Physician Ratio	750:1
Hospitals JCI accredited	0
Recommended Vaccinations	Hepatitis A, Typhoid, Hepatitis B, Rabies, Diphtheriatetanus, Measles, Varicella, Poliomyelitis, Yellow fever
Other Infections	Lymphatic filariasis, Schistosomiasis, Tick-borne relapsing fever, Brucellosis, HIV

Tourism Related			
Population	10,777,500	Reliability of Police Services	24/140
Global Competitiveness	4.65/7	Physician Density	74/140
Tourism Competitiveness	4.4/7	Hospital Beds	83/140
GDP/Capita	$9,774	Quality of Air Transport Infrastructure	29/140
Safety and Security	4.4/7	International Air Transport Network	40/140
Health and Hygiene	5.9/7	Quality of Roads	39/140
Air Transport Infrastructure	3.2/7	Hotel Rooms	21/140
Tourism Infrastructure	3.8/7	Tourism Openness	30/140
Cultural Infrastructure	2.3/7	Attitude of Population Towards Foreign Visitors	20/140
Visa Requirements	16/140		

The smallest country in North Africa, Tunisia is widely known as the land of colors and contrasts. Officially, the Republic of Tunisia, the Maghreb country shares its boundaries with Libya to the southeast, Algeria to the west and the Mediterranean Sea to the north and east. The spices and scents of Tunisia always welcome its visitors to enjoy its natural beauty and traditionally rich culture. With impressive modern infrastructure, great accommodations, connectivity and information, Tunisia has been among the future center of tourist attractions.

Location

As discussed above, Tunisia is situated between Algeria and Libya in North Africa. The main attractions that act as magnets for tourists in Tunisia are the golden sandy beaches, vibrant sunshine, the Atlantic Ocean and the Nile Delta. Most of the part of this country lies in the Sahara desert, which is around 40 percent of Tunisia and is semi-arid. It lies on the shores of the Mediterranean Sea and along Atlas Mountain Range. Its north-south extent further plays a vital role in endowing the country with great environmental diversity. Visitors would sure love to explore Sahel, the world's best area for olive cultivation and the Steppes.

People

Most of the people in Tunisia seriously follow the religion of Islam. The nature of people is very friendly and lively, which can be seen during their festive celebrations. The people enjoy sharing and educating visitors about their customs and beliefs. The population of Tunisia comprises people of mainly Arab, Berber, and Turkish descent. Most Tunisians simply identify themselves as Arabs. However, some practice the Maliki School of Islam of Arab origin, while others practice the Hanafi School of Turkish descent.

Events

Being on the crossroad of diverse cultures, Tunisia's cultural legacy comes to the fore through a wide calendar of festivals and celebrations. Tunisians show tremendous adaptability in terms of combining their deeply rooted customs with the events of international importance. The Techno music festival held in Gammarth substantiates it fully.

Celebrated in Douz, the Sahara International Festival aka the Camel Festival owes its inspiration to the Saharan Bedouin culture. Tunisians, Libyans, Algerians and Egyptians congregate at the event to display their crafts, dance, music, apart from demoing their camel and horse riding skills. While in Tunisia, you cannot afford to miss the Carthage International Festival of Theater, Music and Dance. The festival attracts several artists from Americas, Europe, Asia and Africa.

Next, the Roman amphitheater of El Jem celebrates the El Jem Symphony Music Festival. Here, you could have your chance to listen amazing melodies created by the Italian Chamber orchestras, the Hungarian Symphony Orchestra and the Vienna State Opera. These festivals are celebrated not only by the citizens but also by the tourists visiting this destination.

Weather

With mainly dry summers and mild winters, the climate of Tunisia falls under the category of Mediterranean. The tourists pour in mostly in the month of March to May. The summer is quite popular to attract visitors to enjoy the vibrant landscapes, beaches, and festivals as well.

Medical tourism in Tunisia

Medical tourism is slowly becoming a key sector in the tourism industry along with eco-tourism and spa tourism. Compared to other North African counterparts, Tunisia is heavily marketing to attract potential patients, who love to visit Tunisia for quality medical services at affordable rates. With medical services provided at 50 per cent less cost than in America or Europe, Tunisia has emerged as a popular healthcare destination.

In fact, reports claim that over 70,000 patients hailing from Libya, Algeria and other African nations sought medical care in Tunisian hospitals and clinics in 2009. The International Medical Tourism Journal (IMTJ) reports that Medical tourism in Tunisia has become the country's second highest foreign currency earner.

Healthcare System

The healthcare system in Tunisia consists of public and private sector, which has enabled it to cover the majority of its citizens. The Ministry of Public Health operates the public sector, which is responsible for basic primary care and preventive services.

The private sector's health facilities are comprised of an outpatient network of general or specialized medicine, paramedical treatment and hospitalization facilities. The private health care sector represents 12 per cent of the total capacity in beds and 70 per cent of the top range medical equipment in the country.

Quality of Healthcare

With Tunisia's new reputation as a popular medical destination, the government invests heavily to improve and maintain quality standards in all medical facilities catering to foreign patients. Tunisia has also focused on improving the management process to make its training staff better. The modernization of the billing system further allows the mobilization of additional resources.

Tunisia currently has 80 private clinics with an accommodation capacity of 2500 beds. Most of these clinics have all the latest technologies available. Physicians and other healthcare providers, trained in Europe or America, offer their services in clinics and hospitals to meet the highest standards.

■ TURKEY

General	
Language	Turkish
Time Zone	EET(UTC+2)
Dialing Code	90
Electricity	230V, 50Hz
Major Cities	İstanbul, Ankara, İzmir, Bursa
Currency	Turkish lira
Clothing	Casual dress for most places. No shorts, sleeveless tops or revealing clothing for men or women.

Health Related	
Mortality Rate	6.1deaths/ 1,000 population
Life Expectancy	73.3 M /78.1 F
Patient: Physician Ratio	750:1
Hospitals JCI accredited	48
Recommended Vaccinations	Hepatitis A, Typhoid, Hepatitis B, Rabies, Diphtheriatetanus, Measles and Varicella.
Other Infections	Legionnaires' disease, Cutaneous leishmaniasis, Tick-borne relapsing fever, Louse-borne relapsing fever, Brucellosis, Anthrax, HIV

Tourism Related			
Population	75,627,384	Reliability of Police Services	83/140
Global Competitiveness	4.45/7	Physician Density	73/140
Tourism Competitiveness	4.4/7	Hospital Beds	72/140
GDP/Capita	$10,666	Quality of Air Transport Infrastructure	36/140
Safety and Security	4.6/7	International Air Transport Network	30/140
Health and Hygiene	4.9/7	Quality of Roads	39/140
Air Transport Infrastructure	4.5/7	Hotel Rooms	43/140
Tourism Infrastructure	4.8/7	Tourism Openness	86/140
Cultural Infrastructure	5.2/7	Attitude of Population Towards Foreign Visitors	53/140
Visa Requirements	21/140		

Turkey is an affluent transcontinental country, which provides a decent admixture of Asian and European lifestyle. Officially known as the Republic of Turkey, the country is strategically located mostly on East Thrace in Southeastern Europe and on Anatolia in Western Asia. Displaying a unique blend of eastern and western sensibilities and traditions, it is a perfect convergence point of conservative Asian culture and a somewhat open European way of life. Ranked as the 15th largest economy in the world, Turkey competes with other popular European tourist destinations like Greece, Italy and Spain. Turkey offers middle-Eastern cuisine and Islamic religion allied with a westernized democracy pushing to join the European Union (EU) in 2013.

Location

The Eurasian country is the world's 37th largest in terms of area. Surrounded by seas of three sides, Turkey provides travelers with diverse scenery. It encompasses azure Mediterranean coasts, dusty Anatolian plains, bustling Black Sea ports, pastoral Kurdish territories and the cultural cosmopolitan city of Constantinople, modern Istanbul. In the northwest, Turkey has the Sea of Marmara. East Thrace, i.e. the European section of Turkey, shares its borders with Greece and Bulgaria. The Asian part of the country, i.e. Anatolia, situates itself between the Köroğlu and Pontic mountain ranges to the north, which consists of a high central plateau with narrow coastal plains, plus the Taurus Mountains to the south. It stretches over 1,600 kilometers end to end from the Greek islands in the west, past the limestone cave-worlds of Cappadocia and the snowy forests of the Kashkar, to the Biblical slopes of Mount Ararat on the east with Armenia and Iran.

Climate

Turkey's climate varies from region to region but generally, the north enjoys hot summers and chilly winters with the occasional dusting of snow. The Anatolian plateau forms the center of Turkey and can be extremely hot in summer and freezing cold in winter. However, most visitors head to the Aegean and Mediterranean coasts where winters are mild and often wet. Winters on the eastern part of the plateau are especially severe. The average winter temperature in eastern Anatolia ranges from –30 °C to –40 °C (–22 °F to –40 °F). In the west, winter temperature averages below 1 °C (34 °F). During summers, temperature may rise above 30 °C (86 °F) in the day.

History

Historically, Turkey has seen three of the world's largest empires from the ancient Greeks, some of their key cities (including Troy and Ephesus) are in the modern-day Turkey, to the Byzantines, the 'Eastern Romans' who created their capital at Constantinople, and the Ottomans, who ruled all from Vienna to Iran.

Tourism

Tourism focuses largely on a variety of archaeological and historical sites and on seaside resorts, along with its Aegean and Mediterranean coasts. Turkey is modern enough to be comfortable yet traditional to be interesting. Here, the visitors will have the opportunity to explore 10,000 years old historic treasures.

Istanbul is one of the most-popular destinations among the tourists. Being the only city in the world to have the flavor of two continents, Istanbul offers a rich legacy of mosques, churches, museums and magnificent palaces, coupled up with bustling markets and a vibrant street life.

Turkey offers many types of activity holidays like water sports and yachting, hiking, white-water rafting, mountain climbing and cycling. Turkey may not be the obvious ski destination, but it does have a number of winter sports resorts, generally located on average height, and forested mountains.

Medical Tourism in Turkey

According to a new research report entitled "Emerging Medical Tourism in Turkey," the country hopes to attract a significant rise in the number of foreign patients seeking medical treatments in Turkey. Connecting Asia and Europe, Turkey is poised to be one of the leading destinations for medical tourism with its affordable services and high quality healthcare.

Additionally, government initiatives, including heavy marketing and investment in this sector for creating more affordable hospitals and spas for medical tourists, will further drive the industry forward. The report also identified dental treatment, cosmetic surgery, thermal tourism and infertility treatment as the major areas of growth in the industry.

Healthcare System

The Turkey government owns and manages around 55 per cent of Turkey's healthcare facilities. Private organizations, universities and foreign companies operate the rest of the hospitals. Though private investors entered the healthcare market in early 1990's, the private sector investments doubled within the last decade. Currently, we have 305 private hospitals plus 44 JCI accredited healthcare facilities in Turkey.

Quality of Healthcare

Turkey is currently seeking European Union membership, and will be set to join the coalition by 2014. With its aim to take the right step in the right direction, Turkey has invested a lot of money and effort in establishing and implementing strict standards to have the highest level of quality medical care in both government and private healthcare organizations. The local Ministry of Health is in charge of regulating and ensuring all facilities and providers comply with healthcare standards and guidelines.

Medical facilities catering to foreign patients contain latest medical technologies and have board-certified staff with the majority of them receiving the training abroad. Turkey has 44 JCI accredited hospitals. Many of the hospitals are affiliated with esteemed US organizations like Johns Hopkins and Harvard University as well.

■ UKRAINE

General	
Language	Ukrainian
Time Zone	EET(UTC+2) summer EEST(UTC+3)
Dialing Code	+380
Electricity	220V, 50Hz
Major Cities	Kiev, Kharkiv, Dnipropetrovsk, Donets'k
Currency	Hryvnia
Health Related	
Mortality Rate	6.1deaths/ 1,000 population
Life Expectancy	65.4 M /75.5 F
Patient: Physician Ratio	240:1
Hospitals JCI accredited	0
Recommended Vaccinations	Measles, Hepatitis A, Typhoid, Hepatitis B, Rabies, Influenza, Tickborne encephalitis, Diphtheria-tetanus, MMR, Varicella
Other Infections	Leptospirosis, Anthrax, Crimean-Congo hemorrhagic fever, HIV

Tourism Related			
Population	44,854,065	Reliability of Police Services	105/140
Global Competitiveness	4.14/7	Physician Density	25/140
Tourism Competitiveness	4.0/7	Hospital Beds	4/140
GDP/Capita	$3,971	Quality of Air Transport Infrastructure	85/140
Safety and Security	4.7/7	International Air Transport Network	101/140
Health and Hygiene	6.6/7	Quality of Roads	135/140
Air Transport Infrastructure	2.8/7	Hotel Rooms	94/140
Tourism Infrastructure	4.6/7	Tourism Openness	56/140
Cultural Infrastructure	2.1/7	Attitude of Population Towards Foreign Visitors	127/140
Visa Requirements	91/140		

Thanks to the widespread reforms in Ukraine, the country has now moved beyond the authoritarian rule; thereby, ushering into an era of peace and development. Ukraine has definitely shed away its past Soviet Union connections and has adopted a European Union mentality owing to its close proximity with the Eastern Europe and a perceivable Romanian and Slovak influence. With the newfound freedom, tourists can now expect to witness the creative architectural landmarks of the new generation that gel so beautifully with the historical sites of the past, which further makes Ukraine a very interesting destination to visit.

Location

Ukraine is located in Eastern Europe between 44 and 53 degrees North latitude and 22 to 41 East longitudes, in the continental temperate zone. This destination shares its boundaries with Russia on the east and Belarus on the north, with the Black Sea on the south and, it shares its boundaries with Romania, Moldova, Hungary and Slovakia on the west. Ukraine occupies a total area of 603,700 square kilometers, which is somewhat smaller than the size of Texas; however, Ukraine is the world's 44th largest country.

People

Ukrainians are fun loving people who actively participate in various forms of traditional dances and games to exhibit their culture. Many of these dance forms and games owe their origin to the rural villages of Cossack where one could trace some of the oldest and ancient forms of dances. The Constitution of Ukraine applies the term 'Ukrainians' to all its citizens, who have Belarusians and Russians as their closest relatives. The Rusyns is yet another closely related group.

Events

Ukrainians take pride in their heritage and performing multi-cultural celebrations, which they keep celebrating all round the year. Sorochyntsi Fair or Sorochynsky Fair is a large fair held in the village of Velyki Sorochyntsi near Poltava in the Myrhorodskyi Raion (district) of Ukraine. The fair highlights traditional handicrafts, including Reshetilivka embroidery, rugs, Opishnya ceramics, and theatrical performances. Next, Eurofan takes place in Lviv, Ukraine, which focuses on developing friendship and respect between European fans and instituting sportsmanship spirit. Further, GOGOLFEST is yet another annual multidisciplinary international festival of contemporary art and cinema, which is held in Kiev (Kyiv), Ukraine. Dedicated to the famous writer Nikolai Gogol, the festival highlights literature, theater, music, visual art and films. Humorina or Yumorina is another annual festival held in Odessa, Ukraine on and around the April Fools' Day since 1973.

Weather

As discussed above, Ukraine has temperate continental climate; however, the Crimean coast flaunts a subtropical, humid climate. While the annual temperature in Northern Ukraine fluctuates from 5.5 °C (41.9 °F)–7 °C (44.6 °F), it ranges from 11 °C (51.8 °F)–13 °C (55.4 °F) in the South. Similarly, displaying similar disproportionate distribution, the Western Ukraine receives 47.2 in of annual precipitation; Crimea, however, receives around 15.7 in of precipitation.

Medical Tourism in Ukraine

In recent years, the medical tourism sector in Ukraine has developed at a rapid rate to achieve perfection in all sub-sectors of healthcare. Since the region is well capable of becoming a medical tourism destination, it undeniably is a competitor to the Eastern European countries providing excellent medical tourism facilities to medical travelers. Ukraine has garnered popularity in the world of medical tourism predominantly for dental care, said to be in line with the best in the world. Ukrainian health facilities also excel in reconstructive and cosmetic surgeries.

Many medical tourism centers urge tourists to take advantage of the wonderful cultural heritage sites Ukraine has to offer. These clinics arrange treatments in such a way that travelers have a chance to visit some of the cultural and historical sites as well.

Healthcare System

The healthcare system in Ukraine resembles a similar system seen all around the Europe. The government-aided services are the backbone of the Ukrainian health system, which is free for citizens and long-term residents. The Government of Ukraine oversees all the health services and finances through governmental revenues.

The country also has a prevalent healthcare system with facilities and physicians that operate on a pay out-of-pocket system. Even though the price of healthcare in Ukraine is a fraction of what American or British patient pay, only the wealthy residents can afford to pay for treatments in the private facilities.

Quality of Healthcare

Public and private facilities in Ukraine display a clear distinction. Aside from private or semi-governmental health institutions, the governmental hospitals also provide similar healthcare facilities.

On the other hand, private centers are state-of-the-art facilities that house well-trained and experienced physicians. Considering the fact that there is shortage of health professionals in this region, most of the experienced physicians rather work in the private sector as they can earn more money. This further contributes to a palpable disparity of quality between public and private sector. With their aim to aid rapid recovery, Ukrainian healthcare facilities provide unparalleled dental work, eye surgery, cosmetic surgery, reconstructive surgery and relief from a host of illnesses.

■ UNITED ARAB EMIRATES

General	
Language	Arabic
Time Zone	GST (UTC+4)
Dialing Code	+971
Electricity	220V, 50Hz
Major Cities	Dubai, Abu Dhabi, Sharjah, Al 'Ayn
Currency	UAE dirham
Clothing	Summers are hot hence pack natural material clothing, whereas winter a pleasant take lightweight jacket. Conservative dressing.

Health Related	
Mortality Rate	2.08 deaths/ 1,000 population
Life Expectancy	77 M / 79 F
Hospitals JCI accredited	61
Recommended Vaccinations	Hepatitis A, Typhoid, Hepatitis B, Rabies, Diphtheriatetanus, Measles, Varicella and Poliomyelitis
Other Infections	Brucellosis, HIV

Tourism Related			
Population	8,264,070	Reliability of Police Services	8/140
Global Competitiveness	4.89/7	Physician Density	61/140
Tourism Competitiveness	4.9/7	Hospital Beds	84/140
GDP/Capita	$49,011	Quality of Air Transport Infrastructure	3/140
Safety and Security	5.2/7	International Air Transport Network	3/140
Health and Hygiene	5.1/7	Quality of Roads	2/140
Air Transport Infrastructure	6.1/7	Hotel Rooms	24/140
Tourism Infrastructure	5.7/7	Tourism Openness	41/140
Cultural Infrastructure	3.7/7	Attitude of Population Towards Foreign Visitors	15/140
Visa Requirements	104/140		

Ruled by Sheikhs since time immemorial, the United Arab Emirates is a rich and wealthy country on the eastern Arabian Peninsula. As one leaves behind the Persian Gulf, a federation of seven emirates welcomes him to witness extended shorelines and the starting point for travels in the Middle East. The emirates include Abu Dhabi (capital city), Dubai,

Sharjah, Ajman, Ras Al Khaimah, Umm Al Quwain and Fujairah. This country has been one of the most preferred destinations in terms of tourism, trade and leisure activities. The Arabian country shares its borders with Oman to the east and Saudi Arabia to the south, aside from sharing shorelines with Qatar and Iran.

Location

One of the most exciting and unique feature of UAE has been its varied topography. It has beautiful and vibrant desert landscape with vast sand dunes and dry riverbeds that add to its dry beauty. The 200 islands lying offshore along the Persian Gulf Coast are a treat to explore. Apart from this, there are coral reefs and salt marshes that add volumes of vividness to its beauty.

People

Popularly known as Emiratis or Emirians, the UAE residents owe their origin to the Bani Yas clan, ethnic Persians and ethnic Baluchis. Several people from other races, including South Asians and Africans, have married Emiratis to become UAE nationals. The UAE citizens prefer working in their own country rather than moving outside thanks to more than adequate welfare benefits. The people here are very fun loving and carefree. They lead a very exotic and wealthy lifestyle due to the burgeoning economy. The people are very friendly, hospitable and helpful in nature.

Events

The fun loving residents of this country like to celebrate festivals and events throughout the year. The annual calendar of UAE is full with cultural, religious and other entertaining events that have high participation rates from all the people here. The Abu Dhabi Festival, Dubai International Film Festival, Dubai Lynx International Advertising Festival, Dubai Shopping Festival, Sharjah Biennial, Tropfest Arabia and the UAE Awafi Festival feature primarily on the list of festivals celebrated across UAE's various emirates.

Weather

Lying across the Tropic of Cancer, weather condition in UAE is warm and humid. The winters here are sunny with pleasant temperatures in contrast to the terribly hot and humid summers. Nights here are relatively cold that can even be less than 5 degrees in the desert area. Temperatures in summers are in 40s and higher in the inner areas. The coastal areas are very humid, with level ranging between 50 to 60 per cent and even up to 90 per cent in summer and autumns.

Medical Tourism in UAE

The World Bank ranked Dubai and Abu Dhabi as the second and third most popular medical tourism destinations respectively in the Arab region. The Emirati government invests heavily on marketing and promoting the medical facilities in this region so that the foreign patients could avail excellent healthcare. Medical tourists from the US and UK visit the United Arab Emirates to benefit from high quality medical services and hospitals in Dubai and Abu Dhabi.

The UAE is becoming a prime medical tourism destination due to its strong healthcare infrastructure, foreign-trained specialists and physicians and latest technology housed at state-of-the-art medical facilities. The UAE tourism board is no stranger to catering to foreigners, so coupling a vacation in Dubai or Abu Dhabi with the various medical treatments is becoming increasingly appealing to health-seeking travelers.

Healthcare System

The UAE has a comprehensive, public-funded healthcare delivery system and a burgeoning private health sector that provides a high standard of health care to the population. The growth in medical services has been staggering when compared to the state of facilities just a few decades ago. The Ministry of Health is commissioning large investment projects to widen and expand medical facilities and hospitals, medical centers and emergency services in the seven emirates.

Dubai Healthcare City, a multi-million dollar project has attracted the local and foreign patients to world-class health facilities. This medical zone offers international-standard care with dedicated quality.

Quality of Healthcare

Facilities in the UAE, especially those in Dubai and Abu Dhabi, boast extremely high standard of healthcare quality in all medical facilities. Increased government spending and international regulations have taken the level and standard of healthcare to its next, higher level.

The costs might be higher than they are in other medical tourism regions; however, the medical services are unparalleled. The vast majority of providers are foreign trained. Moreover, the private and public hospitals host most of the latest technologies and medical procedures. With its 47 JCI accredited hospitals, the UAE demonstrates its priority to ensure better health standards, develop new medical facilities and implement its medical policies to achieve the benchmark of international healthcare quality.

■ UNITED KINGDOM

General	
Language	English
Time Zone	GMT(UTC+0) summer BST(UTC+1)
Dialing Code	+44
Electricity	230V, 50Hz
Major Cities	London, Birmingham, Glasgow, Liverpool
Currency	Pound sterling
Clothing	Summers are mild, and winters are extremely cold
Health Related	
Mortality Rate	9.33 deaths/ 1,000 population
Life Expectancy	78.5 M / 82.4 F
Patient: Physician Ratio	417:1
Hospitals JCI accredited	0
Recommended Vaccinations	Influenza, Diphtheria-tetanus, Measles, Varicella
Other Infections	Lyme disease, Leptospirosis, Rabies, Hemorrhagic fever, HIV

Tourism Related			
Population	8,264,070	Reliability of Police Services	32/140
Global Competitiveness	5.45/7	Physician Density	40/140
Tourism Competitiveness	5.4/7	Hospital Beds	55/140
GDP/Capita	$49,011	Quality of Air Transport Infrastructure	22/140
Safety and Security	5.7/7	International Air Transport Network	8/140
Health and Hygiene	5.7/7	Quality of Roads	24/140
Air Transport Infrastructure	5.6/7	Hotel Rooms	30/140
Tourism Infrastructure	5.8/7	Tourism Openness	88/140
Cultural Infrastructure	6.4/7	Attitude of Population Towards Foreign Visitors	55/140
Visa Requirements	12/140		

United Kingdom is an affluent nation, which flaunts diverse traditions, religions and ethnicities. Located in the northern part of the Europe, the United Kingdom is composed of England, North Ireland, Wales and Scotland. A parliamentary form of government system works in close cooperation with a constitutional monarchy to govern this country.

Over the past centuries, many immigrants from the neighboring colonies have settled in UK, which contribute bountifully to its rich and prosperous heritage. The increased number of immigrants from regions around the world has major influences on the culture and tradition of UK including dressing style, living, food and culture.

Location

As we mentioned earlier, UK is located on the northwestern coast in Europe. The island nation has a large collection of islands, which primarily includes Great Britain, the northeastern part of Ireland and other small islands. The Atlantic Ocean, Irish Sea, North Sea and English Channel surround UK from all sides. The Channel Tunnel, the longest undersea rail tunnel in the world connects the island with continental Europe. On its eastern and southern sides, you would find low, rolling countryside; however, the western and northern regions flaunt the while hills and mountains.

Weather

The United Kingdom is a true paradise for those who wish to enjoy a pleasant weather all year around. Touting a temperate climate, the country has plentiful rainfall. Temperature never falls below –11 °C (12 °F) or goes beyond 35 °C (95 °F). The southwestern wind brings the wet and mild weather from the Atlantic Ocean to the mainland, which does not have any effect on the eastern parts. Hence, while the western regions get the major chunk of rainfall, the eastern part remain comparably dry. As the southeast England is closest to European mainland, it flaunts the warmest summers.

People

British people display immense friendliness and compassion while interacting with outsiders. They take immense pride in highlighting their culture in front of the tourists and visitors. They actively take part in their events and festivals all round the calendar year. A short conversation with them is enough to befriend you.

Events

The calendar year of UK is filled with many events and festivals, which are centuries old. Some of the major festivals include Christmas, Easter and Thanksgiving. As we all know, Christmas is celebrated all over the world; however, in UK, people started celebrating it since AD 596. It was in this year, St. Augustine brought Christianity to English shores. Other festivals and events include Twelfth Night, New Year, Mothering Sunday, May Day, Harvest Festival, Halloween, Bonfire Night, Remembrance Day and Boxing Day.

Medical Tourism in UK

Even though the major focus of medical tourism in the UK has been on outbound tourism – British patients seeking healthcare out of the UK due to long waiting list, yet UK remains one of the world's greatest medical tourism destinations. Besides the National

Healthcare System that serves the citizens of the UK, a burgeoning private sector caters to those dissatisfied with the NHS or foreign paying patients.

The healthcare in the UK is more expensive than any other popular medical tourism destinations. However, it never means that we should sideline the importance of medical facilities that potential medical tourists can grab only here. Considering the fact that the healthcare in UK is world-renowned in terms of physicians, technology, facilities and resources, the UK definitely ranks higher than other countries providing medical tourism facilities.

Healthcare System

With several countries modeling their health infrastructure around the British one, the healthcare system in the UK is one of the most popular and well-known systems. The government takes the burden of providing free or very low cost healthcare to all British citizens, thanks to the British National Healthcare System.

This system is generally quite well received by the public as only 10 per cent of the population has private insurance coverage. Those who seek private care tend to be dissatisfied with the long waiting lists that are the norm of public sector systems or are interested in more physician and specialist options. However, when compared to the rest of the world, the United Kingdom takes pride in offering the best medical facilities to its citizens and medical tourists from all over the world.

Quality of Healthcare

Despite the high cost or long waiting times, both the public and private sector offer all the patients with the highest quality healthcare in the world. Since Britain has been providing quality healthcare for such a long time, they have developed the standards and created their own benchmarks commonly found in medical facilities around the world. The Trent Accreditation Scheme accredits several medical tourism hospitals globally.

■ UNITED STATES

General	
Language	English
Time Zone	UTC -5 to -10 summer UTC -4 to -10
Dialing Code	+1
Electricity	120V, 60Hz
Major Cities	New York City, Los Angeles, Chicago, Brooklyn
Currency	United states dollar
Clothing	All sorts of attires are worn, pack according to the season you visit in.
Health Related	
Mortality Rate	8.38 deaths/ 1,000 population
Life Expectancy	76.1 M / 80.9 F
Patient: Physician Ratio	390:1
Hospitals JCI accredited	JCAHO - 11,000 (No JCI in US)
Recommended Vaccinations	Hepatitis A, Hepatitis B, Rabies, Diphtheria-tetanus, Measles, Varicella, Poliomyelitis, Yellow Fever
Other Infections	Lyme disease, Rocky Mountain spotted fever, meningitis, HIV

Tourism Related			
Population	316,650,000	Reliability of Police Services	18/140
Global Competitiveness	5.47/7	Physician Density	49/140
Tourism Competitiveness	5.3/7	Hospital Beds	64/140
GDP/Capita	$49,922	Quality of Air Transport Infrastructure	30/140
Safety and Security	4.9/7	International Air Transport Network	22/140
Health and Hygiene	5.5/7	Quality of Roads	20/140
Air Transport Infrastructure	6.2/7	Hotel Rooms	17/140
Tourism Infrastructure	6.3/7	Tourism Openness	131/140
Cultural Infrastructure	6.3/7	Attitude of Population Towards Foreign Visitors	102/140
Visa Requirements	96/140		

Visitors to the world's biggest economy and fourth largest country, divided into fifty states and five territories, may discover a melting pot of diverse people and cultures becoming part of an equally varied and mind-blowing landscape. United States of America has sixteen of the world's 30 busiest airports.

Location

Located in the North American continent, the United States of America is the world's fifth largest country in the contiguous area. The state of Alaska, which is in the northwestern part of North America, stretches along and across the Bering Strait in Asia. Furthermore, the state of Hawaii is situated in the mid-North pacific. Aside from the mainland, America has five populated and nine unpopulated territories in the Pacific and the Caribbean. All this combines to form a 3.79 million square miles (9.83 million km²) nation, which has now become the world superpower after the downfall of the USSR.

People

Thanks to people who emigrated from several parts of the world, the United States of America is a true mixed bag of several cultures that flaunt unity in diversity. American people are very accommodative when it comes to interacting with strangers or visitors who come to America to explore its cultural diversity and scenic landscapes.

Events

If you wish to enjoy all year around, you would not find any other country in the entire world more suited to your festive frame of mind. Be them the art fans, beer lovers or those wish to explore the food, harvest, music, sports, theater, movies or other cultural occasions, America is the best destination to discover. Among various cultural events and festivals, the Exotic Erotic Ball, Rainbow Gathering, Cain Park Arts Festival, Great American Beer Festival, ComFest, New York Renaissance Faire, International Cherry Blossom Festival and ¡Globalquerque! hold prominence.

Tourist Destinations

All US cities are marked with pulsating life, which makes them home to several attractions. Washington D.C, the capital city is home to the White House. New York has the Statue of Liberty, The Brooklyn Bridge and Central Park: almost all of them are the landmarks for the entire country itself.

Among the top 25 most-visited tourist destinations in the US, the thundering falls of Niagara, the harrowing water- chutes of Disneyland's and Pirates of the Caribbean deserve special mention. Disney World's Magic Kingdom, in Lake Buena Vista, Florida, remains on top in the theme-park world. The natural scenic attractions include the Grand Canyon, Yosemite and Yellowstone National Parks.

The northern states offer many winter vacations and skiing opportunities to those interested in winter sports. When it comes to enjoying sunshine and sandy beaches, the southern states have excellent climate and tourist appeal. Hollywood is famous for its film-loving visitors. Finally yet importantly, Las Vegas is home to casinos, enormous hotels, wedding chapels and an exciting nightlife.

Weather

The climate varies from tropical in Hawaii and southern Florida to Tundra in Alaska and some of the highest mountains. While the South experiences a subtropical humid climate with mild winters and long, hot, humid summers, the North and East experience a temperate continental climate with warm summers and cold winters.

While the humid forests of the Eastern Great Plains have high rainfall, the semi-arid short grass prairies on the high plains abutting the Rocky Mountains have sporadic showers. Arid deserts, including the Mojave, extend through the lowlands and valleys of the southwest, from westernmost Texas to California and northward throughout much of Nevada. Some parts of California have a Mediterranean climate. Forests line the windward mountains of the Pacific Northwest from Oregon to Alaska.

Medical Tourism in the US

Most of the media attention given to medical tourism focuses on the growing trend of Americans seeking out more cost-effective medical services in other countries due to the escalating prices of healthcare in the US. However, the US has always been a key destination for those seeking advanced medical treatments. The US provides patients with highly educated and trained physicians and other healthcare providers that offer treatments to complex and difficult medical cases. The recession and the simultaneous decline in the value of the US dollar in the last decade further attracted tourists to seek the high quality care at a more affordable price.

Healthcare System

The healthcare infrastructure in the US is one of the most complex systems to understand. It includes an amalgam of limited government influence, a dominating private sector and non-profit organizations to pick up the slack that the private and public sector cannot fulfill. The burden of financing and reimbursements of the healthcare costs is placed on the insurance company, which dominates the healthcare industry. The government provides insurance for the elderly and unfortunates, as they cannot afford insurance.

The US is battling several healthcare industry issues, which further prompts for immediate reforms. America spends more than any other country (16 per cent of their GDP) on the healthcare industry and yet, a large percentage of the American population remains uninsured. For those fully insured and/or able to pay out-of-pocket, the quality of medical services are unrivalled to any other medical tourism destination.

Quality of Healthcare

Despite the recent failures of the US healthcare system, many still argue that Americans have the "best health care in the world," pointing to the freely available medical technology and state-of-the-art facilities that have become so highly symbolic of the system. People travel all over the world to avail the fantastic services provided in the US. The amount of emphasis placed on research and technology is unparalleled throughout the world, leading to innovative approaches and treatments.

Several major medical centers and medical colleges have international patient centers that cater to patients from foreign countries who seek medical treatment in the US. Many of these organizations offer service coordinators to assist international patients in arranging for medical care, accommodations, finances and transportation.

■ VIETNAM

General	
Language	Vietnamese
Time Zone	ICT (Indochina Time) UTC+7 (UTC+7) Summer (DST) No DST (UTC+7)
Dialing Code	+84
Major Cities	Ho Chi Minh City, Hai Phong, Hanoi, Nha Trang
Currency	đồng
Health Related	
Mortality Rate	5.94 deaths/ 1,000 population
Life Expectancy	73.1M /78.3F
Hospitals JCI accredited	1
Recommended Vaccinations	Hepatitis A, Hepatitis B, Typhoid, Rabies, Japanese Encephalitis
Other Infections	HIV
Clothing	tropical in south; monsoonal in north with hot, rainy season (May to September) and warm, dry season (October to March)

Tourism Related			
Population	90,388,000	Physician Density	80/140
Global Competitiveness	4.11/7	Hospital Beds	60/140
Tourism Competitiveness	4.0/7	Quality of Air Transport Infrastructure	94/140
GDP/Capita	$220.825	International Air Transport Network	111/140
Safety and Security	4.9/7	Quality of Roads	118/140
Health and Hygiene	4.5/7	Hotel Rooms	92/140
Air Transport Infrastructure	2.8/7	Tourism Openness	46/140
Tourism Infrastructure	2.2/7	Attitude of Population Towards Foreign Visitors	108/140
Cultural Infrastructure	4.1/7		

The Socialist Republic of Vietnam, popularly known as Vietnam, is located in Southeast Asia on the Indo-China Peninsula. The country has China to its north, South China Sea to its east, Cambodia to its south-west and Laos to its north-west. As per the records of 2012, it ranks thirteenth in the whole world in terms of population with 90.3 million people. The climate of Vietnam varies from place to place. November to April is the winter season, which remains dry when compared to the rainy season. Annual temperature is higher in the plains as well as to the south in comparison with the mountains and the north part of the country.

Events and Festivals

The colorful events and festivals in Vietnam are a major attraction for both regular and medical tourists from across the world. Most of them are annual celebrations, which are celebrated with real fervor. The most important festivals include the Lunar New Year Festival, locally known as Tet, which is celebrated in February. Some other popular events and festivals include Dong Da Festival, Chol Chnam Thmay Festival, Hai Ba Trung Day, Hung King festival, Trung Thu, Mid-Autumn Festival, Labor Day, Liberation Day, Doan Ngu, Thap Ba – Po Nagar Festival, Chem Temple Festival, Co Le Pagoda Festival, Elephant Race Festival and many more.

Medical Tourism in Vietnam

Medical tourism in Vietnam has improved significantly over the past few years. In fact, the World Travel and Tourism Council have named it as one of the fastest growing medical tourism destinations. The doctors and surgeons are qualified and the medical services provided are of high standard. Apart from these factors, the cost of treatment is also another aspect that makes it a popular destination for medical tourists. The cost is low when compared to Australia, the United States or European countries. Cosmetic surgery, dental surgery, alternative medical treatments like acupuncture, etc. are some of the facilities, which Vietnamese health experts provide to international medical tourists.

Healthcare System

At present, Vietnam invests only a small portion of the GDP of the country in healthcare. Citizens have to visit private hospitals or clinics to get quality treatment and pay from their own pockets. There is also a huge difference in the quality of medical services provided in the urban and rural areas. The upcoming changes in the system intend to cover all patients under government healthcare facilities. Government is trying to reduce the deficit between medical facilities in urban and rural areas.

Medical Tourism Terms, glossary

1. **Accreditation** – There are several organizations that accredit hospitals, which means that the hospitals have reached a certain set of standards reviewed by self-assessment and external peer assessment. The process is used by health care organizations to accurately assess their level of performance in relation to established standards and to implement ways to continuously improve the service and standards of care. Criteria ensure quality assurance and also medical ethics.

   Some of the international accreditation organizations are:

   a **JCI** – Joint Commission International www.jci.org – represents the Gold Standard for international hospital accreditation

   b. **ISquA** – International Society for Quality in Healthcare http:// www.isqua.org/ - non-profit organization that discusses quality assurance in international healthcare

   c. **ISO** - The International Organization for Standardization www.iso.org - is international agency with close to one hundred member countries and facilitates and organizations compliance to accreditation standards.

   d. **QHA** – Quality Healthcare Alliance http://www.qha-international.co.uk/ - UK based standards agency, using standards based on NHS clinical governance

2. **Ambulatory Care** — Ambulatory care is any medical care delivered on an *outpatient* basis. Increasing numbers of medical conditions do not require hospital admission and can be managed without admission to a hospital. Many medical investigations can be performed on an ambulatory basis, including blood tests, X-rays, endoscopy and even biopsy procedures of superficial organs.

3. **Affiliations:** Hospitals catering to medical tourists that are affiliated to prestigious medical institutes (like Harvard Medical, or John Hopkins) which demonstrates a desire to maintain a high level of quality healthcare at their facility.

4. **Board Certified Healthcare Provider** – This means that the doctor or surgeon has been certified by the medical board of their country. It should be possible to check their credentials and is inadvisable to be treated by someone who is not board certified

5. **Centers of Excellence"** – places that are well known for having the best doctors, services and treatments (i.e. Harley Street in London) 363 Dr Prem's Guidebook - Medical Tourism | **www.DrPrem.com** Dr Prem's Guidebook - Medical Tourism

6. **Consumer Price Index (CPI)** – fluctuating price level of consumer goods and services

7. **Cultural Tolerances (Do's and Don'ts)** – Understanding the cultural, religious and social mores of the destination country

8. **Digitizing Documents** – Putting medical documents and records onto the computer and online to make consultations with foreign doctors more convenient. Can also be used when connecting back with local doctor to show progress of treatment.

9. **Elective Surgery** – making a choice to have surgery, rather than it being a medical emergency. Most commonly seen for cosmetic surgery procedures.

10. **Facilitators:** Are companies which arrange and organize your trip. Some are connected to particular hospitals, other provide a broad service. The term "facilitator" can mean many different things. It is up to the patient to understand exactly what the facilitator they employ does and does not do.

    a. **Hospital Commission** – An extra fee a patient would be required to pay. Medical tourism facilitators offer a lot of convenience but do need to make their money somewhere. This will usually come from a hospital commission, service charge (concierge fee), or both.

11. **Insurance Terms:**

    a. **Air Ambulance Insurance** – insurance for air ambulance cover to transport patient to or from home country and destination

    b. **Co-pay** – payment split between patient and insurance company

    c. **Deductible** – a pre-agreed amount that the patient is responsible before the insurance company pays for treatment

    d. **Medical Travel Insurance** – insurance that specifically covers patients travelling for medical treatment rather than a regular vacation or business travel

    e. **Self-funded** – paying for yourself

    f. **Travel Insurance** – insurance for vacation and business travel

    g. **Underinsured** – patients who do not have enough insurance to cover their bills

    h. **Uninsured** – not having any insurance

12. **Intra-Country Laws** – legal agreements between two countries, can affect legal action taken in the home country against the destination country

13. **Legal issues:**

    a. **Legal Recourse** – legal action a patient can take if something goes wrong

    b. **Enforcement Laws** – where legal terms in contracts are enforceable, either in home country or destination country

    c. **Jurisdiction Clauses** – legal clauses in contracts with hospitals or medical facility

14. **Medical Travel Agencies** – Travel agencies that help people arrange travel for medical treatment abroad. They are different from facilitators because they make more of the practical arrangements but can now get qualifications. One such organization that qualifies travel agencies is the Council for Global Integration of Travel, a voluntary a non-profit organization focused on advancing the development and role of the professional practices, education and research in global clinically integrated healthcare and healthcare administration including medical tourism. (www. cgih.org)

15. **Medical Tourism Complications** – Things that go wrong as a medical tourist either with the treatment or post-operatively or problems with the actual trip.

16. **Medical Tourism Packages** – Special package trips specifically for medical tourists whose purpose is to travelling to seek healthcare abroad. The package usually includes travel, accommodation and medical treatment.

17. **Nationalized Healthcare System** – Healthcare provided free or at a nominal cost to the citizens of the country. Nations that have adopted this system is the United Kingdom's free universal health service known as the National Health Service and Canada's Medicare.

18. **Out-of-pocket treatment** – When an individual takes monetary responsibility for a treatment, without utilizing government provided services or insurance to pay for the procedure.

19. **Patient Medical Records** – Patients should either ask their doctors to liaise with the foreign hospital or take responsibility for their own records. Patients should endeavor to get copies of their patient records and relevant information when travelling for healthcare.

20. **Post-operative complications** – Potential medical discomforts or problems that can go wrong after treatment. Some common post-treatment complications is embolisms and blood clots after flying long journeys before full recovery.

21. **Pre-consultation** – a consultation with a doctor or surgeon before treatment

22. **Quality practice by Healthcare Providers:**
    a. **Quality Indicators** – to find lists and criteria for quality indicators necessary to denote a high quality facility it is best to refer to the JCI and other accreditation websites to find out what they look for.
    b. **Publications** – http://www.healthcaretrip.org/, the International Medical Travel Journal www.imtj.com and the Medical Tourism Association www.medicaltourismassociation.com website are all useful online resources and the Treatment Abroad website www. treatmentabroad.com has the largest resource for medical tourists anywhere on the internet.

23. **Recovery Centers** – a quasi medical place to recover that have the facilities and staff to ensure the medical traveler is able to have post-operative recuperation to heal from their medical treatment.

24. **Standard Practices by Hospital**
    a. **Malpractice Coverage** – Medical malpractice is professional negligence by act or omission by a health care provider in which care provided deviates from accepted standards of practice in the medical community and causes injury or death to the patient. Every hospital and doctor should have malpractice cover/insurance in case something goes and the patient takes legal action
    b. **Local Healthcare Licensing** – where the local facility/hospital/clinic and therefore doctors and healthcare staff are full licensed locally.

25. **Tele-Medicine** – is about Telephone consultations and interactions between doctors and patients through the internet and telephone. Rapidly growing area of practice in medical tourism

26. **Transparency** – Being completely open and honest with the quality and pricing of healthcare services in the Medical Tourism Industry.

27. **Travel Medicine** – Travel medicine includes pre-travel consultation and evaluation, contingency planning during travel, and post-travel follow-up and care. Information is provided by the WHO (world health authority) that addresses health issues for travelers for each country as well as the specific health risks of air travel itself. Also consult the destination country for medical advice on immunization, drinking water etc

28. **Travelers Check** --A traveler's check is a form of money that can be replaced if lost or stolen so it is safer for a medical tourist to carry it than cash.

29. **Types of Tourism:**

    a. **Inbound** – patient coming into a country for treatment

    b. **Outbound** – patients travelling abroad for treatment

    c. **Intrabound** – patients travelling between two countries

Notes

Notes

Notes

Made in the USA
Middletown, DE
19 November 2017